MEN SPEAK OUT

Men Speak Out is a collection of essays written by ⌐   ⌐... In
the essays, which feature original, lively, and accessible prose, anti-sexist men make
sense of their gendered experiences in today's culture. They describe their successes
and challenges in bucking patriarchal systems in a culture that can be unsupportive
of—or downright hostile to—a pro-feminist perspective. In these chapters, a
diverse group of men reflect on growing up, share moments in their day-to-day
lives, and pose serious questions about being a pro-feminist male living, working,
thinking, and learning in a sexist society.

"In the 1970s, the question 'can men be feminists?' led to lively debates. Today, this
is no longer the question. The multi-generational men's chorus of feminist voices
in *Men Speak Out* demonstrates unequivocally that, today, some men are doing
feminist work on many fronts—as teachers, writers, musicians, students, anti-
violence activists, fathers, lovers, and friends. This is an important book to read—
and to savor, discuss, and share with our sons and daughters."

> Michael A. Messner, Professor of Sociology and Gender Studies,
> University of Southern California

"*Men Speak Out* is a book many of us have been waiting for, a passionate collection
of essays by men who are theorizing, reflecting and downright questioning masculinity, gender and feminism. Shira Tarrant has brilliantly gathered a provocative
range of men's voices on everything from athletics, porn and Aztec warriors to
racism in the gay community. Their stories are engaging and have left me feeling
downright hopeful about men and women, feminism and gender. If these men are
willing to ask themselves and each other the hard questions, then it can only be a
sign of better things to come for all of us."

> Daisy Hernández, co-editor of *Colonize This! Young
> Women on Today's Feminism*

"Until I read this book, I did not realize the stunning absence of men speaking
about their feelings. At times, I felt like a self-absorbed spouse, yanked out of my
own preoccupations long enough to REALLY HEAR what my man experiences
in this society. This is an important validation for men trapped in the masculine
construct, for women who wonder about men's role in the feminist movement, and
for all the trannies and queers who negotiate these issues."

> Inga Musico, author of *Cunt: A Declaration of Independence*

"I have always believed that feminism is about gender itself more than women;
with its diverse array of insightful voices, *Men Speak Out* is an important addition
to the growing body of work exploring men's crucial role in the fight for gender
justice."

> Lisa Jervis, founding editor and publisher of *Bitch: Feminist Response
> to Pop Culture*

MEN SPEAK OUT

Views on Gender, Sex, and Power

Edited by Shira Tarrant
with a foreword by Jackson Katz

Routledge
Taylor & Francis Group

NEW YORK AND LONDON

First published 2008
by Routledge
270 Madison Ave, New York, NY 10016

Simultaneously published in the UK
by Routledge
2 Park Square, Milton Park, Abingdon, Oxon OX14 4RN

Routledge is an imprint of the Taylor & Francis Group, an informa business

© 2008 by Taylor & Francis

Typeset in Abode Caslon by Keystroke, 28 High Street, Tettenhall, Wolverhampton
Printed and bound in the United States of America on acid-free paper by
Walsworth Publishing Company, Marceline, MO

Library of Congress Cataloging in Publication Data
Men speak out: views on gender, sex and power/edited by Shira Tarrant;
foreword by Jackson Katz.
p. cm.
ISBN 978–0–415–95657–4 (pbk.) — ISBN 978–0–415–95656–7 (cloth)
1. Sex role—Philosophy. 2. Feminist theory—History. 3. Sex differences
(Psychology) I. Tarrant, Shira, 1963- II. Katz, Jackson.
HQ1075.M46 2007
305.42081—dc22   2007018015

ISBN10: 0–415–95656–0 (hbk)
ISBN10: 0–415–95657–9 (pbk)
ISBN10: 0–203–93506–3 (ebk)

ISBN13: 978–0–415–95656–7 (hbk)
ISBN13: 978–0–415–95657–4 (pbk)
ISBN13: 978–0–203–93506–4 (ebk)

CONTENTS

LIST OF CONTRIBUTORS

Jacob Anderson-Minshall has been many things in his life, including carny, farm boy, park ranger, magazine founder, and a woman. After eighteen years as a butch-identified lesbian, he transitioned to male, but hasn't quite resolved his issues about becoming the enemy: "straight," white guy. Jacob writes the syndicated column, "TransNation" that runs in queer publications from San Francisco to Boston. With his wife Diane, he co-authors the Blind Eye Detectives mystery series that premiers in 2007 with *Blind Curves*.

Brandon Arber was a top-ranked athlete and captain of his college swim team. He majored in political science, graduating with honors. Brandon now attends Boston College Law School.

Ben Atherton-Zeman is a spokesperson for the National Organization for Men Against Sexism and the author of "Voices of Men" (www.voicesofmen. org), an educational comedy about men's violence against women. Ben lives in Acton, MA with his amazing wife and partner, Lucinda. His email is benazeman@hotmail.com.

Greg Bortnichak will soon graduate from college at which time he hopes to put his barista days behind him. Greg plays a mean guitar and a wicked cello in his band, The Sparta Philharmonic. Look for him soon at a city near you.

Andrew Boyd is an author, humorist, and twenty-year veteran of creative campaigns for social change. As Phil T. Rich, he co-founded the 2004 media sensation Billionaires for Bush. His writing has appeared in *The Nation*, *The Village Voice*, and Salon.com and he has published two volumes of "serious" humor: *Daily Afflictions* (W.W. Norton, 2002) and *Life's Little Deconstruction Book* (W. W. Norton, 1998). More info can be had at www.andrewboyd.com.

Prior to graduating with his master's degree in women's and gender studies, **Kyle Brillante** received undergraduate degrees in biology and Chinese. He currently teaches in New York City, and plans to pursue a career in education.

Derrais Carter is currently a junior at the University of Kansas majoring in sociology and African-American studies. With aspirations of obtaining a PhD in American studies, his research interests include representations of black masculinity, visual culture, and black feminisms. In addition to attending college, he is also a motivational speaker and workshop presenter.

Chris Crass is the coordinator of the Catalyst Project, a center for political education and movement building. They prioritize anti-racist work with mostly white sections of the political left with the goal of deepening anti-racist commitment in white communities and building multiracial left movements for collective liberation. Chris's essays on collective liberation politics, anti-authoritarian leadership, organizing strategy and movement building have been published widely in *Left Turn*, *Clamor*, and on Colours of Resistance, ZNet, and Infoshop.org. He was part of the Against Patriarchy Men's Group and is a member of the Heads Up Collective, a group working to bridge anti-war and economic and racial justice movements.

Chris Dixon (chrisd@resist.ca) is a longtime anti-authoritarian writer and organizer. He is currently a PhD student in the history of consciousness program at the University of California, Santa Cruz.

Born and raised in Jackson Heights, Queens, **Nathan Einschlag** attended a liberal arts college in Baltimore, Maryland, graduating in December 2007. He was an elementary education major and a theater minor, and plans to live and teach in New York City. Despite what happened on the basketball team, Nathan wants people to know that he truly appreciated his college experience and never once regretted choosing the school he did. Through college, he has met some truly inspiring people that have changed the course of his life for the better.

Dr. Michael Flood is a Postdoctoral Fellow at the Australian Research Centre in sex, health and society at La Trobe University in Melbourne, Australia. His research examines the sexual cultures of young, heterosexual men. Michael is a co-editor of the *Routledge International Encyclopedia of Men and Masculinities* and the author of academic papers on men and masculinities, heterosexual men's sexualities, men's violence, homosociality, fatherhood and fathers' rights, anti-violence mobilizations, and youth and pornography. Michael also has had a variety of involvements as a pro-feminist educator, speaker, and activist on issues of men and gender. In particular, he is involved in community advocacy and education work focused on men's violence against women. He has conducted anti-violence workshops for young men and women in high schools and colleges and participated in groups such as the White Ribbon Campaign and Men Against Sexual Assault.

Chong-suk Han is a doctoral candidate in social welfare at the University of Washington and a lecturer in sociology at Temple University. A former journalist, his writings have appeared in over two dozen different publications.

Eli Hastings earned his MFA and taught creative nonfiction and English at the University of North Carolina at Wilmington. He currently lives in Barcelona, Spain, with his wife, Lili. His work has appeared in *Rivendell*, *Cimarron Review*, *Pinyon*, *Pedestal Magazine*, the *Seattle Review*, *Wandering Army*, and *The Tulane Review*. An essay published in *Third Coast* was nominated for a Pushcart Prize and an essay at *Alligator Juniper* won their nonfiction contest. His story published in *Whetstone*, "Out of the Blue," is in the pre-production stages as a short feature film by *Westbound Films* (www.westboundfilms.com). He has earned a place on the Fish Publishing contest short list and an honorable mention in a New Millennium Writings contest. A book of essays, *Falling Room*, which was his graduate school thesis and won Best Nonfiction Thesis in 2004, is now out from Bison Books (University of Nebraska Press) in their prestigious American Lives Series. A memoir, *A Cold and Broken Hallelujah*, a collection of stories, *Splitting*, and a novel, *Invading the World*, are all under the knife.

Ryan Heryford was born in Pittsburgh, Pennsylvania, and now lives in San Diego where he is working on his PhD in literature at the University of California, San Diego. He finished his first novel in the fall of 2007 and is currently shopping it around for publication.

Byron Hurt, a native New Yorker, is an anti-sexist activist, writer, college lecturer, and a filmmaker. His documentary *Hip-Hop: Beyond Beats and Rhymes* premiered at the 2006 Sundance Film Festival, and aired nationally on PBS' Emmy award-winning series, *Independent Lens*. Byron is married and currently lives in Plainfield, New Jersey.

Robert Jensen, a journalism professor at the University of Texas, Austin, is the author of *Getting Off: Pornography and the End of Masculinity* (South End Press, 2007), and co-author of *Pornography: The Production and Consumption of Inequality* (Routledge, 1997). He can be reached at rjensen@uts.cc.utexas.edu.

Jackson Katz is an educator, author, and filmmaker, who is internationally recognized for his groundbreaking work in the field of gender violence prevention education with men and boys, particularly in the sports culture and the military. He has conducted hundreds of lectures and professional trainings in the United States, Canada, Australia, and Japan. He is the co-founder of the racially diverse, mixed gender Mentors in Violence Prevention (MVP) program, the leading gender violence prevention initiative in professional and college athletics. He directs the first worldwide domestic and sexual violence prevention program in the United States Marine Corps. He is the creator and co-creator of educational videos including *Tough Guise* (Media Education Foundation, 2002), *Wrestling With Manhood*, and *Spin the Bottle* (Media Education Foundation, 2004). He is the author of *The Macho Paradox: Why Some Men Hurt Women and How All Men Can Help* (Sourcebooks, 2006). He is currently completing his doctorate in cultural studies at UCLA.

After completing his PhD in sociology at the University of California, Berkeley, **Michael S. Kimmel** has taught at Rutgers, University of California at Santa Cruz, Berkeley, and State University of New York, Stony Brook, where he is currently Professor of Sociology. He has worked for the past two decades to build the subfield of masculinity studies—through teaching innovative courses, writing and editing books and articles, and founding and editing the scholarly journal *Men and Masculinities*. One of the founders of the National Organization for Men Against Sexism (NOMAS), he remains a spokesperson for the organization and lectures around the world encouraging men to support gender equality.

Tomek Kitlinski and **Pawel Leszkowicz** are partners in life and in artistic, academic, and activist projects in Poland. They lecture at the Universities of Poznan and Lublin, Poland. Kitlinski studied at Lublin's Curie University, and with Julia Kristeva at the University of Paris. Leszkowicz studied at the University of Poznan, and the New School for Social Research in New York. They have participated in numerous feminist and gay workshops, conferences, and performance art events across Eastern Europe. Their work includes a number of contributions to Poland's feminist and gay publications and a book *Love and Democracy* (Aureus, 2005). Together with Joe Lockard, they authored an essay "Monica Dreyfus," included in the anthology, *Our Monica, Ourselves: The Clinton Affair and National Interest* (New York University Press, 2001).

Bob Lamm is a freelance writer and teacher in New York City. His political articles and personal essays have appeared in more than forty periodicals—among them, the *New York Times*, *Publishers Weekly*, *Ms.* magazine, the *Village Voice*, and the *Journal of Popular Film and Television*—as well as four anthologies. He has taught at Yale, Queens College, and the New School, and currently runs improv comedy workshops for beginners and non-performers at the City University of New York Graduate Center.

B. Loewe is originally from the Maryland suburbs of Washington, D.C. and is currently an organizer and fundraiser for the immigrant workers rights movement in Chicago, Illinois. This essay is the product of three years of writing and wouldn't be possible without the loving support, patient pushing, and thoughtful edits of previous lovers and current friends. Thank you.

Jared Margulies is a college student, studying anthropology and environmental studies. Following graduation, he plans to spend time abroad on a sailing ship or perhaps a sheep farm.

Alfredo Mirandé is Chair and Professor of the Ethnic Studies Department and a professor of sociology at the University of California, Riverside. He is the author of *The Stanford Law Chronicles: Doin' Time on the Farm* (University of Notre Dame Press, 2005), *Hombres y Machos: Masculinity and Latino Culture* (Westview, 1997), *The Age of Crisis* (Harper & Row, 1975), *La Chicana: The Mexican-American Woman* (University of Chicago Press, 1981), *The Chicano Experience* (University of Notre Dame Press, 1985), and *Gringo Justice* (University of Notre Dame Press, 1987).

Bryan Talbot Morris wrote this essay based on his experiences as a Fulbright Scholar to Indonesia in 2005–06. He has an MA in international development from Ohio University and a BA in communications from Mercer University. He is a former Peace Corps Volunteer in the Republic of Georgia and currently works in the NGO and international development sectors.

Rob Okun is Executive Director of the Men's Resource Center for Change (www.mrcforchange.org), one of the oldest men's centers in the United States, established in 1982. He is also editor of the center's magazine, *VOICE MALE: New Visions of Manhood*. His essays and commentaries on men and masculinity, fathering, domestic violence, and women and men collaborating, have appeared in numerous print and online publications and have been broadcast on public radio. His anthology, *The Rosenbergs: Collected Visions of Artists and Writers* (Universe Books, 1988), explores the intersection of art and politics. Rob speaks on issues of evolving masculinity on college campuses around the country. A husband and father of three daughters and a son, he maintains a counseling practice in Amherst, Massachusettts where he is also a justice of the peace. He can be reached at rob.okun@mrcforchange.org.

Ewuare X. Osayande (www.osayande.org) is an activist, poet, essayist, and parent. He is the author of several books including *Blood Luxury* (Africa World Press, 2005), *Black Anti-Ballistic Missives: Resisting War/Resisting Racism*

(Talking Drum Communications, 2003), and the forthcoming *Misogyny and the Emcee: Exposing the (S)exploitation of Black Women in Hip Hop*. He is co-founder of POWER (People Organized Working to Eradicate Racism) and the creator of ONUS, a workshop series on resisting sexism. He lives and organizes in the Philadelphia region.

Tal Peretz is a feminist, queer activist, environmentalist, yogi, Penn State Alumnus, and currently a graduate student in sociology at the University of Southern California. He authored and individualized an undergraduate major in diversity and oppression, focusing on feminist masculinities, and his current studies are interrogating the ways and reasons men enact feminism. He is especially interested in how privileged individuals can learn to recognize their status and reject or redirect it for positive social change.

Jay Poole grew up in rural North Carolina and despite his destiny to become a good ol' boy, he is now a social worker and educator who constantly poses the challenge to his clients and students as well as himself to call all things into question. Jay holds a master's degree in social work and he is a licensed clinical social worker. He is a visiting assistant professor in the Department of Social Work at the University of North Carolina at Greensboro where he teaches and learns from undergraduate and graduate students.

Richard Pringle, PhD, is a senior lecturer in the Department of Sport and Leisure Studies at the University of Waikato in New Zealand. His main areas of research are sport and gender relations, pain, and pleasure. He is the co-author (with Pirkko Markula) of *Foucault, Sport and Exercise: Power, Knowledge and Transforming the Self* (Routledge, 2006). Richard and his marriage partner, Dixie, enjoy parenting Zachary and Luke.

Jonathan Ravarino grew up and still lives in Salt Lake City, Utah, with his wife, Harmonie, and two lovely dogs, Kiley and Nesta. Harmonie and he got married shortly after he graduated with his bachelor's degree in sociology from Pacific Lutheran University in Tacoma, Washington. Following a year of running the rivers he entered graduate school and obtained masters degrees in social work and educational psychology from the University of Utah. His training led him to pursue a doctoral degree in counseling psychology focusing on men's experiences as social justice allies to women in preventing men's violence against women. He wants to recognize several mentors and friends who were instrumental in completion of this essay, including Harmonie Ravarino, Susan Morrow, Carla Reyes, Kristy Bartley, Donna Hawxhurst, Debra Daniels, Marty Licardo, Kevin Laska, and Linda Najjar.

Matthue Roth's newest book, *Candy in Action* (Soft Skull Press/Red Rattle Books, 2007), is a girl-empowerment philosophy book disguised as an actionadventure novel about supermodels who know kung-fu. He's also the author of *Never Mind the Goldbergs* (Scholastic/PUSH, 2006) and *Yom Kippur a Go-Go* (Cleis Press, 2005). He has performed poems at bars and colleges nationally and for Def Poetry Jam, and he keeps a secret diary at www.matthue.com. He and his wife, Itta, live in New York City.

Grantlin Schafer is a social worker and proud alumnus of the 2005–06 One in Four National Peer Education Tour, part of One in Four, Inc. He is extremely grateful for his tour mates Chris, Matt, and Daniel. The Captain, Dr. John Foubert, deserves much praise and deep gratitude for his vision in creating *The Men's Program* and One in Four, Inc. Finally, Dan Carlile, Dante Ricci, and Will Sellers have his sincere thanks for their guidance. More information is available at www.nomorerape.org.

Hugo Schwyzer has taught history and gender studies at Pasadena City College in California since 1993. In addition to teaching courses in Western civilization and women's history, he has developed and taught courses on men and masculinity, beauty and the body, and American lesbian and gay history. He's a popular speaker and workshop leader on issues ranging from sexual harassment in church settings to the role of men in the feminist movement. A sixth-generation Californian, Hugo holds a BA from the University of California, Berkeley, and an MA and PhD from the University of California, Los Angeles. In addition to an academic and professional interest in the pro-feminist men's movement, Hugo is active in animal rights, and serves as president of a non-profit chinchilla rescue. An avid marathoner and ultrarunner, he and his wife make their home in Pasadena. He blogs at http://hugoschwyzer.net.

A graduate of creative writing programs at Stanford University (BA) and State University of New York, Buffalo (MA), **Hank Shaw** is an award-winning writer who runs The Guy with the Tie, a marketing communications firm based in Rochester, New York. He worked with Pete Navratil and Jack Brennick to found an organization of men in Rochester who are working to end gender violence and discrimination. The group is called Stand-up Guys. Hank is the fortunate husband of a remarkable wife, Barbara Kasper, and is the father of Alex Kasper-Shaw, a great young man who will not have to go through the difficult transformation his father went through to embrace the simple fair-minded idea that equality isn't a club for men. In his spare time, Hank writes children's stories and other fiction, plays hoops (one of his great loves), and prepares for his next life as a honky-tonk pianist. Hank can be reached at Time4guys@aol.com and he wants to thank you for taking the time out of your day to read his piece.

Haji Shearer is director of a statewide fatherhood initiative in Massachusetts and a frequent contributor to *Voice Male* magazine. He founded the fathers' program at the Family Nurturing Center, which serves men in Boston's urban communities. He is a licensed social worker who spent many years doing crisis intervention with families. He frequently presents at conferences across Massachusetts on father involvement, male intimacy, and co-parenting. Haji promotes gender awareness through facilitating Men's Healing Circles, Boys to Men Rites of Passages, and Couples Workshops. He is especially interested in seeing African-American and Latino men heal the twin traumas of racism and patriarchy. Haji practices his vocation with his wife of seventeen years and two teenaged children. He is a long-time student of meditation who believes in the power of love.

When an earlier version of this essay was written and originally published in *AlterNet*, **Jeremy Adam Smith** was a stay-at-home dad in San Francisco. Today he is Managing Editor of *Greater Good* magazine and still striving to be the best dad he can be. His articles have appeared in *The Nation*, *Wired*, *Utne Reader*, and numerous other periodicals. Jeremy is also the author of *Twenty-First-Century Dad*, forthcoming from Beacon Press in 2009. He blogs about the politics of parenting at daddy-dialectic.blogspot.com.

Amit Taneja is the Assistant Director of the Lesbian, Gay, Bisexual, and Transgender Resource Center at Syracuse University, New York. He was born and raised in India, and moved to Canada in 1995. He completed his BA in psychology at the University of British Columbia in Vancouver, and his master's degree in college student personnel at Bowling Green State University. He is currently an advanced doctoral student in the Higher Education program at Syracuse University. He also serves as the Education, Advocacy, and Outreach Chair on the Executive Board of the National Consortium of Lesbian, Gay, Bisexual, and Transgender (LGBT) Directors in Higher Education.

Army reservist Sergeant **Marshall Thompson** spent a year in Iraq working as a military journalist. He served in the same capacity in Kosovo, Macedonia, and South Korea. In November 2006, Thompson completed a 500-mile walk across his home state of Utah to protest the war on Iraq and call for withdrawal of U.S. troops. Thompson and his wife, Kristen, have a daughter, Eliza, who was born during Thompson's tour in Iraq.

Marcus C. Tye, PhD is Associate Professor of Psychology at Dowling College in Oakdale, New York. A clinical psychologist, his writing includes both fiction and nonfiction, in addition to scholarly work in the field of law and psychology.

Donald N.S. Unger, PhD is a Lecturer in the Program in Writing and Humanistic Studies at the Massachusetts Institute of Technology. His scholarly interests include tracking changes in the representation of men, masculinity, and fatherhood in both language use and in popular culture. He has been writing about fatherhood—as well as doing occasional commentary for local National Public Radio (NPR) affiliates on the topic—since before the birth of his daughter Rebecca, in 1995.

EDITOR'S ACKNOWLEDGMENTS

I send lots of love to my family, Emilie Tarrant and John Ciulik, and to my parents, Judy and Mark Feingold. Thanks for staying on-call in case of editorial emergencies. Fortunately, there were few. My students, past and present, have been a source of inspiration, insight, and lively conversation: Cara Peckens, Lisa Narinian, and Emma Douglas provided helpful comments early in the project, and Katie Sipes stepped in with feedback when things came down to the wire. Shelby Woods and Jeanette Sanchez assisted in ways both large and small, and Sarah Gomez lent her invaluable, conscientious attention to the manuscript. My appreciation goes to Dave McBride for his enthusiasm for this project and to Steve Rutter and Anne Horowitz for seeing the process through to the finish. Anne has a great sense of follow-through and a wicked good sense of humor. Thanks to Sue Cope and Pearl Chang for their patience and artistry. This book benefited greatly from Sue's keen eye for editorial detail and from Pearl's skill in cover design. I also appreciate the focused efforts of Beatrice Schraa and Joon Won Moon in the Routledge marketing department. Family, friends, and colleagues along the way have been generous with their intellectual and moral support, offering much food for thought and sustenance for the soul. Sara Pollak, Alisa Feingold Savitz, David Feingold, and their wonderful families have a special place in my heart. Of course, Grama Sally is with me always. Finally, here's to all the feminists, pro-feminists, and allies out there, past, present, and future, who have the imagination to picture a different kind of world and the dedication to make it happen.

FOREWORD

Jackson Katz

At first glance, a book entitled *Men Speak Out* might strike some as oddly redundant, if not downright satirical. After all, haven't men—especially privileged white men—had ample opportunity to vocally express their opinions and narrate their own lives? Just what are these (presumably) formerly muzzled men going to speak out about? In fact, as I write this the radio "shock jock" Don Imus was just fired by CBS because, like countless arrogant men in the past and present, he abused his license to speak one too many times by mocking and denigrating people—in this case young African-American women—with much less social power.

The rationale for this book is not that men have been silenced and need to reclaim our voice. That, of course, is a powerful feminist narrative about *women's* voices and *women's* lives. What makes this book special is that it features the stories of twenty-first-century American *men* whose lives have been shaped in unprecedented ways by the social changes catalyzed by modern, multicultural women's movements. As some fascinating essays in this volume attest, feminism inspired a number of self-critical reflections from men. When I was in college in the early 1980s, I read and was moved by a groundbreaking anthology entitled *For Men Against Sexism*, edited by Jon Snodgrass, which was published in 1977. It helped me, and some of my fellow student activists, to envision a number of ways that we as men could contribute to the enormous transformations in the gender and sexual order that were taking place all around us—as well as within us.

Men Speak Out is in its own way a kind of cultural milestone. But it is a book of essays by men that could not have been written a generation ago, because while it was possible in the 1970s to speculate about how men's lives would change in the wake of feminism, there is now an entire generation of men who have lived through, indeed pioneered those changes.

Notably, the authors in this book are men from diverse backgrounds who have learned to see men's lives—their lives—from the standpoint of women's experience. Along with their own conventional and countercultural experiences as straight, gay, or bisexual men, many of the authors have had the opportunity to receive a formal women's, gender, or masculinities' studies education or have been mentored by feminist women. Many are well-read in multicultural feminist and womanist literature. Some have had close relationships with women that have enabled them to "walk a mile in her shoes."

Contrary to those who would dismissively assert that this has feminized or emasculated them, women's input hasn't in any way diluted the power of these men's insights into theirs or other men's lives. Rather, it has strengthened it. As the eminent feminist philosopher Sandra Harding maintains, the "view from women's lives" can illuminate men's lives by creating "a broader context and contrasting perspective from which to examine their own beliefs and behaviors, social relations and institutions."[1]

Harding argues that it is important for men (and whites, heterosexuals, citizens of wealthy Western countries) to learn about themselves through the lens of the experiences of subordinated groups. But she also acknowledges that men must struggle for a kind of self-awareness, a process that is painful for men who find themselves "abandoning cherished beliefs about themselves and their worlds, and choosing new behaviors and life projects."[2]

In the spirit of this struggle, it is altogether fitting that the editor of *Men Speak Out* is . . . a woman. One of the many ironies of contemporary history—both in the U.S. and around the world—is that women's leadership has made possible a more open and meaningful conversation *among men* about a wide range of issues that profoundly affect us. I know that I only started to think critically about men and masculinities—and my own gendered experiences as a (white, Jewish) boy and man—when as a young college student I was first introduced to feminist ideas by women, inside and outside the classroom.

To be sure, the essays contained in this collection advance the project of men thinking openly and meaningfully about our everyday lives as well as our generational location in the grand sweep of history. But this openness is not without its costs, because introspection can be unsettling. Taking a good hard look in the mirror requires a questioning nature and an adventurous spirit, even a certain kind of courage. Consider some of the challenging and provocative questions the authors grapple with: Is it possible to play out conventional heterosexual scripts between consenting adults and still be a committed anti-sexist man? Is there such a thing as a pro-feminist girl-watcher? Can men of color identify as feminists? Where do struggles against heterosexism fit into movements against sexism and racism? Is men's attraction to pornography about desire or power? Can those two concepts ever be separated? When a man has been sexually abused by another man—or by a woman—to what extent does it affect his masculine identity? Are stay-home dads at the leading edge of a cultural revolution? Why haven't more progressive men recognized that working to end men's violence against women is a social justice imperative? How does the destabilization of traditional masculine/feminine categories prompted by the transgender revolution challenge our assumptions about the kinds of folk wisdom embodied in the phrase "boys will be boys?"

These kinds of questions can be quite discomfiting, at least in part because the answers are often complicated, or unsatisfying. There is much more reassurance in simplistic clichés like "men are from Mars" than in the idea that what is considered masculine or "manly" is ever-shifting and contingent on a constellation of economic, social, political, and historical forces. When you factor in the responsibility that members of privileged groups have not only to be aware of their unearned advantages but to work against them, you can see why there is built-in reluctance to set the entire process in motion. Perhaps that explains why many of my academic colleagues who teach college courses on men and masculinity report that it is common for them to have only three or four male students in a classroom of thirty.

In the face of this kind of resistance to introspection, it is tempting to try to reassure men that their lives—including their relationships with women and other men—might actually improve if they have the will to critique and challenge the precepts of traditional masculinity. In fact, many more men would likely be drawn to feminist ideas if they understood that a commitment to gender justice entails deep concern for the wounds of boys and men—wounds that are inflicted by the same oppressive, sexist system that does such harm to women.

Just the same, I believe there are certain privileges men will have to forego if we are ever to be more than rhetorically committed to equality between the sexes. One of those privileges is the ability not to think about our privilege.

During the Clarence Thomas–Anita Hill hearings in 1991, when the mainstream media turned its full attention to the topic of sexual harassment for the first time, many men reacted defensively as the spotlight shifted toward our attitudes and behaviors toward women. Newspaper stories and cable TV programs featured interviews with countless men who hyperbolically asserted that, "It's gotten so bad I'm scared to say anything to a woman anymore." But was it really such a bad thing that men were being asked merely to stop and think about the effects on women of their words and actions? For years now, this type of introspection has been derided as political correctness. But far from being a debilitating burden, self-reflexivity should be seen as an indispensable character trait for members of any dominant group who want to be better, more compassionate people.

In the 1960s and 1970s, women formed consciousness-raising groups in part to help each other draw connections between personal issues in their own family and work lives and those in the broader movement for women's equality. Today, as the number of men who do pro-feminist work proliferates, there is a need for men to do consciousness-raising of a different sort: *self-consciousness-raising*. Of course, in our culture we generally use the term "self-conscious" to mean someone who is nervous and insecure. But that is a rather narrow definition. The great nineteenth-century German philosopher G.W.F. Hegel equated being self-conscious with being self-aware. In our time, when there is so much violence perpetrated by narcissistic, angry men—acting as lone school shooters, rapists, or as agents of state authority at the highest levels of power—encouraging men to be more self-aware would seem to be a task of the utmost urgency.

Fortunately we are in the midst of what the sociologist R.W. Connell calls the "ethnographic moment" in writing about men's lives. In many cultures around the world, growing numbers of men are publicly discussing their personal and political struggles—as well as their joys and triumphs—around issues related to masculinity, violence, sex, and feminism. The willingness of men like the contributors to *Men Speak Out* to engage in what the writer John Stoltenberg calls acts of "revolutionary honesty" is a gift to anyone who yearns and works not only for equality and justice for women—but for men, too, as well as for human rights, non-violence, and an end to so much of the unnecessary suffering in the world.

April 20, 2007

1. Sandra Harding. *Whose Science? Whose Knowledge? Thinking From Women's Lives*. Ithaca, NY: Cornell University Press, 1991, p. 286.
2. Ibid., p. 287.

INTRODUCTION

Shira Tarrant

Feminism is a dirty word. It conjures images of whiny, bitchy women with sanctimonious complaints about men. And the men who call themselves "feminist"? If they aren't simply whipped, then it's a cheap ploy at getting laid. Or so the story goes.

But that's an old version of the story. Fortunately, it looks like we're in the midst of change.

Recently, I was teaching in the women's studies program at a small, East Coast, liberal arts college outside of Baltimore. At first there were only one or two young men among the women enrolled in my classes. Soon there were more. They trickled in from the soccer team, the basketball team, the swim team, and the arts. They majored in physics, political science, mathematics, and dance. *Who were these guys?*, I wondered. *And how could I find more of them?*

Some answers came from conversations that I had with these same young men after class, sitting on the campus lawn. What they asked for was a book of essays written by men who had stories to tell about challenging the concepts of gender. They wanted to know if there were other men out there who were also trying to make sense of their experiences in today's culture, finding some past assumptions about both men and women no longer serve them. They wanted to know that they weren't alone in their thinking, and that it was possible to make a change. They wanted to know that they—and these other men—weren't wimps.

This anthology is a fresh look at gender, sex, and power—and feminism. It is a collection of essays about modern men making their way in a world that is struggling to rethink how it understands manhood and masculinity, just as it is struggling with changing ideas about women and femininity. This is a collection about men—written by men—who are willing to stare down these issues head on. Their attention to the interconnection and impact of gender, race, class, and sexuality is contemporary and vital. Our assumptions about men and women are shifting. We're not always sure where we're heading or where we want to end up. This book helps navigate the course.[1]

I set out to collect a series of essays that are direct and expressive in their interrogation of masculinity and power. I posted my request for essays to a number of relevant websites and listservs. I wanted to compile as diverse a selection as possible. Queries came from activist men, university men, men who used to be women, men from the South, men from the North, and men from places in between. I heard from queer men, straight men, and bi men; from young men, older men, black, Latino, Jewish, and white men. Emails of interest and support poured in from New Zealand, South Africa, England, Australia, Poland, Uruguay, Vietnam, Lapland—you get the picture. Many sent notes just to say thanks in advance for a book they've been waiting for. This response— awesome and humbling—was good news. There are many good men out there actively working to end male pattern domination and the abuse and misuse of power over others. There are so many creating new answers to old problems.

Encouraged by the response, I hatched a plan while preparing for a cross-country move back to California. Armed with over 2,000 photocopied announcements explaining the book and inviting men to send in their written thoughts, I planned to leave fliers behind at every college town and coffee house, truck stop and Bob Evans restaurant, coast to coast. This ambitious idea petered out somewhere around Indiana, where the road ahead looked longer and longer and the days and nights joined together as I drove with my family across the country. I did get the chance, though, to leave fliers at many places: at a corner bar in Athens, Ohio; a Starbucks in Cleveland; the Presbyterian Manor Senior Retirement Home in Salina, Kansas; at a down-on-its-luck casino outside of Reno, Nevada. I papered the National Women's Studies Association Conference in Oakland before heading south to Los Angeles, and stuck my head into the kitchen at a Mexican restaurant along the way to share some fliers. To my utter surprise and delight, the cook there said he'd already seen the call for submissions online. The word was out and the response was tremendous.

Some men in this book recount their personal challenges with living up to the demands of "traditional" masculinity. Others are quintessential guys' guys who love sports and beer. But one thing brings these men together on these pages if not in their day-to-day lives: Each of them struggles, in his own ways, with the personal and political limits that conventional masculinity imposes. Their unflinchingly honest prose tackles the politics of domination and strategies for change. They reflect, with kaleidoscope effect, on the issues of men, masculinity, identity, sexism, and feminism from different angles, revealing new insights and shifting patterns. The essays in this book deal not only with the difficulties of being a man, but also with the challenges of being a man who is grappling with sexism.

What becomes immediately clear is that there is no monolithic meaning of masculinity shared by all the authors. There is, instead, what Josephine Peyton Young describes as the "existence of multiple masculinities."[2] There is tension and interaction between gender, class, race, ethnicity, and sexuality. Age and youth lend additional viewpoints to these issues. There is also an encouraging theme: that we have tremendous potential for personal and political change. Hank Shaw, a writer from Rochester, New York, a self-described "guy off the street who bangs out words for a living," got his feet on the street when he took action against two local pornographers whose willingness to denigrate women seemingly knew no bounds. Tal Peretz, a recent college graduate from Pittsburgh, Pennsylvania, describes the radical transformation of his friend Cliff from a racist skinhead to feminist ally. For other men, complacency was never an option. Chong-suk Han calls out the gay community for its racism and white privilege while simultaneously attempting to stake a claim as oppressed sexual minorities. Nathan Einschlag takes on his college coach and basketball team for their upside-down expectations that place hooking up above personal ethics. Greg Bortnichak wonders out loud how he can remain true to his nonsexist ideals without falling into the trap of paternalistic protection when a much older man wants to hit on his girlfriend. Jacob Anderson-Minshall questions the expectations of straight men who assume he's one of them, and lesbian women who assume he's not. For all these men, asking soul-searching questions is a moral imperative, even if doing so leads to danger, rage, distress, or initial alienation from their peers.

We learn from Tomek Kitlinski and Pawel Leszkowicz that being out and gay in Poland is a risk far greater than we in the United States might imagine, with members of the far-right youth militia hurling stones and threatening their lives. Essays by Byron Hurt, Haji Shearer, Ewuare X. Osayande, and Amit Taneja teach us that there are multiple ways of understanding the intersections of race, nation, identity, and change. On fatherhood, we begin to imagine a world in which men are actively engaged parents, and to consider why some versions of fathers' rights groups do not work in the best interest of women, children, or men. Michael Kimmel and Rob Okun remind us where we came from so we can better see where we're going.

These essays, and the others in this collection, bring personal insight and critical awareness to our ideas about masculinity and feminism. Each is written through the unique lens of individual experience. There may be points of discomfort, and there are certainly questions raised but left unanswered, or only partially answered. There will be women who distrust men writing about feminism, and doubtless there will be men who are suspicious about a woman editing the voices of men. But as I see it, this discomfort can be productive. This anthology is part of a process of discovering the personal and political meanings of progressive manhood and feminist men. This process of discovery is certainly not a destination but it is a solid beginning.

There is a serious and growing movement of men who are committed to addressing problems we live with every day: domestic violence, rape and sexual assault, racism, homophobia, unequal pay, objectification, and standards of gender that are impossible to live up to. It's all part of the same package. There are men out there who stand beside women in feminist struggle, and this book is intended to give voice to those men and to provide role models for others coming up behind them. This book is intended to provide ideas and encouragement for the process of ongoing change.

In feminist theory and practice there is a tradition of coming to voice, of taking personal experience seriously, and of commitment to acknowledging that personal experience is political. We have heard plenty from men over the years, but to date we haven't heard enough from feminist allies about issues of identity, politics, and the potential for change.

Men Speak Out draws on feminist foundations and the work of feminist scholars who identify the ways in which we experience power, domination, freedom, and liberation. Kimberlé Crenshaw writes that people live multiple identities.[3] Because it is possible that we are simultaneously members of more than one community, we can experience both privilege and oppression at the same time. For example, a black man may enjoy gender privilege yet also experience racism. A gay white man may experience skin privilege but suffer the effects of homophobia. Building on this theoretical paradigm enables us to think about the feminist understandings of masculinity. We must take into account, as these essays do, broad differences such as immigrant standing, nation of origin, religion, race, sexual orientation, and trans-status. The potential is here for taking feminist scholarship in new directions, further extending conversations into areas such as research on transnational masculinities or on the efficacy of men as strategic political allies in achieving feminist goals. To this end, *Men Speak Out* adds in a hopefully significant way.

THE ESSAYS

The authors write about men and feminism, growing up male, recognizing masculine privilege, taking action to change the imbalance of power and privilege, and the constraints that men experience in confronting sexism. The essays describe individual authors' successes and challenges in confronting patriarchal systems in a culture that can be unsupportive if not downright hostile to this perspective. Some of these stories reflect on growing up, whereas others are vignettes of a day in the writer's life. Several authors draw from their academic expertise or political experience, while others ask tough questions about being a pro-feminist male who is living, working, thinking, and learning in a sexist society.

The essays in this collection are thematically organized into five parts beginning with Masculinity and Identity. In this part are a variety of perspectives: an athlete writes about the pressures of hooking up; a man who used to be a woman describes his transition; a boyfriend mulls over his girlfriend's love of Eminem. These authors explore issues of experience and agency, and they raise questions of race and masculinity, while suggesting answers to the puzzle of living as a man in a highly gendered world. The essays in part II, Sexuality, are about sexual desire, sexual assault, and sexual orientation. These forthright discussions look at men's use of pornography, what happens when lust from the waist down interferes with politics from the neck up, the media's assumptions about bisexuality, racism in the gay community, and male sexual assault. In the third part on Feminism, the reader will explore dynamic views on men, masculinity, and identity. The writers here do not agree on what feminism means, or even if it is a title they want to claim. What they do share, however, is an interest in gender equity and healthy masculinity, and a dedication to figuring out what this means. The essays in part IV, Points and Perspectives, include authors' recollections of the early women's liberation and anti-war movements, accounts of fatherhood, musings on being a man in academic women's studies, and the necessity of integrating public and private beliefs in equality. The title of the final part is Taking Action, Making Change. Some of these authors have chosen very public forms of activism that we readily associate with political action while, for other men, progressive change takes the form of deeply personal transformation.

HOW TO USE THIS BOOK

Men Speak Out is strategically positioned at the intersection of feminist literature and masculinity studies. This book is designed to appeal to curious readers, students and professors, activists and organizers alike. Admittedly, this is a tall order, but the essays are written in first-person accessible prose. These are not disembodied perspectives but voices coming from real people. The brief introduction to each section is intended to satisfy readers wanting an overview of the theoretical issues and an introduction to supporting resources that can be used for further investigation. I hope that readers will select from this combined material as each sees fit.

Taken as a collective whole, the essays in this anthology highlight the personal struggles, changing viewpoints, and learning that the authors have undergone in negotiating a wide variety of experiences of masculinity and ethical concern. These are forthright accounts that I think will enable the reader to better understand these personal and political issues. I hope that this book provokes discussion and that readers will relate to, argue about, agree and disagree with, expand on, and improve upon the ideas presented here.

1. The field of masculinity studies is rapidly growing. For examples of representative work, see the collected essays in Rachel Adams and David Savran, eds. *The Masculinity Studies Reader*. Malden, MA: Blackwell Publishing, 2002; and Judith Kegan Gardiner. *Masculinity Studies and Feminist Theory*. New York: Columbia University Press, 2002. In contrast to these theoretical accounts, *Men Speak Out* explores masculine identity and feminist politics primarily through narrative and personal experience.

2. Josephine Peyton Young. "Review: *Masculinities, Gender Relations, and Sport*." *Gender and Society*. Vol. 15, no. 5 (October 2001): 779.

3. Kimberlé Crenshaw. "Demarginalizing the Intersection of Race and Sex: A Black Feminist Critique of Antidiscrimination Doctrine, Feminist Theory, and Antiracist Politics." In Katharine T. Bartlett and Rosanne Kennedy, eds. *Feminist Legal Theory: Readings in Law and Gender*. Boulder, CO: Westview Press, 1991. For discussion on structural and political intersectionality in policy-making see Mieke Verloo. "Multiple Inequalities, Intersectionality and the European Union." *European Journal of Women's Studies*. Vol. 13, No. 3 (2006): 211–28.

Part I

Masculinity and Identity

INTRODUCTION

When it comes to gender, we are living in interesting times. Warrior masculinity is reinscribed and reinforced through military conflicts in Iraq, Afghanistan, and around the globe.[1] At the same time, the term "metrosexual" rolls easily off our tongues. TV commercials are full of grown men acting like developmentally arrested twelve-year-olds, and pop culture foists lad lit on us, replete with bumbling male incompetence. There is serious, ongoing, male-on-male gang violence at the same time as more American men are contentedly doing domestic work.[2] Advances in medical technology make it easier to sync up our bodies with our genders, and we know that masculinity is not only for men, but music videos like Nelly's "Tip Drill," with its infamous credit-card swipe down a woman's backside, are not unusual. The first national study on eating disorders reveals that 25 percent of all anorexic, bulimic, and binge-eating adults are now male.[3] So what, exactly, does it mean to be a man in the twenty-first century?

The essays in this section are written by men from many walks of life who explore the issues of power and masculinity. They dispel homogenous stereotypes about what it means to be a man.

These essays are timely since there is growing interest in the subject of masculinity. There is increasing curiosity about how it might be possible for men to "do" masculinity differently; that is to say, in ways that are not limiting or harmful to any of us. Susan Faludi's recent book, *Stiffed: The Betrayal of the American Man*,[4] drew mainstream attention to the subject. *Bitch*,[5] a magazine of feminist response to pop culture, devoted its entire Spring 2005 issue to masculinity. Rebecca Walker's book, *What Makes a Man: 22 Writers Imagine the Future*[6] and Daniel Jones's *The Bastard on the Couch: 27 Men Try Really Hard to Explain Their Feelings About Love, Loss, Fatherhood, and Freedom*[7] explore questions of manhood and masculine identity, and enjoy continuing strong sales.

In academic circles, critical gender studies, masculinities studies, and queer theory are dissecting the assumptions of biological essentialism. Genetics may explain a lot, and biological arguments about how men's and women's behaviors and traits are "hard-wired" are in vogue. But we also know that culture has deep effects on the social construction of gender and masculinity.[8] Michael Kimmel and Michael Messner's book, *Men's Lives*, is a key text for university masculinity and gender studies courses. In *Manhood in America: A Cultural History*, Kimmel makes the case that manhood is a constantly shifting cultural construction. R.W. Connell's *Masculinities* complements the recent stream of academic publications, offering suggestions on how we might study masculinity in the interest of progressive gender politics.[9]

Connell proposes that there is not *one* true version of masculine identity. Instead, there are many aspects of, and multiple ways of performing, *masculinities*.[10] But there are also tenacious mainstream assumptions about what it means to be a man. Conventional manhood—and its close cousin, hegemonic masculinity—can be summed up in three short words: no sissy stuff.[11] This imperative for masculine leadership dominates our collective imagination by invoking unrealistic expectations that men are by nature stoic, unemotional, aggressive, and interpersonally detached. In keeping with these stereotypes, physical contact is never okay unless it takes place on the wrestling mat, on the football field, or in a fight.

This picture of masculinity is restrictive to men and oppressive to all. Moreover, it is just plain inaccurate. Conventional masculinity is a style of manhood that many men are complicit in upholding, although few actually embody. There is nothing traditional, universal, or eternal about our current conventions of masculine gender. The more pertinent issue is, rather, "how particular groups of men inhabit positions of power and wealth, and how they legitimate and reproduce the social relationships that generate their dominance."[12]

The default setting for a masculinity defined by male dominance and aggression also makes the invalid assumption that all men are white, heterosexual, American, able-bodied, and middle class. Yet masculinity comes in many forms and packages and these multiple masculinities are informed, limited, and modified by race, ethnicity, class background, sexual orientation, and personal predilections. As Kimmel points out, hegemonic masculinity not only involves men dominating women, but men exerting power over other men, as well.[13] This particular version of manhood *may* use force or violence to uphold itself, but force is not necessarily required. Iris Marion Young explains how oppression or submission of the target group requires only the threat of violence to be effective.[14] By the same token, men—as members of the dominant group—can also be harmed by hegemonic masculinity. Experiencing harm is different, though, from being oppressed or subjugated because although "sexist notions of masculinity prevent men from showing emotion, for instance . . . failure to cry does not routinely cause men to lose out on the best jobs or receive lower pay."[15]

Dominator versions of masculinity continue to exist by recreating situations where men can exert power over women in general and various subordinated groups of men: immigrant, gay, or effeminate men, for example. The interplay between the powerful and less-powerful "is an important part of how a patriarchal social order works,"[16] but this isn't the end of the story. The dominance of any group of men is open to challenge and to change.[17]

Standards of masculinity are a cultural ideal, not a reality. The images of "real men" that public media show us do not correspond to the actual personalities of most men. Let's face it: How many guys are John Wayne, Rambo, James Bond, Barry Bonds—or even want to be? Yet many of us are complicit in upholding the masculine mystique. Doing so results in perceived gratification or the promise of a positive reward such as comradery, or vicarious aggression, or a passive sense of accomplishment. Going along to get along can also help guys avoid such negative sanctions as ostracism, ridicule, violence, and discrimination.

There is also the possibility that hegemonic masculinity, which is usually defined with fixed, negative connotations, might be transformed into a positive force. "It is quite conceivable," writes Connell, "that a certain hegemony could be constructed for masculinities that are less toxic, more cooperative and peaceable, than the current editions."[18] Scholars such as Demetrakis Z. Demetriou disagree, however, cautioning against prematurely celebrating the improved forms of masculinity that Connell claims are possible at new historical junctures. Patriarchal masculinity has a long history and is more persistent and sly, he claims. The hegemonic bloc may appear to change but in very deceptive ways through negotiation and appropriation, and "through the transformation of what appears counter-hegemonic and progressive into an instrument of backwardness and patriarchal reproduction." In other words, Demetriou explains, we ought to "avoid falling into the trap of believing that patriarchy has disappeared simply because heterosexual men have worn earrings."[19]

bell hooks's theories indirectly modify these arguments. She highlights the politics and patterns of domination—not of men or masculinity, *per se*—as the core area of concern for liberation struggle. The sociopolitical dynamics of exploitation and subjugation describes a broader abuse of power that is not necessarily limited to individual practitioners, although there are certainly individuals whom we can hold accountable for bad behavior. For hooks, social, political, economic, and cultural domination is predicated on what she calls white, supremacist, capitalist patriarchy.[20] This model of masculinist power is played out by dominating groups on the backs of subjugated peoples.

While we continue to question the assumptions that accompany privilege, we do well to remain concerned about the effects of hegemonic masculinity. It harms women—and men—because it is the strategic institutionalization of men's dominance over others. Maintaining this more complex political and social definition of power and subjugation is important in creating a more accurate understanding of identity and what it means to be a man.

The men writing here about masculinity build on popular trends and academic groundwork. But they are also creating an invigorating history of their own by speaking out about how gender ideals can operate in constricting ways, and the limitless possibilities for change. This section on masculinity and identity explores the myths and realities, and the doubts and certainties, of men's lives. The voices are those of real men reflecting on their own experiences. These essays put an active face on what Rachel Adams and David Savran describe as the process of unsettling assumptions "that govern dominant understandings of masculinity."[21]

Men Speak Out opens with Byron Hurt—hip-hop head, former college football quarterback, and creator of the acclaimed film *Hip Hop: Beyond Beats and Rhymes*. Hurt explains that as he learned more about sexism, violence, and homophobia in hip hop, he became more conflicted about the music that he loved. This conflict led Hurt to turn on the camera and create his film about masculinity in mainstream hip-hop culture. In his essay, "Daytona Beach: Beyond Beats and Rhymes," Hurt chronicles the hypermasculine behavior, the crude objectification of women, some women's complicity in the game, and the complicated issues of race, gender, violence, and sex that he sees played out while filming in Florida during BET's Spring Bling celebration. The limitations of hypermasculinity and the violent crime and homicide rates affecting young black men are serious issues. Yet the corporate media continues to record and distribute monolithic images of masculinity, providing limited models for becoming a man. Perceiving few options, many continue to go along with it. While the rap-star images we see on TV are slick and well edited, Hurt reveals the more complex gender politics behind the scene. Back from filming the crowds and interviewing fans at the Spring Bling in Daytona, Hurt's got eight hours of footage in the can and a story to tell.[22]

In the next essay, "The Real Slim Shady," Ryan Heryford writes about navigating heterosexual relationships and his sense of self as a feminist-minded man. Heryford's perspectives on gender conflict with those of his girfriend in unexpected ways: She likes Eminem; he prefers the Dixie Chicks, contradicting gendered stereotypes about masculinity and "being hard." Heryford tries to understand why some women prefer guys who treat them badly and wonders why these women put themselves in the path of violent, dangerous men. Heryford's best friend Matt is in a relationship with just such a woman. Matt, a gentle sort of guy, tries to get tough with his girlfriend Sarah. When this backfires they break up, and both Matt and Heryford are left questioning the meaning of masculinity, aggression, love, control, and tenderness.

In "The Enemy Within," Jacob Anderson-Minshall writes about his transformation from a young girl growing up in rural Idaho, to an adult lesbian woman, to becoming a straight white man living in the Bay area. Anderson-

Minshall's sexual trajectory has taken him deep undercover: He's had intimate access to the worlds of both heterosexual men and lesbian women. Since for Anderson-Minshall, sex and gender have been transitional states—not biological givens—he is able to raise provocative questions about both masculine and feminine identity.

In "Redefining Manhood: Resisting Sexism," Ewuare X. Osayande, an activist and writer from Philadelphia, ties together male entitlement and domination, feminism, and the black liberation struggle. His story is profoundly personal: Osayande's father was murdered in January 2000. The killer was the abusive ex-boyfriend of a woman who was dating Osayande's father. Osayande details how the murderer "resorted to the most violent expression of male domination. In his sexist mind, the woman was his property. She had no agency or capacity to create a life outside of his desires." When she started dating Osayande's father, this violent man struck out at both of them in the most extreme manifestation of sexism and hegemonic masculinity. Complicating efforts to resolve sexism, Osayande claims, has been the racism of some feminist white women. Osayande points to this as limiting the radicalizing potential of feminism within the black community in part because "sexist black men" have successfully used racism within feminism "to trump any real discussion of sexism within the black community."[23] Osayande's commentary draws from his personal observations of sexism and racism in the black community, and speaks directly to the need and possibilities for improving feminism.

On a different note, Jared Margulies describes his outsider status during six years as a member of a Slavic folkdance troupe beginning when he was ten years old. In "Straight Guys Can Dance, Too" Margulies lightheartedly wonders why people would assume that a boy who dances must be gay—and why he would harbor this own fear about himself. A rather large article about his dancing career, including full-page color photographs, appeared in Margulies's Ohio hometown newspaper, *The Columbus Dispatch*. Once this article appeared, writes Margulies, his middle school's jock population found it necessary to bar his entrance to the cool kids' table in the cafeteria. Although Margulies is funny in writing about his experiences, the issues he raises about ostracism and male identity are incredibly serious.

Nathan Einschlag recounts his life-changing and heartbreaking experience playing college basketball at a school filled with privileged—and in many ways protected—young students. Growing up in the immigrant neighborhood of Jackson Heights in Queens, New York, Einschlag saw things that the guys on his team "only read about in magazines, or saw on TV." During high school, playing ball kept Einschlag off the streets and out of trouble. Now in college, Einschlag finds himself surrounded by teammates who think that excessive drinking and sexual conquest are equated with their ability to be a guy and play the game. Einschlag faces a difficult choice: to play college basketball and go along with the expected standards of masculine behavior, or stay true to himself and possibly leave the team behind.

"*Hombres y Machos*," is the title of Alfredo Mirandé's essay on machismo and Chicano/Latino masculinity. Mirandé recalls his experiences growing up in an extended family in Mexico, and reflects on how stereotypes of machismo are at odds with his memories of boyhood. This disjuncture led Mirandé to conduct empirical research investigating issues of machismo and masculinity in Chicano and Latino culture. Mirandé launched this project because although patriarchy, machismo, and "excessive masculinity" are assumed to be prevalent among Latino and Chicano men, there has been little research to establish this. Until recently, Mirandé writes, these generalizations about machismo "were based on meager, nonexistent, and misinterpreted evidence."[29] With *Hombres y Machos* Mirandé corrects the record. This project is of particular importance because of the ways in which images of machismo are used to perpetuate negative conceptions, and legitimize the economic and political subordination, of Mexican and Latino men.

1. While both women and men are involved in war, there are gendered aspects of global violence that are worth attention. The Summer 2007 special issue of the journal *Signs* titled *War and Terror: Raced-Gendered Logics and Effects* cites, for example, the gendered logic of masculine warrior ethic by which "peace is commonly associated with 'feminine virtues' and war with regimes of masculinity. . . . Depending on the definition of war there are between sixty-five and two thousand sustained wars ongoing in the twenty-first century." Recent feminist scholarship suggesting that "deep-seated cultural, racial, and gender stereotypes" intensify during wartime thus becomes particularly relevant. See "Call for Papers." *Signs: Journal of Women in Culture and Society*. Vol. 31, no. 1 (Autumn 2005): ix. For discussion about gendered discourse and thinking about war (as distinct from gendered participation in war) see Carol Cohn. "Wars, Wimps, and Women: Talking Gender and Thinking War." In Michael S. Kimmel and Michael A. Messner, eds. *Men's Lives*, seventh edition. San Francisco: Pearson, 2007. For further discussion about militarism, war, and contemporary gender politics see, for example, Cynthia Enloe. *Bananas, Beaches and Bases: Making Feminist Sense of International Politics*. Berkeley, CA: University of California Press, 2001; Bonnie Mann. "How America Justifies Its War: A Modern/Postmodern Aesthetics of Masculinity and Sovereignty." *Hypatia*. Vol. 21, no. 4 (Fall 2006): 147–63 ; Francis Shor. "Hypermasculine Warfare: From 9/11 to the War on Iraq." http://bad.eserver.org/reviews/2005/shor.html. Accessed January 31, 2007; Shira Tarrant. "Who's Accountable for the Abuse at Abu Ghraib?" *off our backs*. September–October 2004.
2. Lakshmi Chaudhry. "Growing Up to Be Boys." *In These Times* www.alternet.org/story/33801. Posted on March 23, 2006. Accessed on October 10, 2006.
3. Denise Gellene. "Men Found to Be Anorexic, Bulimic Also." *Los Angeles Times* February 1, 2007, A12.
4. Susan Faludi. *Stiffed: The Betrayal of the American Man*. New York: Harper Perennial, 2000.

5. *Bitch: Feminist Response to Pop Culture.* Issue #28 (Spring 2005).

6. Rebecca Walker, ed. *What Makes a Man: 22 Writers Imagine the Future.* New York: Riverhead Books, 2005.

7. Daniel Jones, ed. *The Bastard on the Couch: 27 Men Try Really Hard to Explain Their Feelings About Love, Loss, Fatherhood, and Freedom.* New York: Harper Paperbacks, 2005.

8. For discussions about how biological explanations came in and out of fashion as the dominant paradigm for explaining gender during the twentieth century, see Shira Tarrant. *When Sex Became Gender.* New York: Routledge, 2006. See also Martha McCaughey. *The Caveman Mystique: Pop-Darwinism and the Debates Over Sex, Violence, and Science.* New York: Routledge, 2007.

9. This list is, of course, only partial, but it is evidence of the burgeoning critical interest in men, masculinity, and contemporary society.

10. R.W. Connell. *Masculinities.* Los Angeles: University of California Press, 1995.

11. Deborah S. David and Robert Brannon, eds. *The Forty-Nine Percent Majority: The Male Sex Role.* Reading, MA: Addison-Wesley, 1976.

12. Tim Carrigan, Bob Connell, John Lee. "Toward a New Sociology of Masculinity." In Rachel Adams and David Savran, eds. *The Masculinity Studies Reader.* Malden, MA: Blackwell Publishing, 2002, p. 112.

13. Michael S. Kimmel. *The History of Men: Essays on the History of American and British Masculinities.* Albany, NY: State University of New York, 2005. For resources on global masculinities see the Global Masculinities Series (series editor, Michael S. Kimmel) published by Zed Books. Titles include, for example, Victor J. Seidler, ed. *Young Men & Masculinities: Global Cultures and Intimate Lives.* London: Zed Books, 2006; Lahoucine Ouzgane, ed. *Islamic Masculinities.* London: Zed Books, 2006; Adam Jones, ed. *Men of the Global South.* London: Zed Books, 2006.

14. Iris Marion Young. *Justice and the Politics of Difference.* Princeton, NJ: Princeton University Press, 1990.

15. Kelly Rae Kraemer. "Solidarity in Action: Exploring the Work of Allies in Social Movements." *Peace & Change.* Vol. 32, no. 1 (January 2007): 24.

16. R.W. Connell. *Gender and Power: Society, the Person and Sexual Politics.* Stanford, CT: Stanford University Press, 1987, p. 183.

17. R.W. Connell. *Masculinities.* Los Angeles: University of California Press, 1995, p. 77. Challenging this domination is a key aspect of the essays in Part III.

18. R.W. Connell. "Reply." *Gender & Society.* Vol. 12, no. 4 (August 1998): 475.

19. Demetrakis Z. Demetriou. "Connell's Concept of Hegemonic Masculinity: A Critique." *Theory and Society.* Vol. 30, no. 3 (June 2001): 355.

20. Sut Jhally, dir. *bell hooks: Cultural Criticism and Transformation.* Northampton, MA: Media Education Foundation, 1997.

21. Rachel Adams and David Savran, eds. *The Masculinity Studies Reader.* Malden, MA: Blackwell, 2002, p. 337.

22. The Black Youth Project, led by Dr. Cathy Cohen, Professor of Political Science at the University of Chicago, collected empirical data to answer questions about black youth and empowerment, including a content analysis of rap music. The project

conducted in-depth interviews about (among other things) political efficacy, gender and politics, and hip hop and politics. See http://blackyouthproject.uchicago.edu for further information.

23. See Winifred Breines. *The Trouble between Us: An Uneasy History of White and Black Women in the Feminist Movement*. New York: Oxford University Press, 2006. Despite efforts in the 1960s to embrace antiracist politics and build interracial political movements, Breines argues that white women's "staunch commitment to universal feminism revealed insensitivity to the differences between Black women and themselves." Although black and white feminists have achieved some success working together, "legacies of racial divisions and racism linger in contemporary social movements." Verta Taylor. "Review. *The Trouble between Us*." *Gender & Society*. Vol. 21, no. 1 (February 2007): 137–8. For writings by women on contemporary issues of transracial identity and the feminist movement see Lisa Weiner-Mahfuz. "Organizing 101: A Mixed-Race Feminist in Movements for Social Justice," and Rebecca Hurdis. "Heartbroken: Women of Color Feminism and the Third Wave," in Daisy Hernández and Bushra Rehman, eds. *Colonize This! Young Women of Color on Today's Feminism*. Emeryville, CA: Seal Press, 2002; and Susan Muaddi Darrraj. "Third World, Third Wave Feminism(s): The Evolution of Arab American Feminism," in Rory Dicker and Alison Piepmeier, eds. *Catching a Wave: Reclaiming Feminism for the 21st Century*. Boston: Northeastern University Press, 2003.

24. Alredo Mirandé. *Hombres y Machos: Masculinity and Latino Culture*. Boulder, CO: Westview Press, 1997, p. 5. For discussion about machismo and Puerto Rican men see José B. Torres. "Masculinity and Gender Roles among Puerto Rican Men: Machismo on the U.S. Mainland." In Michael S. Kimmel and Michael A. Messner, eds. *Men's Lives*, seventh edition. San Francisco: Pearson, 2007.

DAYTONA BEACH: BEYOND BEATS AND RHYMES

Byron Hurt
April 2003

Daytona Beach, FL—I'm at BET's annual Spring Bling, an event fashioned after MTV's Spring Break, a yearly-televised weeklong party and hedonistic mating ritual. Like the MTV version, BET's Spring Bling looks like mad fun on television, and is well attended. One big distinction between the two music television shows (both are under the corporate banner of Viacom): MTV's Spring Break is largely white with some faces of color sprinkled throughout the crowd; BET's Spring Bling is clearly black space. White folks here are mostly cultural tourists.

I am here to shoot footage for my yet-to-be-released film *Hip-Hop: Beyond Beats and Rhymes*, a documentary about manhood in rap music and hip-hop culture. I am hoping to interview rap artists and fans about their thoughts and feelings about sexism and misogyny in mainstream hip-hop music.

There is a lot of energy here, and it is shaping up to be the type of event I've been to many times before—from the annual Greek Fest on Long Island's Jones Beach, to July Fourth weekend at Martha's Vineyard, to Atlanta's Freaknic, to the Grand Conclave of my fraternity, Omega Psi Phi. At thirty-five years old, this kind of thing ain't new to me. I've seen it all when it comes to social events for young black folks like this one. I'm older, and it's been awhile, but amazingly, I still feel comfortable in this crowd.

The morning starts out mildly, with young black men and women from all walks of life congregating in hotel lobbies, chilling on the popular strip, and out on Daytona Beach. Hip-hop music thumps in the background. Before lunchtime there are hundreds of hip-hop heads on the scene, doing what has become typically hip-hop—promoting parties, shamelessly plugging and passing out CD demos and mix tapes, igniting impromptu freestyle battles, and, of course, lots and lots of flossin'. The party at Daytona Beach has officially begun. And everyone, including myself, loves a good hip-hop party.

Just before my trip, BET denied my request for press credentials and backstage access—a last minute curveball. But I am here anyway, hoping to somehow bullshit my way behind the scenes to score interviews with A-List rappers. Once here though, I find BET's on-location headquarters to be well organized. Security is extra tight. At the press check-in table, I politic for an "elite access" badge, claiming I never received a declination of my credentials request, which I have with me, hard copy in hand. The polite but firm BET event coordinators recognize my name and the name of my film production. They assure me that my request had been seriously considered, but tell me that unfortunately, the powers that be at BET denied my request.

They turn my crew and me away, and ask me to step aside so they can help the next production crew in line. Malik, my production assistant, Caleb, my soundman, and Bill, my director of photography, are all here with me. As the film's director, I must come up with a Plan B.

We head back through the hotel lobby, which is now a spectacle. Dudes are freestyling and waging MC battles ten feet from the hotel's concierge. A street team comprised mostly of black men dressed in black and white short-sleeved tees hold placards on wooden sticks high above their heads. Bold white letters on the black laminated poster boards read "Let's Get Free," promoting rapper Freeway's upcoming new album. Men fully dressed in summer gear ogle scantily dressed women who pass by. How hotel security manages all of this traffic, I don't know.

Throngs of men, donning du-rags underneath carefully placed baseball caps, slightly tilted, and barely touching the scalp, perform a brand of hip-hop masculinity reserved only for true thugs, pimps, and playas. A few folks, some older and black, some white and un-hip-hop, are clearly not associated with the event and look uncomfortably out of place.

With all of the video cameras, throwback jerseys, tricked-out rides and bling, I am starting to feel like I am in a real live, hip-hop music video. Everyone comes, it seems, to play a role. The men behind their cameras (and it is mostly men with video cameras) shoot black female bodies at camera angles intended for the male gaze. Men in hip-hop drag do their best G-Unit impersonations on camera. Instead of throwing up the Roc (Rocafella Record's world famous hand gesture in the shape of a diamond), they throw up homemade hand signals repping their hood or fledgling record companies. And the women, well, some of the women at least (save the ones disinterested in serving as props), play the role of the sex kitten—the object of the men's desire.

The main drag now is a car show. 50 Cent's *P.I.M.P.* is ubiquitous on the strip and blares out of tricked out cars with brilliant color combinations. One car, a refurbished '74 Chevy Impala, is money green with burnt orange trim. Twenty-two inch rims spin, even as the car stands still in bumper-to-bumper traffic. As the car slowly passes a large crowd, the passenger, clearly a showman, opens his door revealing a bucket seat with a fuzzy wool seat cover. He spins the seat 360 degrees. The crowd is awed, and in unison, everyone screams "oooohhhh!" By today's conventions, this is all so hip-hop.

As the day grows longer, the energy increases, and all of the elements for this live hip-hop video are in place. Everyone is ready on set. Lights, camera, action.

As I stand on the busy sidewalk with my Angela Davis T-shirt and blue New York Yankees fisherman's hat pulled down just above my eyes, it does not take long to find Plan B. The story reveals itself. What my crew and I catch on camera next is far more important, alarming, and compelling than backstage access or any interview with an A-list rapper could provide.

A BET performance lets out, and now there are thousands of hip-hop fans on the strip. It is hot. Very hot. Men drape their shoulders with white hand towels and occasionally wipe away their sweat. Some let their towels hang long from their back pockets, a hip-hop fashion statement. They all swagger. I quickly realize that this is not just black space—this is black *male* space. The masculine energy is palpable. Women in small groups stick close together as they walk to their next destination. Suddenly, as if a tacit agreement among the men had been reached, the men begin to make life difficult for the women. As women in skimpy bathing suits exit the beach area to cross the crowded Daytona strip, men with video cameras follow. One unfortunate threesome (one white, one black, and one Latina) get stuck at a crosswalk and wait for their turn to cross the street. The men with video cameras descend. A man with audacious gumption lifts the white woman's blue and white sundress, and records her bare ass. As he tilts his camera upward, she swipes at his hands and spins. Simultaneously, the light turns red, as if to save her from further distress. She begins to cross the street. Her two friends try to prevent themselves from being recorded, but to no avail. The men capture their bodies on camera, without their approval. Who knows where these women's likenesses will end up?

On the same sidewalk, about twenty yards ahead, a man in a red, white, and blue T-shirt hustles homemade DVDs from last year's Spring Bling. Titled *Dirty South*, an image of a black woman's behind graces the cover. You do not see her face, just her buttocks and legs. I tell my cameraman to get a shot of him. Realizing he is on camera, he hams it up. Holding one DVD close to the lens, he endorses his product like a hip-hop Donald Trump. He knows his target audience—young, male, with hip-hop sensibilities. He looks directly into the camera when he speaks, and then to me when he is done. He has no clue I am an anti-sexist activist. No one here does.

I blend right in the crowd because I am a man. Not even my Angela Davis T-shirt gives me away.

I head up the street with my crew behind me. I tell Bill to stay close to me as we move through the thick crowd. The men form lines on both sides of the sidewalk as the women walk through the center. It is clearly a set up. One by one, as women with various shapes, skin complexions, and hairstyles walk through, the men—showing no restraint—grab at body parts. Arms, shoulders, hands, chests, and asses, nothing is off limits. Some women yell, "Stop! Quit!" and "Get off of me!" Others helplessly ask, "What are you doing?" Most remain silent; one out of maybe ten of the women swings violently at a male offender. They are the courageous ones. Resistors this brave are rare. The others seem to endure it.

Then, out of nowhere, I hear a roar. I turn around and see a young man, probably in his mid-twenties, pulling down a heavy-set woman's bikini top. She stands there, smiling. She is complicit, but doesn't seem well. She looks mentally challenged. I watch as he and his boy stand around the woman, smiling, pointing at her bare breasts. Video cameras, including mine, roll. As an anti-sexist activist, my first instinct is to intervene. But I remember I am here to document this event, not to be a proactive bystander. My inaction fills my body with inner-conflict. I feel tense, uncomfortable, nervous. I am vexed at what I see, but I remain focused on capturing the moment on film for the greater good of revealing the prevalence of misogyny in hip-hop culture, and how normalized it has become. No one challenges the two men at all. In fact, men cheer from the sidelines, rewarding the duo's sexual violence. In an instant, I muster the courage to approach the two men. I walk closer to the scene. Bill and Caleb are in tow. "What makes you feel like it is okay to pull this woman's top off like this in public?" I ask. The one caught in the act sheepishly grins, revealing braces on his teeth. He tries to be coy. "Nah, see what happened was, I was walking past her, right, and she grabbed my ass, so I grabbed her tits," he says. I look him straight in the eye as if to say, *Yeah right, man. Don't try to play me*. I repeat my question. His husky friend, apparently his road dog for the weekend, jumps in. He begins to break down the situation on behalf of all black men in America. "Look here," he says. "The white boys got their *Girls Gone Wild*, now this is our *Girls Gone Wild*, you see? Why should the white boys have all the fun? They have their MTV Spring Break, now this is our Spring Break. The white boys do it. Why can't we? We're not trying to hurt no one; we're just trying to have a good time."

Unmoved, I reframe my question. "What if someone did something like that to your daughter or your sister?" He becomes defensive. "Aw man, why you trying to play me out like that, brother?" He then motions to Bill to turn the camera off. I give Bill a quick, sharp look—nonverbal communication for *Don't you even think about turning off that camera*. The guy, realizing now that I was dead serious about challenging their behavior tries to shift the conversation, and questions my racial loyalty. "Yo man, how you gonna play the black man out like that, man? Don't make us look bad on camera like that, man." Then he says, "Look, we're brothers, right? Why would you play us out like the white man? The white man always plays us out like we're bad people, man. Don't be like the white man."

Admittedly, this taps into my concern about revealing negative black male behavior to a largely white PBS audience. I am fearful about reinforcing stereotypes of black men as oversexed to an audience of unsophisticated, conservative white people. I almost retreat. But just before I do, I come up with a comeback line that I think might work. "But she's a black woman, though," I say. "How could I be against the race if I am supporting a black woman? It's not like she's white, or green, or an alien," I say, growing more confident in my position. "This is a black woman you are disrespecting and you're challenging my blackness?"

Stumped, he tries to deflect by pointing at my shirt. "Who is this?" he asks, looking down at the iconic photo of the Afro-wearing woman on my chest. "She's a Black Panther, right?"

"Yeah," I say. "This is Angela Davis."

"My daddy was a Black Panther," he says. "I got mad respect for the Panthers." "Well, not only was she a Black Panther," I tell him, "but she is also a black feminist."

"Oh, word?" He seems to lose interest.

"Word," I say. "And she would never approve of you treating black women this way."

Moving closer to me he as if to share a well kept secret, he says, "Dawg, I know its wrong, but if the women let us treat them this way, then we're going to treat them this way, *you-know-what-I'm-sayin*'? It's just how it is."

I smell alcohol on his breath and realize this conversation is only going to go so far. I tell him that it doesn't matter if women allow us to mistreat them, it's still not cool. Just as I was making my point, a tricked out car passes by which catches everyone's attention. Suddenly, the interview is over.

I looked away for a second, and the two men were gone.

At dusk, the scene at Daytona worsens. The men here are completely out of control. Check that. The men here are completely *in control*. They are benefiting from the type of male privilege that transcends race. Even the police officers, who are white, remain silent. If the women were white, I wonder if they would be so nonchalant about enforcing the law. The women, save but a few outspoken voices, are too complacent, too accepting of sexist behavior without resistance. My crew and I grow tired of shooting scene after scene of sexual assaults, and take a break. We find a place on the strip that is not as crowded, and sit down on the curb. My soundman, Caleb, asks if we can go home. "I knew it was going to be wild down here, but I didn't expect this," he says. Stunned by the enormity of the situation, I sit with my head cradled in my hands. My young production assistant, Malik, seems less disturbed than the rest of us. "I'm going to get some pizza. Do y'all want anything?" he asks. There is a long silence. No one answers. Then Bill, who is white, says softly, as if he's unsure if it is cool to say aloud, "This is exactly what white people think of black people. You know that right, Byron?" I sigh. His question is genuine, honest, and perfectly timed. I am thinking the same thing, but don't want to admit to Bill. To outsiders we look really bad to people who do not understand our complex history and culture. Shit, we look bad period, no matter the spectator. There's no comeback for Bill's sad-but-true admission. I feel disappointed in my people, both male and female. I sit thinking about my work as an anti-sexist activist—a man who speaks to groups of men about rape and sexual assault—and how much work there is to be done before this kind of male behavior becomes socially unacceptable. I think also about women who, just like men, internalize sexism, and how so many participate in their own degradation. I feel sad and overwhelmed.

Later in the evening during another break, I run into a woman who sticks out like a sore thumb. She wears a natural hairstyle, locked, and reminds me of some of the gender conscious women I know back home. Unlike many of the women here who seem aloof—even validated by the negative attention some men give them—she seems like she is studying her environment. She is here with a group of friends from New York. She looks pensive, and is deep in thought. I strike up a conversation, and we talk about the Daytona scene. This is her first time at BET's Spring Bling. She says she is working on her PhD, and is here on spring break. She "needed to get away," she tells me. Her university is predominantly white, and she wanted to be around black people and have a good time this weekend. She, too, is disappointed. I have lots of questions for her. I am thinking about interviewing her for the film, but right now, the camera is off. I ask her why women come to events like this, and why women put up with this kind of behavior by men? Her answer hits me over the head like a club.

"I don't know," she tells me. "I think most women put up with this kind of treatment because we live most of our lives dealing with men who are assholes," she explains. "We expect y'all to act like this. It's almost a fact of life, so we grin and bear it and try to have a good time despite trifling brothers who act like they've never seen a woman before."

Wow. What a powerful statement. What strikes me most about her comments is the fact that when describing men's behavior, she uses the word y'all to describe all men. Without knowing my feminist sensibilities, this woman sees no difference between me, and the "typical" man on the strip. Who could blame her?

Still, something about her not distinguishing me from the rest of the men stings. Like the men on the strip, she doesn't know I am an anti-sexist activist. I flash back to my own past, before I became a gender conscious male, before I learned about sexism, before I understood the reality of women who live in a rape culture. Back then, I was just as typical as some of the men here today in Daytona: male, privileged, selfish, unconcerned about women's issues, guarded about the image of black men, defensive, and insecure about my masculinity. Fortunately for me, I had the opportunity to learn about gender issues in ways many of these men have not. That's the only thing that separates me from them.

Other than that, we are all the same. We are men who learn sexism from myriad places in the culture. Hip-hop is just one place that informs us about how to treat women.

A month later I'm home watching BET on a Saturday afternoon. Spring Bling is on television and it looks like nothing but fun for all who attended. The final package is slick, well edited, and entertaining. You see concerts, hip-hop executives, celebrities, star struck fans, tons of bling, and interviews with A-List rappers—all of the footage I would have shot had BET given me the backstage pass I requested. But what you will never see on BET is what happens away from all the glitz and the glamour at this particular Spring Bling—men gone wild, and women who came here for a party, but who go home as sexual assault survivors.

With eight hours of footage in the can, I have a story to tell.

THE REAL SLIM SHADY

Ryan Heryford

I usually miss. Something always goes wrong. My knees buckle, or the dryer bell rings in the other room. I turn my head and my hips follow. My dick sways too far to the left or sometimes to the right, and a splash lands on the rim or the back of the seat, sometimes onto the puke orange rug we keep at the base of the toilet. I'm always stealthy. I snatch a tissue square and wipe off the stray drops, throwing them back into the bowl. I've never been caught. OK, I've only been caught a few times.

My girlfriend believes it is romantic to have that freedom of walking in on me while I pee. Perhaps, it is through this little ritual of ours that all of my elaborate masks which I have polished for her, all of my adorned statements about nothing at all, are reduced only to this: a body, pale, untrimmed, with a dick that usually sways too far to one side, dripping piss onto the white tiles below. So that she might say—"You peed on the floor."

"I'm sorry. I'll clean it up."

"No you won't. You'll clean some of it up. And some it will seep into the cracks, or make a puddle behind the toilet bowl. And it will dry and get warm when I turn the heat up. And it will stink like all hell. But you won't notice. You never notice. Only I do."

"I'll clean it up. I'm sorry. This is ridiculous anyways. Why don't they ever put urinals in people's homes? Only seats. It's unnatural. It isn't natural to pee into a seat. Even with the rim up. The diameter isn't wide enough. It's like a carnival game without prizes. Only punishments."

"Don't be a prick about it. If it means this much to you, don't clean it up at all. I'll just suffocate from the stench. And when my body is cold and dead on the bathroom floor, you can pee all over it." She usually sighs now, and then she says: "Christ, you're just like every other guy I've ever dated."

This is when the fight begins.

We fight precisely because I am not at all like any other guy she has ever dated. I am lanky, uncoordinated, and my cologne smells like a teenage girl's body wash. I go to bed by eleven and I am up at seven. I usually skip breakfast. I eat soy processed imitation meat patties for lunch. And sometimes, if I'm feeling adventurous, I'll go and see a movie in the evening. But only after reading numerous reviews and repeatedly verifying the show time. If my car broke down on the way to the theater, I wouldn't even know how to open the hood. I would probably call my mother. Most likely, I would cry.

These traits are incomparable to the other men who have come and gone throughout her life: a Jewish cocaine dealer with a pit bull and Samurai swords; a high school rugby all-star who punched out the coke dealer during a gang fight at the homecoming dance; a car mechanic with a pot farm in his basement and a gold chain that read, *Ain't No Secret I'm a Full Grown Man*. At this point in the argument, I will bring up each one of these characters by order of their deficiencies, and then tear them down by order of my insecurities. The truth is, I am severely jealous. While they dueled out their shortcomings with the sharp edges of their inflated masculinities, mine shrivels away, deflated in its holster. And the only link that I have to any of them as men is that we have all dripped pee along the rim of our girlfriend's toilet seat.

She would tell me not to panic. She never really cared for any of them. When they made love, she would always close her eyes. She would fantasize about someone else, someone who ultimately understood her. Often, she would conjure up the image of her favorite musical artist—Eminem.

I imagine that the image isn't too hard to conjure. His figure is plastered all across the bedroom. A *Rolling Stone* clipping of Marshall Mathers in a suit and tie with roses in his arms, lying in his unsealed grave, is tacked up next to her nightstand. Slim's very own plastic action figure hangs above our door, a three-centimeter chainsaw glued to his left hand. My personal favorite is the poster, duct-taped to the ceiling above the bed, where he's standing tall, stark naked, holding a two-foot bong over the patch of poster where his dick ought to be.

When we make love, when she is on top, I don't have to conjure up anything at all. There he is, his dark brown eyes staring hard into my baby blues, that lifeless expression on his face which seems to say—"Yeah, I trickled a little bit of piss onto the toilet seat. So what, pussy?"

I asked her to take them down. It wasn't happening. She's been playing his albums since she was thirteen. "What the hell is so fascinating about him, anyways?" I asked. "He's a misogynist pig, a racist, anti-Semitic. He hates homosexuals. He hates everything and everyone just for the sake of hating."

"Because he never backs down," she told me. "He'll always be the last one standing."

"Standing for what?" I asked.

"Standing for his pride, his manhood."

My best friend Matt is a skinny feminist with knee problems, lactose intolerance, and an extensive collection of Ani DiFranco records, who thinks that he stands stronger than any of the Slim Shadys out there. But Matt doesn't have to stand up, he tells me in our ongoing e-mail conversations. Matt "relinquishes power! Saying, 'yeah, I have power; but here, you fucking take it.' That is hard! And all the fucking cock-wielding assholes (whose heads I've fought myself from wanting to tear off, whose throats I've fought myself from wanting gleefully to defecate down). They're the real unformed ones."

But he doesn't really mean any of this.

"Actually," he writes, "that line about wanting to tear off their heads is a slightly altered rendition of wanting to wash their feet. I turned it around toward anger, frustration, and fury, because I wanted to seem a little hard, which I am not really. But I keep it alive for the sake of other's passions."

Dirty feet can be sexy sometimes. They are a sign of one's rugged, untamed manhood; that brown-eyed expression that says, "So what, pussy?" But dirty feet grow calloused, gather diseases; they become unfit to walk upon. Matt's need to clean these feet doesn't come from hatred. It comes from a desire to love.

Matt has always told me that to love the one you are with is to love everyone they've ever loved. "What you must love is the entity," he writes, "that part of your girlfriend which was and is that previous relationship. You must love her love (all bad and good included). I think one of the biggest flaws is what I call 'historical re-visioning' of relationships. That's when we look back on an old relationship, based on where it ended, and revision everything that happened. This is often an important phase of recovery or learning to live with the relationship's end. But it can't stop there. At some point, we must go back and learn to love the relationship on its own terms, particularly for those involved, and also for their new partners."

I've taken Matt's advice into my own heart. I have gone back through the catalog of all my girlfriend's ex-boyfriends and attempted to envision the love that was once there. I have spent hours alone on our bed, listening to each of Slim's tracks, my eyes tracing the muscles of his plastic action figurine, juxtaposed with my own scrawny flesh and bones reflecting off the bedroom mirror.

But I listen to folk music. I listen to soft and deftly placed guitar rhythms, honky-tonk pianos and bluesy vocalists who dwell upon each word they echo. I detest thumping bass beats, cars with rims and sound systems, weight rooms that smell like testicles and chlorine. If she and I had never met, had never loved one another so deeply, I wouldn't even have befriended these men, we wouldn't have even struck up a conversation. I would have tossed Slim Shady's CD out the window of my Jeep Wrangler, the one with the Dixie Chicks slogan taped to the bumper.

To love those men whose piss has already stained your partner's toilet seat is a dangerous task. It requires endless self-comparison, reflecting on all that it means to be both human and the socially conditioned monster that we call "man."

Even Matt was ultimately destroyed by his own manifesto. In order to love his girlfriend, Sarah, he not only needed to love Garret, her manic depressive ex-boyfriend, but he also needed to love the man with whom she was having an affair.

Sarah met Garrett when she was fourteen years old. They started fucking right away. It wasn't particularly romantic. He held a switchblade to her throat. In the parking lot behind the middle school cafeteria, in the back of her aunt's station wagon. He held a switchblade to her throat and he fucked her until he had finished. Then they would walk back to her mother's house. If she didn't hold his hand tight enough, or if she looked over toward the tanned German boy who spread mulch across her neighbor's front lawn, Garrett would slap her hard across the mouth and remind her of what a goddamn slut she could be. They did this for five years, and then he disappeared. He was found, a few months later, dead from a heroin overdose, outside of a Los Angeles erotic massage parlor.

Sarah graduated from her small-town, blue-collar Connecticut high school, and moved to big-town, blue-collar Baltimore where she met Matt. I can't imagine that their love for each other was ever perfect. I can't imagine perfect love. But the role that Matt played in Sarah's new life was drastically different from her ex-boyfriend. He was sensitive, communicative, thoughtful, and always kind to her. They carried this love for three years, and then, in the fourth, things began to wither.

"She wasn't connecting physically to me anymore," Matt tells me by e-mail. "She wasn't interested at all in sex. She didn't find me physically attractive."

Despite the anguish and trauma that Garrett had brought into her life, Sarah still yearned for a man who would stand up and be a Real Slim Shady, someone who would subjugate her, dominate her, set her in her place so that she might know where she sat. With Matt, things were more complicated. All of the power structures that Garrett had laid out to define her as a woman were gone and now she had to learn what it meant to live as a human. In a moment of retreat, she found Ben, a computer graphics designer who lived in the apartment below, who had fighter jets tattooed across his biceps, and sixty-pound weights lying beside his leopard-print comforter.

"One thing was for sure about Ben," Matt writes. "He was condescending to her. This much she said. He looked down on her, and treated her like a sex toy. And the idea that she would allow herself to be treated like that was so disturbing because of how much I valued her."

Matt's efforts were based in love, at first. Despite his own hurt that he felt inside, Matt asked Sarah more and more questions about Ben. He tried to know and love Ben as something separate from the violent, masculine images that he had conjured up for himself. But the more that Matt learned about

Ben, the more hatred he felt toward him. And through his hatred, he slowly started to become the thing that he most feared and detested.

"I literally tried everything to revive our relationship. The most prevalent and prominent of which was to go hard, to become a cock-wielder, to try and demand that she stay, to put up a fight."

It was when the boundaries were broken that Matt's own persona became the most dangerous and violent part of their relationship.

"Just before the Ben incidents, we had been trying simulated rape (wrestling sex, anyways). And so I thought I would try to spring that on her spontaneously."

He tossed her spine against the wooden backboard of their bed. He pulled her hair back into the space between the metal frame and the wall. He held her hands over her head, and wrapped the space between his thumb and his index finger, tight around her neck. He unzipped his jeans. She started to cry. And then she started to scream.

"The desperation of my attempted role play made it too real. That type of thing has to happen when trust is at its strongest, not weakest. It really broke down. She was very upset, almost crying. Crunched up in a ball on the bed. I was apologizing. Saying that I didn't know how to let her go. And then I saw myself in her full-length body mirror, which was at the foot of her bed, leaning from the ground to the wall, behind a milk crate, on top of which was an open laptop. When I saw myself in the mirror, several things happened:

1. I wanted to lose control of myself.
2. I hated myself for wanting to lose control.
3. I wanted to do whatever it would take to win her back. Anything to make her stay. In a way, it all culminated in a particular loss of control. Although somewhat dramatically contrived, in the end it was not."

Matt punched the mirror from a kneeling position by their bed. He hit where the mirror's hypotenuse was furthest from the wall. It burst, into his knuckles, all over the floor, into Sarah's laptop keys. Blood was everywhere. He went to her and apologized again. He kissed her on the forehead.

"Perhaps more gently than I ever have in my life with anyone."

He told her he was going and then he left. It was the end of their relationship.

Matt's single now. Sarah has taken up with an army reserve trooper named Bill. They live in an apartment above Bill's father's hardware store in a suburb of Chicago. Matt has moved back in with his mother. He's still learning how to love and how to be human. He sent me another e-mail yesterday:

I read an incredible, incredible line last night in a book, while I was in bed. Two people in love were about to have a sexual encounter. It was building up. And one of them, he felt such a forceful and urgent surge to love—not just to touch, but to love. I think it was described as a river pushing through a small culvert in a mountain ridge. A force—*"It was the violence that made him gentle, for it frightened him."* And that's exactly it, sometimes for me. It is the sheer, untamed force of feelings, the violence of emotion that causes me to be so gentle. Because I am frightened of what it could do to her and to me.

Sometimes, in my own dreams, I tear down my girlfriend's posters along the bedroom walls. I lay them out across the cold white tiles beneath the toilet bowl. I unzip my pants and begin to dribble thin streams of urine across the curves that move over the chest and the shoulders and the arms of the Real Slim Shady. Some nights, I catch my reflection in the bathroom mirror. I see my own baby blues wither and shrink, the dark black of my pupils consuming everything as I let out a few last drops onto the poster's hard, brown eyes, thinking—"So what, pussy?"

THE ENEMY WITHIN: ON BECOMING A STRAIGHT WHITE GUY

Jacob Anderson-Minshall

I've seen the enemy and he is me. But it hasn't always been that way.

From the time I was in pre-school I've been agitating for social change. I accompanied my mother to women's rights rallies, and door-to-door campaigns for ratification of the Equal Rights Amendment. In high school I joined anti-nuclear protests. In college I worked against apartheid and marched in support of women's reproductive rights. After graduating I canvassed for the anti-nuclear group SANE/FREEZE and made phone calls on behalf of NARAL Pro-Choice America before turning my attention to gay and lesbian rights, then joining the environmental fight against the destruction of the natural world. The demographic of most protests leaned heavily toward the female gender, while those being protested almost always shared their own set of characteristics: They were primarily straight white men. At the time, I was a white lesbian woman.

Today, when I look in the mirror, I find a man looking back and I wonder if, in the coming years, I will lose my feminist sensibilities. I recently read *The Testosterone Files*, the memoir of Max Wolf Valerio, a man who, like me, is a former lesbian feminist. A writer featured in the seminal work of feminists of color, *This Bridge Called My Back*, his hormones have now engulfed him and he can't remember these days what it felt like to be a woman. Max now gets accused of being sexist—a charge he *never* thought would be leveled at him. In a lot of ways I am just beginning my own journey, and I wonder if I will follow in Max's footsteps or blaze my own trail.

My own struggles with gender identity and expression, my discomfort with my physical body, and my attempts to come to term with the labels assigned me, started early and continued for decades. I was born a girl, but I like to say that I was raised a boy. My parents didn't seem to care that I was a tomboy and they allowed me to wear boys' clothes, roughhouse freely, and play with action figures and cars instead of dolls. At home, especially after we moved to a small farm in rural Idaho, I was allowed to be pretty much as masculine as I wanted to be.

The same could not be said about my experience at school. Our move to the farm dropped us into a conservative religious community to which we didn't naturally belong and to which we failed to assimilate. We were left uninvited to most social functions and children were directed by their parents to avoid us. But there was also an incredible increase in the communal pressure for me to conform to gender expectations. When I was ten years old, for example, I was called into the school's administrative office where the district psychologist proceeded to interrogate me. He demanded to know why I only hung out with a group of boys and suggested that I would be much happier if I had female friends. I experienced the confrontation as an implicit threat: Stop hanging out with the boys or start seeing the shrink more often. I quickly became a loner.

Influenced by my mother's spirit of social justice, I chose to attend a small Quaker college. I took women's studies classes and majored in Peace and Global Studies. I adored Audre Lorde, the writings of Barbara Smith, and Adrienne Rich's theory about compulsory heterosexuality. I learned to recognize the oppressive patriarchal system, to acknowledge my own privileges, and to view straight white men as the oppressive enemy.

Although I came out as a lesbian in college I wasn't comfortable with this identity until I blended my college's compulsory academic-feminist-androgynous-lesbian look with dive-bar, old-school, blue-collar dyke and found solace in the guise of a butch-identified lesbian. Dating women and dressing in men's attire, I finally felt at home until I'd pass a mirror and notice that my reflection didn't reveal the physical person I felt I was.

In graduate school, I co-founded a student LGBT organization, ran for homecoming king, met my wife, and continued to inform my studies with a feminist perspective. I wrote my master's thesis, "Lesbianism as Confrontational Rhetoric," in which I argued that it was not just the words lesbian women used or the political actions they took, but lesbianism itself that was confrontational. In the study of social movement rhetoric, the level of institutional response can be a fair indicator of the threat that is perceived in a group's confrontational actions. Now I recognize that it's not merely sexual orientation, but gender variance, that provokes discomfort in individuals and institutions. This discomfort and perceived threat results in violence and discrimination against gender non-conformists.

The Combahee River Collective's "A Back Feminist Statement" could have been written about transgender people rather than black women. To paraphrase their argument, cataloging the cruel, often murderous treatment black women and transgendered people receive indicates how little value and how much fear has been projected on our lives.

Gender variance doesn't just threaten patriarchal gender/sex roles; it seems to intimidate some feminists as well. QuestioningTransgender.org raises the point that transgender people might undermine the argument "that the gender classes of men and women are socially created."

And maybe we do.

Maybe transpeople, along with intersex people, threaten conservative assumptions that there are two, and only two classes of human beings—men and women—and radical assumptions that gender classes are entirely socially created, rather than having some biological roots. Although studies of transgender individuals are sparse, findings seem to indicate that hormone-disrupting environmental pollutants may impact the development of a fetus's brain and their gender identities by producing, for example, male-brained persons with female genitalia.

Anecdotal accounts of transmen also seem to indicate that biology can out-maneuver socialization. Despite being raised female, years on hormonal treatment seem to produce men as diverse as the rest of the world's guys including those who are sexist jerks.

In order to transition from one sex to another, you first spend a great deal of time speaking with a psychiatrist about your gender issues. The first time I verbalized my feelings about my gender to a shrink, I said, "I'd hate to be the woman that proves Freud right." It's hard to admit to penis envy when women, especially lesbians, have been struggling against that misconception for over a century. I was worried about being seen as a gender traitor and losing a twenty-year relationship I had with the lesbian community—a community to which I still feel a great deal of allegiance.

When I was younger, I spent many years with little or no interaction with straight men. My friends were women and gay men. I worked in women-only businesses. My mother used to worry that I'd never meet a nice guy by hanging out in all-lesbian venues. She was right. When I was a woman, I didn't meet a lot of so-called nice guys hanging out with straight people either. Every time I thought I was making a friend, guys apparently thought I'd just given them permission to hit on me.

For me, men's advances were as unwanted and unappreciated as they would be to a homophobic man. I found their sexual gaze offensive. I didn't understand why they didn't see the man inside of me. Now that I live as a man, I don't mind at all when the gay boys think I'm hot. I know they're seeing me as a *man*, and that makes all the difference in the world.

I didn't decide to transition because I was thrilled by the men I met. I accepted my masculinity despite the bad examples. After thirty years trying to convince myself that I was just a different kind of woman, I've found comfort in defining myself as a different kind of guy.

As a transman I still see myself as a little queer, but now my queerness, my *other*ness, isn't readily visible. Straight men assume I'm one of them and suddenly treat me as a member of a special club, swapping inside jokes and slapping me heartily on the back. In the lesbian community that has been my home for twenty years, some now view me as a straight white man and reject me as such. I am no longer a welcome contributor to certain publications. My trans status threatens to give my lesbian wife a bad name and could even cost her her career. Now that the woman she married is a man, my wife hears up-front doubt that she's still a lesbian and vocal criticism about the fact that she edits a lesbian magazine. Like an estranged family member, I find myself defending my personal sense of allegiance to the lesbian community. Other transmen have accused me of discounting my own masculinity by repudiating my alignment with straight America, and some lesbians doubt my ability to be an ally in this new man's body.

Masculine transpeople are assumed to be renouncing femininity by their transition; they are often accused of gender treachery. Gender theorist Judith "Jack" Halberstam argues that even for female-to-male transpeople, misogyny goes hand-in-hand with masculinity.

I don't *think* I'm a misogynist. So far, even under the influence of testosterone I continue to believe that institutions of patriarchy and the minutiae of male indoctrination are in place to deny women's power. I believe that women have natural power that comes not only from their sexuality, but also from their ability to make life. Men, on the other hand, have institutional power that comes from controlling the governmental, medical, religious, and educational institutions. Indoctrinating socialization distracts women from recognizing their own power and keeps them at the mercy of men. And it disguises its real purpose from men, so most men have no idea that their actions promote the current patriarchal regime. They're just being men.

As a white person I've always had racial privilege and I know my life and options would have been entirely different if I hadn't. Although the trips to thrift stores and the reliance on our homegrown food might have confused me as a child, my family was first generation middle class. I haven't always lived up to my economic heritage—I've been a carny making less than a dollar an hour, I've lived out of our vehicle, I've worked as a day laborer—but I do have resources unavailable to the working poor and outright destitute.

As a transperson who appears male and straight I now have even greater privilege. It doesn't evaporate just because you don't want it. And I do want some. After twenty years, I am tired of being a starving lesbian writer. I want to be well paid and make the full dollar instead of the seventy-seven cents. Don't we all want that? I want that for all of us. But what's the appropriate, feminist response to this added privilege? What are my responsibilities? What should I do if I'm offered more for a job now than I was as a woman? And will I stop noticing these differences at some point?

As soon as I changed my name from Susannah to Jacob, I started to be treated differently. It started even before I began hormone treatment; commencing in cyberspace and slowly rippling out into the real world until now I pass in almost every arena. Men grant me greater respect and are willing to see me as an authority. Women and men alike stopped being courteous. Women no longer appreciate me expressing my opinion. Traits like being outspoken that were formerly lauded as feminist, are now seen as just another guy's propensity for interrupting and valuing their own opinions over women's. I wonder how long it will take before being treated differently will make me a different person. I have more questions than answers and I'm not exactly sure how to bridge my feminist past with my male future. Coming to terms with my place in this oppressive patriarchal system means learning how to balance being a feminist with being a man. Maybe that means constantly evaluating the manner in which I'm expressing my masculinity.

Recognizing the inherent privilege in my situation doesn't mean that privilege can't be taken away because of my trans status. I'm always at risk for my biological beginning being discovered and held against me. My place in the power hierarchy can always be reiterated through rape or other violence. In most locales in America it is still legal to discriminate against transpeople. Like women, a lot of transpeople are being shafted—just differently. In fact, as the authors of the 2006 anthology *Transgender Rights* explain, the same institutionalized, sexist assumptions that keep women down are used in legal settings to deny transpeople their rights. For example, in determining which binary sex to ascribe a transsexual defendant, some modern-day courts have relied on antiquated notions of femaleness like defining female sex as the ability to be sexually penetrated within the confines of "normal" heterosexual intercourse.

Becoming a man has opened my eyes and I no longer see all men—even straight, white, natal men—as inherent enemies to women or peace or the environment. That's not to say that it isn't mostly men who are controlling the political and economic power in this country. They are. Those holding the axe over our collective heads are more likely to be men. That said, there are a great number of men who are suffering intensely from our current economic woes: men who are imprisoned by their masculine roles; men who are sent to their death in the name of freedom; men who long for women to take on more responsibility.

A patriarchal system keeps our country in the control of men, and that male-domination clearly denigrates all things feminine. But the male-centric nature of our society doesn't—by itself—explain America's racial and economic stratification. If patriarchy is not the sole cause of men's oppression (be these men minorities in race, religion, class, sexuality, gender-identity and expression, or ability, etc.) then there is certainly something else going on here as well. This deserves our attention especially since the difficulties that some men face these days don't seem like signs of patriarchy crumbling. (If patriarchy was the only source of oppression, and if it was collapsing, there would presumably be a leveling out of privilege, wealth, and power. And I don't think we can argue this has happened.)

There are a lot of awful problems in the world today, and to solve them we need to make allies and build bridges to other movements seeking change. We need to accept the problems of others as our own. Until we understand that the unbelievably high rate of African-American incarceration is an American tragedy not just a black one, we won't be addressing racial inequities. Until we see that rape, domestic violence, and childcare are not women's issues but our issues, we won't improve women's status or win their respect. Until we truly accept same-sex marriage we are not honestly striving for sexual equality. Until we demand universal healthcare we will continue to allow people just like us to die on the streets.

To start, here's what I have to say to all my brothers: Until being called pussy, girl, fag, and pansy isn't the worst thing in the world, we won't eliminate misogyny. We do have different expectations for women and men, although there is some leeway for women to be masculine because our society values masculinity. But the fact that men can't be feminine without being punished by our society is proof that we still don't value femininity: It's treated as reprehensible—at least when it appears in men and boys.

One day when I was walking my dogs in the local park I passed a group of Little League boys running sprints while their coach yelled motivational phrases. *"What are you? Pussies? Is that all you can do, girls?"* This shit stuns me. I can't believe that we're still teaching our boys to push themselves harder by threatening that if they don't, they'll be girls and that being a girl is a terrible thing. If we really believed that the sexes are equal this wouldn't happen.

When we respond violently to those who question our (hetero)sexuality— say with taunts of "sissy" or "pansy"—isn't that just another example of fearing our own femininity? Homophobes fear nothing more than being feminized by another man's sexual gaze. To avoid being seen as woman-like they are willing to deprive fellow citizens of their civil rights and even, in some cases, their lives. This again begs the question: What's so awful about being women?

I have one advantage in this arena: I'm a man who was called a girl, not occasionally, but every day, for decades. Even when I excelled at sports or academics. Sure, it felt wrong, because it wasn't accurate, but it wasn't a put down. Not then, not now. I'm comfortable enough in my masculinity to not have to prove it. When someone calls me a pussy I don't get offended. I've had one. I've been one. Being a girl wasn't right for me, but it sure as hell wasn't the worst thing in the world.

REDEFINING MANHOOD: RESISTING SEXISM

Ewuare X. Osayande

"**D**on't you grow up to be a black man!" The words would echo in my young and impressionable mind for years. They belonged to my mother. The source of her message was the combination of internalized oppression as a black woman living in a white supremacist society, and her pain and frustration with the men in her life who abused and misused her. I came to understand my mother's outcry as a desperate plea for her son not to grow up and be like the men she knew.

I saw the worst of patriarchal abuse in the tragic murder of my father, caught in the path of a jealous man who thought that women were his property. Despite these traumatic experiences, I am today a proud, self-loving, heterosexual black man. I have decided to respond to my mother's lament by working to redefine what manhood means to me and to the men I come in contact with. This means confronting racism, sexism, and masculine violence when and where I see it.

I did not have many men to look up to during my childhood. Soon after I was born, my father joined the Army and eventually ended up stationed in Germany. My mother's first marriage was to a man who was hardly ever around. When he was, he never showed any real interest in my life. As I became a teenager, I promised myself that I would never be like either of my fathers. Although I did not know what to do, I certainly knew what not to do. But it wasn't until I got married that I came face to face with my own issues of manhood.

The marriage lasted less than three years. I quickly realized that I was not able to fulfill the socially ascribed role of being the "man of the house," even though I tried to the best of my ability. The pressure of providing for a growing family and finding affirming work became overwhelming. The marriage quickly dissolved even as my self-criticism and awareness was beginning to evolve. There is nothing about masculinity in that period of my life that makes me happy or proud. I am ashamed of the man I was, and I remain ever-vigilant to prevent the man I was from becoming the man I am. But my early confusion led me to a process of political self-awareness that has rooted me ever since.

I don't remember how I first came across the work of feminist writer bell hooks, but I do know that I read her book, *Sisters of the Yam*, in one sitting. Although written for black women, this book helped me make sense of the problems I experienced in my marriage and it helped me make sense of myself. I had heard about feminism before, but never paid it much mind. I dismissed it as "that white women's stuff."

I had long been involved in black liberation struggle. I went from being a staunch black student activist in college to being a respected community activist in Philadelphia. Like many black men, I believed that racism was the only oppression that required our community's attention. Reading bell hooks helped correct my vision and revise my understanding. I now see that sexism is as important as racism in liberation struggle. Black women and men have to address white dominant society as well as male domination from both within and outside the black community. Black feminist thought has broadened my understanding of how various forms of oppression criss-cross and often collide.

I now also see that my experience of trying to live up to a "man-of-the-house" sex role is shared by many of the men in my family. I watch my male relatives mask their depression with jokes that project their sense of worthlessness onto the women in their lives. I worry for them and more so for the women they claim to love. I see how the men's penchant for domination in the home has wreaked havoc on their partners. There is a cloud of anxiety that covers these women. That cloud is the threat of violence that lingers in the air after the man has publicly ridiculed, demeaned, or yelled at her. I am torn up inside even as I try to figure out how to intervene.

I once feared that any act of intervention would be met with resistance by the men and would result in increased violence in the home. I now better understand the root causes of this pain and anger. Rather than being a model for healthy relationships, patriarchy is actually the very force responsible for their demise.

I try to speak affirmatively to these men in my family, offering them alternative ways of viewing themselves as men, keeping myself accountable to the pain and anguish that I know very well. I know that I must not wait for a tragedy to occur. I must remain in constant communication with the hope that conversation can offer a process for change. I share with my family and with myself the belief that love is justice in its most intimate embrace. As such, we men must make every effort to see the women in our lives as equal partners and we must respect them as individuals with ambitions and desires that transcend our own.

It has been ten years since I embraced feminist thought as a guide for my personal life and political activism. In that time, I have given talks and workshops on resisting negative socialization and internalized oppression. One of the issues I am constantly confronted with is how to talk about the matrix of oppressions in a way that is both direct and accessible. I find that all too often some folk want to hide behind their personal oppression. For example, when I give talks on racism and how race impacts our understanding of sexist oppression in the United States, it's not unusual to meet resistance from white women in the audience. More than one white woman has tried to deflect any consideration of how she may experience white privilege even as she must contend with sexism. At the same time, I often meet white men who claim a profeminist outlook but who approach me with questions that suggest male domination only exists within the black community. There is a continuing challenge to appreciate the ways that race and class impact how sexism is experienced in this country.

There is a different gendered experience for a black woman or a woman of color and a white woman. Women of color scholars and activists have written about this for years. I have witnessed an increased interest in feminist thought in the black community thanks to the works of bell hooks, Angela Davis, Alice Walker, Joy James, Barbara Smith, Audre Lorde, and many others. My black female peers are pioneering a body of scholarship and engaging in feminist activism that speaks directly to this hip-hop-inspired generation. Yet progress is still slow. While the legacy of racism has made it difficult for feminist thought to have the radicalizing effect it could have within the black community, sexist black men have used that racism to trump any real discussion of sexism within the black community.

In the United States, black masculinity is a manhood that, in the main, has braced itself against the onslaught of a biased and bigoted society. Racism constantly threatens our well being and our very existence. This defensive posturing often leaves us detached from our feelings. In a society that views us as predator and prey, we are inclined to be on guard at all times. Yet our self-protective posturing often manifests in a hypermasculinity that is predicated upon domination and that sees violence as a primary option to resolve problems.

This perversion of manhood took its ultimate and most personal form in the murder of my father in January 2000. My father had recently begun dating a woman who had left an abusive relationship. My father's murderer was this woman's former lover who resorted to the most violent expression of male domination. In his sexist mind, the woman was his property. He did not recognize her agency or her right to create a life outside of his desires. When she began dating my father, this man struck out. He ambushed and attacked my father and his woman friend. My father was stabbed so severely that he died before the rescue workers arrived. The woman spent a few days in the hospital recovering from her wounds.

The murderer was a respected man of the community who was considered upstanding by most people who knew him. He was not crazy. He was socialized to view women as mere property and to exercise power even to the point of violence, especially when he believed his so-called manhood was being challenged.

As long as domination and violence are considered central parts of masculinity, I worry about the future for my two boys. At ages eleven and eight, they are still becoming aware of themselves in the world. I am learning how quickly sexist socialization can take place. The system is relentless; it bombards my sons with sexist and racist messages on a daily basis. Their mother and I go to great lengths to provide our sons with alternative ways of understanding themselves as boys so that they can resist sexist indoctrination. Yet, despite all our intervention, it seems that every aspect of their young lives is filled with sexist instruction. The same old sexism has been revamped for the computer age.

Female cartoon characters are portrayed as damsels in distress who are in constant need of a male hero to save them. In video games, the same is true but with added violence and grossly sexualized images of the female body. My response is to aid my sons in making better choices about the kinds of cartoons they watch and video games they play. I read books with them about women athletes who excel in sports. Their mother has taken them to see the WNBA play live.

It is my fervent hope that anti-sexist, anti-racist interventions will serve my sons well as they grow from boys into men. I will certainly be there to provide an example of manhood that is not an expression of force, superiority, and violence but rather an expression of love, respect, justice, accountability, integrity, and peace.

STRAIGHT GUYS CAN DANCE, TOO

Jared Margulies

My career as a dancer began when I was in fourth grade. Through a series of circumstances that I'd rather not expand upon, my audition for a southern Slavic folk dance company led to a peculiar six-year period of my life during which I was, for all intents and purposes, a dancer.

I was originally cast with my brothers and sisters in an annual performance of "Christmas in Croatia." It was one of several shows put on every year by the dance company, *Živili!* (To life!). Soon after this inaugural show, my siblings and I got involved in other dance productions and did some regional touring as well.

My role as a dancer in *Živili!* was professionally inconsequential, but personally significant because it rendered me an outsider both at home and at rehearsal. I could never let my friends know what I was up to during those months of late-night and weekend rehearsals. What respectable thirteen-year-old boy wants his buddies to know he spends all of his time dancing? I kept those two worlds as separate as possible.

Much of this seemed quite tumultuous and devastating at the time. No doubt it had something to do with prepubescent fears that dancing would turn me gay. Today, as a college-age male with a well-developed sense of self, I'd like to say that my insecurities reflect the naiveté of youth. But the fact is that I haven't put on the tights, so to speak, ever since I left my comfort zone with *Živili!* The closest I've come to dancing has been attending an occasional performance and taking one ballroom dance class, although I don't think spending seven weeks skimming over the foxtrot and the cha-cha to get my college PE credit really counts. I find myself asking, *Why can't I muster the balls to sign up for Modern Dance 101?*

After much reflection, I realize that the answer is because, as much as I like to think of college students, myself included, as bright-eyed, open-minded, enlightened souls, the very act of enrolling in a modern or ballet class would tear my testicular brethren right out of their comfortable habitat. It would provoke even the most tempered of my peers to think, if not ask, "So, is he a queer?"

It's curious that there are so few male dancers at my campus, which is known for its dance department. And out of the small number of male dancers that exist at my college, how come their sexual preference seems so ambiguous? Just for kicks (no pun intended), I interviewed one of the male dancers at my school. He spoke to me on the condition of anonymity. "We male dancers range from overtly homosexual to completely straight," he said. "But if you are a straight male dancer there is pressure to have a girlfriend. If you don't, your sexuality gets questioned."

To be honest, I was surprised by this response. I assumed that all of the male dance majors were gay. While my assumptions were wrong, it seems the straight guy dancers work hard to maintain the public image of their sexual identity. I get this, though, especially considering that in the past I have simply mentioned the idea of taking a dance class, only to be summarily disregarded as joking—even by female dancers.

Straight men can dance, so where's the problem? Should I blame my closed-minded fellow students for scraping away any last vestige of courage I had to enroll in ballet? Is the issue that homophobic society thinks less of gay men and thinks that dancing is somehow gay? Or is this just a personal issue that I've tried to pass off as a larger social problem? Maybe a closer investigation of what led me to this state of living sans jazz/tap is in order.

My fifth grade musical. Because of my participation in *Živili!*, I owned a modest stage makeup kit. In retrospect, I guess I should have known not to bring a personal makeup set with me to the show. Let's just say the other boys were not dazzled by my talent for blending foundation lines.

My sixth grade musical: same as above.

Eighth grade. A rather large article, including full-page color photographs of my family dancing in *Živili!*, appeared in *The Columbus Dispatch*, Central Ohio's largest newspaper. While a few teachers enjoyed the Von Trapp exposé, my middle school's jock population found it necessary to bar my entrance to the cool kids' table in the cafeteria.

The list of discomfort continues through high school and beyond. But what is important are not the quirks of my personal history, but the widespread unease so many men and women continue to have when guys do things our culture deems outside the masculine arena. And although I'd be hard pressed to find someone who actually uses words like "faggot" and "queer" in a purposefully malicious way, I know that these words are still thrown around casually and often.

And I have to say I use them, too. In fact, I use these words a lot. I don't really care if a friend calls me gay for going folk dancing with my girlfriend. I recognize it isn't actually meant as a personal attack. It's just part of the everyday banter so many of us embrace as humor. But why do we think this particular brand of mockery is funny?

We are so inundated by a constant stream of disapproval under the guise of wit that it is often difficult to separate jest from scorn. Eventually, these repetitive messages stick, and as benign as their original intentions may have been, what was once merely jocular conversation becomes malignant.

I'm not suggesting that we censor the use of words like "faggot" and "queer." But if we pay better attention to the power of language then maybe the next fourth-grade boy who just wants some tap shoes to dance around in won't be too embarrassed to take Dance 101 in college ten years down the line.

STEPPING OUT OF BOUNDS

Nathan Einschlag

One day the shit just hit me. I understood. Everything that I had questions about, everything that I had stressed about for the last year of my life, finally seemed to have an answer. I simply wasn't like them. I'm six feet tall and weigh one-eighty. I can bench press 225 pounds. But on the team, I stuck out like a weed in the concrete. In the locker room, on the basketball court, in the words I spoke, by my actions. Everything about me was different. I saw things differently. I was from a different place.

Growing up in the immigrant neighborhood of Jackson Heights in Queens, New York, I had seen things that the kids at my fancy college only read about in magazines, or saw on TV. I knew what happened to the drug and alcohol addicts: They died. I saw young abused girlfriends pushing strollers on the way to the local elementary school to pick up their sons and daughters. It was routine to pass prostitutes on my way to the subway late at night. I was from a neighborhood where my senses were trained to keep me aware and out of harm's way. I always watched one block ahead, spotting shadows, and keeping my distance from the men on the corners. I never went down a too-quiet block for fear of what might lie ahead. My actions made me strong. I walked with my head up and a swagger that can only be learned in New York City.

I made a decision when I was young that I would be focused, and not be dragged into the streets like so many before me. I put my heart and soul into basketball and the senses that I honed walking those late night blocks all my life did not fail me. It was love. Basketball embraced me. Sophomore year I made the varsity basketball team at Fiorello H. Laguardia's High School of Music, Art and Performing Arts. My junior and senior year I started. Senior year we were division champs with a thirteen-three record. It was a high point in my life and an experience I will never forget. It would be time to move on, however, and I said goodbye to my high school team.

Soon after graduating I walked onto my college men's Division III basketball team. I thought I was ready. I had no idea that college would be so much different from high school. Things changed drastically for me my freshman year.

Girls approached me all the time. Drunk girls. Eyeliner girls with their eyes halfway shut, holding red plastic cups full of beer. Those same girls would be all over the lacrosse players who would call them sluts later that same week. Girls didn't see the guy I was, just a freshman trying to get to know people. They saw the basketball logo and didn't need to know anything more about me. They thought I must be like all the other guys who pushed up the girls' skirts as they walked by or pretended to trip while grabbing girls' breasts. "Dude, get a drink. Stop being so uptight," they'd say. I didn't want a fucking drink. Where were the kids who wanted to listen to music and get on the dance floor?

I once came back to my dorm room where I stepped over two girls lying on the floor in my hallway. They could have been waiting for me, or for anyone one who walked by and was interested in quick, easy sex. College was nothing like I had expected.

The kids on my high school team were the most creative and talented teenagers in New York City. We didn't pound 40s on a Monday night. We didn't drive drunk for fun like my college teammates did. All we needed was a ball and a court. Nothing made us happier. Off the court we argued about who had the flyest sneakers or who was a better rapper, Nas or Jay-Z.

We didn't buy sixteen-ounce cans of Miller Lite instead of eight-ounce cans, thinking that the girls would get drunker because they have twice as much alcohol. "The girls don't notice," my college teammates assured me. I didn't enjoy being affiliated with this team I was on now. This didn't seem to matter to my teammates, though. I was only seen as a freshman athlete who needed to be broken in.

When I turned down drinks, girls would ask my teammates what was wrong with me, and why I was such a weirdo. They called me strange because I would not objectify them. The gender roles at my school were like nothing I'd experienced. Girls were doing male athletes' laundry while the players poured beer on the girls.

To make matters worse my coach was not playing me. He didn't seem to take a liking to me either. At practice, I was serious and I listened, two qualities I learned from the coaches for my previous teams. The other freshmen were rowdy and rude. Some upperclassmen were hotheaded and didn't look Coach in the eye when he talked to them. I thought it was disrespectful, but Coach seemed to respond well to their bad behavior. He took my silence as a sign that I was lethargic and unmotivated. I had such a strong desire to play, but my coach decided instead to question my masculinity. "I need to HEAR you NATE! TALK LOUDER!" he'd yell. "GODDAMNIT! SCREAM SOMETHING!"

Talking is a vital part of basketball and I didn't have a problem doing it. But it was more intense with Coach. No play was done hard enough or loud enough. Maybe if I had brought beer to practice and pictures of me taking advantage of a passed out girl (like some of the other guys did) then I would have been seen as a real basketball player and gained my coach's acceptance. But at the time the thought hadn't crossed my mind. And I wouldn't have done it, anyway.

Off the court people treated me differently, too. I'd hear things like, "Dude, if you weren't on the team I'd probably make fun of you, too. Fuck it, though. You're cool. Bitches seem to like you." Thankfully, girls showed me attention. At least I was a cute weirdo on the basketball team and not some freak-fag theater major, they'd tell me. I couldn't tell my teammates that I was minoring in theater. I didn't need to give them any more ammunition.

I loved basketball, but it was ruining my life. I wanted to show Coach that basketball was my priority. I stopped telling him I'd have to miss practice for tutoring sessions or class requirements. I would show up at study groups late and still sweaty from practice. I'd convince the ushers at the theater to let me in late. I feared missing practice.

Coach seemed to love his players' bad attitudes. They were rich kids who didn't think about their parent's money or care too much about education. Their father's business would hire them, so what did a C-minus or a D-plus here or there matter? My priorities were different. I didn't have time to stay and bullshit about "bitches and beer" in the locker room. I didn't care if Susan was wearing a low-cut shirt today in Philosophy, or that she almost fell down the stairs drunk last night at the soccer party. *It wasn't their fault that they gave her the beer. No one told her to drink so much. This is college not kindergarten.*

I had reading to get done. I had papers to write. I had college to attend to. I always felt like the odd man out, but now I started not to care. This isn't what I wanted from a basketball team. I didn't feel like part of a team, even if the school saw and treated me like I was on one. Something was changing; it was me.

I'd talk to my old friends on the phone about school. I'd tell them that things were going well and that I was adjusting fine. The next party I went to, I bought in for a red plastic cup. It was soon full of beer. "Maybe they're right and I do need to loosen up," I thought. I had practice late the next day, and wouldn't have to worry about being hung over. If I teased a few girls that night, cursed and yelled, and tried to be like one of the guys, maybe I'd finally get some playing time. If Coach saw that the guys liked me better, then maybe he'd take notice of my game and play me more.

Not only was I slow in practice the next day, but Coach laid into me extra hard. The guys didn't see me in any new light, and I still felt like the odd man out. Nothing was going to change the situation I was in. My teammates were sexist and ignorant. It would be so easy to be like them. I could just kick back, get wasted, and blame my actions on intoxication. But I wasn't about to let this happen. I made a decision that would separate me from the team and cost me one of the things that I held closest to my heart.

I quit the basketball team after a year and a half. Feeling more comfortable at school now, I shed the basketball reputation. I am no longer the cute, weirdo athlete on campus, but Nate, "the quiet kid who I see in the library and I think is gonna be in that play next week." The girls are a little shyer when they approach me now, especially the ones from the parties I used to go to. I'm not like the other guys and they feel embarrassed and a little ashamed. I still hear them whispering about when I was on the team and what they thought I was like, but I also hear the truth now. "That's Nate. He's such a man."

Had I known what a shock I was going to be in for when I started college, had I known it was going to be so much different from what I was used to at home, in high school, I would not have taken a backseat to my teammates' obnoxious behavior. Had I understood the hypermasculine jock culture that existed in Division III sports before I joined the team, I would have promised myself that I would be more vocal, challenging the things that my teammates thought were fun. Instead I was silent. I let people categorize me, and let them think I had the same beliefs and interests as the guys on my team. I never told my coach how I felt until the day I quit the team. He'd had the wrong impression of me, about how to approach me. I will always look back and wish I had been more honest with the staff and my teammates about how I was feeling.

But I will also look back at my college basketball career as one of the most influential times of my life. I learned more about myself during that year-and-a-half of struggle than I did during my entire life before that. By turning my time on the team into a learning experience, and growing from that experience, I know that I made the right decision to leave college basketball. The athletes at my school haven't changed their behavior, but by sticking to my principles and by not letting people categorize me, I have stayed true to myself. I can fight gender stereotypes with my words and with my actions. I know there's another way for men to be.

HOMBRES Y MACHOS

Alfredo Mirandé

My formative years were spent in México City in the *colonia* of Tacuba, near *el árbol de la noche triste* (the tree of the night of sorrows), a tree where according to Mexican folklore and legend Hernán Cortés was said to have wept after the Aztecs soundly defeated his forces. Over the centuries the tree had been bent by the force of its own weight and was now almost on the ground. I did not understand the historical significance of the old tree at the time, but it was very much a part of my daily life as a child.

We lived in Tacuba near *el árbol de la noche triste* in an extended family with my mother's oldest sister (Márgara) and oldest brother (Juan), and their respective families. *Los* González-Ochoa were from the village of Sayula, a historic community in the state of Jalisco. The first house on the right as you walked in the front gate, which was always open, was occupied by my Tío Juan, his wife Mariana, and their two sons. Tía Márgara, her husband Miguel, and their two daughters occupied the second house. I lived in the last and smallest of the houses, "*el tres*," with my parents, Rosa María and Xavier, and my two older brothers, Alex and Gordo.

The most lasting impression I have of my *tíos* is that they were sort of *matones* (tough guys), burly, pot-bellied men who smoked, swore, drank tequila, and carried weapons. They were much like the Mexican bad guys in films like *El Mariachi*, *Desperado*, and *Somewhere in Mexico*. Tío Miguel was a military man, a general in the Mexican army, who dressed in his uniform and carried a .45. Juan was a civilian, sold tequila wholesale for a living, and also often carried a gun and shoulder holster. Another *tío*, Manuel, lived in Puebla. He was married to my mother's sister, Ana Luisa. Manuel was also in the military, had entered the Mexican Revolution when he was only fourteen, and had become a professional military hit man. He was said to have executed

47

hundreds of men during (and after) the Revolution, executions that were both formal and informal. My father was never in the military and never carried a weapon. He was athletic and strong, and he didn't smoke, drink, or swear.

Our extended family and neighborhood was like a small community. One of the most vivid memories that I have of Tacuba was an incident that happened when I was around six. It was in the afternoon. There was a lot of noise and yelling, as the entire neighborhood gathered around Tío Juan's house. We could hear arguing, screaming, and swearing. Juan was drunk and beating Tía Mariana. My father jumped over the short picket fence and attempted to stop the beating. Because it was unheard of for one household to intervene in the private affairs of another, and because we could sense the danger, it was a very dramatic moment as we watched my drunken uncle coming after my father. My dad was a skilled boxer. He hit and jabbed at Juan and then deftly circled around him, intending more to dissuade him than to seriously hurt him. As my uncle's face bloodied and it became clear that my father was getting the better of the fight, Juan ran into the house and emerged from the kitchen with a butcher knife. My father looked frightened and was certainly alarmed but he didn't run. He continued to dance and jab with Juan pursuing, coming forward, threatening him with the knife. What happened next was even more incredible, as my mother somehow entered the yard and stepped between her husband and her older brother. She proceeded to belittle Juan, asking, and pointing at her brother,

How can you call yourself a man if you go around beating up defenseless women? What kind of a man needs a knife to fight an unarmed man? Put down the knife and let's see what kind of a man you really are.

Humiliated, Juan put down the knife and went inside the house.

I never thought much about the incident, but in retrospect I believe that it had a profound effect on my development, my identity, and my notions of what was considered good and bad behavior in a man—and in a woman. I learned early, for example, that one of the worst or lowest things that a man could do is to hit a woman. I also learned from this and other examples that it is important and honorable to stick up for and defend people who are wronged, abused, or treated unjustly. But most importantly, I learned that strength of character and valor are not gendered qualities.

My *noche triste* occurred when my father returned from location in Morelia where he had been working as an extra in the film *Captain from Castille*, ironically a film about Cortés and the Conquest. My father had been gone for a long time. I was happy to see him and he brought us a lot of presents. But later that evening, there was a big fight, and after my parents argued all night, they separated. Years later my mother related how after she had been fighting with my dad and was very sad and depressed, she had gone to *el árbol de la noche triste*. As she cried by the tree she said she thought about how both she and Hernán Cortés had been in the same situation: depressed, weeping, and alone.

When my parents separated, my brothers and I moved with my father to live with his mother, Anita, and my great-grandmother, Carmela (Mama Mela) in Tacubaya. Grandmother Anita was a petite, energetic woman, while Mama Mela was tall, dark, and stately. In Tacubaya, we were surrounded by family again, but now it was the Mirandé-Salazar family on my father's side. His family was smaller because he was an only child and because his father's two siblings, Concha and Lupe, never married or had children. My grandfather, Alfredo, died when I was about two years old, but I remember him.

In Tacubaya we lived in an apartment house that my grandmother owned. We lived in the first apartment, and my great-aunts, Concha and Lupe, lived in *el seis* (number six). Concha had been an elementary school teacher and Lupe was an artist. They were retired but very active; both did a lot of embroidering and Lupe was always painting. I was very fond of *las tías*. They always seemed old and very religious, but I was very close to my aunts and loved them deeply. They wore black shawls and went to church early each morning. When I wasn't playing on the patio, I was usually visiting with my aunts. They taught me catechism, and Lupe was my *madrina*, or godmother, for my first communion. I would spend hours with *las tías*, listening to their conversation and stories about my grandfather and about the Mexican Revolution.

I was named Alfredo after my grandfather and I strongly identified with him. My family said he was a great man and that they would be very proud and happy if I grew up to be like him some day. Actually, I had no choice—my family expected that I was destined to be like him, since I was his namesake. They said I had the privilege and the responsibility that came with the name, and, like him, I too would be a great man some day. To my family, my grandfather and I were linked because we were both Mirandé and Alfredo, but also because we were both men. I did not realize it at the time, but my teachers—*las tías*, my grandmother, Mama Mela, and my mother and her sisters—were socializing me into my sex role.

I don't know very much about my Grandfather Alfredo, except that he was of humble origins and he was a self-made man who pursued a career as a civil engineer. He was committed to bringing about social justice and distributing the land held by the *hacendados* (landowners) among the Mexican *peones* (laborers). He served as a civilian under Emiliano Zapata, making cannons and munitions. According to historian John Womack, my grandfather was one of Zapata's key assistants and worked for some time as a spy in Puebla under the code name Delta. While he was in hiding, my grandmother took in other people's clothes to mend and launder to earn money so that the family could survive. My aunts said my grandfather grew disillusioned, however, as the Revolution did not fulfill its promise of bringing about economic and social justice.

Tía Concha and Tía Lupe had several photographs of Alfredo in their tiny, crowded living room. In one picture he is standing proudly in front of a new, experimental cannon that he built. The story I was told was that a foolish and headstrong general, anxious to try out the new cannon, pressured Alfredo to fire it before it was ready. My grandfather reluctantly but stoically complied and when the cannon exploded he suffered severe burns all over his body, almost dying as a result. It took my grandfather months to recover from the accident.

As I think back on these stories I was told as a child, I understand that most were designed to impart certain morals and values. What I learned directly from my *tías* and, indirectly, from my grandfather, was that although it was necessary to stand up for one's principles, war and personal conflicts should be avoided, if at all possible. I understood that I should strive to be on a higher moral plane than my adversaries.

Alfredo was intelligent, strong, and principled. But what impressed me most was that he was said to have been incredibly just and judicious. Everyone who knew him, including my mother, said he treated people of all educational and economic levels fairly, equally, and with dignity and respect. Alfredo lived in a society and a historical period in which women were relegated to an inferior status and were largely controlled by men. Yet I also know that he and my grandmother shared a special intimacy and mutual respect.

I now realize that I was raised by strong and powerful women, and that most of what I understood about being a man was learned from women. My great-grandmother, Mama Mela, possessed an uncommon dignity. My Aunts Concha and Lupe were traditional, strong, and independent. But the woman that stands out most in my mind is my mother's oldest sister, Tía Márgara.

Márgara was a large, imposing figure and probably weighed well over two hundred pounds. In her youth Márgara was a tall, attractive woman, and she had a wonderful sense of humor and an incredible singing voice. But *la tía* also had a foul mouth and seemed always to be complaining about some *desgraciados* (bastards) or *hijos de la chingada* (sons of bitches). Ironically, she embodied many stereotypically macho traits. She swore, was a chain smoker, gambled, drank tequila, and loved to sing *rancheras* (Mexican country ballads) and belt out the *gritos* (yells) with the songs. She was the female counterpart to my stereotypically macho *tíos*, but more memorable because she was a woman.

What I remember most about *la tía* were the numerous confrontations and fistfights she had with both women and men. Márgara liked to knit, but she also liked to fight. She usually carried long, sharp knitting needles, which she would often use as weapons. I recall one incident in particular: Márgara got out of the car during a traffic dispute, pulled a cab driver from his vehicle, and proceeded to beat him with her fists. Everyone said, "*Era muy brava*" ("she was very tough"). Her physical assaults were of legendary proportions and were always, it seems, accompanied by verbal abuse and denunciation of her victims, so that in the end, her adversaries were not only physically bested, but also subdued and humiliated.

The problem was that these stories from my childhood were at odds with the images of men and women that were prevalent in popular conceptions of Latinos and in academic social science literature. Latinos in general, and *mexicanos* in particular, have been characterized as heirs to a cultural heritage that is said to be driven by the simultaneous veneration of the male and denigration of the female, a heritage in which men are powerful and controlling and women weak and submissive. Because of my own biography and my increasing concern with portrayals of Latino masculinity and machismo, I was drawn into a project to separate the macho myths from the realities of manhood.

From my social science training and from watching my own family, I knew that this machismo stereotype couldn't possibly be the whole story of Latino manhood. My father and my grandfather were not stereotypically macho, and my mother and aunts, especially Márgara, were hardly passive and dependent. Even if there is a cultural concern with outward displays of masculinity and *hombría*, this is certainly not unique to Latino cultures. There are many societies that have focused on manhood, that have ritualized masculine rites of passage, and that value outward masculine displays.

I decided to research the historical roots and contemporary manifestations of Latino masculinity because I wanted to explore the diversity and variety of masculinities. I wanted to understand Latino men but in the end, the results revealed as much about me as they did about the men I studied. I launched my research project on masculinity by doing in-depth interviews with Latino men because I was dissatisfied with the images of Latino men and masculinity found not only in the academic social science literature but also in society at large. These images had been used to perpetuate negative conceptions of *mexicanos/as* and to legitimate our economic and political subordination and maintain our subordination.

My goal, both personal and professional, was to conduct a study of Latino men that did not begin with the premise that Latino culture and Latino masculinity was inherently pathological and negative. I wanted to look at Latino men in a way that reflected the richness and complexity of Latino culture—a study, in other words, that would incorporate those who were as different and diverse as my father, my uncles, and my *tías*. I wanted to capture the images that Latino men themselves have of machismo, masculinity, and fatherhood. I felt it was important to learn more about how Latino men saw their roles as fathers, as husbands, and as men, and the qualities or attributes that they most respected and admired in a man. Finally, I wanted to place my research findings within a meaningful historical context.

I found in a roundabout way that contrary to what many scholars claim, negative machismo, or exaggerated masculinity, was neither a response to the Conquest nor an extension of pre-Columbian warring Aztec society. Instead, like Catholicism and many deadly diseases, negative machismo was imported and imposed on the indigenous population via the Conquest. The small band of *conquistadores* who conquered and subjugated millions of indigenous people under the leadership of Hernán Cortés appears to be the historical prototype of negative machismo. Though it is said that the Conquest was divinely ordained in order to convert the "heathen natives," the *conquistadores* proved to be cruel, violent men who committed numerous atrocities and *chingaderas* in the name of God, crown, and king. The *conquistadores* appear to have embodied what Evelyn Stevens calls "The Seven Deadly Sins of Machismo": extreme pride, wrath, lust, anxiety, callousness toward women, an obsession with the number of conquests, and belief in male hypersexuality.

Aztec society was hierarchical, militaristic, and characterized by a clearly delineated sexual division of labor. But war and violence were not ends in themselves. War and the sacrifice of enemy prisoners were justified as necessary in order to satisfy the gods and continue the cycle of life. Across social classes, the Aztec masculine ideal also included such attributes as being humble, modest, contrite, selfless, and not giving in to impetuousness or self-indulgence.

Two polar and conflicting images of Mexican masculinity emerged from my project, corresponding roughly to Spanish and Aztec conceptions of men. A majority of my respondents did not identify with being macho. They saw machismo as a negative or synthetic form of masculinity, characterized by profound feelings of inferiority or inadequacy in men, male dominance, and the subordination and denigration of women. This finding calls into question the idea that machismo, at least as it has been traditionally conceived, is somehow a positive or desired cultural trait or value.

Although a minority of respondents identified with being macho and had a positive conception of the term, these men were careful to distinguish between being macho (male) and being *machista* (sexist). Rather than linking machismo with pathology, violence, or the denigration of women, for these men, like my dad, it meant adhering to a code of ethics—similar to the Aztec code—that guided behavior and included attributes such as being honest, respectful, modest, sincere, loyal. Perhaps most importantly, this perspective on machismo includes the expectation that men ought to stand up for their rights and beliefs. The worth of a person, according to this view, is measured not by external attributes, such as physical strength, sexual prowess, fighting ability, or drinking behavior, but by internal qualities and especially the strength of one's character. A man who claims to be *muy macho*, who thinks he is *chingón*, who goes around holding his genitals and committing numerous *chingaderas*, who beats up women, or who is otherwise fixated on proving his manhood is, by definition, not macho. A real macho is confident in his sense of self and in his masculinity and doesn't need to prove it to anyone, and most certainly not to himself.

Another important, and paradoxical, conclusion is that the positive sense of being macho is essentially an androgynous quality, as *la hembra* (the female) is the feminine counterpart of *el macho*. *Hembrismo* (femaleness) is similarly demonstrated by internal qualities such as pride, dignity, courage, perseverance in the face of adversity, and selflessness, not by external attributes like toughness, physical beauty, large breasts, sexuality, or excessive femininity.

Looking back on my youth, I saw that I was provided with a wealth of positive and negative images of masculinity and femininity. As I reflected on the family folklore about my father confronting Tío Juan as he was beating up his wife, I realized it took bravery for my father to get involved in a family squabble and to stand up to his brother-in-law. But I also came to realize that it probably took even more courage for my mother to intervene. She was, after all, the youngest of seven children, and a woman. She grew up in a small village in an era when women ostensibly occupied subordinate roles and did not interfere in the affairs of men. By intervening in the physical confrontation between two grown men (her older brother and her husband), my mother not only challenged her older brother but also, indirectly and symbolically, challenged her husband and the (allegedly) traditional subordinate role of women. Perhaps gender roles are not as rigid or as predictable as mainstream thought would have us believe.

Machismo and conventional conceptions of masculinity (and femininity) have typically been associated with backward rural Chicano/Latino culture. The assumption has been that modernizing and adapting to American culture would eventually lead men to reject traditional gender roles. My research, however, revealed something quite different.

Men who had greater ties to Latino culture—those who were born outside the United States or who preferred to be interviewed in Spanish—generally had more negative views of machismo and were less traditional in their conceptions of gender. Although most men responding to my survey thought of machismo as something negative, the men with stronger ties to Latino culture were *overwhelmingly* negative in their views of machismo. What's more, the men with stronger ties to Mexican/Latino culture and those with lower socioeconomic status were more likely to identify being self-centered, or *egoísta*, as a negative quality in a man.

What this means is that contrary to stereotypes about poor and working-class Latino men being macho, there is actually a distinctive Mexican cultural ethic surrounding manhood and masculinity. A man's success is measured not so much by external qualities, such as wealth, education, or power, but by internal ones such as being honest, responsible, and hardworking, sacrificing for one's children, and, most of all, not being selfish. In the working class, a man who has an honest job, who works hard to provide for his family, and who is responsible is considered a success and a good man and father. One who does not look after his family is not considered successful as a man, regardless of how much money he has or how important his job is. One of the lowest things that a man can do, according to this ethic, is to be selfish and irresponsible (*egoísta*) or to succumb to such personal vices as drinking, drugs, gambling, or womanizing. Worst of all is to fail to take care of the family.

These contradictory views of machismo and masculinity can be reconciled if we see masculinity in Chicano/Latino cultures not as conforming to either the positive or negative conception of machismo, but rather as representing the horns of a dilemma or choices faced by men. Since there is not one, but various, masculinities, a man is evaluated according to whether he is being responsible or irresponsible, honest or dishonest, *egoísta* or selfless. The findings also call into question the assumption that poor or working-class men are more likely to be more patriarchal and that as people get more education and better-paying jobs they will become more gender egalitiarian. My research findings did not support the assumption that socioeconomic status is a critical determinant of gender role attitudes and behavior or the related assumption that traditional masculinity is somehow more prevalent in the working class. Unfortunately, since racial oppression and class oppression go hand in hand, it is often difficult, if not impossible, to separate the relative influence of race and of class on beliefs and behavior.

The Bem Sex Role Inventory (BSRI) is a measure of masculinity and femininity that has been widely utilized in social science research. Contrary to what I expected, men who had more education or higher incomes, those engaged in professional occupations, and men who opted to be interviewed in English, scored higher on the masculine component of the BSRI and were less—not more—androgynous.

Surprised by these findings I developed a second tool to measure the data: the Mirandé Sex Role Inventory (MSRI), which looks at masculinity and femininity within a cultural and situational context. The MSRI produced findings that were more consistent with my expectations. Respondents with more education, higher incomes, and those who were professionals, were generally less traditional on this measure.

What this told me was that much of what we assume to be universal when it comes to gender roles and masculinity and femininity is, in fact, culture specific. The dominant sex role paradigm that has prevailed in the social sciences, for example, assumes that aggression and assertiveness are masculine traits, and that being emotional, affectionate, and showing one's feelings are feminine qualities. Ironically, the stereotypical view of a "macho man" as cold, insensitive, and emotionless is actually more consistent with Anglo than with Latino conceptions of masculinity. Superheroes like Rambo, Superman, and Batman epitomize this image of white masculinity. In Chicano/Latino culture it is permissible and desirable for men to be emotional, to show their feelings, and to kiss, hug, be affectionate with male children, and to even cry on occasion. Latino men can at once be warm, loving, and tender, and self-reliant, self-sufficient, and willing to take a stand. And I assure you that if we had a Superhero, he most certainly would cry.

R.W. Connell, one of the leading voices in the new masculinity scholarship by men, points out the complicated nature of what he calls "masculinities" and calls for us to reject hegemonic masculinities. Ironically, Connell and other new scholars interested in men and masculinity have engaged in their own brand of hegemonic discourse by ignoring masculinity among Latinos and other subordinated communities and by assuming that we can understand all masculinity by focusing on Euro-American theoretical models. In Connell's book *Masculinities* he talks about working-class masculinity and mentions in passing Robert Staples's pioneering work on black men. But Connell largely ignores other people of color. This oversight isn't unique to Connell, but he certainly represents the problem. I fully endorse the call for ending hegemonic masculinities and believe that perhaps the most important conclusion that can be drawn from my research—along with what I know from growing up male in my family and the culture—is that there is not a single Chicano/Latino masculinity, but a variety of masculinities that are not only different, but often contradictory. We should remember that these masculinities are not a subset of the dominant masculinities and that they are as complex and varied as Euro-American masculinities.

Part II

Sexuality

INTRODUCTION

In this section men write about pornography, lust, and male sexual assault and articulate some provocative views on homophobia, biphobia, and racism in the gay community. These writers navigate the minefields of power, domination, and consent, and move our collective efforts one step closer to understanding the contemporary sexual landscape in more accurate and nuanced ways. These crucial conversations bring discussions about sex out of the locker room and out of the classroom.

In "Just a John?" Robert Jensen argues that pornography is not really about sexing up and getting off: Pornography is actually about gender inequality and women's subjugation. Because we live in a culture that buys, sells, and trades women's bodies, Jensen asks men who use porn to take a cold, hard look at why they do. Pornography, he argues, is just another form of buying women's bodies. Instead, there are creative possibilities for new ways of enjoying sex and pleasure that do not require the old tropes of male violence and sexual control of women.

The issue of pornography, pleasure, and power has been ground zero for ongoing feminist debate.[1] The arguments fall roughly into two camps. Some feminist thinkers claim that pornography—and by extension, sex work—is a legitimate source of women's and men's pleasure and employment.[2] Recent feminist exposés from inside the sex industry, and the popularity of gigs like The Suicide Girls or The Pussycat Dolls, reflect the viewpoint that feminism means doing what you want and flaunting it if you feel like it. By the same token, civil libertarians like Nadine Strossen argue that to quash the supply or distribution of pornography amounts to censorship.[3]

An alternative argument about pornography, represented most ably by Andrea Dworkin and feminist legal scholar Catharine MacKinnon, is that pornography is a form of forced sex, and that it institutionalizes gender inequality and eroticizes male supremacy and female subjugation. To MacKinnon, pornography does not simply harm women, it *is* harm.[4] For black women, and other women of color, this issue is exponentially complicated because of America's "brutal history of racialized sexual coercion and violence."[5]

Some who oppose pornography want to get rid of it. Others argue that having more women in positions of power as sex industry executives and directors will improve pornography's impact on women. Feminist women who describe their experiences consuming or producing pornography force us to rethink the line between empowerment and exploitation. Women who run Internet porn companies or video companies, or who work as porn actors and models, claim these options provide ways to earn money and, for some, to creatively explore their sexuality. Jensen, however, is unconvinced that pornography is anything but exploitation. Fear of censorship, he argues, prevents us from confronting what pornography actually reveals "about the cruelty of our culture, and the white supremacy and misogyny that abounds in America."[6]

In the next essay, Hugo Schwyzer shifts the focus to sexualized communication between young men as he writes about girl-watching and sexual lust in "Staring at Janae's Legs." Schwyzer is a college professor who also works with teenagers in his church youth program. During one warm spring month, the planned discussion topic for his youth group was sexuality and dating. Schwyzer notices the boys can't stop talking about their classmate Janae's hot legs. Using this teachable moment, Schwyzer introduces the concept of homosociality; that is, guys' interest in performing their masculinity for each other.[7] Homosocial relations are not necessarily sexual, but involve males viewing females sexually and without empathy in order to form connections with each other.[8] Schwyzer explains how heterosexuality is played out and reinforced through homosocial practices. After all, Schwyzer notes, if catcalls and wolf whistles rarely help guys "get the girl" then what is the purpose? The fact, he explains, is that these practices are less about the girls and more about the boys—how males form homosocial bonds with each other using peculiarly sexist means.

In the essay, "Trying to Be Sexy and Anti-Sexist . . . at Exactly the Same Time," Andrew Boyd wonders whether consenting adults can choose to play with power in sexually charged, yet nonsexist, ways. In other words, can a man appreciate a sexy female body without being considered sexist? And if a woman chooses to overtly display her body and her sexuality, can he really be faulted for wanting to play along?

The first part of this essay takes place at a party in the Red Hook neighborhood of Brooklyn, New York. Boyd sees an attractive woman from across the room. More specifically, he sees her breasts. It seems to Boyd that this woman is intentionally deploying her sexuality as a tool of power and that she wants to be wanted. He is more than happy to comply, but is torn. If he tries to hook up, does that mean he is guilty of objectifying women? Or would this simply mean he was responding positively to her sexual agency? Boyd thinks she's sexy, but doesn't want to be "that kind of guy." He senses a friction between female self-objectification and the feminist politics of male desire. In the process, Boyd reflects confusion over the new vogue of consensual objectification and the notion that this is empowering.[9]

In the second part of his essay, Boyd is on a date with a different woman. Boyd wonders whether he will be expected to pay for dinner because he's a man, even though she earns far more money than he does. Moreover, if she pays for dinner, will she expect that he'll put out at the end of the night like men once expected of women? Boyd hopes that his date will pay and expect a sexual quid pro quo, thus hinting at the uneven risk and penalty of sex and power that remains, even as men and women negotiate new rules. Some may find Boyd's essay offensive or confused, while others may read it as a refreshingly honest account of one man struggling to figure out the shifting expectations of sex and dating while struggling to avoid an expected party line.

Marcus C. Tye's intellectually incisive essay, "Bye Bye Bi?" raises the issue of biphobia, the fear of bisexuality. Tye explains how academic research on sexuality is conducted and interpreted in ways that leave bisexual men like himself invisible. When academic research refuses to acknowledge male bisexuality, men are led to believe that they have only two sexual options: to be either homosexual or heterosexual.[10] When, in turn, the media assumes that men are either homosexual or heterosexual, our cultural biphobia is revealed and reinforced. Tye raises important questions about how we conduct research on sexuality, how mainstream media interprets this research, and how unexamined bias and presuppositions about sexuality precede this. Mainstream media love bisexual women, but fear bisexuality in men. And when bisexual men remain invisible and unrecognized, fears about masculinity and sexuality are encouraged to flourish.

In "Darker Shades of Queer," Chong-suk Han addresses the problem of racism in the gay community. "By now," Han writes, "I've listened with a mild sense of amusement as countless gay leaders, an overwhelmingly white group, attempt to explain that their oppressed status as sexual minorities provides them with an enlightened sense of social justice that enables them to understand the plight of those who are racially oppressed." Yet queer neighborhoods, magazines, storefronts, and bars within the gay community bring new meaning to the term "whitewash." One need only look as far as the personal ads to find phrases like "No femmes, no fats, no Asians." "Sadly," writes Han, "racism isn't just about how we are treated, it's also about how we treat ourselves."[11]

In their essay "Let Us Be Seen," Tomek Kitlinski and Pawel Leszkowicz describe how risky it is to be out and gay in Poland. Poland is dangerously homophobic, they explain. Some high school textbooks still teach that being gay is an illness. Furthermore, homophobia goes hand in hand with misogyny and anti-Semitism in Poland: At feminist and gay demonstrations, counter-demonstrators commonly shout, "To the gas! We'll do to you what Hitler did to Jews." In their essay, Kitlinski and Leszkowicz describe a bold and public nationwide photography project that featured same-sex couples on billboards and in art galleries. The campaign was intended to confront the issue of gay and lesbian visibility in Poland and to resist the country's homophobia.[12] The authors believe that activism, art, and academic research are effective forms of dissidence, and hold out great hope for the "day when prejudice, discrimination, and violence will be abandoned—in Poland and globally."

In "How We Enter," B. Loewe reflects on how stories about invincible male power and chronic male sexual desire impact our ability to accurately understand male sexual assault. The idea that men are always stronger than women and that rapists are predatory strangers, for example, are myths that perpetuate rape culture and prevent acknowledging that men can also be victims of sexual assault.[13] "The existence of male survivors actually interrupts these myths," Loewe explains. "Our existence creates a space for redefining or abandoning constructed male identity." Loewe's exploration of sexual violence and masculine identity draws from his experience as a political activist and as a survivor of an assault by two adult women when he was sixteen years old. Loewe's analysis brings insight to the subject of sexual assault, and in doing so, helps end the silence that surrounds it.

1. Some of the late-twentieth-century feminist perspectives on sexuality are chronicled in Ann Snitow, Christine Stansell, and Sharon Thompson, eds. *Powers of Desire: The Politics of Sexuality*. New York: Monthly Review Press, 1983. See also Carole S. Vance. *Pleasure and Danger: Exploring Female Sexuality*. London: Pandora Press, 1989. Publication of this latter anthology followed the contentious 1982 Scholar and Feminist Conference on the politics of sexuality, held at Barnard College, New York.
2. Carly Milne, ed. *Naked Ambition: Women Who Are Changing Pornography*. New York: Caroll and Graf, 2005; Jill Nagle, ed. *Whores and Other Feminists*. New York: Routledge, 1997; and select essays in Merri Lisa Johnson, ed. *Jane Sexes It Up: True Confessions of Feminist Desire*. New York: Four Walls Eight Windows, 2002. The term "pro-sex feminists" has been used to describe so-called third wave feminists who support the freedom to do sex work and to use pornography. This is a misnomer. I am unaware of analogous feminists who could be called "anti-sex." The central issue is, rather, power and sexual consent not whether one is for or against sex.
3. Nadine Strossen. *Defending Pornography: Free Speech, Sex, and the Fight for Women's Rights*. New York: New York University Press, 2000.
4. To support her argument that pornography does not represent harm but is in and of itself harm, MacKinnon compares pornography to signs appearing above water fountains in the race-segregated South. Just as pornography is harm, a sign stating, "Colored" does not represent harm, but is itself the harm. Catharine A. MacKinnon. "Not a Moral Issue," *Yale Law & Policy Review*. Vol. 2 (Spring 1984): 325.
5. Mireille Miller-Young. "Hardcore Desire." *ColorLines*. (Winter 2005–06): 35.

6. In his 2007 article titled "A Call for an Open Discussion of Mass-Marketed Pornography," Jensen suggests that just as we would not mistake concern about McDonald's nutritional content with being anti-food, "pursuing a healthy sexuality does not mean we have to support toxic pornography." Only four days after this article was originally published, it generated more than 400 online comments and copious reader debate. See http://alternet.org/mediaculture/47677 and www.alternet.org/sex/47987.

7. See Michael Kimmel. *Manhood in America*. New York: Free Press, 2005.

8. Sharon R. Bird. "Welcome to the Men's Club: Homosociality and the Maintenance of Hegemonic Masculinity." *Gender & Society*. Vol. 10, no. 2 (April 1996): 120–32. See also Beth A. Quinn. "Sexual Harassment and Masculinity: The Power and Meaning of 'Girl Watching.'" *Gender & Society*. Vol. 16, no. 3 (June 2002): 386–402.

9. For feminist arguments that self-objectification can be sexually liberating or empowering, see select essays in Merri Lisa Johnson, ed. *Jane Sexes It Up*.

10. Mainstream interpretations of the Academy Award-winning 2005 film *Brokeback Mountain* is a prime example of Tye's point about bisexual invisibility. The protagonist characters are routinely described as gay cowboys, but the film actually shows them as bisexual. The public misframing of this film "results from our culture's ongoing tendency to polarize, dichotomize, and oversimplify issues of sexuality and sexual orientation." See Harry Brod. "They're Bi Shepherds, Not Gay Cowboys: The Misframing of *Brokeback Mountain*." *Journal of Men's Studies*. Vol. 14, no. 2 (Spring 2006): 252. Jennifer Baumgardner raises similar points in her book, *Look Both Ways*. See Jennifer Baumgardner. *Look Both Ways: Bisexual Politics*. New York: Farrar, Strauss and Giroux, 2007.

11. For self-reported accounts by young gay Asian males living in Anglo-Australian environments and discussion about the impact of white archetypal masculine ideals on body-image concerns, see Murray J.N. Drummond. "Asian Gay Men's Bodies." *Journal of Men's Studies*. Vol. 13, no. 3 (Spring 2005): 291–300.

12. Kitlinski and Leszkowicz further explore art, xenophobia, homosexuality, democracy, and activism in their co-authored book, *Love and Democracy: Reflections on the Homosexual Question in Poland*. Krakow: Aureus, 2005.

13. For resources and information about male survivors see Male Survivor (http://malesurvivor.org), and the Rape, Abuse and Incest National Network (RAINN) (www.rainn.org).

JUST A JOHN? PORNOGRAPHY AND MEN'S CHOICES

Robert Jensen

There has been much talk about the need for men to love each other and be willing to speak openly about that love. That is important; we need to be able to get beyond the all-too-common male tendency to mute or deform our emotions, a tendency that is destructive not only to ourselves but to those around us. Many have spoken about our need to nurture each other, and that's important, too. But it's also crucial to remember that loving one another means challenging ourselves as well.

I would like to challenge us all—in harsh language—to address men's use of pornography. In an unjust world, those of us with privilege must be willing to do this, especially out of love. The challenge is this: Can we be more than just johns?

Let me start with a story that a female student at the University of Texas told me. She was on a bus traveling from Austin to Dallas for a football game. The bus was chartered by a fraternity and many of the passengers were women. During the trip, someone put into the bus' VCR a sexually explicit video. Uncomfortable with the hardcore sexual images of women being used by men, the female student began a discussion with the people around her about it, and one of the men on the bus agreed that it was inappropriate. He stood up and said to the other men, "You all know me and know I like porn as much as the next guy, but it's not right for us to play this tape when there are women on the bus."

No doubt it took some courage for that young man to confront his fraternity brothers on the issue, and we should honor that. But we should recognize that his statement also communicated to his fraternity brothers that he was one of them—"one of the guys"—who, being guys, naturally like pornography. His objection was not to pornography and men's routine purchase and use of women's bodies for sexual pleasure, but to viewing it with women present. He was making it clear that his ultimate loyalty was to men and their right to use women sexually, though that use should conform to some type of code of chivalry about being polite about it in mixed company. In doing that, he was announcing his own position in regard to sex. He was saying *I'm just a john.*

PIMPS AND JOHNS

A john is a man who buys another human being for sex, typically through an intermediary; the pimp. Men sell women to other men for sex: pimps and johns.

There is a lot that could be said about the current cultural practice of using the term "pimp" in a wide variety of other contexts—for example, the MTV show "Pimp My Ride." We live in a world in which men who sell women are glorified. It is also a world in which the dominant white culture implicitly defines a pimp as black and then alternately celebrates and denigrates them. The confluence of racism and sexism in these cultural trends deserves discussion. But I want to concentrate here not on the pimps, but on the johns, on the men who buy women for sex.

I assume that many men reading this masturbate, or have masturbated, to pornography. That makes us johns. I don't mean that most men have necessarily bought a woman from a pimp in prostitution, though no doubt some of us have. I'm talking, instead, about the far more common experience of pornography. In my childhood and young adulthood, I was sometimes a john. Virtually every man I know has been a john.

In pornography, the pimp is called a publisher or a video producer, and the john is called a fan or a pornography consumer. But that doesn't change the nature of the relationship: It involves one person (usually a man) selling another person (usually a woman) to a third person (usually a man). What this means is that pornography is a mass-mediated conglomeration of pimps and johns. When you masturbate to pornography, you are buying sexual pleasure. You are buying a woman. The fact that there are technologies of film or video between you and the pimp doesn't change the equation. Legally, it's not prostitution and, legally, you're not in trouble. But you are still a john.

THE PORNOGRAPHY THAT JOHNS LIKE

At this point, let me define a few terms. Pornography comes in all forms and all kinds of people consume porn. In this discussion, however, I'm specifically referring to heterosexual pornography. I'm using the term to describe the graphic, sexually explicit material that is consumed by heterosexual men. These DVDs, videos, and Internet sites comprise the bulk of the commercial pornography market. There are three consistent themes in heteronormative pornography:

1. All women want sex from all men at all times.
2. Women naturally desire the kind of sex that men want, including sex that many women find degrading.
3. Any woman who does not at first realize this can be turned on with a little force.

The pornography industry produces two major types of films: features and gonzo. Features mimic, however badly, the conventions of a Hollywood movie. There is some minimal plot, a little character development, and a bit of dialogue, all in the service of presenting the sex. Gonzo films have no such pretensions; they are simply recorded sex, usually taking place in a private home or a starkly decorated set. Gonzo porn often starts with an interview with the woman or women about their sexual desires before other men or women enter the scene.

All these films have a standard series of sex acts, including oral, vaginal, and anal penetration, often performed while the men call the women "bitch," "cunt," "whore," and other, similar names. As they are penetrated, the women are expected to say over and over how much they like the sex. As pornography like this has become increasingly normalized—and readily available through-out the country by increasingly sophisticated technology—pornographers have pushed the limits of what is acceptable in the mainstream. As one pornographic film director put it, "People want more . . . [so we] make it more hard, make it more nasty, make it more relentless."

The adult film industry produces about 11,000 new hardcore, graphic, and sexually explicit films a year. Although *Adult Video News* (an industry trade magazine) sets revenues at $4 billion dollars a year, a 2001 *New York Times Magazine* article estimated annual revenues of the pornography industry in the United States at between $10 billion and $14 billion. Worldwide revenues have been put at $57 billion a year. By comparison, the Hollywood box office was $9 billion in 2005. Because there is no way to chart the amount of money generated by pornographic websites, and because other segments of the industry are almost as difficult to track, any estimates of the industry's revenues are rough and may well be underestimates. In any case, figures indicate that there are lots of johns and a lot of profit for the pimps.

MEN'S CHOICES AND RESPONSIBILITIES

We know there are women who consume pornography and a few women who make it. In this society, that's called progress. Feminism is advanced, some argue, when women can join the ranks of those who buy and sell other human beings.

This argument is a predictable result of the collaboration of capitalism and patriarchy. Take a system that values profit over everything, and combine it with a system of male supremacy, and you get a situation where pornography is increasingly mainstream and normalized; it is made into everyday experience. Pornography is profitable when men take it as their right to consume women's sexuality. When women join in the patterns of producing and consuming pornography, they join in a practice of exploitation and objectification.

When confronted with this, men often suggest that women choose to participate in pornography, so there's no reason to critique men's use of porn. We should avoid the temptation to take that easy way out. I'm going to say nothing in regard to what women should do, nor am I going to critique their choices. I don't take it as my place to inject myself in the discussions that women have about this.

I do, however, take it as my place to talk to men. I take it as a political and ethical responsibility to engage in critical self-reflection and to be accountable for my behavior, at the individual and the collective level. For men, the question is not about women's choices. The real issue is about men's choices. Do you want to participate in a system in which women are sold for sexual pleasure, whether in prostitution, pornography, strip clubs, or in any other aspect of the sex industry? Do you want to live in a world in which some people are bought and sold for the sexual pleasure of others?

When we ask such questions, one of the first things we will hear is: These are important issues, but we shouldn't make men feel guilty about buying sexual pleasure. Why not? I agree that much of the guilt people feel is rooted in attempts to repress human sexuality. This sort of guilt is unfortunately part of our society's cultural and theological history, and it is destructive. But guilt also can be a healthy emotional and intellectual response to the world and one's actions in it.

Johns should feel guilty when they buy women. Guilt is an appropriate response to an act that is unjust. Guilt can be a sign that we have violated our own ethical norms. It can be part of a process of ending the injustice. Guilt can be healthy if it is understood in political, not merely religious or psychological, terms.

Buying women is wrong not because of a society's repressive moral code or its effects on an individual's psychological process. It is wrong because it hurts people. It creates a world in which people get hurt. And the people who get hurt the most are the people with the least amount of power. When you create a sex-class that can be bought and sold, the people in that group—in this instance, women—will inevitably be treated as lesser, as available to be controlled and abused.

The way out of being a john is political. The way out is feminist analysis. And I'm not referring to a superficial exercise in identifying a few "women's issues" that men can help with. To borrow from Karl Marx, feminist analysis provides ruthless criticism of the existing order. Feminist analysis of pornography will not shrink from its own discoveries. Nor will this analysis shy away from conflict with the powers that be.

We need to engage in this ruthless criticism. Let's start not just with pornography, but with sex more generally. One discovery, I think, is that men are often johns, and that the way in which johns use women sexually is a window into other aspects of our sexual and intimate lives. For many men, sex is a place where we display and reinforce our power over women. By that, I don't mean that all men use sex that way all the time. What I mean is that this pattern of relationships is readily visible in our society. Women deal with it every day, and at some level most men get that.

The issue is not just about pimps and johns, and the women who are prostituted. It's about men and women, and sex and power. If you've been thinking, "Well, that's not me. I never pay for it," don't be so sure. It's not just about who pays for it and who doesn't. It's about the fundamental nature of the relationship between men and women, and how that plays out in sex and intimacy.

And if you think this doesn't affect you because you are one of the "good men," then take a closer look. I'm told that I am one of those good men. I work in a feminist movement. I have been part of groups that critique men's violence and the sex industry. And I struggle with these issues all the time. I was trained to be a man in this culture, and that training doesn't evaporate overnight. None of us is off the hook.

WHAT IS SEX FOR?

No matter what our personal history or current practice, we all might want to ask a simple question: What is sex for?

A male friend once told me that sometimes sex is like a warm handshake, nothing more than a greeting between friends. Many people claim that sex can be a purely physical interaction to produce pleasurable sensations in the body. At the same time, sex is said to be the ultimate act of intimacy, the place in which we expose ourselves most fully, where we let another see us stripped down, not just physically but emotionally. Certainly sex can be all those things to different people at different times. But isn't that a lot to ask sex to carry? Can one human practice really carry such a range of meaning and purpose? And in a male-supremacist culture in which men's violence is still tacitly accepted and men's control of women is often unchallenged, should we be surprised that sex becomes a place where that violence and control play out?

This isn't an argument for imposing a particular definition of sex. It's an invitation to confront what I believe is a crucial question for this culture. The conservative framework, often rooted in narrow religious views, for defining appropriate sex in order to control people is a disaster. The libertarian framework that avoids questions of gender and power has also failed.

We live in a time of sexual crisis. That makes life difficult, but it also creates a space for invention and creativity. The possibility of a different way of understanding the world and myself is what drew me to feminism. I was drawn to the possibility of escaping the masculinity trap set for me, and the chance to become something more than a man, more than just a john. I was drawn by the possibilities of becoming a human being.

STARING AT JANAE'S LEGS

Hugo Schwyzer

In my work as a pro-feminist professor who teaches gender studies courses, there are few concepts more essential to convey to students than homosociality. Homosociality is the idea that men are raised in our culture to be more eager to please other men than women. According to this view, women are pawns used to prove one's masculinity. It doesn't take much in my classes to get heads nodding in agreement when the subject comes up.

To use one cheap and easy example, homosociality explains catcalls and wolf-whistles. Women often ask me why men whistle and hoot at them from construction sites or passing cars. "Do they think this actually 'works' to pick up women?" they inquire.

The thing is, men rarely catcall when they're alone. They almost always do it when they're part of a group of men. So why do they do it? Seen through the lens of homosociality, the explanation is obvious: Men whistle and yell to connect with other men. Women are devices for creating non-sexual, same-gender bonds. This doesn't explain all catcalling behavior, but it goes a hell of a long way toward doing so.

One of the most significant difficulties (and opportunities) in pro-feminist men's work is that it challenges homosocial norms. Pro-feminist men are often characterized as "wimps"—that is, soft, gentle men with submissive natures. Actually, pro-feminist men who work to match their language and their lives have to be remarkably brave. Few things are more difficult than speaking up against sexism in all-male environments. To do so means risking anger, ostracism, and sometimes, even violence. Given the intense desire for male approval that many young men have, it takes guts to stand alone in all-male environments.

When I was younger, I quickly mastered non-sexist talk. Around female friends, I was a thoughtful, polite, and intelligent critic of gender roles and the patriarchy. But get me alone with my buddies (especially with a beer or two) and I spewed the same objectifying garbage that they did. There were many reasons for this. First off, I was deeply ambivalent about feminism. Being alone with the guys gave me a chance to blow off steam; the more I tried to match my words, actions, and politics in mixed groups, the more I felt the overwhelming need to act boorishly around my guy friends when we were alone together. Second of all, I was desperate for male approval. In college, most of the guys I hung out with were pre-law or engineering types. None of my guy friends were humanities or art majors, much less interested in taking women's studies classes. I knew that criticizing their words and actions would mean losing their companionship and, at that stage of my life, the craving for friends won out over my ethics, hands down. I often made fun of the very material I was studying, as if to reassure my friends that I didn't take it too seriously, and thus could be trusted to remain one of the guys.

This kind of double life left me feeling ashamed and fraudulent.

It wasn't until I was in my thirties that I grew comfortable challenging men in single-sex environments. I'd like to think I do it politely, but firmly. I certainly don't do it every time I hear sexist humor or beliefs expressed. Like most folks, I've learned to pick my battles—and frankly, sometimes, I'm just too tired or busy to speak up. But what has given me the courage to do so—when I do—has been the support of other men. It wasn't until I started to do men's work with other pro-feminist men that I began to feel sufficiently empowered to start calling guys on their (sometimes) unintentional misogyny. Doing male retreats through church, and my work with groups like Men Can Stop Rape put me into contact with guys who didn't just share my politics, but had spent far longer than I had living pro-feminist beliefs as strong, courageous men.

When I talk about these issues with younger men and boys, they almost invariably acknowledge the tremendous power of homosociality. Many of them are receptive to feminist ideas, but cannot even imagine actually speaking up about them when they are alone with other guys. I know first-hand how difficult it is to match language and life in the face of homosocial pressure to conform. I am particularly careful to stress to the younger men I know that just because someone isn't ready to speak up yet doesn't mean that they are a fraud. The key thing, I tell them, is finding male allies who will support them in taking small steps toward personal change. Making this sort of change requires battling our own insecurities and doubts, and dealing with the periodic pressure to chuck our ethical commitments and just "go along to get along." But I've seen change happen, and I've seen it work.

I've had many chances to encourage this change and many opportunities to refuse to "go along with the guys." One forum has been my local progressive Episcopal Church's Wednesday Night Youth Group. I've been volunteering with the senior high students at All Saints Episcopal Church in Pasadena, California, for several years now. Working with teenage boys and girls gives me a chance to walk my talk and practice what I preach. Kids can smell hypocrisy a mile away.

A couple of years ago, the Youth Group kids were in the midst of a month-long program that involved four consecutive Wednesday nights talking about sexuality, dating, and Christian ethics "All Saints Pasadena style." As we always do, we spent some time in single-sex groups. There were just two Youth Group leaders at the time, and my female colleague took the girls off to one room, while I went to another room with the boys.

It was May. The weather was warm. One girl in the larger group, widely regarded by all the kids as one of the hottest girls, had worn very short shorts, flip-flops, and a tiny top to Youth Group that day. As soon as I got the boys alone in the room, two of them started talking excitedly about what "Janae" (name changed, of course) had been wearing. One of the boys said, "Dang, when I look at those shorts all I think is how much I want to hit that!" The other boys all laughed, and then turned toward me with sheepish grins. Yes, their youth minister was in the room, but they were operating under the homosocial assumption that even in church, it's okay to objectify women and girls as long as only other men are around.

A younger Hugo would have rebuked them sharply. I could so easily have given them the "Janae is your sister in Christ, boys!" lecture, and tried to shame them. An even less mature Hugo might have validated what they were saying by agreeing about Janae's attractiveness, if for no other reason than to affirm my masculine *bona fides* by showing them that I, too, was, after all, "just another guy" who enjoyed looking at pretty girls.

But since the discussion subject was supposed to be sex, I figured I'd use Janae's shorts as a teaching moment. So I asked the boys, "What's it like when a girl like Janae is showing a lot of skin? How do you feel?" The replies came fast and furious: "Dude, it's so awesome!" "I love it when you can see so much!" And, of course, "I can't stop looking!" The boys laughed and got rowdy. Then I asked, "When you say you can't stop looking, what does that mean? Do you have no choice?"

Silence. One boy, "Aaron," blurted out, "No way. No choice. Girl that fine, can't control my mind." Again, the other boys laughed. I waited and then followed up. "Do all of you feel like Aaron feels? None of you think you can control what your eyes do and where your mind goes?"

More silence. "Roger" spoke up. "I guess it's kind of a choice. I mean, when you first see a pretty girl, you can't help but look. But you can choose whether or not you keep staring at her legs or her tits. You don't have to make the girl feel uncomfortable." Several other boys quickly agreed, and Aaron found himself on the defensive: "I don't know, dude. I don't know how you can say you really like girls and not be totally distracted by something so fine." I smiled inwardly. It was clear what was going on. Aaron was trying to bully the other boys by threatening their masculinity if they didn't take his side.

What followed was a serious discussion. With my prodding questions, the boys debated their own ability to control themselves. In the end, even Aaron grudgingly admitted that he, too, has choices about how he looks at girls. Roger, his foil, high-fived him at this and said "Hey, Aaron, welcome to reality!"

What I said to the boys was something like this: "I don't think that there's anything wrong with noticing girls. I don't think there's necessarily anything wrong with fantasizing about them. I do think there's something very wrong when your focus on their bodies makes it impossible for you to see them as people, as friends, as human beings. When you find yourself noticing a girl's body and staring at her skin, I don't want you to beat yourself up. But I don't want you to objectify her, either."

"Next time you're looking at Janae's legs, Aaron," I said, "I want you to gently remind yourself that Janae is more than just her body. It's okay to think she's sexy. But she's not only a pair of legs or breasts. She may be hot, she may want you to look at her body, and she may want to be wanted. But I'd put money on it that she hopes you'll also see her as a human being. And no matter how hot she is, you've got it in you to never forget that." Aaron nodded solemnly, but I don't know if he really heard me or not.

Other boys did, though, and a couple of them came up to thank me for the discussion and to talk more about the subject. Boys almost never hear that they have *choices* about how they direct their thoughts and their lust. I don't deny that guys can be very, very horny. But the myth that young guys are easily overcome by their uncontainable, raging, male libido is a powerful story, and one that gets reinforced in our culture and through homosocial relations.

My goal is to reach young men where they are with a message about their sexuality that is realistic, loving, and authentically pro-feminist. Ultimately, I don't want any of my Youth Group teens—male or female—to feel ashamed of their desires. I don't expect them not to lust for each other. But what both pro-feminists and Christians can insist on, even for young men, is that sexual desire, no matter how powerful, cannot be used as an excuse to rob our brothers and sisters of their humanness. Whether Janae is wearing sweats or shorts, how the boys perceive her is ultimately their responsibility. Libido is a powerful thing, but so is the patriarchal objectification of women. We do well, I think, when we don't fear all that raging sexual energy. We do well to acknowledge it, even celebrate it, and then ask that it always be tempered with recognition of the other's essential humanity. That's a far more effective strategy than either demeaning boys for lusting or asking girls to cover up in order to prevent the boys from doing so. Or, worse yet, not talking about it at all.

TRYING TO BE SEXY AND ANTI-SEXIST . . . AT EXACTLY THE SAME TIME

Andrew Boyd

ARE WOMEN SEX OBJECTS?

I respect women and regard them as my equals. So what am I supposed to do at parties? Especially, when there's a hot redhead over by the liquor table. I notice her all the way across the room. Okay, it's her breasts that I notice all the way across the room.

The room we're in is a vast, eat-in, work-in, live-in, sleep-in, kitchen-like space in a recently reclaimed loft in Red Hook. Techno is pumping from a makeshift dance floor on the other side of the far wall. It's close to midnight, the place is packed, and from all the way across the room I notice her breasts.

But do I want to be the kind of guy who notices her breasts from all the way across the room? I certainly don't want to be the kind of guy who notices her breasts from all the way across the room, then walks up to her breasts, makes small talk with her breasts, asks her breasts out, and has a short-lived, emotionally dishonest relationship with her breasts. Granted, the going-home-with-her-breasts part has great appeal. A full-bodied, magnetic fascination, in fact. But I don't want to be that kind of guy.

Women get catcalled, hit on, and over-sexualized all the time. I don't want to add to that. I'm watching her and thinking how the media and mass culture typecast women into narrow, sex object roles. Trophy bride, sex goddess, ball-buster, slut. I'm thinking about *Baywatch*, porn, beer commercials, marriage customs, Howard Stern. On the other hand, I'm also thinking: I definitely want to hit on her—if only to find out if there's chemistry between us, and also to be nearer to those breasts, those superb breasts.

I flash back to my last visit to the Met—one of the most famous museums in the world—and note how even high culture typecasts women. For every

Reubens who celebrated the full-figured female form, there's a Willem DeKooning who portrayed breasts as if they were evil disembodied curved pieces of meat pulsating in wild colors shouting out my name. I remind myself how trapped, and often degraded, women feel when men force them into these roles.

But I'm different, I remind myself. I'm not an asshole. I'm one of the good guys. Other men may not be aware that they are lustful, objectifying, breast-obsessed, sex fiends—but I am. Now, if only she knew that I knew, then I might be able to get somewhere with her. But she doesn't. She has no idea of the strenuous ideological gymnastics I'm putting myself through on her behalf. She doesn't know how valiantly I'm trying to treat her right, how severely I'm policing my own gaze, how hard I'm struggling not to stare at the straining buttons on her shirt. It's a huge struggle. A struggle against millions of years of socialization or evolutionary hard-wiring (I'm not really sure which), a struggle against the primal synchronization between my brain and her body. A struggle that I'm losing. I try not to feel guilty. This is why she's curved in the first place, I tell myself. Well, that, and the evolutionary utility of child-bearing hips.

I took a women's studies class my sophomore year of college. I know objectification is demeaning and dehumanizing. I know a woman is not defined by the male gaze. I know all this. But I also know that objectification happens, whether I want it to or not. And what's the big deal, really? I get off on the Victoria's Secret catalog. So what? Doesn't everyone operate by some internal, body-image calculus? Doesn't desire itself require some level of objectification? "Just because I objectify her, it doesn't mean I can't also relate to her in other ways," I tell myself. My *glands* might experience her as a sex object, but I don't always have to treat her as one. Can't I honor the integrity of her whole being at the same time that I fetishize my favorite part?

And, so, I lift my gaze off her chest and look her in the eye. And lo! She smiles. Our eyes lock together for a moment. Unfortunately, this moment only lasts a micro-fraction of a second because my eyes involuntarily dart back to her chest. Again, I raise my eyes to meet hers. Back again to her chest. Her eyes. Chest. Eyes. Aaahhgh, what could she be thinking now? I'm pretty certain it's not, "Why hasn't he noticed my breasts?" I'm dreading that it might be, "Jeez, it's so gross the way he's checking me out." At this point I'd be willing to settle for, "Hmmm, I think that guy's interested, and look—oh, how sweet—he's trying so hard not to stare dead on at my cleavage." And maybe that is what she's thinking, because although she doesn't want me to stare at her breasts like a deer caught in onrushing headlights, I think she wants me to notice them. In fact, she's probably gone through a hell of a lot of trouble to support, maintain, possibly enhance, display, and deploy her breasts. Not only does she want them noticed, she wants me to notice each painstakingly choreographed detail about them: that inviting shadow of cleavage, that suggestion of nipple, that rising Bezier curve, that perfectly calibrated bounce as she moves. And I do. I do notice all this—in excruciating, aching, longing-inducing detail.

I try to imagine how differently things might turn out if I just go over to her, talk to her, relate to her as a complex, fully human, breast-less being. With such a sympathetic approach, it's quite possible that she'll squeeze my hand meaningfully and say, "You're such a dear. But let's just be pals, OK?" Instead, should I be more aggressive? Maybe give her a long hard look over? A move like that would signal interest and up the ante. And she might welcome it. And that would be great. But if she doesn't welcome it and I persist, I've become an asshole—and my sexual come-on has become a degrading act of power. Objectification should be fun, I remind myself. Degradation is only fun if she's a professional and she's brought new toys.

Clearly there are problems with both the all-breast and no-breast approach. The crux of the issue: A woman is a complex human being. The other crux of the issue: She has breasts. She doesn't want to be treated like a piece of ass, but she also doesn't want me to work so hard at not being sexist that I end up not being sexual. I wonder: Can a guy be sexy *and* anti-sexist? From experience I know that women get offended when I treat them as sex objects. I also know that sometimes they want me to treat them as sex objects. The trick, I figure, is to understand when, where, how, and how much. For example, I probably shouldn't treat a woman as a sex object when she's giving birth, giving me a raise, or standing next to my wife. However, it seems fairly safe to treat her as a sex object when she's fucking my brains out.

And that seems to be the basic rule: A woman is a sex object when she wants to be. Not when I want her to be one, not when the culture wants her to be one, but when she wants to be one. When she chooses to be a sex object, she is deliberately adopting a limited part of who she is. She's playing a role and she's looking for someone to play with. But what does a woman actually want when she wants to be treated as a sex object? She certainly doesn't want to be groped. She probably doesn't want 100 guys staring at her breasts. Maybe she wants to feel her sexual power. Maybe she wants some guy to be completely captivated by her. Maybe that guy is not me.

But it could be me, couldn't it? Yes it could, and I'm going to go right over there and talk to her. So, what's my opening line? How can I possibly communicate the grand nobility of my dilemmas? What opening line is seductively powerful enough to provoke sexual interest, gracefully nuanced enough to leave her alone if she so wishes, and also open-ended enough to let her exercise her own discriminating sexual agency? Maybe "Hi." Yes, "Hi" would probably do fine. Then I can flirt, or have a real conversation, or both, feeling things out as I go.

The beautiful irony here, I'm thinking, is that all this tortured, altruistic concern for women can actually advance my own naked self-interest (not to mention the interests of my naked self). Treating a woman as a full human being is not only the decent thing to do, it's also the royal road to lots of hot sex over the long-term. Because the more you recognize and respect her for all that she is, the more she'll trust you—follow closely here—and the more she trusts you, the more comfortable she'll feel letting you treat her as a sex object.

Because, in the end, a woman doesn't want to be with an asshole (no matter how sexy she might find his cocky disregard for boundaries), but rather with a decent guy who can play the bad-boy role when called upon. This guy knows when a woman wants to be a sex object and when she doesn't. He treats her as a sex object because she's sexy, not because she's a woman. And he's always open to engaging in the sexy power play she invites. It's not just about breasts; it's about everything that makes her sexy: her voice, her power, her presence, the way she moves, how she handles the room. He recognizes the total package of self-objectification that she presents.

With this ideal embodiment of male savvy and sensitivity firmly in mind, I have found my pole star, a distant vision of my best possible self. I don't know exactly what I'm going to do or say (except maybe "Hi"), but I am finally ready to make my move. As I search for her among the partygoers (she's not in the kitchen anymore, maybe the back fire escape?), I see clearly now that this amazing creature is not the sum of her body parts. She is a complex and deeply human, deeply sexy woman whom I am ready to treat with respect, equality, and wet buckets of lust. If only she hadn't already left the party.

WHO SHOULD PAY THE TAB?

The waiter approaches our table, bill in hand. He sets it down almost exactly between Karla and me, yet ever so slightly closer to me. The conversation misses a beat. We glance away from each other—only for a moment, but it's quite noticeable since we've been staring quite steadily at each other for most of the past hour. Karla is smart and together and, tonight, in her blue, spaghetti-strap dress, in the three-quarter light of this cozy, Italian place in Brooklyn, she's looking quite lovely. It's another first date with another independent-minded career woman. Unlike most of the other dates recently, this one is going well. Until now.

The waiter briefly nods to us and walks away. A gauntlet has been thrown down. The two of us have only just met and already we're at a turning point in our relationship. It is a true test of manhood, and in a culture singularly lacking in meaningful male rites of passage, I cannot afford to let it go by unmet. I gather all the studied self-assurance that a contemporary red-blooded American male can muster and immediately begin a confused and panicked conversation inside my own head:

"Be a man," I tell myself.

"Huh?" I reply to myself.

"You know, act like a man."

"Hey, look, do you want me to *be* a man or just *act* like one?"

"Huh?"

"Like, do I need to somehow *become* a man, or can I just *pretend* I'm a man for this situation?"

"Pretend?"

"Yeah."

"What kind of man are you?"

"Well, who's this man you want me to act like?"

Without betraying a hint of the inner turmoil raging in my brain, I smoothly pick up the bill and reach for my wallet—but only because I've asked her out. If she'd asked me out, I might let her pay. But before I'd let her pay, I'd offer to pay. Well, actually, I'd gauge her independent-mindedness on a one-to-ten scale, and if it were seven or above, I'd offer to split. However, if neither of us had clearly asked the other out, and we both sort of just fell into the date together, then I'd suggest a clean fifty-fifty split—unless I made a whole lot more than she did, in which case I would offer to cover the whole bill. If, however, she made a whole lot more than me, I might let her pay. All this is moot, of course, if she's very politically minded. In that case, it's important to keep the big picture in mind and split the bill according to the current disparity between male and female incomes in society at large—which at 77¢ on the dollar, would have me paying exactly 56.5 percent of the bill.

While the first date can be a little tricky, it only gets worse. If Karla and I were to survive this crucial moment of decision and ambiguity and have a second date, then I'd also have to factor in how she's interpreting the way we split the bill on the first date. Does she think that's the pattern that will be followed from now on? Or just a special case? Or was it the first in an alternating series of he-pays, she-pays evenings?

There's the added complication of multi-part dates. Maybe Karla and I will go see a movie after dinner. If we're splitting, would we split the dinner and also split the movie? Or should I cover the dinner and let her get the movie? And what if we were to have a drink after the movie? If we're alternating, are we alternating whole dates? Or are we alternating dinner-movie-drinks within dates? And does that mean that if I got the last sub-unit of the previous date, she should get the first sub-unit of the next date?

Sometimes special circumstances overrule all of these delicate negotiations. In such a situation I would pay the tab date after date after date until she dumps her other boyfriend or I go broke.

Eventually, Karla and I might find ourselves in an actual relationship. Then I could relax a little. What happens with the tab each evening would be less important. Instead, we'd both be keeping a monthly balance sheet vaguely in mind. Sometimes we'd split, sometimes we'd alternate. It would all come out in the wash. However, I'd try not to fall into a too-predictable routine. Every once in a while I'd take her out for a special evening that wouldn't figure into the balance sheet. I'd do it in style and pay for everything. Maybe on another occasion, she'd do the same for me.

Money is an expressive medium. In the old days, paying the tab on that first date was a simple, non-verbal way to say: *I am interested in you. I am a generous person. Tonight you are worth $28.45 plus tax.* The feminist revolution changed all that, making things more equal, but turning dating from a simple minefield of sex, power, and money to a far more complicated minefield of sex, power, and money. Now nobody is quite sure what mix of new rules and old rules anybody else is playing by. If you pay, will she think you are a traditional romantic, a chauvinist, or a savvy modern guy who is versatile enough to also play the gentleman? And if you let her pay, are you economic dead weight? Or a man at ease with powerful women? And if you split, what are you saying then? That you are a cheapskate? Or only half interested in her? Or the kind of man who's willing to do half the housework and go down on her half the time?

Tonight, as it turns out, my date is a TV producer. Karla makes more money than I do. A lot more. She insists on paying, and I consent. I believe in equality. I believe in it very strongly. And yet, as she casually snaps her platinum advantage card on the table—its sixteen ribbed silver digits glistening like a robust economic muscle, its embedded hologram glowing like a pre-Minoan earth goddess straddling the center of the world—I feel like I've been bitch-slapped.

But guys are not the only ones suffering from gender-role meltdown. The woman at the other end of the table might get to play both sides of the game, but not without her own anxieties. She resents that her hard-won economic independence can be an intimidating turn-off to some guys. But she also knows that if she wants to feel taken care of—and sometimes even the most fiercely independent women do—she can choose to sit back and let the man see to everything. Yet when she does, her feminist conscience torments her. *I'm perpetuating the system, I'm giving up, I'm not wielding the economic power my foresisters-in-struggle sacrificed their valium-chilled suburban lives to achieve.* Then again, if she needs to make it clear to the guy that things are going to be on an equal footing, she can always choose to split the bill. If the guy insists on paying, fine, but at least she's being clear that it won't buy him what he really wants.

Tonight, what I really want is to take this sexy TV producer home with me. The traditional method—fork over some big bucks and press on—is no longer an option. Anyway, women like Karla can rarely be seduced by such things. Whether I bought her a burger or a banquet, I couldn't expect her to fuck me for either. However, since *she's* buying, I can at least try to give her the impression that I expect that she expects that she'll get to fuck me. Who knows, it might work.

BYE-BYE BI? BAILEY, BIPHOBIA, AND GIRLIE-MEN

Marcus C. Tye

I am standing in front of an electric sliding door to the library. It doesn't open. I flap my hand over my head toward the sensor. Still the door doesn't open. Long seconds pass, with three thoughts running through my mind.

1. Did I look vaguely effeminate with all the hand flapping?
2. Decades into a supposed feminist revolution, what is a trained psychologist doing with 1950s' notions of what type of hand motions are manly and womanly?
3. Perhaps, as the *New York Times* had recently suggested, I didn't exist. Maybe that was why the door wasn't opening.

The *Times* didn't say that I, Marcus C. Tye, didn't exist, but that week published an article stating that male bisexuality, and male bisexuals, aren't real. We're all gay, straight, or lying: gotta pick sides, which I'd rather not. So does that mean I don't exist? And why do men have to pick teams?

Every now and then the *New York Times* has an article on male sexuality. It usually becomes the most frequently emailed article, especially if it concerns sexual orientation. "Straight, Gay, or Lying?" (July 5, 2005) almost topped the charts for a whole week, mostly holding steady at number two, trumping even reports on the London Underground bombing. It was only topped by Brooke Shields' earlier op-ed reacting to Tom Cruise's psychiatry-phobia.

While this suggests that the supposedly liberal, East Coast educated elite are actually closet *E!* cases, it also suggests a certain public fascination with male sexuality. A consistent theme emerges over the years: Articles on the down-low, brokeback marriages, and the like all reach the conclusion that males are straight or gay, and anyone who doesn't pick sides is being dishonest.

I think this says more about mainstream notions of masculinity and how scientific research is interpreted in popular media than it says about male sexuality (bi or otherwise). But first I should explain the "Straight, Gay, or Lying" article.

As one might expect, the original scientific paper that underscored the *Times* report is filled with quadratic regressions and absolute residuals. The statistics tell a very different story from the one reported in the media, even the supposedly veridically exhaustive *Times*.

The original paper was written by Gerulf Rieger, Meredith L. Chivers, and J. Michael Bailey of Northwestern University. Of the three, Bailey is by far the most well known, a tenured professor and former chair of the psychology department at Northwestern. He's a heavy-hitter in the research field of sexual orientation and gender, who got somewhat bloodied by transgender activists for his book, *The Man Who Would Be Queen*, and his theories on transsexuality.

This particular paper on sexual arousal in males involved taking self-identified heterosexual, bisexual, and homosexual male volunteers, recruited from gay-oriented magazines and an unidentified "alternative" newspaper. As is typical in these experiments, participants are instructed on how to put a small, rubber-band-like device on their penis, and then are shown straight or gay porn as well as visual stimuli that, for most people, are completely non-sexual. (Think carrots. Although there have been reports of men with erotic attraction to carrots, it's so rare it doesn't even warrant a special name.) The plethysmograph records how stretched the band is, i.e. how engorged the penis is.

A great many people won't participate in this type of research, so samples suffer considerably from selection bias. Of the ones who are willing, some men are intimidated by the situation and have no arousal at all: what we in the psychological science business call a floor effect. Their floppy data are thrown out. Some men are generally very horny and highly aroused throughout the experiment. Their rock-solid arousal becomes statistical noise that cancels out, too: a ceiling effect. A running joke in the field—partly true—is that this ceiling effect happens especially often when the volunteers are young male college students.

So what we're left with are guys in the middle range of arousal, a subset of a subset of half the population. Arousal studies are possible with women, and show less of a relationship between genital arousal and subjectively reported arousal than with men, but that's a topic for another essay, as the Rieger paper only looked at males. Sorting through all the statistics, the results were simple: Rieger, Chivers, and Bailey found that gay men got hardest looking at gay porn, and straight men got hardest looking at straight porn. A no-brainer. More interesting was that most self-identified bisexual men got much harder at gay porn. And, these bisexual men responded no more to straight porn than the straight guys did to gay porn. So, from their penises' perspective, they responded like the gay guys. A few were opposite: They got much harder from straight porn, and gay porn didn't do anything more than it did for the straight-identified men. Sounds like the *New York Times* got it right, right?

But what's most interesting about the study, and what wasn't reported at all in any mainstream press, is that all three groups in the study—gay, straight, or bi—showed more arousal to any of the porn than they did to neutral stimuli.

The media misreported that bisexual men expressed "exclusively" gay or straight arousal, meaning they got aroused by depictions of men or women, but not both. But what Rieger, Chivers, and Bailey actually found and reported in their study was that the bi men responded *like* straight or gay men: Straight guys actually got somewhat hard at the gay porn, gay guys got somewhat hard at the straight porn. Sure, they got much harder to their preferred stimuli, but they all showed moderate arousal to their non-preferred stimuli, higher (and statistically significant) than to neutral non-sexual stimuli, so we're not talking about a ceiling effect.

The authors could have concluded from their data that the bi-identified men were just being honest about experiencing some bisexual arousal, which, based on their research, is evidently almost universal in men. Instead they concluded that male bisexual identity isn't consistent with the data, that there are really just two teams, like most people continue to believe. There were other problems with the study that fueled the misreporting, such as the use of Alfred Kinsey's earliest pioneering-but-outdated, one-dimensional scale of sexual orientation, rather than a more modern grid like Fritz Klein's that separately identifies arousal to males and females, and more importantly breaks out attraction, behavior, fantasy, preference, and emotional bonding. Instead, they collapsed Kinsey's seven-point scale (0, exclusively heterosexual, to 6, exclusively homosexual) into a trichotomous "what team are you on?" identity question.

The media headlines could have—and *should* have—read that the 96 to 98 percent of guys who identify as heterosexual are in fact bisexual to a statistically significant degree, because if you get down to it and show them gay porn and check out their penises, you're going to find they aren't quite so 100 percent straight as they say. Even if some of the straight-identified men were closeted homosexuals, it wouldn't account for the fact that some arousal to gay porn was typical of the average straight male. Most gay men openly acknowledge an occasional heterosexual experience, so I think it's more interesting to consider the unacknowledged same-sex sexual potential of the 96 to 98 percent of guys who identify as heterosexual.

So, why didn't the *Times* hit on this? Why not title the article "*Bi* or Lying?" Why the ongoing focus on the closeted gay male living on the down-low or in a brokeback marriage, the barely disguised biphobia? Isn't it even more newsworthy that the overwhelming majority of straight-identified men apparently are experiencing and suppressing moderate same-sex arousal? After all, straight men are not generally socialized for sexual restraint.

I think the answer is because the myth of the straight male is integral to our culture's conceptualization of masculinity. Acknowledging the truth is too threatening—both for men and women. Furthermore, keeping the myth alive is essential to social conservatives' goal of keeping gender and sexuality in check. This is nothing if not a power issue.

EVERY MAN'S FANTASY?

In 1998 in a shopping mall in Sydney, Australia, I saw a poster of two women, looking like very attractive identical twins, about to embrace. Their unbuttoned shiny jackets revealed large bosoms about to make contact. Underneath was the caption, "Every Man's Fantasy." Bisexual behavior among women is a frequent element of heterosexual male porn, suggesting that quite a few women are at least a little bit bi (or at least, their heterosexuality will not be diminished by a little experimentation).

Notwithstanding all the suggestiveness of semi-naked, buff young men cavorting with one another in Abercrombie & Fitch advertising, the suggestion of male bisexual behavior remains just that, a suggestion. The guys are just horsing around. Unlike the women in the ad in Sydney, they're not really about to start making out. Men and women both take great pains to ensure that male–male sex is a line that just isn't crossed by "real" men, no matter how homoerotic the horseplay gets. I have yet to see a caption stating "Every Woman's Fantasy" underneath an image of two guys about to get it on.

Despite the alleged popularity of *Queer as Folk* with straight women, a lot fewer women actually report the fantasy of a guy-guy-me three-way, than straight men report the fantasy of a woman-woman-me three-way, so it's a taboo that is reinforced by women just as much as by men. Gay men can go there, but not straight men. And remember, you've got to pick sides.

It's clear there is a cultural double-standard about same-sex behavior in heterosexually identified men and women. A careful read of the literature produced by Rieger and others shows that the 100 percent "red-blooded heterosexual male" turns out to be a myth (or almost as rare as the exclusively gay male; that is, 2 to 4 percent of the population). Research suggests that the typical heterosexually identified male experiences some arousal to same-sex erotic stimuli. The amount of arousal is modest, but is far more than nothing. I'm not suggesting we're bonobo chimpanzees at heart, and that absent the prohibitions of culture we'd all be rolling around under the rainforest canopy. That would be a misread of our evolutionary heritage, which suggests that it is impossible to separate out the interaction of culture with biological tendencies in *homo sapiens*. It's an intellectual fallacy to suggest there is a single natural state of human behavior. Instead we observe behavioral tendencies that vary between individuals and even within individuals across time, with culture shaping the likelihood that such behavioral tendencies will occur, the manner of their display when they occur, and whether we feel guilty or proud about the behaviors.

It *is* natural for culture to influence our behavior, but its greatest influence is on our beliefs about our behaviors and our identities. When it comes to having sex, culture has a far greater influence on our sexual identities and how we feel about our sexual practices than on the sex itself. Into carrots? Whether you're ridden with guilt and believe this desire is a hellfire-damning abomination, or whether you think it's no big deal, is culturally determined. Men are a little bit bisexual, but whether most men recognize or accept this is the result of social learning.

So, why aren't we now reading articles about expanding horizons of male bisexuality? Why don't we see the fantasy played out on TV commercials for the enjoyment of straight women, whereas we see female bisexuality played out for men? Why do research articles gloss over their own findings that show that exclusive male heterosexuality isn't really that exclusive? And why do we see most heterosexually identified men continue to vehemently say they are 100 percent exclusively heterosexual? I think the self-brainwashing is strongly related to what I'll call "the girlie-man effect."

At its heart, the joke of the girlie-man involves a male who violates gender role expectations: a physically weak male, one who has an unmanly wave of the wrist, an unmanly mode of speech, an unmanly build. It's a joke that doesn't apply to women. Certainly, women who violate gender role expectations of femininity may face disdain, discrimination, and often violence, and certainly, women face enormous pressure to conform to ideals of thinness and beauty, but there is no exact female-on-female equivalent to the nervous locker-room laughter from males that mocks another male who fails to live up to expectations of strength and masculinity. Strong women may have their sexuality mocked, and androgyny has in recent years been good fodder for *Saturday Night Live*, but there is no feminine analog of the girlie-man, no boyly-woman touchstone of mirth. We certainly don't have contemporary female politicians publicly suggesting that their female opponents are boyly-women or ball-busters. It doesn't fit in quite the same way.

That's because the entire hypermasculine man's man image (like Arnold Schwarzenegger) is one of exaggerated secondary sexual characteristics and traditional male gender roles: pumped biceps the size of tree trunks, a booming voice, physical strength and conquest, provider and protector—the opposite of the girlie-man. The man's man doth protest too much: As many scholars have noted, women today have more flexibility in normative roles—even in clothing—than men. Social conservatives are upset about feminism not just because of expanded opportunities for women, but because equality means a sharing of privilege previously reserved for men, and a diminishment of male power and control. The battle against feminism has been lost in the courts, and so threatened and diminished males cling to antiquated archetypes of masculinity for their sons. These sons in turn perpetuate the myth that maleness is defined by vast innate differences, and exaggerate those differences that do exist. No "real" boy wants the shame of growing into a girlie-man.

No longer assured of being head of state, head of corporation, or even head of family, the average boy still receives the vestigial imperative of former male privilege: a message that he must still be a real man, and that all real men are strong, and are powerful. No wrist flapping, no girlie pretentions, and certainly no acknowledging of non-heterosexual impulses. That's grudgingly OK for the gays, but not for the rest of mankind.

Of course, daughters are indoctrinated into this cultural ideal, too, and they perpetuate it just as strongly. Most heterosexual adolescent females desire a pumped-up "real man" over a metrosexual, and many adult women would be horrified if "their" man turned out to have any sexual interest in other men. The main reason bisexuality among males isn't acknowledged yet is that if it were, it would accelerate the perceived erosion of male power.

That most women still prefer the heterosexual male myth shows just how far we still have to go. That so many sexuality researchers and journalists cooperate in the myth of exclusive male heterosexuality shows how ingrained the myth is, how difficult it is to see beyond our own childhood indoctrination. So, we collectively sideline the real findings of the plethysmograph, and instead falsely conclude that science shows an absolute dichotomy between male and female, gay and straight, rather than the dazzlingly complex diversity that science truly reveals, and that feminism frees us to celebrate.

Of course, there is a cost to males for holding on to these vestiges of male power. The consequence for the typical, mostly heterosexual man, goes far beyond a diminished range of sexual partners. It is a confining prison of gender role conformity, of having to be manly in gesture and speech and body. It results in men amping up innate biological differences, heightening secondary sexual characteristics such as muscle mass and lately even height, with parents administering growth hormone to boys. The prison of traditional masculinity fuels steroid abuse, limits career choices, and involves a continuous barely conscious self-monitoring, a self-censorship, a mismatch between potential and what is realized in many aspects of life. Women are not spared either. A corollary is the popularity of breast augmentation among women, again amplifying innate but modest differences in physique.

Our ideas about masculinity are still easily threatened. We see this in the ways that bisexuality in so-called straight men is covered up and ignored— even feared. More radical, accepting change has been kept at bay, for now. But on the insightful edges of our culture, a willingness among both men and women for ostensibly heterosexual males to explore and acknowledge bisexual behavior (if not identity) suggests that liberating forces will eventually come for men, too.

DARKER SHADES OF QUEER: RACE AND SEXUALITY AT THE MARGINS

Chong-suk Han

By now, I've listened with a mild sense of amusement as countless gay leaders, an overwhelmingly white group, attempt to explain that their oppressed status as sexual minorities provides them with an enlightened sense of social justice that enables them to understand the plight of those who are racially oppressed. As sexual minorities, they say they share a history of oppression. This "shared history of oppression," they explain, provides them with exceptional insight and somehow absolves them of blame when it comes to the racial social hierarchy. Certainly, this view is not unique. People of color also believe that they possess special insights when it comes to social justice. Yet, two things are bitterly clear about our "shared" American experiences. One, a shared history of oppression rarely leads to coalition building among those who have been systematically denied their rights. More devastatingly, such shared experiences of oppression rarely lead to sympathy for others who are also marginalized, traumatized, and minimized by the dominant society. Rather, all too miserably, those who should naturally join in fighting discrimination find it more comforting to join their oppressors in oppressing others. In fact, they trade in one oppressed status for the other. Doing so, many gay white folks become more racist than non-gay folks while many people of color become more homophobic. As a gay man of color, I see this on a routine basis, whether it be racism in the gay community or homophobia in communities of color. And it pisses me off.

Psychologists have theories, I'm sure, about why such things happen. Perhaps some of us feel some comfort in the ability to claim at least a small share of the privileges and benefits of belonging to the so-called majority group. Maybe gay white folks use their race to buy into the mainstream while straight people of color use their sexuality for the same purpose. If they have something in common with those with power, perhaps some of that power will trickle down or rub off on them. I doubt it, but it's easy to believe. It's even comforting. What easier way to make oneself feel better than to marginalize others. But for now, it doesn't really matter why they do what they do. I'm not interested in why it happens. Rather, I'm interested in exposing it, condemning it, shaming it, and stopping it. Many gay activists want to believe that there aren't issues of racism within the gay community. As members of an oppressed group, they like to think that they are above oppressing others. Yet, looking around any gayborhood, something becomes blatantly clear to those of us on the outside looking in. Within the queer spaces that have sprung up in once neglected and forgotten neighborhoods, inside the slick new storefronts, in trendy restaurants, and on magazine covers, gay America has given a whole new meaning to the term "whitewash."

Whiteness in the gay community is everywhere, from what we see, what we experience, and more importantly, what we desire. Media images now popular in television and film such as *Queer as Folk*, *Queer Eye for the Straight Guy*, *The L-Word*, and the like promote a monolithic image of the gay community as being overwhelmingly upper-middle class—if not simply rich— and white. These images aren't new. Flipping through late night television, I'm often struck by how white and rich gay characters are whether they are on reruns of the *Golden Girls* or rebroadcasts of *Making Love*. The only difference now is that there are more of them, and they aren't so angst ridden about their sexuality. We now live in a country where gay TV characters are out and proud instead of languishing in perpetual shame, hiding in the shadows. They revel in their sexuality, at least on the screen. I can't help but think, though, that their revelation comes largely from their privilege of whiteness, the privilege to "be like everyone else," with only one minor difference.

Even the most perfunctory glance through gay publications exposes the paucity of non-white gay images. It's almost as if no gay men or women of color exist outside of fantasy cruises to Jamaica, Puerto Rico, or the "Orient." To the larger gay community, our existence, as gay men and women of color, is merely a footnote, an inconvenient fact that is addressed in the most insignificant and patronizing way. Sometime between Stonewall and *Will and Grace*, gay leaders decided that the best way to be accepted was to mimic upper-middle-class white America. As a sexually marginalized group, the idea is to take what they can from the dominant group and claim it as their own. Rarely a day goes by when I don't read something, by some gay "leader," about the purchasing power of the gay "community."

Sometimes, racism in the gay community takes on a more explicit form aimed at excluding men and women of color from gay institutions. All over the country, gay people of color are routinely asked for multiple forms of identification to enter the most basic of gay premises, the gay bar. Some might argue that this is a minor irritant. But in a country where gays and lesbians are expected to hide their sexuality while in public spaces, gay bars and other gay businesses provide us with the few opportunities to freely be ourselves. Denied access to the bars, gay men and women of color often lose the ability to see and socialize with others like us who also turn to these allegedly safe places for not only their social aspects but for their affirming aspects, as well. Isolated incidents might be easily forgotten, but news reports and buzz on various online forums expose such practices as endemic in gay communities. From New York to Los Angeles, from Seattle to Miami, the borders of gayness are patrolled by those who deny the existence of gay men and women of color. And much like a neighborhood with more than six black families is quickly labeled "black" and, hence, avoided by many white buyers, a bar with more than six non-white folks is quickly labeled "ethnic" and avoided by the white clientele. Except, of course, those on the prowl for something "different" to wet their sexual appetite. In so many ways, their actions are nothing more than a cheap version of sexual tourism.

More importantly, gay men and women of color are routinely denied leadership roles in gay organizations that purport to speak for all of us. In effect, it is the needs and concerns of a largely middle-class gay white community that come to the forefront of what is thought to be a gay cause. Interjecting race in these community organizations is no easy task. On too many occasions, gay men and women of color have been told not to muddy the waters of the primary goal by bringing in concerns that might be addressed elsewhere. When mainstream gay organizations actually address issues of race, gay white men and women continue to set the agenda for what is and is not considered appropriate for discussion. During one community forum on race, the organizers, again an overwhelmingly white bunch, informed the audience that we would not actually talk about racism, as "everyone is capable of racism." With one sweeping generalization, this group of white men, trivialized the everyday experiences of the men, and a few women, of color in the audience by denying our personal experiences and by turning the accusation back on us. It's a funny feeling to sit in an audience as an Asian gay man and watch as middle-class white men claim victimhood in racist America. Ultimately, isn't that what their claim that "everyone is capable of racism" boils down to? Isn't what they're really saying that they are also victims of racism?

Sadly, racism isn't just about how we are treated. It's also about how we treat ourselves. The primacy of whiteness in the gay community often manifests as internalized racism. In his 2002 online essay, "No Blacks Allowed," Keith Boykin argues that "in a culture that devalues black males and elevates white males," black men deal with issues of self-hatred that white men do not. Boykin argues that this racial self-hatred makes gay black men see other gay black men as unsuitable sexual partners and white males as the ultimate sexual partners.

This desire for white male companionship is not limited just to black men, and neither is racial self-hatred. Rather, it seems to be pandemic among many gay men of color. Even the briefest visit to a gay bar betrays the dirty secret that gay men of color don't see each other as potential life partners. Rather, we see each other as competitors for the few white men who might be willing to date someone considered lower on the racial hierarchy. We spend our energy and time contributing to the dominance of whiteness by putting white men on the pedestal while ignoring those who would otherwise be our natural allies.

The primacy of white masculinity in the gay community is no accident. It is a carefully choreographed racialization of men of color that mimics the masculine hierarchy in straight communities. Related to the "middle-classing" and "whitening" of gay America, images of gay men have mirrored the mainstream. No longer the Nellie queens of the 1960s, stereotypical images of gay men have changed from swivel-hipped sissies to muscle-bound he-men. So ingrained is the image of the "ideal" man within the gay community, "straight-acting" is a selling point in gay personal ads.

But masculinity doesn't exist in a vacuum. Masculinity is built upon the femininity of Others. Lacking female femininity, the gay community thrusts this role upon Asian men. Given the way that Asian men are gendered in the mainstream, this isn't a difficult task. If gay white men are masculine, they are masculine compared to gay Asian men. If masculinity is desirable and femininity is not, then clearly white men are desirable but Asian men are not.

While black men have escaped the feminization inflicted on Asian men, their masculinity is also heavily gendered. Rather than lacking masculinity, they are hyper-masculine, outside of the norm and thus, to be feared. Gay Latino men and gay Native American men fare no better in the gay imagination. In the gay white mind, they are exotic beings who exist for the pleasure of white male consumption. Much like heterosexual male claims to the right of sexual consumption of women, many gay white men have claimed the right to pick and choose what they want from their sexual partners by positioning whiteness as a bargaining tool in sexual encounters.

Ironically, we strive for the attention of the very same white men who view us as nothing more than an inconvenience. "No femmes, no fats, and no Asians," is a common quote found in many gay personal ads, both in print and in cyberspace. Gay white men routinely tell us that we are lumped with the very least of desirable men within the larger gay community. In this way, we are reduced to no more than one of many characteristics that are considered undesirable. Rather than confronting this racism, many of my gay Asian brothers have become apologists for this outlandish racist behavior. We damage ourselves by not only allowing it, but actively participating in it. We excuse their racist behavior because we engage in the same types of behavior. When seeking sexual partners for ourselves, we also exclude "femmes, fats, and Asians."

The rationale we use, largely to fool ourselves, to justify the inability of seeing each other as potential partners and allies is laughable at best. Many Asian guys have told me that dating other Asians would be like "dating [their] brother, father, uncle, etc." Yet, we never hear white men argue that dating other white men would be like dating their brothers or fathers. This type of logic grants individuality to white men while feeding into the racist stereotype that all of "us" are indistinguishable from one another and therefore easily interchangeable.

Some of us rely on tired stereotypes. Boykin writes about the professional gay black man who degrades other black men as being of a lower social class while thinking nothing of dating blue-collar white men. The Asian version is that they are "Americanized" and looking for "American" men. In effect, we help white men oppress other men of color by buying into the racial social structure that the former group has created.

This self-hatred and willingness to join our oppressors in oppressing others is clearly evident in an April 4, 2006 column posted on Advocate.com. Jasmyne Cannick, a self-described black lesbian, argues that we should not extend any rights to "illegal" immigrants until gays are granted full rights. When did equality become a zero-sum game? Does extending human rights to immigrants somehow limit the amount of equal rights left for us? This is as absurd as claiming that extending marriage rights to gays and lesbians would somehow weaken heterosexual marriages. Extending rights to immigrants does not limit our rights in any way. To the contrary, it reinforces the commitment to equality and fairness for everyone, including gays and lesbians. As for Cannick's argument that these immigrants are "illegal," I might remind her that until the Supreme Court ruled on *Lawrence v. Texas* in 2003, millions of us were engaging in the horribly illegal activity of loving someone of the same sex. Thousands of us also got married "illegally." Why does Cannick believe that we have the right to challenge laws that brand us or our actions illegal, while others do not share this right? Clearly, those with the real power at the *Advocate* wanted to make a statement and found a pawn in Cannick. Her willingness to stand so firmly against granting rights to "illegal" immigrants simply reinforces the erroneous belief that it is acceptable for some members of society not to have the exact same rights enjoyed by others. Shamefully and unapologetically, Cannick quotes Audre Lorde at the very same time she uses the master's tools to build a fence around another oppressed group.

If we are invisible in the dominant gay community, perhaps we are doubly so in our own communities of color. If we are a footnote in the gay community, we are an endnote in communities of color—an inconvenient fact that is buried in the back out of view. We are told by family and friends that being gay is a white problem. We are told, early in life, that we must avoid such stigma at all costs. When we try to interject issues of sexuality, we are told that there is precious little time to waste on trivial needs while we pursue racial justice. Cannick writes that "lesbians and gays should not be second-class citizens. Our issues should not get bumped to the back of the line in favor of extending rights to people who have entered this country illegally." I've heard that exact sentence elsewhere. In fact, nearly verbatim, except "entered this country illegally" was replaced with "chosen an immoral lifestyle." See how that works? Master's tools.

I've seen those who are marginalized use the master's tools in numerous instances, now too legion to list. Citing Leviticus, some people of color who are also members of the clergy have vehemently attacked homosexuality as an abomination. This is the same Leviticus that tells us that wearing cloth woven of two fabrics and eating pork or shrimp is an abomination punishable by death. Yet not surprisingly, rarely do Christian fundamentalists picket outside of a Gap or a Red Lobster. If hypocrisy has a border, those yielding Leviticus as their weapon of choice must have crossed it by now. It must be convenient to practice a religion with such disdain that the word of God need only be obeyed when it reinforces one's own hatred and bigotry. How else do we explain those who condemn *Brokeback Mountain* based on their religious views while, in the same breath, praise *Walk the Line*, a movie about two adulterous country singers?

More problematic is that we choose to practice historic amnesia by ignoring the fact that Leviticus was used by slave owners to justify slavery by arguing that God allowed the owning of slaves and selling of daughters. Anti-miscegenation laws, too, were justified using the Bible. In 1965, Virginia trial court judge Leon Bazile sentenced an interethnic couple who were married in Washington, D.C., to a jail term using the Bible as his justification. In his ruling, he wrote, "Almighty God created the races white, black, yellow, malay and red, and he placed them on separate continents. The fact that he separated the races shows that he did not intend for the races to mix." Scores of others also used the story of Phinehas, who distinguished himself in the eyes of God by murdering an interracial couple, thereby preventing a plague to justify their own bigotry. Have we forgotten that the genocide and removal of Native Americans was also largely justified on biblical grounds?

Have we simply decided to pick and choose the parts of the Bible that reinforce our own prejudices and use it against others in the exact same way that it has been used against us? Have we really gotten so adept at using the master's tools that he no longer needs to use them himself to keep us all in our place?

Given the prevalence of negative racial attitudes in the larger gay community and the homophobia in communities of color, gay people of color have to begin building our own identities. For gay people of color to be truly accepted by both the gay community and communities of color, we must form connections with each other first and build strong and lasting coalitions with each other rather than see each other as competitors for the attention of potential white partners. We must begin confronting whiteness where it stands while simultaneously confronting homophobia. More importantly, we must begin doing this within our own small circle of gay people of color. We must confront our own internalized racism that continues to put gay white people on a pedestal while devaluing other gays and lesbians of color. Certainly, this is easier said than done. The task at hand seems insurmountable. In Seattle, a group of gay, lesbian, and transgendered social activists from various communities of color have launched the Queer People of Color Liberation Project. Through a series of live performances, they plan on telling their own stories to counter the master narratives found within the larger gay community and within communities of color.

Certainly, gay people of color have allies both in the mainstream gay community and in our communities of color. Recently, Khalil Hassam, a high school student in Seattle won a national ACLU scholarship for opposing prejudice. Hassam, the only Muslim student at University Prep High School, decided to fight for justice after a Muslim speaker made derogatory comments about homosexuals. Despite his own marginalized status as a Muslim American, Hassam confronted the homophobia found within his own community. Examples such as these are scattered throughout the country. Nonetheless, there is much more that allies, both straight and gay, can do to promote social justice. We must see gay rights and civil rights not as exclusive, but as complementary. All too often, even those on the left support "other" causes out of a Niemoellerian fear of having no one left to speak up for us if the time should come. I propose that the motivation to join in political efforts should come not from such fears, but from the belief that there are no such "other" causes. Rather, as Martin Luther King, Jr. reminded us, "an injustice anywhere is a threat to justice everywhere." We must remind ourselves, contrary to what Cannick may want us to believe, that social justice is not a zero-sum game. Granting rights to others does not diminish our rights. It is the exact opposite. Ensuring that rights are guaranteed to others ensures that they are guaranteed to us.

Ultimately, the crisis for gay men of color is one of masculinity. The centrality of masculinity within the gay community leads to rejecting all those outside of the masculine norm. Likewise, the centrality of masculinity in communities of color leads to stripping away masculinity based on stereotypical perceptions of homosexuality. Gay men of color are told, by both communities, that we are somehow not masculine enough to be full members in either community. Some of us have tried to attain this mythical masculine norm. We spend hours at the gym toning our bodies and building our muscles to fit with the gay masculine norm. Some of us disguise our speech, alter our style, and watch our steps in an effort to appear more straight to the untrained eye. And while a few of us may escape the cage of the masculine abnormality, we leave our brothers behind. "You're pretty masculine for an Asian guy," we are told. "You don't act like a black guy," they say. Ironically, both of these betray the cage of acceptable masculinity that binds us to the mythical norm. Asian men are not masculine enough, black men are too masculine. The narrow range of acceptable masculinity is reserved for white men—gay or straight—because, ultimately, it benefits them. Rather than see the explicit racist statement embedded in this compliment, we secretly blush and giggle at the attention. I can't speak eloquently or competently about lesbian experiences with the expectations of femininity they experience. Yet, whenever I listen to my gay

Asian sisters speak of needing to be more lipstick to attract the butch white woman, I wonder what's happening over there in the lesbian community. It sounds vaguely familiar.

The real solution lies not in mimicking the masculinity found in the larger society, but in abolishing it. We need to think about re-envisioning what it means to be masculine and, for that matter, what it means to be feminine and the social value we place on each of these categories. Sadly, I don't have the answers, at least not yet. But I can't help yet feel that feminist scholars who attack the gendered hierarchy have a point. Perhaps one of them will find the answer some day. Until then, I can continue to make sure that concerns regarding race are brought up in the gay community and homophobia is confronted in communities of color. Perhaps one day, I won't need to do either.

LET US BE SEEN: GAY VISIBILITY IN HOMOPHOBIC POLAND

Tomek Kitlinski and Pawel Leszkowicz

It was a freezing Sunday afternoon in the winter of 2003. We stood holding hands in the heart of Poland's capital, Warsaw, in a park next to the Monument of the Unknown Soldier. The statue of this soldier represents the model Pole. But we had made a decision to participate in an unsoldierly, non-military, civil campaign to resist Poland's homophobia in an action of gay and lesbian visibility. In front of us a young photographer, Karolina Bregula, held her camera, asking us not to pose, but to be natural and smile. The smile was a problem. We remained stiff and cold because two men holding hands as a loving couple was a very unusual thing to do in Polish public space.

The park was crowded with strolling people who pretended not to look at us. After thirty minutes of discomfort we welcomed the end of the session with relief. Now we could go back to passing for straight. By giving our real faces for a public campaign we joined twenty-nine other gay and lesbian couples in contributing to the first, large-scale, coming out event in Poland's history.

The "Let Us Be Seen" campaign for gay and lesbian visibility was inspired by feminist art; the idea that art can be a participatory tool used to demand our rights. This project was intended to counter Poland's prejudice and gay invisibility through positive and viewer-friendly images. It ignited a storm of hatred. The far-right militia group, the All-Polish Youth, threatened the exhibit, and some community leaders refused to host the show. In the end, though, the photo exhibit provided visibility and strength for Poland's gay community. At equality parades where gay demonstrators are frequently attacked with stones, eggs, bottles, and slurs, activists now shout back, *Let us be seen!*

POLITICS

A bit of background is in order to better understand the importance of the "Let Us Be Seen" photo exhibit.

In our opinion, Poland's political transition has gone terribly wrong. In the 1990s, totalitarian communism gave way to fundamentalism instead of liberation. This has meant free elections and travel without granting sexual freedom to women and minorities. Social and economic constraints have not only remained, but increased. Poland is currently misogynist and homophobic. Some high school textbooks still teach that homosexuality is an illness. On May 7, 2004, one week after Poland joined the European Union, members of the nation's leadership, the ultra-conservative League of Polish Families, attacked the Krakow Feminist and Gay Parade of Equality with caustic acid.

The All-Polish Youth is a subset of this far-right political party. With its roots in Poland's interwar anti-Semitism, the League of Polish Families and the All-Polish Youth are staunchly homophobic and actively anti-gay. They also aim to deprive women of rights. Abortion has been criminalized in this country since 1993, but the League wants a total constitutional ban. In the early twenty-first century, far-right ideology isn't at the margins, but at the very center of Poland's politics.

Anti-gay arguments are made in the media about religious prohibition, sin, medical pathology, unnatural behavior, gay men's promiscuity, and gay men as pedophiles. In order to scare Poles into voting against EU membership, the League of Polish Families argued that Western liberalization promotes homosexuality. Posters appearing in the far-right and nationalistic press featured images of a same-sex couple with a child to symbolize Western Europe's moral depravity.

In a country where Roman Catholicism currently underscores a virulently conservative political ideology, gay men and lesbians in Poland bravely appeared in the public photos for "Let Us Be Seen." The project started in March 2003 and was initially planned as a public art campaign displaying same-sex portraits on city billboards. In this way, same-sex couples holding hands would inhabit the streets with straight couples and other passers-by as equal parts of society.

But the billboards were only seen for two weeks. The Mayors of Warsaw and Krakow would not support the use of public space for the exhibit. The commercial company that owns the billboard sites withdrew from the project. Although the photos were deliberately hung high enough to deter vandals, paint was splashed on them in hostile attempts to destroy our efforts.

Since the streets proved inhospitable, art galleries instead functioned as alternative platforms for exposure. The All-Polish Youth threatened gallery openings with violence and members of the group were responsible for a fear campaign directed toward the exhibit. Yet although some cities banned the shows and skinheads destroyed many of the photos, "Let Us Be Seen" was still very successful in Warsaw and Gdansk. To promote continuing success, as small as these steps may seem, a feminist–gay alliance is badly needed.

Feminism helps us survive in Poland. Women's struggle for equality inspires the gay rights movement. Feminists teach us to resist oppression in a country where gays are despised, disrespected, and discriminated against. Moreover, misogyny and homophobia go hand in hand with anti-Semitism. At feminist and gay demonstrations, counter-demonstrators commonly shout, "To the gas! We'll do to you what Hitler did to Jews."

Feminists spearhead opposition to this sort of prejudice and hatred. The civil rights activities that started in the 1980s in conjunction with international feminism have become stronger every year. The Gay Pride Parade, organized in Warsaw since 1995, is increasingly visible in spite of bans and attacks. Similarly, the liberal Jewish community also supports the gay rights movement under the motto "minority for minority." In a statement by Poland's reform synagogue, Beit, for example, the congregation openly spoke out on behalf of Warsaw's Gay Parade of Equality on June 10, 2006.

Recently, the director of a large public art gallery in Poland organized a town-hall meeting about gay and lesbian rights to welcome the exhibit of "Let Us Be Seen." There was an unexpectedly high turnout of activists and academics. The All-Polish Youth also came. Pawel was asked to moderate the meeting. We asked for police protection.

There was a crowd of friendly allies, and a small hostile group that was outspoken and visible. Pawel had to control a militant group of skinheads and religious fundamentalists from the All-Polish Youth and the League of Polish Families. These men wanted to speak the most, voicing their prejudices against gay men. The rest of the participants—around one hundred people, mostly students and some local journalists—occasionally stood up to the attackers.

Pawel managed to calm the members of the All-Polish Youth by allowing each person to speak, if only once. Miraculously, this worked and many opinions were presented. Our face-to-face meeting with far-right funda-mentalists confirmed for us that post-Communist nationalism in Eastern and Central Europe is carved from racialized, sexualized, masculinist hatreds and that, in a context of limited visibility and political power for marginalized groups, coming together to talk is an even more pressing need. Instead of excluding women and sexual minorities from discussion, there is an urgent need for openness and political hospitality.

HOPE

There is also another, more optimistic, part of the story. "Let Us Be Seen" provoked not only hostile reaction, but also positive media support. There was a debate on TV, on the radio, and in the press. The Polish edition of MTV had a regular ad featuring portraits of same-sex couples from the photo campaign.

Polish video clips with fragmentary images of same-sex love started to appear. The photographed couples were suddenly sought by the media to participate in talk shows and journalistic photo-stories. For a while "Let Us Be Seen" was a hot subject.

The challenge, though, remains serious. Men enjoy a monopoly of Poland's power. Mainstream media (particularly the state-run media) foregrounds misogynist and homophobic sitcoms, commercials, and news broadcasts. The ideology of the heterosexual reproductive family is relentlessly circulated. Homosexuality is still largely invisible and taboo. But alternatives are possible.

Poland's feminist band Duldung sings that ours is a "dictatorship of white beetroots," slang for macho, militarist, homophobic Poles. It is our conviction that activism, art, and academic research are forms of dissidence. We believe that writing, discovering, and interpreting the history of women and gays is a crucial political task. We promote democracy, pluralistic society, human rights, equality, and toleration. We believe that contemporary knowledge about the variety of human sexuality, and freedom from religious pressure are important. Together, we dream of a day when prejudice, discrimination, and violence will be abandoned—in Poland and globally. We shall overcome.

HOW WE ENTER: MEN, GENDER, AND SEXUAL ASSAULT

B. Loewe

My mother took me aside from my eighth birthday pool party to scold me. It was 1990, the summer after third grade, and we'd set up a big tent in our backyard. My sister wasn't allowed to sleep in it at night. My mom gave her the same reason she gave for Kate not being able to play in the woods, only this time the evening news agreed. All the mothers were talking about the "Silver Spring rapist." Pat McCall didn't know what rape was. So he and I snuck around to the soda machines and I explained in a whisper in his ear, "Rape is when a man forces a woman to have sex with him," and we ran out screaming toward the shallow end of the pool until I heard my mom call my name in mid-stride. She said that my friends and I were very young, and that I shouldn't share such things because their parents might not want them to know about it yet.

That summer my friends and I inherited our first lesson in sex education: rape mythology. We crafted a common imagery in hushed tones in each other's basements out of earshot of our parents who would be sure to censor us. There were dark men stalking alleys or, in our suburbanized version, the surrounding woods. And there were unsuspecting, helpless women who fell victim to their attack, as these men carried out their plot, pushing themselves on top of women and forcing them to have sex. For our young, uneducated, but highly imaginative minds, the story always stopped there. We had no concept of what sex actually was, other than that it was something dirty, wrong, and to be desired like grass stains on church clothes. It was something that women could give us and that some men took from them. We saw the potential power we, as man-boys, were to inherit; the manhood we were to adopt and avoid. We affirmed our own moral purity in knowing that we would never misuse that power. We learned that men are stronger than women, but that rapists are predator-types who abuse the power all men rightfully hold. As far as we knew, potential abusers remained relegated to alleys and bushes, living as a lurking threat. They were not people who played a role in any other part of our lives; not as mothers or fathers, not as neighbors, relatives, partners, or religious leaders. Surely we didn't know any rapists. And, surely, we could not be abused.

As we've grown up, so have many of our understandings about sexual assault. However, the way men respond to sexual assault is still often based on these lessons we first learned as children. And so these attempts at addressing sexual assault perpetuate patriarchy rather than breaking it down. Working with a framework of men-as-attackers and women-as-survivors, our conception of power can only rest in the hands of men. In dealing with sexual assault, this makes "good men" the protectors and avengers and in general makes women preyed upon and in need of prayers. If this is our story, then gender is determined not by our biology, but rather by which end of the knife we're on. If some of our earliest ideas of manhood depend upon having control over women, what does it mean to let go of that handle? Or even further, what does it mean when men feel the steel against their own throats?

Men's groups dedicated to anti-sexist work have done their darnedest to raise consciousness about these issues. Feminist men's groups I've been involved with focus on defying stereotypes by examining how we fit them. In these groups, we get emotional about not being in touch with our emotions. We patiently listen to each other talk about our impatience with our partners. With good reason, we focus on patriarchy as something we, as male-socialized people, do to others. We look at the outward effect of behavior we've internalized in order to be better organizers, better partners, better friends to the people in our lives. Whether we're describing scenarios that involve dominating conversations or dominating other people's bodies, from our position of masculinity, we analyze ourselves as potential perpetrators, always identifying with the person in power. We're willing to examine in depth our effect on a fairy-tale She-ra but we're unable to see ourselves as anything other than a He-Man, Master of the Universe. Examining our own moments of weakness is rarely a topic we talk about. Weakness would be too sharp a point to bring near our identities so inflated with masculinity. We are always strong, always the actor, never the acted upon. Thus, it is difficult to see ourselves as potential survivors, potentially vulnerable.

With patriarchy so pervasive, it's no wonder that men have to struggle so hard to unravel their myths of supremacy. In order to do so, men must confront the very basis of their identity, to acknowledge our own vulnerability, and to begin rethinking and rebuilding meanings of power. This self-examination requires the very tools that the process of becoming men convinces us to abandon. From the time we are young, boys are taught we should not cry or express hurt. As bell hooks explains in *All About Love*, boys "must be tough, they are learning how to mask true feelings. In worst-case scenarios they are learning how not to feel anything ever." At every point that we might imagine living without absolute control, without being masters of our destiny, there is another road sign rerouting us toward expressway erections.

But what happens when our lives and our lessons contradict? More specifically, what happens when men are the victims, rather than the perpetrators, of assault? For me, it took years before this possibility could be considered anything other than a joke.

I never classified my experience as sexual assault because it never fit my definition of abuse. It wasn't forced. It wasn't violent. It was inappropriately discreet; the epitome of "bad touch." Importantly, I was a man-boy and they were women. I knew that as a "red-blooded American teenage boy" I was supposed to want sex all the time and welcome any chance at it.

I believed that I held the social power in that room and I wasn't going to let these two women affect that. I wasn't going to let them affect me. I walked out of that room confused. In all my previous ideas about abusive sexuality, the powerful man overtook or ignored the will and desires of the less-powerful woman. If a woman could do this to me, what did that say about my power and my masculinity? Besides, wasn't this supposed to be kinky? Men are always supposed to want sex so this must be a joke. *Women could never have power over me.*

And thus, as long as I stayed in my manhead, this encounter when I was sixteen years old wasn't an assault. It was a funny story to tell friends because the idea that I could have been acted on instead of being the crafter of my own universe, Charles in Charge, unaffected by the world around me, was absurd.

As long as I relied upon these early lessons of masculinity, sexuality, and power for my self-definition of manhood, I could neither deal with the reality of my own world nor effectively act in solidarity with the women and gender variant people in my life. My desire to maintain my own sense of power debilitated my ability to participate in efforts to actually end sexual violence. Without a broader systemic analysis, activist men's groups deal with every assault case as another individual man gone wrong. For these groups, it's up to men to use our strength and rationale to either bring the perpetrator back into the fold of appropriate manhood or expel him from the circle. This approach perpetuates patriarchy rather than finding strategies to redraw the systems that shape our world.

It wasn't until I was in a men's discussion about sexual assault where, in go-around fashion, people could make comments like "I passed out drunk and when I woke up, someone was on top of me having sex," and then move on to the next person without any emotional content, that my male bonds began to break down. When we wrapped up the group, all I could say was how inadequate it was. The clock struck two hours and we were done. I walked to the nearby rocks and cried.

Later my partner at the time confronted me about the group's collective lack of emotion in the discussion. She asked, "How can you all expect to struggle against sexual violence when you don't let it affect you? When you don't feel it?" I defended the group and said that men deal with things intellectually and that it's a different, not a lesser, way of processing than emotional ways. I pointed to how I treated my own experience of being abused as an example. Then things shifted. This conversation with my partner forced me to realize that I did not have a different experience or a different relationship to my body. I had a detached one, an absence of a relationship with my body. She said, "It's not a different experience, it's half an experience." I agreed. I wanted to be whole.

Most literature on male survivors of sexual assault describes a "feminization process" where men feel "less like a man" after being abused. Often, this state of being is described as standard but temporary, with multiple appeals to survivors to reclaim their traits of traditional masculinity: to be strong, to be courageous. Many resources available to male survivors assure men that they are still "real men" and explain that abuse causes most to question their sexuality and gender identity.

No one should have to survive abuse. But, at the same time, I don't think it's a bad thing for men to have to critically think through gender socialization. One of the effects of having social power, of having privilege, is the ability to live *without* questioning one's identity; to assume, in this case, that hegemonic manhood is natural, normal, and preferred.

The existence of male survivors actually interrupts these myths. Our existence creates a space for redefining or abandoning constructed male identity. Patriarchy may not be the knife whose handle men firmly grasp and wield, but, rather, a double-edged blade that targets some and cuts us all.

It is not in redirecting, but in redesigning, our relations that all of our wounds can heal. With this new framework, I could neither be the Superman hero with the shadowy stranger in the alley as my foil, nor could women remain hapless objects in a world that I, and other men, create.

While men must grapple with the privilege and responsibility that socialization allots us, we can also un-puff our chests and end the posturing. We can strive to be something other than the action figures of our collective imagination.

Having lived through a harsh denial of our invincibility, having our scripts interrupted, we have the chance to either deny our experience—as I did for half a decade—or we can reject the role we're expected to play and improvise a new place for ourselves. We can reinvent a world of sharp contrasts and create a space amongst the subtler tones, to dance in the hues between poles. We can stop viewing life in polar opposites and start becoming human as a way to own up to and fight against male privilege, and to end masculinist patterns of domination over others.

More often than not, discussions about male sexual assault are used by men to avoid responsibility for the power and privilege they maintain. The topic of men as victims, especially victims of the actions of women, is used to obscure the prevalence of male sexual violence. Worse yet, these are used as cloaked conversations coated with allegations of reverse sexism meant to maintain, not reexamine, men's power. Recognizing this dynamic creates an even bigger challenge to understanding that, according to the National Alliance to End Sexual Violence, one out of six boys will experience sexual assault by the time they reach eighteen. By comparison, though, one in three women will be sexually assaulted in her lifetime. What this means is that we need to include men as victims in conversations about sexual assault without decentralizing women's experience and without taking away from the leadership of women and gender variant survivors. We must recognize that while sexual assault affects everyone, it is also a tool of patriarchy that specifically and disproportionately targets those assigned less social power.

Male socialization kept me from understanding that I had been molested, and women's support finally enabled me to identify as someone who was—five years after the fact.

I bring this up crying on a bus ride with a guy friend. I tell him that he doesn't know a thing about my past and I accuse him of assuming that I haven't been abused. In doing so, I assumed the same of him. I was wrong. But he says he never thinks about it. It never registers. But then what do men let register with them? Are we so out of touch with ourselves and so in touch with trying to maintain power that we must deny our vulnerability to everyone? With no space to talk about ourselves as victims, we maintain the tough-guy persona that patriarchy demands of us. As bell hooks writes (again in *All About Love*), "patriarchal masculinity requires of boys and men not only that they see themselves as more powerful and superior to women but that they do whatever it takes to maintain their controlling position." If this is true, what must men do if we are ever to play an effective role in challenging sexual assault in our communities? What is at the core of our identities if we remove superiority over women and moral purity compared to more abusive men? What will give us permission to express our own vulnerabilities? What does real, positive masculinity look like?

To be honest, I rarely feel emotionally equipped to deal with these questions or mentally prepared to write about them. I get a knot in my stomach every time I think about sexual abuse and I have spent days in an inexplicable fog after reading or hearing yet another survivor's account of assault. But I know that we can do better, that our conversations can become more inclusive, that our approach needs to change in order for all our attempts, from pummeling to processing, from ostracizing to education, to ever be effective. I write this because I want to get past the shock, the shock at my presence in survivors spaces and at my tears in men's groups, to get past the bravado and the bitter days, the binaries and the ghosts I bring to bed. In this society, everyone comes out damaged goods. In setting out to transform the world we must also be ready to transform ourselves. Toward a world of healing, tomorrow is ours.

Part III

Feminism

INTRODUCTION

the problem with most movements is
that they
move alone
a house divided
—S.A. Griffin, "A House Divided"[1]

Feminism is a practice, a perspective, and a process. It involves constructing new frameworks for understanding politics and power while simultaneously setting concrete goals for change.[2] Feminism is a theory that puts gender at the center of how we see the world. It is a social and political movement interested in improving the conditions of all people, in particular women. The question is this: If feminism is primarily concerned about the status of women, then what is—or what ought to be—men's role in this movement? Is there room in the picture for men?

The following eight essays explore sexism, harassment, oppression, and equality. They investigate the intersecting impact of gender, race, nation, and sexuality. They raise questions about men's relation to feminist movement as allies, activists, and observers. They talk about how to stand up and get involved while avoiding the pitfalls of protectionism. Some ask whether or not feminism is a title that suits men well, even when they are committed to gender justice.

Regardless of whether men engage the title "feminist," the movement for gender and social justice benefits from men's participation. Because most women and men live among each other, without men's active engagement with gender justice, efforts to solve the problems are ultimately limited. If men do not take active roles in resolving the politics of housework, male violence against women, hiring and wage disparities, or gender bias in the media, then women are talking into a feminist echo chamber.

As things stand, however, there is a tendency to conflate the term "feminist" with women. Given this inclination, how we can better understand and imagine new possibilities for men and feminism? We need to do so because assuming that feminism is only a woman's problem raises serious existential questions (Can I be a guy and be a feminist?) and pragmatic questions in regard to political strategy and activism (Who will set the agenda, who will do the talking, who will make the coffee?). It's important to face these questions head on. Feminist strategy is stifled in achieving its goals of gender justice if it remains an exclusionary movement based on essentialist assumptions about who can join the movement, let alone if it is suspicious of men who do. Linking feminism with women and basing feminist knowledge production on identity is problematic, reinforcing the same dichotomies and gendered traits of masculinity that feminism claims to oppose or wants to subvert.[3]

As long as feminism *itself* gets lumped with women, and as long as we continue to suppose that women know something special *as women* and in particular as *feminist* women, then sex/gender identity as the foundation for feminist politics and theorizing remains problematic by virtue of placing women within feminism and leaving men on the outside.[4] Melding masculinity with men, and femininity with women—and femin*ism* with women only—leads to the assumption that the term "feminist men" is oxymoronic. According to this train of thought, as Michael Kimmel puts it, a feminist man is either a) not a "real" man or b) cannot be a real feminist.[5] These misconceptions keep intact the gender binaries which feminism sees as underscoring the very power and privilege inequities it seeks to eradicate. In writing about their perspectives on and experiences with feminism, the authors in this section direct our thinking away from these binaries. Yet at the same time that men in feminism has advantages, there is the possibility that a feminism with men will lose its focus on women.

The puzzle is this: How can we a) make room in feminism to account for men as "our comrades in struggle,"[6] while b) retaining a central focus on women, yet c) avoid reinscribing the gender binaries that feminism-as-female invokes? To borrow awkwardly from Charlotte Bunch, what would it mean to feminism if we "added men and stirred"? The essays in this section consider what it looks like when men promote women's issues as strategic political allies, and when men use feminist tools for enhancing gender justice for all.

Feminism benefits from men's inclusion in several ways. First, including men as feminist allies helps break down a gender dichotomy where feminist-equals-female, and where it therefore becomes extremely strange or weird to think of a man as being a feminist. Similarly, thinking of feminist-as-female excludes genderqueer or intersex people, which is inconsistent with the principles of gender justice. There is also a practical advantage: There is strength in numbers and feminism could use more allies.[7] Third, there is an enriching effect that comes from men and women defending feminist views together. Feminist men can be unsettling to detractors and can help shift the terms of dialogue.

A fourth benefit of men participating in feminist politics is that there are times when men, because of past involvement with sexist practices and institutions, such as hardcore pornography, gender discrimination, or violence against women, can be helpful in exposing and critiquing these practices. Finally, including men in our conceptualization of feminism helps build a politic that is broadened by the integration of interlocking oppressions.

Because of the overlapping experience and impact of race and class, many black women—and other women of color—have been unwilling to ignore men in the community in favor of a feminism that focuses solely on women *as women*.[8] Patricia Hill Collins writes that black women expressed ambivalence about feminism during the 1960s and early 1970s less because they rejected feminism's core ideas, but rather because they hesitated "to work with White feminist groups exclusively on gender issues while neglecting issues of class and race."[9]

Feminism today exists under this hangover. Feminism has had to face its history of separatism and internal racist dynamics, a history that overlooks important strategic and ideological alliances between women and men. It is simply not true that all men are "always dominant over all women in all things"[10] at all times and places, and in all cultural contexts. Nor is it true that male domination is the only social justice issue at hand. When men reflect on experience and politics to construct feminist perspectives on gender and social justice, as they do in this section, we can more effectively respond to the challenges and demands of intersectionality. An expanded, male-inclusive feminism can help account for issues of race, class, ethnicity, sexual orientation, and gender. This allows for alliances within and across communities. Coalition building and dialogue across differences is critical to feminist development.[11]

Another way to think of feminism as a politic that has room for men is to conceptualize feminism as a movement committed to issues of global concern, domestic improvement, access to rights, and freedom from political and personal oppression. In *The Fire This Time* Vivien Labaton and Dawn Lundy Martin define contemporary feminism as the process of "women and men doing social justice work while using a gender lens."[12] Following Labaton and Martin's lead, feminism clearly has room for men without necessarily losing its focus on women. Current threads of feminist theory (especially those informed by postmodern and queer theory) tend to resist essentialist notions of womanhood and instead complicate what we mean by sex and gender. With this sort of feminist analysis, "masculinity" stands to be critically problematized, just as concepts of "femininity" have been. This can be done without depoliticizing concepts of subjugation, domination, or oppression by claims that sexism affects all equally.

Still, there are legitimate reasons to be cautious about men as feminists. Some, of course, fear that including men's perspectives might simply erase women from feminism, or at least diminish their central role. In *Feminism Without Women: Culture and Criticism in a "Post-Feminist" Age*, Tania Modleski argues that when men become a feminist mouthpiece, we dangerously re-contain women within a masculine universalism by "returning critical practice to a 'pre-feminist world'" in which men produce knowledge.[13] A second reason for caution is that feminism may be co-opted to focus on the ways in which men are oppressed by masculinity instead of on the physical and material manifestations of gender inequality like rape, domestic violence, and wage disparity. Third, celebrating men as feminist partners may inadvertently reinforce the idea that if men are doing something it must be good, although feminism has long recognized this as a problematic assumption and promoted the legitimacy of women's perspectives and demands. Fourth, some might be suspicious that feminist men are just cashing in on the opportunity to promote their own self-interests (for example, getting academic jobs or dates with progressive women).

The essays included in this section are not self-serving apologies for reactionary men's rights. They are not exposés on men as victims. They do not invoke the so-called crisis of masculinity that alarmist pundits claim is afflicting boys today. The eight authors in this section, instead, consider the issues of feminism and gender justice by drawing on their personal experience and in doing so expose some important concerns.

In his essay, "How Two Aspiring Pornographers Turned Me Into the Ultimate F Word," Hank Shaw explains how a beer-and-hoops-loving guy (him) finally "opened his eyes to the *huge* local, national, and international problem of violence against women and girls." Shaw describes how two local cable-access television hosts aired a show so full of pornographic "humili-tainment" that it was impossible to ignore the links between misogynistic culture production and violence against women. The issue got Shaw off the couch and into the streets, transforming him into a feminist activist.

Recently back in the United States after a tour of duty in Iraq, Marshall Thompson describes his shock and concern about the sexual harassment of female Army officers and enlisted military personnel. According to findings published in the *American Journal of Industrial Medicine*, the military environment condones sexual harassment (intentionally or not), and allows sexual assault and trauma to occur. Twenty-eight percent of women veterans surveyed for the journal's report claimed they were raped while in the military.[14] In similar findings released by the Citadel, a public military college in South Carolina, nearly 20 percent of female cadets reported that they had been sexually assaulted since enrolling at the school.[15] With Army Spc. Alyssa Peterson's 2003 suicide after serving in sexually loaded circumstances in Iraq and Spc. Suzanne Swift's 2007 court martial following her refusal to return to Iraq where she had been harassed by three of her commanding officers, Thompson's observations take on particular urgency. Thompson describes what he saw and reflects on this experience in his essay, "Exposed in Iraq: Sexual Harassment and Hidden Rank Structure of the U.S. Army."

In "Why I Am Not a Feminist," Haji Shearer explains why he rejects the term. A social worker from Massachusetts, Shearer is professionally committed to improving gender equality and healthy masculinity in the black community. He suggests that "healthy manhood advocates for the equal rights and responsibilities of women and men." Shearer's essay raises important issues about race and feminism, and "how race consciousness and feminism can both converge and be at odds."[16] Yet because Shearer has good reason not to describe himself as a feminist, this prompts us to consider whether it is the feminist title or one's political intent that is more important.

In "Preaching to the Choir," Matthue Roth, a punk-rock Orthodox Jew, recalls his experience as a male member of the radical feminist group, Womyn's Issues Now. Roth admits that part of the initial appeal in joining was that hanging out with lesbian grrls was socially comfortable and sexually non-threatening. But Roth soon finds himself actively involved in antiviolence work, organizing the men's auxiliary to the annual Take Back the Night March, and speaking out on behalf of his best friend who was sexually assaulted when Roth was fifteen years old.

When Greg Bortnichak was in college he worked at Starbucks foaming lattes and brewing coffee. This job brought a steady stream of customers his way, a microcosm of the social universe Bortnichak was studying in school. Bortnichak explains that, for him, feminism could include many things like working to change unjust laws, or eliminating damaging media stereotypes. But in "The Starbucks Intervention," Bortnichak makes the political personal as he deals with misogynist customers, and sexist and racist co-workers. Derrais Carter, also a college student, writes about how hip hop led him to feminism in his essay, "This Is What a Feminist Looks Like." Carter describes his personal trajectory and personal experiences with womanism, stereotypes, and being a self-proclaimed black male feminist.

Amit Taneja grew up in India, later moved to Canada, and now lives in the United States. A "poor, immigrant, big-boned, non-Christian, gay person-of-color," Taneja draws from a broad, transnational experience in describing his perspectives on masculinity, sexuality, identity, oppression, and power. Taneja's essay, "From Oppressor to Activist," concludes with a demand for action in which he challenges readers to make a personal and political commitment to social justice activism.

Brandon Arber, a law student and former college athlete, recalls the derision and negative reactions from guy friends when they found out he was taking women's studies courses. Arber defines feminism as opposing rape, abuse, and discrimination against women and girls. To Arber, feminism is about improving conditions for all by erasing apathy. Raised to believe that fighting for women's rights is synonymous with fighting injustice in general, the idea that men can be feminist is, Arber claims, "Just Common Sense."

Feminists include all those who identify the unequal and unjust distributions of power and resources as a problem. Including men in a feminist agenda can be strengthening for all of us, as these authors clearly show. Those who identify with feminist politics and perspectives share the perception that gender disadvantage occurs systematically, even if they lack consensus about the solutions.[17] Men's participation will require a political and ethical commitment based on recognizing "the need to eradicate the underlying cultural basis and causes of sexism and other forms of group oppression."[18] Understanding how power works in terms of gender—but also in regard to class, race, sexual orientation, nation, age, ability, religion—is central to feminist thought and action.[19] Feminism does not reject men, but the abuse of power, *per se*.

1. S.A. Griffin. "A House Divided." In *Unborn Again*. Los Angeles: Phony Lid Books, 2001.

2. For an overview of feminism and feminist theory see, for example, Rory Dicker and Alison Piepmeier, eds. *Catching a Wave: Reclaiming Feminism for the 21st Century*. Boston: Northeastern University Press, 2003; Carole R. McCann and Seung-Kyung Kim, eds. *Feminist Theory Reader: Local and Global Perspectives*. New York: Routledge, 2003; Robin Morgan, ed. *Sisterhood Is Forever: The Women's Anthology for a New Millennium*. New York: Washington Square Press, 2003; and Rosemarie Putnam Tong. *Feminist Thought: A More Comprehensive Introduction*, second edition. Boulder, CO: Westview Press, 1998. For essays on men and feminism see Tom Digby, ed. *Men Doing Feminism*. New York: Routledge, 1998.

3. Feminist practice has deep theoretical and historical roots in identity politics. A core aspect of feminist strategy lies in making personal experience both visible and political. However, there are potential pitfalls with this approach in regard to women, men, and experience as an epistemological foundation. I argue this point in "Stepping Out of Bounds: Feminist Men and Political Organizing." Unpublished paper presented at the Western Political Science Association Annual Conference, Las Vegas, Nevada, March 9, 2007. For other discussions on feminist epistemology and feminist standpoint theory see, for example, Sandra Harding, ed. *Feminism and Methodology*. Bloomington, IN: Indiana University Press, 1987; and Linda Alcoff and Elizabeth Potter, eds. *Feminist Epistemologies*. New York: Routledge, 1993.

4. Patrick Hopkins "How Feminism Made a Man Out of Me." In Tom Digby, ed. *Men Doing Feminism*. New York: Routledge, 1998, p. 42. As Judith Grant writes, "feminism cannot simultaneously be the lens through which experiences are interpreted, and also find its grounding in those experiences. That is, the feminist interpretive lens cannot be grounded on women's point of view . . . To ground feminism in women's experiences and then to look to feminism to interpret those experiences is a tautology. To the extent that feminist standpoint theory accepts this tautology, it cannot accomplish what it sets out to do." Stated somewhat differently, a theory cannot be tested on the same data used to build that theory. See Judith Grant. *Fundamental Feminism: Contesting the Core Concepts of Feminist Theory*. New York: Routledge, 1993, p. 101.

5. Michael S. Kimmel "Who's Afraid of Men Doing Feminism?" In Tom Digby, ed. *Men Doing Feminism*. New York: Routledge, 1998, pp. 60–1.

6. bell hooks. *Feminist Theory: From Margin to Center*. Cambridge, MA: South End Press, 2000, especially chapter 5, "Men: Comrades In Struggle."

7. The second, third, and fourth points are made by James P. Sterba. "Is Feminism Good for Men and Are Men Good for Feminism?" In Tom Digby, ed. *Men Doing Feminism.* New York: Routledge, 1998, p. 298.

8. Black women have challenged the implicit and overt white racism within the feminist movement. The 1977 Combahee River Collective articulated these concerns noting that material conditions prevent most black women from upsetting "both the economic and the sexual arrangements that seem to represent some stability in their lives." At the same time, black women and black men frequently share commonly situated experiences of race and class in a capitalist, white imperialist society. See Combahee River Collective, "A Black Feminist Statement." In Carole R. MacCann and Seung-Kyung Kim, eds. *Feminist Theory Reader: Local and Global Perspectives.* New York: Routledge, 2003, p. 170.

9. Patricia Hill Collins. "Book Review: Separate Roads to Feminism: Black, Chicana, and White Feminist Movements in America's Second Wave." *Acta Sociologica,* Vol. 49, 2006, pp. 231–2. Internal racism has troubled the American feminist movement most obviously during the abolition/suffrage era and again during the black liberation/civil rights/women's liberation movements of the late 1960s and early 1970s. The problem hinged on white feminists' unexamined race and class-privileged assumptions that women's issues could be separated from race and class issues.

10. Judith Grant. *Fundamental Feminism: Contesting the Core Concepts of Feminist Theory.* New York: Routledge, 1993, p. 162.

11. Patricia Hill Collins. *Black Feminist Thought: Knowledge, Consciousness, and the Politics of Empowerment.* New York: Routledge, 2000, pp. 35–6. Collins's discussion pertains specifically to the development of black feminist thought. By extension, her insights are useful in considering how to create feminist politics and knowledge that is expansive enough to include men, without losing the advantages of women's self-defined knowledge.

12. Vivien Labaton and Dawn Lundy Martin. *The Fire This Time: Young Activists and the New Feminism.* New York: Random House, 2004, p. xxiii.

13. Discussed in Robyn Wiegman. "Unmaking: Men and Masculinity in Feminist Theory." In Judith Kegan Gardiner, ed. *Masculinity Studies and Feminist Theory.* New York: Columbia University Press, 2002, p. 36.

14. Anne G. Sadler, Brenda M. Booth, Brian L. Cook, Bradley N. Doebbeling. "Factors Associated With Women's Risk of Rape in the Military Environment." *American Journal of Industrial Medicine.* Vol. 43, Issue 3 (March 2003): 262–73.

15. Jennifer Zahn Spieler. "Soldier's Harassment Claim Leads to Court Martial," run date March 3, 2006. www.womensenews.org/article.cfm/dyn/aid/2980/context/cover. Accessed January 24, 2007.

16. Andrea G. Hunter and Sherrill L. Sellers. "Feminist Attitudes Among African American Women and Men." *Gender & Society.* Vol. 12, no. 1 (February 1998): 81. See also Patricia Collins. *Black Feminist Thought.* New York: Routledge Kegan Paul, 1991; Paula Giddings. *When and Where I Enter.* New York: Bantam, 1984; bell hooks. *Ain't I a Woman: Black Women and Feminism.* Boston: South End Press, 1981; Gary Lemons. "A New Response to 'Angry Black (Anti)Feminists': Reclaiming Feminist Forefathers,

Becoming Womanist Sons." In *Men Doing Feminism*, Tom Digby, ed. New York: Routledge, 1998.

17. Shira Tarrant. *When Sex Became Gender*. New York: Routledge, 2006, p. 32.

18. bell hooks. *Feminist Theory from Margin to Center*. Cambridge, MA: South End Press, 2000, p. 33.

19. See Gloria E. Anzaldúa and Analouise Keating, eds. *This Bridge We Call Home: Radical Visions for Transformation*. New York: Routledge, 2002; Judith Butler. *Gender Trouble: Feminism and the Subversion of Identity*. New York: Routledge, 1990; Patrick Califia. *Speaking Sex to Power: The Politics of Queer Sex*. San Francisco: Cleis Press, 2002; Cherríe L. Moraga and Gloria E. Anzaldúa, eds. *This Bridge Called My Back: Writings by Radical Women of Color*. Berkeley, CA: Third Woman Press, 2002; Michelle Tea, ed. *Without a Net: The Female Experience of Growing Up Working Class*. Emeryville, CA: Seal Press, 2003; bell hooks. *Killing Rage: Ending Racism*. New York: Owl Books, 1996. hooks writes that the institutionalized structure and patterns of domination negatively impacting women are repeated in all other arenas wherever particular groups of people are suppressed, oppressed, or subjugated. See also bell hooks. *Where We Stand: Class Matters*. New York: Routledge, 2000.

HOW TWO ASPIRING PORNOGRAPHERS TURNED ME INTO THE ULTIMATE F WORD

Hank Shaw

Around the turn of the century, with the help of a friend, I produced a booklet to educate guys about violence against women and girls. The title? *It's Time For Guys To Put An End To This.*

Our goal was simple: We wanted to talk about the problem in a down-to-earth way. So more guys would recognize the problem. And start working to end it.

Since the sixteen-page color booklet was first printed in 2000, more than 50,000 copies have been distributed in North America. Even today, several years after publication, I still get requests for copies from colleges, batterer education programs, church groups, sexual assault prevention programs, activists, and others working to make the world safer and fair for women and girls.

Sometimes people ask me how I got involved in this feminist cause, because I'm not a professional educator or expert: I'm just a guy off the street who bangs out words for a living. Besides, you don't just wake up one morning and say, "Hey, that feminism-thing looks fun! Let's try that!" So here's the story that explains how a beer-and-hoops-loving guy (yours truly) finally opened his eyes to the *huge* local, national, and international problem of violence against women and girls. It's also the story of how I became the ultimate F word.

What happened was this. My wife belonged to a group called Women Against a Violent Environment—WAVE, for short. The group was trying to raise awareness about violence against women and girls. And I was mildly supportive. "Yes dear. That's awful. Terrible! Pass me the Doritos, would ya?" Sometimes I even offered advice, which made me feel like I was contributing. But I didn't actually have to do anything. What's not to like about that kind of gig?

Besides, I had this sneaking suspicion that my feminist friends—including my esteemed co-mortgage holder—were blowing this whole violence against women thing *way* out of proportion. I mean, if it really was as big a deal as they said it was, then everybody'd be talking about it. And since everybody wasn't talking about it . . . well, you can see where I'm going with this. Then suddenly I was drafted into the cause. And my days as a happy-go-lucky Armchair Activist came to an end.

The particular form that this Draft Board summons took was a cable TV show called *Life Without Shame*. The show popped up in Rochester, New York, which just happens to be the final resting place of one of the founders of modern feminism: Susan B. Anthony.

The *Shame* show began on public access, then jumped to leased access to sell advertising. It was hosted by a couple of dumpy-looking dudes who took you into exotic dance halls where you could see Genuine American Nudity right there in the comfort and convenience of your own living room without paying any de-scrambling fees.

Well, naturally, the show attracted a lot of attention. Of course there were also the inevitable uptight complaints about godless nudity. But it wasn't the moving pictures that bothered my friends in WAVE. It was the commentary that invited guys to have lots of sex with lots of women and girls without worrying about annoying details like their age, or inclination, or consent. Here are some examples that give you the flavor of *Shame*'s philosophy of modern-day gender relations:

• "If I had a girlfriend and sent her over to your house," a guest asked the host, "what would happen?" "I'd be f-ing her in a second," the host says, "whether she wanted it or not . . . tied up in the air." "Exactly!" says the guest.
• "What's she doing? Putting a bag over his head?" one of the hosts says, as a topless dancer puts a bag over a patron's head. "Just like we put a bag over the heads of ugly women when we f- 'em."
• "Watching her makes me want to go home and rape my Barbie doll."
• "I think that any time there's any slapping of the genitals . . . like the slapping of the dick across a girl's face . . . that's a great thing, because it shows true love."

In addition to these romantic insights, *Shame* featured real-life footage of executions and circumcisions. The show even hosted the world's first Bum Olympics: Homeless alcoholic men got free booze for (among other things) licking whipped cream off the private parts of blow-up dolls. I guess the *Shame* boys beat the Fox network to that one. But what was most remarkable about *Shame*'s programming was the public endorsement of activities that are listed under R in the criminal code.

"What do you call a man who sleeps with teenage girls?" the hosts asked as they stood in front of a billboard designed to raise awareness about the sexual abuse of minors. "Someone who watches our show! It's a crime! Don't do it . . . unless you can get away with it!" Then they turn to each other with big cheesecake grins. "You pedophile!" "You rapist!"

You can imagine how the members of WAVE viewed this howling misogyny. But the *Shame* boys put a different spin on it. As they told a TV reporter, "We just try to be light-hearted and funny."

The "lighthearted and funny" content was bad enough. Then young guys started showing up in junior high and high school wearing *Life Without Shame* T-shirts. Even more amazing was this: The show started to attract advertisers. And they weren't all gun shops and porn emporiums. Ads started popping up for a famous local pizza parlor, a family restaurant, a comic book store, and a popular car stereo place that was an authorized distributor for the local phone company. I'm not making this up.

Since the rest of the community was more concerned about free public nudity than full-tilt medieval misogyny, WAVE launched a letter-writing campaign asking advertisers to drop their support for the show. The stereo shop owner said it was simply a "business decision" to advertise on *Shame*. The bargain-basement TV ad rates were too cheap to pass up. The comic book storeowner sent a letter back that began "Dear KKK." None of the other businesses responded. It was about this time that WAVE decided to do a little public consciousness-raising.

To raise the issue that advertising on the *Shame* show might not be in the best interests of, say, half the world's population, WAVE decided to boycott one of *Shame*'s loyal supporters: a pizza restaurant that had once been deemed the best in the city.

The place not only advertised on the *Shame* show, it even hosted an unforgettable episode in which a drunk patron with his pants at half-mast tried to grope an exotic dancer while they were both gyrating on top of the bar. Now this is not the image I want in *my* mind when I order pizza. But maybe I'm just being picky.

At any rate, the purpose of the protest was not to condemn dancing, nudity, or pizza (or even nude dancing with pizza), but to publicly question why any advertiser would publicly endorse a misogynistic worldview. WAVE simply wanted to raise awareness about violence against women and girls, which is the depressing global reality that made *Shame*'s attitudes so thoroughly vile and revolting.

Anyway, it was at this point in the feminists vs. pornographers battle that I faced a critical decision: Would I continue in my time- and labor-saving role of Armchair Activist? Or would I put my own feet on the street?

Since I string words together for a living, I decided to help my feminist friends by putting together a quick little flyer for their protest with some basic info about rape and domestic violence. So I grabbed some low-hanging facts from the Net, and I typed them up.

Hopefully, they would help people—including the local media—understand why WAVE was protesting the *Shame* show. Here's what I put together:

- A woman is battered every eighteen seconds.
- Every six minutes a woman is raped.
- Four women a day are killed by their husbands or boyfriends.
- America's rate of sexual assault is higher than that of every other industrialized nation in the world.
- Nearly 60 percent of all rapes are committed against girls younger than seventeen.

"Man, there's a lot of sick shit happening out there that guys aren't facing up to," I thought as I banged away on the keyboard. Then my old doubts resurfaced. *Hey! Things can't be this bad or everybody would be talking about it!!*

Right then and there I made a mental note to do an in-depth check on these facts in the future. In the meantime, however, the *Shame* boys' comments had riled me up enough that I decided to join in on the protest . . . despite some major-league anxiety about what my hoops-and-softball homeboys might think.

That fateful decision officially launched the WAVE Men's Auxiliary, unofficially known as HAVE (Hank Against a Violent Environment). And so, one cold November day in 1996, WAVE and HAVE and a couple of other earnest male supporters appeared out of the fog on the sidewalks in front of the famous local pizza joint with our signs and rhyming chants and all the other stuff that comes in your basic Sixties-Style Protest Kit.

There were maybe fifteen or twenty of us marching as the street filled up with rush-hour traffic. Then the media showed up. And then the *Shame* guys showed up with cameras rolling. And that launched a brou-ha-ha that reached epic proportions: a federal court case . . . inquiries from national TV news magazines . . . an article in the *New York Times* . . . a debate with a *Shame* boy on a nationally syndicated radio show . . . fisticuffs in the Op-Ed section of the paper. All this was in the future.

At the time of the protest, we wanted the community to recognize *Shame* for what it was: toxic programming in an age of violence against women. But it was harder, much harder, to get this point across than I ever imagined.

The local newspaper reporters kept calling the *Shame* show "risqué." It was another way of saying, "This show's way too cool for middle-aged conservative people and feminists." From my point of view, that single word served up a bigger endorsement than Roger Ebert's thumb.

There were other signs that media types in Susan B's town weren't ready to *get it*. For example: One radio talk show guy went so far as to publicly criticize the mean old feminists of WAVE for picking on a poor little pizza parlor. (He stopped this rant after we faxed him some verbatim comments from the show.)

Other people in the community seemed content to parrot the *Shame* boys' party line: If you don't like the show, all you have to do is change the damn channel!

Even more disturbing to WAVE was this: Hardly anyone in local media bothered to mention the issue of violence against women and girls in their coverage of the ongoing protests. An editor from Rochester's daily newspaper told WAVE, "Violence against women isn't news." Others seemed to think the connection was too far-fetched to bring up.

After all, if violence against women was as big a deal as WAVE said it was, then the national media would be talking about it. But they weren't. And since there was free TV nudity involved, it was much easier to characterize WAVE as your basic fun-hating male-bashing anti-pornography group, which is what one newspaper columnist did, conveniently ignoring minor details like what WAVE's name actually stood for.

These experiences helped me realize the strange language-processing quirks that can occur in these media situations. You think you're saying, "I'd like to talk to you about an important issue that often gets overlooked: violence against women." But what gets heard on the other end is this: "I'd like to waste your valuable time by talking about *a really annoying issue blown totally out of proportion by us man-hating feminazis!*"

Given the fact that misogyny isn't ready for prime time, I began to fear that we'd never make a boycott work. Then a minor miracle occurred. Our community education effort got a big boost from a surprising source: the *Shame* boys themselves.

Years ago, I sent some scripts to *Saturday Night Live*. The producers ping-ponged them right back. That was the extent of my TV writing career until the *Shame* boys gave me another chance. They grabbed the little flyer I put together for the pizza parlor protest, and they used it as raw material for one of the most impressive exhibitions of dumb-ass misogyny in the history of the planet.

Sitting in front of the camera with a rash of happy face decorations in the background, they went through the stats on my flyer one by one, adding their inimitable color commentary in the process.

- "A woman is battered every eighteen seconds. Is that it? If it was up to us, it would be every nine seconds."
- "Every six minutes a woman is raped. How can you go that often? I just can't get it up that quickly."
- "Nearly 60 percent of all rapes are committed against girls younger than seventeen. Well, of course. You don't want someone that's thirty-five years old. She'd probably like it. And they get stronger as they get older. You've got to get someone more docile. When they're that age, they're a lot tighter and wetter."
- "Four women a day are killed by their husbands and boyfriends? We have no facts on this, but if they're the kind of broads who go f-ing around on their

boyfriends . . . a knife in the throat is deserved." (Note: This is an edited version of the actual comment, which tops out the Richter scale in terms of woman-hating content.)

• And let's not forget the all-time *Shame* classic: "If she's dressed like a Catholic schoolgirl, you want to get in there and f- her. The younger, the better."

I was really ticked off when I first saw this episode, complete with ads from sponsors. How could anyone say such things? How could any self-respecting advertiser support them? But after I thought about it for a while, I felt like sending the *Shame* boys a candygram. After all, they had just given WAVE some great material to work with.

So with the help of Tim Shea, a videographer-and-softball buddy who lost a daughter to an act of domestic violence, I put together a five-minute Lowlights video that included the revealing comments above. Then we held the international premiere at a press conference called by former New York State Senator Rick Dollinger, a longtime advocate of women's rights.

Previously, we had faxed information and verbatim comments from the show to every politician in town. *Shame*'s comments about Catholic schoolgirls didn't sit well with Rick. He's Catholic and just happened to have a school-age daughter. He was the only pol in Susan B's town with the guts to get involved in this mess.

The press conference was held in the office of the public access station where *Shame* made its cable TV debut a year or so before. As the Lowlights video rolled, some women in the audience broke into tears: They couldn't believe that grown men (one of these guys was in his mid-forties) could actually say such hateful things about women.

On the other hand, one of the TV reporter guys had his hand over his mouth to keep from laughing: He thought the *Shame* guys were hysterical. Further proof that a lot of men don't get it about this whole violence-against-women thing. After that, things got even crazier. Time Warner kicked the show off the air for six months for submitting indecent programming. And that gave the *Shame* boys more attention than ever.

While their show was banned from leased access, the boys returned to public access. But that was only a temporary fix. After all, they couldn't sell advertising on public access. So they couldn't make a living.

The boys sued Time Warner. And they did a smart thing. They promoted themselves as First Amendment Heroes. "Hey, everybody! We're just two struggling entrepreneurs, but we're willing to put everything on the line to take this case to federal court and protect everyone's right to free speech!"

They did a good job of it, too. Die-hard *Shame* viewers started calling the boys champions. A woman photographer from the local paper even thanked the guys for defending the First Amendment during a photo shoot.

Unfortunately, no one in the media bothered to point out that a feminist boycott might also be an expression of free speech. And they were clueless to the fact that the *Shame* boys had a slightly different view about the First Amendment rights of feminists or anyone else who opposed them. This point was as obvious as a corpse in a living room to anyone who had actually bothered to watch the *Shame* show.

On several occasions, for example, the *Shame* boys had gone after a popular drive-time radio host with whom they'd had a public feud. On one episode, a *Shame* boy waved around a sword and boasted about how he was going to carve up the radio guy's ex-wife and sexually assault her in the wound.

When I heard this, I called the D.A.'s office. I couldn't believe you could publicly threaten someone like that on TV. But guess what? You can! Especially if you're being light-hearted and funny. And here's what the *Shame* boys had to say at the end of their flyer-bashing show about WAVE:

> In closing, we love protests. Women— gee, we don't want to get in a debate with you and all that shit, but you are ignorant, carpet-munching sluts. Just watch the movie *Thelma and Louise* while you're fingering each other at home. And that's about it. F-ing teach all your children—especially your daughters—how to become muscle-bound little f-ing whores so they can beat up men. OK? We'll see you. Junkyard Stripper's coming up soon . . .

The *Shame* boys also had fun on TV with a blow-up doll labeled "WAVE." I'll let you fill in the blanks on their antics. Of course, all of this trash talk was a slight departure from the position taken by most real First Amendment Heroes, which usually goes something like: "I disagree like hell with what you're saying, but I'll defend to death your right to say it." But then the *Shame* boys weren't really into the First Amendment. They were just a couple of small-time guys trying to cash in on the billion-dollar porn boom. And they took exception to anyone who might get in the way.

In 1997, the Time Warner–*Shame* case went to federal court. It was a big deal because the decision would affect the right of a cable operator to exercise control over leased access programming. Clearly, there were national implications.

When it was time for the hearing, WAVE and HAVE showed up along with Time Warner, Time Warner's attorneys, the *Shame* boys, their attorney, the New York Civil Liberties Union, Senator Dollinger, the local media, and a growing mob of media types from outside the area. The only thing missing was Trixie the dancing elephant.

The arguments went back and forth. Time Warner pointed out that it should have the right to exercise control over its programming. The *Shame* boys claimed that Time Warner had violated the First Amendment. They also objected to the unfairness of the suspension, which "banned the programmers instead of the programming."

Both sides made good points. But the highlight of the hearing was when the *Shame* boys' attorney admitted that he couldn't stomach one of the banned shows—the "Tribute to Violence"—which just happened to include a movie scene in which a man slits a woman's throat and beats her with a meat tenderizer. I guess that was just *too risqué*.

WAVE played a bit part in the courtroom drama, too, thanks to Senator Dollinger, who had drafted a friend-of-the-court brief that included our Lowlights video, information on violence against women, and letters from leading experts on sexual abuse and gender violence.

By now, the story was ready to go big time. NBC's *20–20* contacted WAVE. So did a producer for Bryant Gumbel's short-lived evening news-magazine. For a brief dizzying moment, we felt like we might finally, *finally*, get our side of the story across. We might actually get everybody talking about violence against women and it would be certified as an Important Public Issue.

We argued about which show would be the best forum. Finally, we opted for *20–20*, because the guy who contacted us had been so encouraging and supportive. "The *Shame* boys' comments were awful! Terrible! And yes, there's way too much violence against women and girls in the world." The guy could've been our therapist.

So we made our decision. We shipped the Lowlights reel off to NBC and waited to make the leap into the national spotlight. But before that happened, another scandal jumped out of a rabbit hole, and the national media went howling off in a different direction.

Repeated calls to our good buddy at *20–20* were routed straight to voice-mail. A week or two later, our Lowlights reel was returned in the mail with a big crack in the cassette as if somebody had dropped a barbell on it. I'm not making this up either.

The Court's decision came down in September 1997. Time Warner had the right to ban indecent programming, but they couldn't ban the programmers. Frankly, it seemed like a fair decision. But neither side was happy, and the *Shame* boys appealed. The case ended up in the U.S. Court of Appeals, which upheld the original ruling. That was on June 14, 1999—two-and-a-half years after our pizza protest, at the tail end of the twentieth century.

Of course, the *Shame* boys didn't give up. They launched an infomercial on cable access for gun shops, cigar shops, tattoo parlors, and porn video rental establishments. The show featured scantily clad women with prior exotic dance experience. But there was no free female nudity. And without that powerful ingredient, the show finally went off the air.

After that, the *Shame* boys . . . just . . . sort of . . . disappeared—moving on, I imagine, to a place more hospitable to aspiring pornographers with a particular view about women.

I think everybody in Susan B's town was glad to get this whole sorry episode in the rearview mirror. And to tell you the truth, I was delighted to be done with the thing, too. The public mud fight had taken an enormous amount of time. I didn't really dig the glazed looks I got from my male friends when I talked about what was wrong with the *Shame* show. It wasn't all that much fun to have people in the media view me as a wacked-out extremist. And I was dying to put my energy to better use. There comes a time when you'd rather plant a garden than fight a reeking landfill.

So I went back to the fact sheet that I put together for the pizza protest. I decided to turn it into a brochure, thinking that there might be some open-minded guys out there who would own up to the problem of violence against women if they could get the straight scoop in down-to-earth, guy-to-guy terms.

I started from scratch, checking out sources, looking for new research, and shit-canning facts that didn't hold water. I worked on it whenever I could smuggle time into my schedule. A few hours here. A few days there. Sometimes, when day gigs slowed down, I'd put an entire week into the project. Three years later, I reached the finish line. It took that long before the facts and words felt right. By that time, what was originally intended to be a simple collection of stats had grown into the booklet *It's Time For Guys To Put An End To This.*

Daniel Hoh, a graphic-designer friend of mine, donated more than $10,000 of his time to make my words look great on paper. We published the booklet in June of 2000, right around the time of the sexual assault riot in New York City's Central Park.

Since then, more than 50,000 copies of have zipped out across North America with help from Michael Kauffman and Jack Gagliardi of the White Ribbon Campaign, Joe Kelly of Dads & Daughters, and Jackson Katz, who (among other accomplishments) founded the revolutionary gender violence training program in the United States Marine Corps. All of these guys have dedicated their lives to making the world safer and better for women and girls. These guys—and many others—are all heroes in my book.

So where did I end up after all this? I ended up in a new and different place. I saw a lot and I learned a lot, and it changed the way I viewed everything from world history to house chores. I saw how—at the end of the twentieth century—you could develop a popular TV show by mixing free female nudity with a rape-ain't-no-crime platform.

I saw how local businessmen could blithely justify their sponsorship of *Shame* on the grounds that the TV ad rates were cheap. Which brings up the big question: Would they have supported a show that violently trashed religious or ethnic groups? (We all know the answer to that one.) During my time on the *Shame* beat, I saw how quickly the local and national media jumps on anything that smacks of racism. But misogyny? It's not even up there with the snail darter. I also had a brief Orwellian moment when I was asked to remove the word "boycott" from my anti-*Shame* Op-Ed piece because, the editor said, the word was "too strong." This was the same paper whose reporters continuously characterized *Shame's* violent, women-trashing content as "risqué."

As I got farther and farther away from my armchair, I saw how easily feminist issues are dissed and dismissed, because a lot of people just aren't going to cave in to a bunch of hysterical, humorless, nit-picking women. Even when they're not hysterical or humorless. Even when they're only trying to get people to think for five damn seconds about serious stuff that dispro-portionately affects some three-plus billion XX-chromosome people. Even when the feminists in question are not, actually, women.

During my research for the brochure, I discovered other things I'd never thought about. I learned about female genital mutilation, dowry burnings, acid attacks, female infanticide, state-of-the-art sex slavery, child sexual abuse (which has to be human history's most shameful secret), and the use of rape as a time-honored military strategy. I learned that there may be as many as sixty million women and girls missing on the face of the earth due to assorted acts of discrimination. I learned that guys around the world have *a lot* more political power, property, and wealth. Plus, they get better jobs, more education, better health care, you name it. And it's all because they lucked out in the old chromosome-shuffling card game played at conception. Last but not least, I learned that there are a lot of decent, fair-minded, nonviolent guys out there who come home after a hard day on the job and stick their wives with most of the crap work—for a simple reason: Their wives are women.

Just the other day I looked one of these guys in the eye: I was shaving at the time.

As you might imagine, my efforts to size up violence against women permanently extinguished any doubts I had about the significance of the problem. There were too many headlines, too many statistics, and too many personal anecdotes from women I knew for this to be a feminist fiction.

I had also begun to see a pattern that connected the glass ceiling in the corporate world, the second shift women face at home, the never-ending series of stories about pro athletes who beat up their wives and girlfriends, sexual harassment and discrimination on Wall Street, Eminem's rants, the Texas-based business that sells "Wife Beater" T-shirts, the Brazilian hit song that makes domestic violence seem sexy, the chilling preference for boy babies in parts of Asia, mass rapes in Bosnia and Rwanda, the reports of Catholic priests raping nuns in Africa, the crazy-ass decisions by the Italian Supreme Court about rape and sexual harassment, and the countless other acts of violence, harassment, and discrimination that women and girls have to deal with every day on every continent in the world.

The *Shame* boys were a small flower on this centuries-old vine.

Bad shit. All of it. And my apprehension of this fractal pattern could have been paralyzing—except for one dazzling thing: I knew there were women and men out there who were working hard to make a difference, despite the obstacles and resistance. Despite the patronizing looks from colleagues and friends. Despite the crazy-ass radical reaction you get from pillars of the community and members of the media.

What's more, I knew that some of these people were giving up lucrative professions to do this work; others were risking their lives, because they believed so deeply in the cause. There are no award shows for these people. No gala parties with paparazzi straining at the ropes. But I knew there was one reasonable way to honor them. I could keep trying to *do some damn thing* instead of throwing my hands in the air and heading back for the Armchair.

And so it goes: A story that began with my uncertain support of a pizza parlor protest ended with my firm conviction that the ultimate F-word— feminism—is one of the coolest things to hit this planet in the past couple centuries. After all, this quietly growing international movement has the potential to make life better for half the people in the world. (Some would argue, *all* the people.) What's not to like about that?

And, in case you haven't noticed, feminism is already working wonders, opening up new opportunities for women and girls in every time zone, and fighting discrimination and violence with mind-blowing spirit and conviction.

No question about it. Feminism is writing a great chapter in world history. And once I saw that, I could finally call *myself* a feminist—without flinching or adding asterisks or worrying what my buddies think. So from here on out, I've got a job to do. I'm going to keep trying to get more guys to realize that violence against women and girls isn't a feminist myth: It's a crime. And I want to encourage these guys to start talking to their buddies about the problem. So *those* buddies will talk to *their* buddies. And we start to change the attitudes that make it okay to hurt people because of their gender.

Of course, I'm a realist–idealist. I know that right now there are only a couple guys in every crowd who are ready for this. But if we reach them—and if they reach others—we can start a chain reaction that will, over time, reach around the world. Anyway, that's the story about what I'm doing, and how I got into this, right here in Susan B. Anthony's town. Right near the beginning of the twenty-first century.

EXPOSED IN IRAQ: SEXUAL HARASSMENT AND HIDDEN RANK STRUCTURE OF THE U.S. ARMY

Marshall Thompson

When William Cohen started his job as Secretary of Defense in 1997, he made cracking down on sexual harassment in the military one of his top priorities. "We are going to make it very clear from the very top officials to the lowest in the chain of command this is not acceptable conduct," he said. With such a clear directive from Cohen and from many other military leaders, it would seem a simple matter for every disciplined, oath-bound soldier to comply. Unfortunately, it just doesn't work that way.

In May 2006, I was knee-deep in a one-year tour of duty as a military journalist in Iraq. One of my coworkers, a female sergeant, came in one morning and threw herself down in her chair without saying hello to anyone. I decided to give her some room. After all, there are plenty of good reasons for being in a bad mood in Iraq, like the constant fear of death or the balmy 130-degree weather.

About a half hour later, she couldn't stand it any longer and started venting to me about being sexually harassed the day before by a first sergeant and company commander. They had hounded her to get naked, lie across a humvee, and let them photograph her.

"I'm sorry," I said. "How did that make you feel?"

"Like a piece of crap," she replied.

I was shocked. I'd been in the military for seven years and I'd never seen people in those kinds of leadership positions treat a woman so poorly. For a long time now I've considered myself a feminist, and at that moment I considered myself an extremely pissed off feminist.

"Do you want me to talk with them?"

"No," she said.

"Do you want me to beat them up?"

She just laughed.

"I'll help you file a complaint," I said.

"No, I just want to forget about it."

I didn't want to pressure her, but I had to remind her that if she didn't make a statement, these guys would continue to make other women feel like crap. She said she understood, but the perceived cost of complaining was just too high. Currently, the U.S. Armed Forces do not have a confidential reporting system for sex crimes. If a woman wants to report sexual harassment or a sexual assault, she has to make her name public.

"Those other girls will just have to deal with it," she said.

The next day, I left the office to cover some stories in Al Anbar province. Long hours in helicopters and convoys gave me time to reflect on how I'd become a feminist. Until I was a junior at Utah State University, I thought only women could be feminists. This all changed when one of my favorite male journalism professors wore a T-shirt to class that read, "This is what a feminist looks like." Intrigued by the idea, I tried the title on myself.

"Hello, my name is Marshall and I'm a feminist," I said aloud as soon as I was alone. It felt good. Later I found that Karen Offen, a historian specializing in feminism, defines a feminist as anyone, female or male, who protests against the institutions and ideas that promote inequalities between the sexes.

This definition appealed to me on a personal level: Since my youth, women had been some of my most respected role models, the foremost of whom was my mother's mother known simply as "Granny" to my siblings and me. Granny earned a bachelor's and master's degree in sociology during the Great Depression. When she married, she inspired her husband so much that he went back to school to get his master's in sociology. They worked together as social workers for a few short years. He died of a heart attack when my mother was eleven and my Granny never remarried. She worked full-time and raised four children. One of my earlier memories is seeing hundreds of coworkers honoring my silver-haired Granny at her retirement party. I also noticed how my father treated her. He would lean in and confer with her about the plans for the day, like a cabinet member discussing an important issue with the president.

My reverie ended as I stepped off a Black Hawk helicopter at Camp Al Asad in western Iraq. I boarded a shuttle bus that would take me to the unit I was looking for. I walked to the back and sat down behind a male lieutenant colonel, a male sergeant major, and a female sergeant. I'm a constant eavesdropper and as I stared out the window at the vast fields of dust, I listened closely to their conversation.

They were the advanced group for their National Guard unit, which would be coming to Al Asad in a few weeks. Eventually they started talking about housing. The lieutenant colonel turned to the sergeant and said, "Of course, you'll be rooming with me, just don't tell my wife."

I thought the sergeant major might stand up for his soldier and remind the commander of the sexual harassment policy.

"No, sir," said the sergeant major. "You've got it all wrong. Sgt. X is rooming with me."

The female sergeant laughed quietly and shook her head.

"You laugh," the sergeant major said. "But you know you're gonna give it up before you leave here."

I was disgusted. This was the second time in two days I'd heard of unit commanders sexually harassing their subordinates. I wanted to say something, but I was still scared. After all, maybe she enjoyed the jokes. If she were offended, it would be her responsibility to say something, not mine. Right?

I said nothing. The bus stopped, I got off, and met up with the unit I was covering. The unit commander cancelled my convoy and told me I'd have to wait a few days. Writing stories about units on the base kept me occupied, but at night, I had nothing but time to think.

Were women treated much worse in Iraq than in the United States? And if this were true, was it because the rules in Iraq were different? For instance, I would never think of pointing a loaded weapon at somebody back home, but in Iraq, that was a perfectly normal thing to do. Perhaps this shift in standards had caused some soldiers to reevaluate what they knew about sexual harassment. Out here in the desert with little to no chance of punishment, maybe it seemed okay to make objectifying and degrading comments to women. Is that what they were thinking?

Now that I was paying more attention to sexual harassment, it seemed to be popping up everywhere, and not just from superiors. In many cases, it was coming from peers.

While I was killing time before my convoy, a couple of soldiers invited me up to their motor pool to photograph their weekly basketball game. Out of eight players, only one was a female, Pvt. Y. When it came time to determine which team would play in their camouflage tops and which team would play in their brown undershirts, the players invoked a standing rule: Pvt. Y's team would play in their undershirts.

"You'll see why," one soldier said to me as he winked.

I'd met Pvt. Y a few days ago and she'd left a favorable impression. She was young and a little bit goofy with thick glasses and a boy's haircut, a skinny kid from the Midwest. When she took off her camouflage top, all the male players hooped and hollered. Her tight brown undershirt revealed that she had a larger than average chest. She blushed and almost bowed as she set her top on the ground.

"Hey Sergeant," one of the players yelled to me. "Are you gonna get some pictures of Pvt. Y's big ol' titties bouncing around?"

"No," I said.

I didn't feel comfortable saying anything more at that point because I didn't want to embarrass Pvt. Y. However, her response to the comment was anything but embarrassed. She grabbed her breasts and shook them, an action that elicited even more cheering from the crowd.

I'm still not sure what was going on during that game. If I took what I saw at face value, I'd have to assume that Pvt. Y actually enjoyed what other women and men would consider criminally offensive. It's not completely ridiculous to assume that a woman raised in a society that puts such a high value on physical attractiveness would find sincere pleasure in the lavish attention that her body garners. I've heard this line of logic explained often by soldiers complaining about the strict sexual harassment policy in the military.

The male soldiers at the basketball game, however, were not simply complimenting their peer. It's almost comical to think they would ever use the same sort of language to describe each other's physical appearance. As if a male soldier would remove his shirt and his fellows would make catcalls and yell, "Wow, Joe, your pecs are luscious."

Pvt. Y wasn't that naïve to assume the lascivious comments were simply compliments. So why did she play along? Maybe it was a defense mechanism— an easier way to deal with the problem than filing a public report after every basketball game. But why did the female sergeant on the bus merely laugh and shake her head when her male commander made a joke about them sleeping together? Why wouldn't my coworker file a complaint against the men who had made her feel so worthless? For that matter, why hadn't I said anything when I witnessed these things happen?

The military structure requires teamwork and obedience to orders from superiors. Drill sergeants pound these ideas indelibly into the minds of every recruit. If you don't follow orders, military trainers say, people will die. So when a high-ranking person says something to you, your first response is to do exactly what they say. The last response is to question them. And when you find acceptance in a group, your first response is to cling to it. Fitting in and working as a team is necessary to survival.

It's this dynamic, however, that made former-Secretary of Defense Cohen so intent on ending the military's addiction to sexual harassment. Instead of accepting sexual harassment to retain superficial comity in the ranks, he demanded that it be eliminated.

"We're talking about men and women putting their lives on the line at some point," Cohen said in 1997. "We can't have that kind of dissension, that kind of discrimination or morale problem within the unit."

Eight years later, it seemed service members decided to ignore this command while putting their units in actual danger by allowing the sexual subjugation of women in the Armed Forces to continue. It has become such a problem that at least one female soldier has refused to return to Iraq.

Spc. Suzanne Swift said that during her tour in Iraq she was constantly sexually harassed by superiors, exposed to sexual banter, and coerced into a sexual relationship with her immediate supervisor. She was brave enough to file complaints, but the perpetrators received no real punishment. Because of her year of sexual degradation in Iraq, she has refused to return. For that, the U.S. military court-martialed her.

This seems like a total reversal from Cohen's zero-tolerance policy. Sadly, the military's current policies that reinforce sexual inequality and female repression go further than court-martialing. On Sept. 15, 2003, they took a life.

Originally, the military reported Alyssa Peterson's death as an "accidental discharge." But as family and local journalists dug deeper, the details of her suicide became clear.

Peterson was a devout Mormon and served as a volunteer missionary for eighteen months in the Netherlands. She was fluent in Dutch and had a gift for languages, so when she enlisted to serve her country she signed up as an Arabic interpreter. When she got to Iraq she was assigned to an interrogation unit called "the cage." The details of what went on in the cage are classified, but other female interrogators have described some of the process. Guards brought male prisoners into the cage blindfolded and then stripped them down. When the guards removed the blindfolds, the first thing the prisoners saw was a female interpreter. Superiors instructed the female interpreters to insult the prisoners' genitalia. In other cases, female interrogators wiped fake menstrual blood on prisoners, molested them, and performed strip teases. The U.S. Army has set a new low mark in sexual harassment; they turned it into a torture device.

When superiors ordered Peterson to use her sexuality as a base torture device, not only was she expected to make Iraqi men suffer, but military officers also unwittingly forced Peterson to defame the divinity of womanhood that is so core to Mormon religious beliefs. After two days in the cage, Peterson refused to continue. She changed assignments, but she didn't get over what she had done. A few weeks after leaving the cage, Peterson committed suicide.

At the time of the bus ride with Sgt. X and the basketball game with Pvt. Y, I didn't know Peterson's story and I didn't know about Swift's court martial. If I'd known then how dangerous sexual harassment could be, I'd like to think I would have done more. I don't know what happened to Sgt. X or to Pvt. Y, but I hope they're okay.

The next morning I got up hours before sunrise to catch my convoy to Camp Hit, a small outpost near the Syrian border. When I arrived at the isolated camp, I found a handful of female soldiers living and working among the male infantry soldiers and Marines. At this point, this seemed like a recipe for sexual harassment and sexual assault. I was determined to expose the problem in a story. I interviewed all five women. They each told me that nobody treated them any differently because they were women.

I started to feel optimistic. Maybe the last week was just a fluke. Maybe it wasn't all that bad. I started to look for a different angle for the story. I'd noticed that all the soldiers spoke highly of their commander, Capt. Z. This is unusual because most soldiers like to complain about their commanders. I decided to seek out this exceptional captain who, also, just happened to be a woman.

"Do you know where Capt. Z is?" I asked a passing soldier.

"Oh, yeah, she's the hot one," he said.

"Do you know where she is?"

"Just walk that way until you see a hot captain."

It didn't bother me that he said she was hot. I even laughed a bit. Out in the middle of the desert surrounded by a bunch of ugly male grunts, they had probably built this captain up to be an Aphrodite reborn. It was still an objectifying comment, but since this soldier sounded legitimately infatuated, it seemed more innocent to me at the time. Maybe it was because he was a lower rank than Capt. Z and his comment made him seem more like an adoring puppy dog than an oppressive pervert.

When I found Capt. Z, she was pretty and, more importantly, very competent. I was impressed with the efficiency with which she ran the logistics for the base. I thought to myself, "Here is one of the best and brightest of the military." I decided I might do a sidebar personality feature on her because an officer who knows her job is definitely newsworthy these days.

As a precaution, I asked Capt. Z if she felt other soldiers treated her any differently because of her sex. She said definitely not. "Great," I thought, "I've just had a bad week."

I finished up the interview and was about to ask if I could follow her around and get some photos when a male master sergeant butted in.

"Hey, Sgt. T," the guy said to me, "you should get some photos of her with her top off."

She blushed and played it off as if it were just part of being in the Army. But I could hear her voice crackle ever so slightly with emotion. All the guys laughed as if it were some clever repartee. I didn't laugh. She didn't laugh. And I didn't dare ask her right after that comment if I could take pictures of her.

The foul minds and untamed tongues of undisciplined soldiers took something innocent and good and made it seem vulgar. They were power tripping.

I was the lowest ranking person in the immediate area and I froze, yet again. At the time, I was astounded. I thought that a captain in the U.S. Army wouldn't put up with that kind of a degrading comment. What I didn't understand at the time was that hegemonic sexism meant that anyone sexually harassing Capt. Z automatically outranked her. Sexism literally usurped the structure and discipline of the U.S. military.

I decided that day that I would no longer tolerate sexual harassment. I would speak up even if I were subordinate, even if I were poking my nose in other people's business, and even if I were afraid of embarrassing myself. I made a preemptive strike in my unit and informed everyone that if I heard anyone using the language of sexual harassment, I'd file a formal complaint myself, because it offends me personally. When men harass women with viciously sexual language, they don't only degrade the women, they degrade themselves. They demote themselves ethically and morally. But when men treat women with the honor they deserve—that *all* people deserve—then men become truly noble as well. In the end, we're all the same species and in the same military. The degradation of one degrades us all.

My personal stand hasn't changed the military culture of female repression in the slightest. But maybe a few men got the message that sexual harassment is unacceptable. And, still, I think speaking up may have helped a few women who felt outnumbered in a combat zone, and that's a start. After all, we feminists need to stick together.

WHY I AM NOT A FEMINIST

Haji Shearer

I am not a feminist. Applied linguistics prevents me from adopting the title. Feminist is derived from feminine, referring to the female sex. As an African-American man who supports equality for women I don't feel it's necessary, or even beneficial, for me to feminize my personhood in order to do the right thing *vis-à-vis* gender. I know men who identify as feminist, but that doesn't work for me. Even among women, the term feminist has had less acceptance in the black community than among whites. Feminism is defined in my *American Heritage Dictionary* as a doctrine that advocates or demands for women the same rights granted to men. I am all for that. I support equal rights and responsibilities for women without injecting the confusing etymology that implies being feminist is akin to being feminine or female.

There is no comparable male term in English for feminist. Masculinist doesn't work. It might be more accurate to coin a new phrase to identify men who support women's full humanity. True manhood must advocate for equal rights and responsibilities for women as a component of its' own integrity. In fact I consider it a short-sighted compromise for a man to identify as a feminist. Does a white person identify as black to do anti-racism work?

Men who stand up for women's equality are valuable educators within the patriarchal camp precisely because we are men. We shouldn't minimize that advantage. I need not make my feminine side primary in order to honor my mother, sister, or daughter. Because so much viciousness has been committed in the name of false manhood, some have confused the most toxic aspects of patriarchy with true manhood. That is a mistake.

We must reclaim the essence of manhood from thugs and pimps, corrupt businessmen, imperialist warmongers, and juiced up athletes. Manhood needs to be defined by its peaks, not its valleys. Healthy manhood acknowledges the inner feminine and inner masculine of each human being. Healthy manhood advocates for the equal rights and responsibilities of women and men. Healthy manhood honors the inherent value and goodness of all people.

I am a man. African-American, urban, happily heterosexual, conceived in 1961. Some of my earliest memories are of social movements. Blue Hill Avenue burning during the 1967 riots, Dr. King assassinated in 1968, being one of the first black children voluntarily bused to an almost all-white sub-urban school in 1969. My father was a star among his nine brothers and sisters, avoiding the drug addiction that captured his father and several siblings, he founded a successful, community-based, medical laboratory. My mother, unlike many in my neighborhood, was able to full-time parent until I, the youngest of their three children, was fully ensconced in primary school. After that she worked in the family business with my father in a position of shared authority.

As the youngest child and the only boy, I was privileged. The division of labor I most remember among my siblings was the nightly chores. My sisters took turns washing the dishes. I took out the trash. Not only did my trash duty take far less time to finish compared to washing the dishes but on top of that, I had more freedom to explore the neighborhood than my older sisters. My mother encouraged my sisters to stay in the safety of the yard while I replicated Fat Albert and the gang all around the block. And then, of course, there was the sexual double standard.

Although my mom denies it today, I recall getting the message from her, and from society at large, that it was okay for me to have sex before marriage, but it wasn't okay for my sisters. The only message I got from my dad on the subject was his late nights out.

Despite these discrepancies, as a child and young man, racial tension was always more apparent to me than gender injustice. I remember claiming to be a Black Panther as a child in the late 1960s so the white bully who was harassing me would back off. A decade later I joined an organization started by former Panther, Stokely Carmichael (who was then-named Kwame Ture). The All African People Revolutionary Party (AAPRP) was open only to people of African descent and was dedicated to uniting the African continent under one socialist government. When I joined I didn't know about Carmichael's infamous remark about women as social activists. Asked in 1964 what position women in the Student Non-Violent Coordinating Committee (SNCC) could take, he reportedly answered, "Prone." Given the leadership of many women in the AAPRP, Ture's assessment of his sisters' ability had improved in the intervening decades.

Truth be told, I was not a very dedicated revolutionary. I felt like I had missed the glory days of the 1960s: the police shoot-outs, the so-called Free Love, the ubiquitous drugs. I wanted not only the chance to bask in some of that glow, but I wanted some action! When it became apparent that there were no weapons stashed in AAPRP safe houses to confront the pigs and that all these revolutionaries actually did was study books and have discussions, I boogied.

But, in what would be a reoccurring theme in my life, I was attracted to powerful women in the organization. In fact, a female friend introduced me to the group in the first place. She was a beautiful and intelligent sister and, surely, a large reason for joining was to get closer to her. (I would discover, alas, that I was not the only would-be revolutionary motivated, at least in part, by sex.) Fortunately, she and I became close friends. Although the sexual component never developed between us, it did between me and another comrade.

Both of these beautiful black women taught me about politics, history, and interpersonal relationships. Yet, I don't recall either of them ever calling themselves a feminist. And as I befriended and worked with other progressive black women the word feminism rarely was uttered, or it was disdained as the purview of wealthy white women. I understood that addressing the inequalities foisted on women by men in the ruling elite was not something that immediately concerned those of us in the black community. The main issue at hand was racism. The feeling was, *Let's get that worked out first and then we'll turn to gender.*

Another brake on the widespread adoption of feminist ideology in the black community is that bastion of male privilege, the church. One small example: A few years ago my wife and I co-facilitated a couples' workshop in a local church, with a dynamic female pastor assisting us. Our group started with seven hetero-couples, but early in the program almost every man's attendance became sporadic. Only two of the men managed to complete the ten-week course. Despite the men's lackluster performance, the pastor spoke one evening about a Bible verse that states a man is the head of his household.

One of the women in our couples group was having none of that. She passionately detailed the neglect and ill-treatment her man had inflicted on their family—including abandoning her that evening—and she described the extra burdens she had to bear because of his irresponsibility. How, she demanded, could he be considered the head of the household when he was too much of a punk to even attend a little couple's workshop? The pastor, usually an eloquent advocate of her position, had no convincing reply.

In my own family, my wife and I consciously try to share the roles of both head and heart of our home. Growing up amidst the gender awakening of the 1970s surely affected my ideas. As a child, I could sense the disruption in the social fabric of traditional relationships. I remember hating the fact that my father was never around. Granted, he was mostly working and he provided a decent income for the family (especially admirable considering his own primary role model for manhood/fatherhood was a drunk). But I remember as a boy thinking that I would be around for my children because it hurt me so much that my father wasn't around. That's why the most important place I practice gender equality is within my marriage and family.

I married an independent-minded woman dedicated to exercising her full rights and accepting her full responsibilities (although like many of us, she often seems more concerned with the former than with the latter). Even though we are both African-Americans, I understood from the beginning of our relationship that, as a man, I hail from a more privileged group and was committed to trying to level the field.

After my wife, Jasmin, and I conceived our first child, I spent some years volunteering with a black-woman-led, community-based childbirth organization where my wife had started working as a midwifery apprentice and breastfeeding counselor. These women were engaged in the revolutionary act of reclaiming the birth experience from the medical industrial complex. They understood the downside of the patriarchal birth experience that became standard practice in this country after World War II. Midwifery was destroyed, women were disempowered, infants were abused, and people of color were disrespected. And even these progressive black women did not call themselves feminists. So eager were they to eschew the feminist label they adopted the word womanist, a term coined by Alice Walker, to differentiate themselves from their white, middle-class, feminist sisters. With such a strong group of black, female role models distancing themselves from the feminist label while upholding the ideals of gender equality, it's little wonder I turned a cold shoulder to the term. I support the goals of feminism—equal rights of women in the home and workplace, for example—but I never related to the culture of feminism.

Eventually, I became a social worker and, because there was a void in serving this population, working with men became my specialty and one of my passions. As I began practicing family support work with fathers, I saw that men were often ignored by female social workers who were supposed to service the whole family. The need to engage men was crucial because it was obvious that much of the conflict in families came from the inability of parents to communicate. Some of this was the long-standing failure of couples to engage in truly intimate relationships. Some was due to the transformation in relationships inspired by the 1970s-era women's movement that resulted in a shifting power dynamic between family members leaving many men confused and angry. Some men I work with are angry about a perceived loss of power in the home. It seems to them that both women and children had been empowered by changes in social policy over the last thirty years. *So guess who lost power?* they ask me rhetorically.

Initially, most of the men I counseled were African-American or Latino, working-class or lower-income. Talk with these men about Affirmative Action in the workplace and they easily understand that a systematic pattern of discrimination has prevented them from excelling in society. Therefore a pattern of favorable treatment is a reasonable remedy to correct historic wrongs resulting from slavery, Jim Crow, and institutionalized prejudice perpetuated by society's dominant group of whites. I've found some success in helping men of color accept the radical shifts in gender equality thrust upon them by equating it to Affirmative Action for relationships.

Most men can acknowledge a historical burden experienced by women. Even black or Latino men who have been excluded from the old boy network still have the ability to physically oppress women. Most honest men can acknowledge seeing or hearing of a woman being beaten, raped, and/or financially exploited both in romantic relationships and in the community at large. Sometimes women very close to them were hurt in these ways. This well-established gender terrorism is akin to blacks being oppressed by whites for generations. If you acknowledge the similarities, you can see the need for similar restitution.

In discussing the legacy of slavery, some whites fall back on the old excuse, "I never owned slaves" and "I didn't benefit from slavery." In reality, though, a third-grader could draw a direct line from the resources and benefits accrued by whites during slavery to the downtrodden condition of blacks today. Likewise, as men we benefit daily from a conspiracy of male privilege and are burdened with some of the collective karma of our gender's actions. For example, I never raped anyone, but another man sexually abused my wife. As she and I became intimate, and as we worked through the healing process, some of her anger at her stepfather's depraved behavior was transferred onto me. Would it be fair for me to cry, "Hey, don't associate me with him. I'm not like that. I'm different"? Possibly. But that wouldn't eliminate the association in her mind and, one way or another, we'd have to deal with that.

The more effective way to deal with it might be to accept that men have oppressed women for generations. Men consciously working to undo that oppressive history, interpersonally and socially, unleash a powerful healing force in the world. Activating this force requires men of goodwill to listen to our sisters and even abdicate some of our power to them because men have exploited our position in almost every global culture that exists. One need not be a feminist to understand that.

PREACHING TO THE CHOIR

Matthue Roth

Back in high school, all my friends were girls. It just ended up that way. I went to a special-admissions high school which required a hundred different tests before they would let you attend. So, in addition to the standard teenage insecurities—girls don't like me, boys think I'm gay, my clothes suck, I don't know enough about pop culture, pop culture doesn't speak to me in the first place—we also had to deal with academic insecurities. You were afraid you were smarter than everyone else and that made you weird. You were also afraid that you weren't smart enough, that you didn't deserve to go to this special school, that all your good academic grades only came from going to a sucky ass school in a dead-end white trash part of town where people only knew math in terms of football scores.

In high school, I couldn't deal with dating. Instead I made girl friends— that is, girl-*space*-friends. I hung out with girls all the time. My best friend was a girl who liked girls. That made it easier to have a crush on her, since I'd never have to do anything about it or worry about rejection or disappointment or the politics of juggling school and friends and a lover. It was all so much to fit in my brain.

The times that I still hung out with guys, between classes and in my synagogue's youth group, everyone thought I was incredibly lucky. The youth group at my synagogue was trying to make us all Orthodox zealots. They encouraged us to follow more stringent rules, to obey the minutiae of all the laws, and to behave modestly. Friendship between boys and girls, they told us, was something we'd grow out of. When I came to youth group events with stories about my best girl friend's new girlfriend and the Saturday night riot grrrl show at the 40th Street Unitarian Church, they were scandalized. They wanted to know everything.

The reality was a lot calmer. I loved the high of telling people about riot grrrl, even though I wasn't sure if it was a genre of music, a political movement, or a crowd of friends. Really, it was all of them. It was sexy to see a bunch of all-girl bands in short, skanky skirts screaming about empowerment and taking over the world. It seemed like it would be a fun world.

It was even sexier to be at the concerts. We hung out on South Street and I learned how to sit and walk like a girl. The girls I knew, the ones I knew from school and, more often, the girls were friends of friends whose names were a blur of first letters in my mind, were like a backdrop, a hundred nameless teachers who totally made me into the person I am. They spoke in lisps and half-formed sentences when they wanted to be vague, and then they could be exact and verbose and brainy when they spoke to each other.

They used their submissiveness as a form of control. They acted helpless on the pay phones with their much-older semi-asshole boyfriends, "I can't come see *you* cause I'm out of money—*please*, baby, come to South Street and pick me up? Oh, and could you stop at Harmony and get some vegetarian General Tso?"

They loaned me their Bikini Kill and Babes In Toyland and Liz Phair tapes, and I played them on my new sports Walkman (bright yellow, but I stuck band stickers all over the case so it didn't look trendy) on the long bus ride home to the Northeast. I had to transfer buses at Five Points in front of a place called the Imperial, which had a neon and plastic sign that said *King of the Go-Go Bars*. My family used to drive by on the way home when I was a kid, and I always thought it meant like candy bars. Then one day on the subway, Cristin was talking about the place as a strip joint and everything suddenly connected.

Every day after that, I waited for my bus on the dirty red brick stoop in front of the Imperial, watching the sad-looking women, mascara stained into their eyes in black rings that looked permanent. I wanted to tell them about Bikini Kill's radical activist messages, and that not all men suck. But I never did.

Cristin rode with me to Five Points, then she took the bus the other way, toward the suburbs. Sometimes she'd wait in front of the Imperial with me and talk until one of our buses showed up and we ran wildly across Cottman Avenue to catch it. It would take a while, though, twenty or thirty minutes, because Philly buses are so bad. While we waited, Cristin catalogued the songs that played inside the club. Usually it was loud, guitar-solo based rock, which confused me because I thought dance music like Prodigy and The Electric Slide would be easier to strip to. But sometimes it would be something weird, something we identified with, like Nirvana or "Hurt" by Nine Inch Nails. Once, they played a Tori Amos song. We looked at each other and Cristin took my hand under our big heavy coats and we both wanted to cry.

I went to a different city for college, Washington D.C., where everything was bigger and all the architecture was classical Greek like a history textbook. I went there on a whim because Washington seemed like a good idea. I could work at the Smithsonian and hang out at the monuments late at night and go clubbing in Dupont Circle, where all the gay people lived.

But, when I got to the university, this homogeneously white student body who wore polo shirts and backwards baseball caps stared at me. Nobody got me. I'd been so sure I could survive anything. I was punk rock. When I went to concerts, it was rougher than their gym workouts. Girls who didn't like boys liked me.

In college, none of this mattered. If the frat boy prototypes were impressed by me, they didn't show it. If they were frightened by me, well, they only showed it by staying far, far away.

I was marooned in this ocean of straightness. Not even straightness—straight-*laced*-ness. I wasn't sure how to find the queer kids—not because I needed to come out as gay or find a boyfriend or anything, but because I had this pretty solid notion that gay people had more fun. They stayed up later and dressed better and went out more and I even think their beer tasted better.

I remembered this place we went in high school, called the Attic. It was a Friday afternoon club that was held in a municipal building so queer kids could meet each other. They must have something like that in college.

They did. I went to the fourth floor of the Student Center, where all the club offices were. There was a Straight and Gay Alliance, a GLBT Student Union, and Womyn's Issues Now. The first sounded too much like a PBS documentary, and the second, a Gay/Lesbian/Bisexual/Transgendered Student Union, was probably where all the gay kids went to find dates. Womyn's Issues Now had the appeal of being hard core ("the boy in Womyn's Issues Now!") and they were probably more into making each other Ani DiFranco mix tapes and planning the revolution than in sleeping with each other. I scribbled down their meeting place and time in my three-ring binder.

The meeting was mercifully light on the New Age self-love. A dozen of us sat in a circle and I assessed their queerness and their likeability. There were a few bareheaded, bullish dykes with wire-rimmed glasses who might have looked promising if, like most of the juniors and seniors I'd seen around campus, they didn't look so old. Like, *legitimate* old. They almost looked like adults.

But there were a few best-friends-forever potentials. Enough to make me come back, anyway. At the beginning of the meeting I asked everyone if it was okay for me to be there and they looked at me like I was crazy. Affectionately, maybe. I had to stand up in front of everyone and say why I was there and what I expected out of Womyn's Issues Now. I said that I wanted to fight for women's rights and that I didn't usually spell *womyn* with a y but I could learn, and that all my friends were girls because I was kind of afraid of testosterone.

I started calling Monday nights my estrogen nights. We planned the revolution. We stuck pins in Barbie dolls and melted them, we played music loud on the beaten-up Womyn's Issues Now stereo, and everyone but me traded stories about dates from hell. The president and a bunch of her friends were Latina, and sometimes they would fall into Spanish, which I understood but couldn't keep up with. I became a backseat passenger in those conversations, and it felt natural, comfortable; conversation as a spectator sport.

The first step of the revolution was Take Back the Night, an all-women's march around campus, which Womyn's Issues Now did every year to protest how it's unsafe for a woman to walk alone at night. I always thought Washington was a liberal city, because cities are supposed to be liberal and because it wasn't that far from Philadelphia, but lots of students at the university were from the deep South, and about 90 percent of the students there wanted to hold political office some day, and so the student population ended up being very conservative and careful. One year, the Student Union showed the John Wayne Bobbitt porno movie at a campus party and thought it was no big deal. (Bobbitt's the guy who raped his wife who then cut off his penis.) Something as in-your-face as a women-only march fell somewhere between an earthquake and a volcano explosion.

As the date of the march approached, everyone on campus buzzed about it. My roommate, the president of his high school's Young Republicans chapter, requested a transfer down the hall. I started to hang posters that said "my body, my rules," and "Rape Stops Here" on the door and he wouldn't take them down, just added his own poster to the door, one that said "Vote! It Makes America Yours." When people in our hall asked him about Take Back the Night, and what was up with his bedroom door, he shrugged and said it was a free country.

Although I wasn't allowed to march, there was a rally before the march that everyone took part in. When the women marched, we would hold a men's workshop, and they wanted to put me in charge of that.

I cringed. Besides the inevitable New Age flair of a men's bonding group, it sounded kitschy and trite. I tried to bail out. "Maybe we shouldn't let men in at all?" I suggested at one meeting. The next week, I said I was going to be too traumatized after speaking at the rally. One Monday afternoon at lunch, Julia slid into the booth where I was eating. We made a deal that I would co-manage the men's group with her boyfriend Ward, a friendly, activist-positive stoner who was in Delta Thi.

"Delta Thi?" repeated Flora, the president, at our meeting that night.

Julia wasn't even one of the hardcore WIN members. She had long, blond hair and preppy clothes that screamed White America. But she was adamant, she insisted that Ward was cool and a feminist and, when she brought him in, most of the girls ended up liking him more than they liked Julia, big surprise.

Ward was tight. He got worked up whenever he talked about the men's bonding meeting, and he balled his big beery hands into fists and banged them on the table whenever we hit an idea that he really liked, "That so *ROCKS*!" he shouted, banging the table, and gave my back a friendly slap. Ward took everything at face value, never protested any of the menial tasks that the WIN girls gave him. Everybody used him for Xerox duty and made him wait in line to file all our permits. Ward took his orders and followed them, never complaining. Also, he never once questioned me about how I got involved in Womyn's Issues Now. I liked that about him.

I was working overtime on Take Back the Night, too. My favorite band in the universe was Fugazi, who lived in Washington and wrote a lot of lyrics about politics and social issues. They had this song "Suggestion" that was about rape—"Why can't I walk down the streets/Free of suggestion," Ian MacKaye moaned in his raging howl, filled with righteous aggression. He slammed the shit out of his guitar on the breakdown—angry, but justifiably angry. Like he thought singing this song could really beat the sexism out of America. Back in Philly, in high school, Becky Aaronson told me that Ian MacKaye was listed in the D.C. phone book and you could just look him up and call him. Looking him up was one of the first things I did when I arrived in Washington. But calling him was another story. I mean, it was cool enough to know that your teen idol was reachable, real enough to be in the white pages. I didn't need to tell him how cool I thought that was—for a while, it was enough to know that I could.

But now I had a reason to reach out and touch.

I called and got the answering machine. I think it was actually the number for his record label. But I left a message and we played phone tag back and forth, and I still have the first sheet of paper that said *While You Were Out/Mr. Ian MacKaye of Dischord Records called* and I still think he's incredible. Even if they did have to play a show in Finland on the night of Take Back the Night, we tried to work it out, me and my heroes.

On campus, things were heating up even more. For years, two fraternities had shoes dangling on the trees outside their frat houses. At the beginning of the year, rumors started that each pair of shoes represented a woman who'd had sex with two different frat brothers. Nobody knew if it was true, although the frats always said it was. In October, a bunch of frat brothers were quoted about it the school paper. We rerouted the march to stop in front of each of the trees and the frat houses. We scheduled a moment of silence in front of SAE, this one frat house that the university refused to do anything about, even though there were reports that the upstairs bedrooms could only be opened from the outside, and once a girl was in there, she couldn't get out unless the brothers allowed her to.

Everything was escalating. In the tiny WIN office, which we shared with two other student groups, we fielded calls daily from local newspapers around the country, and the *Washington Post* and a few other heavy players. None of us knew anything about being quoted, what you were allowed to say and what people expected from us when we gave interviews. Flora got in trouble, minor trouble, for quoting someone directly when she actually said "And then the Dean told me blah blah blah," but for the most part, we were incredibly lucky that the frats didn't send lawyers after us. This girl Jess and I wrote to the *New*

York Times and William Safire devoted a column to telling us how lame we were. It only made us more ecstatic. We were getting trashed by the big guys.

Meanwhile, I was dreading the men's workshop more each day. I didn't have any ideas for it.

"That's okay, man," said Ward. His voice wobbled with empathy.

Ward told me that he was planning a massive video demonstration. "Trust me," he said, that stoner determination shining in his eyes. He had pages and pages of notes, ideas for camera angles, script pages written in that artistic furor that nobody but the artist will ever be able to read. He let the pages fly open at the Womyn's Issues Now meeting that night. We were all impressed. He was our Golden Child.

I trusted him. I scribbled a list of three or four topics we could discuss at the Men's Workshop, just in case, and left the rest to him.

That night, after the speeches and the rally and everything we'd planned, I watched the cavalcade of women careening down H Street, the main street of the university. I felt a little lost. The sight was overwhelming—imagine your school or office or the place you see affluent assholes smoking and cruising and eating hot dogs every day, and then imagine it overrun with hundreds of women singing your favorite song, all together, off a photocopied sheet, and you'd get chills, too.

Everyone poured themselves into that microphone. Flora spoke about how her family in Lima sent her out of the country after she told them she was gay. Julia talked about feeling like a sex object and how this professor had offered her an automatic A if she would unbutton her shirt in his office. I thought about going up and telling my story, too, but it didn't feel like the right time.

We opened the mic to everybody, and people from the crowd stepped forward. This girl talked about being raped in the SAE house, and we cried even though none of us had ever met her before. She wore a J. Crew blazer and a white baseball hat, the kind of girl none of us would even think of being friends with. There were all these guys there that night, too, some friends of mine from classes, some frat honchos spying on us, and some people who just walked by and watched. The crowd was huge, numbered in the hundreds.

And now I watched the guys, slipping away, going to their regular Thursday night clubs or dinners or whatever they had planned. I wanted to call after them or catch them in a giant fishnet, drag them inside. I could feel Ward's work going for nothing. My WIN sisters were all bonding under the stars, and I was about to endure the men's workshop. I hoped Ward wasn't planning on holding hands and singing Kumbaya.

I went in. There were six or seven guys sitting there. I didn't know any of them and I don't think Ward did either. The lights were off, and a tranquil blue screen was broadcasting on the wall, reflecting off all their faces.

Ward cleared his throat. "Hi, everyone," he said. "This is an average day in a woman's life. As we watch this, I'd like for you to stop and think about what it's like to be a woman in our society, and all the hardships they have to endure."

He pressed play.

A picture of K Street appeared. The camera was at eye level, Georgetown in the distance, cars passing occasionally. The camera moved forward. The cameraman was walking down K Street.

We watched. The camera bounced, jagged, uncertain. My skin started crawling, like it does before bad things happen.

Minutes passed by. Ward—the cameraman—turned down 23rd Street. Somebody coughed.

"Uh, what is the point of this video?" someone else asked, in a high, nasal voice. From the way he annunciated *video*, you could tell he was expecting something more cinematic.

"You're supposed to *imagine*," Ward said. "When a woman walks down the street, there is not a single moment of peace. Everyone is checking her out. She is constantly being evaluated by her physical appearance and *nothing else*, and we can't even, like, *get* it."

"Uh, right," said the challenging guy, like he didn't buy a word of it.

"Did you shoot this yourself?" somebody else asked.

"I did," Ward replied.

"So what you did is you walked down the street?"

"Uh, yeah," Ward said, on the defensive. "But you see how the people aren't paying any attention to me? It's *male privilege*."

"But imagine," I floundered, trying to come to Ward's defense, "imagine if he was a woman. Or even if he was wearing a dress, or in—drag, I guess"— Ward's shoulders were broad, his beard scruffy and Phishlike, it was hard to imagine him ever looking like a woman—"and imagine how easy our lives are, just by being born male. Isn't it fucked up?"

Ward stopped the tape and flipped on the lights. This seemed to be as good a time as any to start the discussion.

"So, what do you all think?" I said.

There was a beat.

One guy, the nasal-voiced one, stood up like it was Catholic school. He cleared his throat. "I find it utterly wrong that men are not allowed to take part in the Take Back the Night march," he announced.

I sighed. There had been two editorials that week in the school newspaper about men in the march.

"Yeah, it sucks. But men can already walk the streets alone and it's not nearly as dangerous. Tonight, we're just trying to *reconnect*." Reconnect. I was pulling out my Zen vocabulary.

"Well, I think we should start a petition," suggested another man who hadn't spoken yet at all. He pulled out a clipboard with an official masthead and spaces for names, telephone numbers, and email addresses. "This is from the International Socialist Organization. We strongly support anti-rape activities, and we oppose any organization that discriminates based on sex, racism, or attempts to fight the working man!" He passed it to the next man, who eagerly scribbled down his name and relevant information. Then *that* guy handed it straight to Ward, who was looking more perturbed by the minute.

"Hey, guy," said Ward. "How about if we put this on hold till *after* we share our feelings?"

"These *are* our feelings," said the second man. "I support the International Socialist Organization in all their campus activities. I think it's a travesty that less than 2 percent of all students on campus are registered socialists."

That was about when I realized he was wearing an International Socialist T-shirt. I grabbed the clipboard and looked at the names on the paper. "Can I ask how many of you all are from the ISO?"

Nervously, hesitantly, all the men in the room besides Ward and me raised their hands.

"Well," I said, standing up, "I think that about covers it for the night."

Ward and I started packing up his camera equipment and the bowl of sour cream and onion potato chips we'd brought, thinking that free food might open people up. One of the socialists tried to snag a handful on the way out, but Ward shot him an I-can-beat-you-up look.

We walked around for a while outside. Ward and I each carried a bag of equipment slung over our shoulder. We circled the campus, avoiding the places where the march was supposed to stop. Ward popped into a liquor store for a second and emerged with a big emerald bottle of malt liquor that was barely tucked into a brown paper bag. We continued on that street, turned, wound around an office building that predated the Declaration of Independence and crossed back into campus. We ended up on a red brick wall outside a shopping center, across from the vigil where the Take Back the Night march ended. Hundreds of candles burned on the quad, with silhouettes of women sitting with their heads bowed, voices talking too quiet for us to hear.

Ward cracked open the bottle, took a deep gulp, and passed it to me. I took a swig and handed it back.

"So that's what it was," said Ward. "Crazy night, huh?"

"Fuckin' A."

"You're really into all this shit, man. What do you do all it for, anyway?"

I grabbed the bottle, swilled some, let it sit in my mouth. Small carbonated bubbles popped against the roof of my tongue. I swallowed.

Someone tried to rape my best friend when I was fifteen, is what I wanted to say. For the first time in years, I actually felt like telling someone. In my mouth the beer tasted fresh, cool, like soda water.

"They're cool to hang out with," I said. "They're fun and they listen to good music. And they're all dykes, so it's not like I can make out with one of them and fuck up my friendships with everyone else."

"Makes sense." Ward contemplated this. We both stared across the street in silence, watching the individual candles flicker.

After a while, he was the one to break the silence. "They're really all lesbians?"

"Mostly."

"And you never wanted to get with any of them?"

"Nope."

"Do you think any of them are hot?"

I stared hard at the murky silhouettes of women across the street, wondering if I could see the outline of their breasts. I couldn't. From this far away, they all looked like dolls.

"Julia is. No offense—I mean, not like I'd *get* with her or anything, but she is. We tell each other our secrets and insecurities and stuff, and it makes us all so vulnerable to each other. So, no. Even if they were straight, I couldn't get with any of them. It would feel too sleazy."

The crowd of women across the quad shifted. Silhouettes of people were standing up, candles were being huffed out. Ward drained his beer, tossed it into a recycling bin, and we hopped off the brick wall. We walked silently to Dupont Circle, where Flora's apartment was. We walked slowly, so we wouldn't be the first ones to get there.

The next few weeks were a blur of events in sped-up motion. None of us was ready for the backlash from the administration and the frats, even Ward's frat, who egged the WIN office and denounced us as freak radicals and whistle-blowers, and the national newspaper columnist who said Flora had overblown estrogen, or the article in *Playboy*, which didn't come out till the summer, anyway, that treated the whole thing like a joke with no punchline. The matter of the shoe trees would actually come before the president of the university, that squirmy walrus of a man who had actually attacked students in print before. He dismissed it, saying that it was a student prank on both sides and he didn't want to get involved.

And then there was the court case. A few weeks after our protest, Flora was running late for her Environmental Geology final, running across Fraternity Row. It was a fall day, almost winter, the sky overcast and the weather a second away from rain. Washington D.C. gets blustery in the early winter, blustery enough to blow trash cans around and untie American flags from their poles and, even, blustery enough to knock a single shoe off the SAE shoe tree.

It nailed Flora straight in the head.

The event was witnessed by a handful of brothers from other frats, along with an entire class of third-grade students, whose teacher had wanted to show them the trees that grew shoes, unaware of the whole controversy. Flora, quick as a whistle, called the city police on her cell phone. They subsequently fined the frat for misuse of municipal property—the trees, that is, which sat on the sidewalk that belonged to the city of Washington—and the frat paid an undisclosed amount to Flora for podiatric assault. She could have sued, but she still wasn't a U.S. citizen, and also, it was a soft-tip shoe and she didn't even have a bruise.

The money Flora got wasn't a lot, but it was enough to fly her home to see her mother on a long weekend, and enough to get Womyn's Issues Now through the next few months of funding, now that the administration had an official reason to resent us.

Take Back the Night had wiped most of us out, and everyone on campus was freaked out enough by the shoe tree incident, so that we were all feeling, more or less, like we'd made our mark. When spring came, and the D.C. sky turned from a cold, dingy gray to a bright, at-least-it's-not-raining type of gray, and people started coming out of their dorm rooms at night again, we threw a coffeehouse—a little impromptu event with a rented espresso machine in the rec room of one of the dorms.

Flora brought a full-size xylophone onstage and played a note-perfect rendition of "You're So Vain." Julia did birdcalls from several varieties of New England finches. Karen read aloud from *The Color Purple*.

"So," said Flora, who'd been hosting the afternoon. "Does anyone else have anything to do?"

I took a breath. I walked onstage. Those three wooden steps leading to the slightly raised platform in the bottom of Riverside Hall Cafe had never seemed so steep, or so intimidating. I could feel sharp inhalations of breath; I was sure that, with every step I climbed, people were walking out of the theater, ready to move onto the rest of their evenings.

But one way or another, I was standing in front of that fuzz-heavy microphone, staring at the audience, and I saw that it was just the other Womyn's Issues folks. It had only been them all along.

I closed my eyes, and it felt like it was just me and Cristin, sitting on that stoop outside of school.

And I started to talk.

"When I was fifteen," I said, "my best friend was sexually assaulted."

I don't know if that was why I started hanging out with girls. I don't know if that's why I wanted to do all this antiviolence work, so it would never happen to anyone else again, or if that was why I felt this security around lesbians, girls who there'd never be a threat of sexuality with. But I leaned up against that microphone like it was an ear to whisper into, and I did my poem.

the way girls learn how to make boys
work for them
i learned how to make girls
hide me away
i was the ultimate stuffed animal,

buried deep in their beds
but afraid to
try
anything.

It was a different kind of activism. That afternoon, we weren't trying to bring a capital-I Issue to anyone's attention, we weren't fighting anything in specific, and we weren't trying to save people's lives, except maybe our own. But it might have been more important than getting that shoe tree knocked down; might have been more powerful or emotional or passionate or just plain meaningful than the protest that day, or any protest that any of us had ever attended. Sometimes, you need to fight a war, and sometimes, you need to take a moment to reassure yourself that you're not a casualty of one.

The rest of the Womyn's Issues Now people and I, we weren't those college friends who kept in touch forever. We graduated different years, faded slowly from each other's lives, passed into the rest of our own. We were like old combat buddies: You have a mission to do. You do it. And you dust your hands off, drop your gun at the base, and get back to the rest of your life.

Did we change anything, doing what we did? Did we make anyone realize what was wrong with the system, what was so fundamentally fucked up about the shoe trees?

Maybe not. Maybe we were just preaching to the choir.

But maybe, sometimes, the choir needed to hear it.

THE STARBUCKS INTERVENTION

Greg Bortnichak

I'm the kind of twenty-something guy you would expect to work in a coffee shop. I play guitar and cello in an experimental punk band and have some cool downloads on Myspace. I'm tall and lean, with an explosive mess of dark hair that makes me look like the love child of Edward Scissorhands and Blacula. Most people correctly guess that I'm artistic and a bit to the political left.

What they may not realize is that I am a self-defined male feminist. Being a feminist is mighty powerful stuff because staying true to ideals about equality and justice involves consciously altering the way I behave. The bottom line is that I try to reject personal acts of subjugation, and I do my best to combat the systems that enable others to be oppressive. As the saying goes, the personal is political.

My brand of feminism is all about not imposing patriarchal power on the women in my life, and hoping to set an example for the boys and men I meet.

From the time I was seven and too short to play ball with the big kids, to the time I was thirteen and too sensitive to party with the cool kids, to now when I struggle with masculinist ideology, I have always felt that dominant culture only truly benefits a select few. So I do my best to reject it. I do it for me. I do it for my partner, and for every man who feels alienated by the expectations that culture places on guys who do not quite fit the "man's man" mold. I do it for anyone who feels constrained by the music videos on MTV because they see both women and men reduced to sexual commodities. But the question remains, *how do I do my feminism*? And, more importantly, how am I a *male* feminist?

It's tricky. And the truth is that a lot of time I feel friction between being a man and being a feminist. Problems come up when I want more than anything to take feminist action—to act in defense of someone who is being victimized by patriarchal power—but my aid is unwelcome or inappropriate or potentially does more political harm than good.

Allow me to illustrate: I work at Starbucks. I spend roughly twenty hours each week serving coffee to strangers, sometimes as many as several hundred each day. And you better believe I see it all. Customers reveal all kinds of personal details. So do my co-workers. I put up with a lot from them: sexist and racist jokes, routine descriptions of masculinist sexploitation, flat-out ridicule for my feminist views. And at the end of the day when my feet feel like they're ready to fall off, and my entire body reeks of espresso grinds, I think back and try to make sense of it.

Winter 2006

A customer comes in and begins telling us about this scheme he has to buy a wife. What he really wants to do is hire a housekeeper, but he thinks it's funnier if he tells us that he's wife shopping today. He complains about doing housework, saying he'd rather pay a cute, young girl twenty bucks an hour to do his chores for him rather than do them himself, or worse, get re-married to have yet another woman sit at home all day, take his money, and bitch at him when gets home from work. He keeps saying there is nothing worse than married life, to which the guys I'm working with chuckle in agreement. The only girl working at the time, Joy, is offended. She tells the customer that marriage won't be bad at all for her husband—she will do all the housework and more (wink, wink) for her husband. For free. Joy wants to be a housewife, and she gives me a hard time for being feminist. The customer tells Joy that she's sweet but that she won't be sweet forever. He's expecting his purchased "wife" to be totally obedient and pleasant every hour of every day. Then, as an afterthought, he mentions that he has no problem getting his "non-domestic" (wink, wink) needs met elsewhere for not much more than it's going to cost him to buy this wife of his.

Later, my girlfriend, Ana, decides to come by and do some homework, keeping me company as I work. She is sitting alone in a far corner, completely engrossed in her studies. A man with slicked-back silver hair, white guy, probably in his fifties, and appearing to be quite wealthy (gold jewelry, designer golf shirt, the works) steps into line and begins staring at Ana. He makes no effort to hide this, and gets out of line to walk around behind her and get a better look. Then he gets back into line and cranes his neck to see down her shirt and up her dress. I see all of this, and I'm simultaneously disgusted and pissed off. He's such trash. I would love to call him out, or lay him out right then and there, but I risk losing my job if I'm rude to the customers. So I bite my tongue. It gets to be his turn in line and he still won't stop staring at her, not even to place his order. He's holding up the line, people behind him are starting to get flustered, and I lose it.

"What's so interesting over there, Sir? You seem to be looking very intently at something," I ask as innocently as I possibly can. "That girl in the corner," he says like he's ready to eat her. He doesn't take his eyes off Ana once. "Oh yeah, what do you think?" I'm trying now to sound as sleazy as I possibly can in an attempt

to lead him to believe that I'm going along with the shameless objectification of Ana. "I think she's a real pretty girl in that little dress of hers." He licks his ugly thin lips and makes a face that screams "pervert." I've caught him red-handed at his patriarchal bullshit, and at this point, I'm done: "Well I think she's a friend of mine, and I think she'd feel violated if she knew you were staring at her like that." I say it low and threateningly beneath my breath so as to not cause a scene. "I think she should get used to it," he replies. There is no hint of apology in his tone. It's like I'm wrong for telling him not to lech at a girl who could be his fucking granddaughter! I glare at him like I want to burn a hole in his face with my eyes and growl, "I think you need to learn a little respect." He leaves. I'm shaking.

I go to Ana and ask her if she saw what just transpired. She says no, that she was completely unaware. When I tell her what happened she is visibly upset. She thanks me for sticking up for her and waits for me to finish my shift without returning to her homework. The woman in line behind the silver-haired man approaches me before leaving and wishes me goodnight, smiling at me in a way that I could only interpret as solidarity.

That night I had nightmares about the silver-haired man. He was so ruthless in how he visually dismembered Ana that he put me in touch with a very distinct fear. No one had ever made me so mad, or provoked such a reaction from me. But was it even my place to step in on Ana's behalf? Was I being over-protective? Despite Ana's appreciation for my fast action, I still could not get this encounter out of my mind. The silver-haired man obviously saw nothing wrong with what he did. I even had a co-worker poke fun at me for bothering that "poor old man." The woman in line behind the silver-haired man was my best assurance—as iffy as it was—that speaking up was the right thing to do.

Yet I could not help but feel unsettled about how I chose to respond. After all, I don't doubt that if Ana looked up at the right time, she would have reacted more strongly and defended herself far better than I. And if Ana had been the one to terminate the encounter, perhaps she would have a stronger feeling of closure or justice. I had to wonder what it meant that I defended Ana instead of simply bringing her attention to what was happening. Did my chivalrous feminism reflect some duty I feel to protect her? And if so, does that mean that on some level I think she is incapable of protecting herself? Even worse, what if my actions actually revealed a sense of possession or ownership over Ana? And what about that burst of anger I felt? How stereotypically masculine to feel angry in light of something another man did to my girlfriend. This encounter with the silver-haired man raises so many difficult questions for me about whether pro-feminist men ought to step in to help women or instead focus our efforts on enabling women to protect themselves.

On the night of the scuffle in Starbucks, Ana happened to be wearing a gorgeous dress that was short, with a very low neckline. She has gotten upset in the past over men leering at her when she wears this dress. Sometimes I think about gently suggesting to Ana that she shelve the dress, but I don't think it's my place to say so. I do not want Ana to continue feeling violated by these tactless creeps but, at the same time, I do not want her to compromise her own sense of beauty, self-expression, and sexuality. I also don't want to be perceived as controlling or paternalistic. It is not Ana's fault that some men feel it's their right to stare crudely at young women. But still, it upsets Ana, and it happens less when she does not wear this particular dress. It is clear who is at fault. It's the voyeurs like that silver-haired man at Starbucks. But if men like that deny responsibility, and if women have the right to wear whatever they damn-well please, and if I happen to see what's going on, then shouldn't I step in and speak my mind?

I've run into a dilemma: It's true that men can deflect unwanted attention, but in doing so we risk offending or patronizing women who are capable of protecting themselves, or insulting women who like this sort of thing. I know that some women rely on the male gaze to feel attractive and some may dress in ways to get attention on purpose. Women have the right to express themselves through their clothes and demeanor in any way they see fit. But I risk sounding sexist if I advise a girl not to go to certain parts of the city looking a certain way, and I risk feeling guilty knowing someone could get hurt if I don't speak up.

The problem lies in knowing when it's okay to intervene; in knowing when to act on my personal feminist beliefs, and knowing when to hold back. Mastering this discretion is something I grapple with each day. Sometimes I get to thinking that I'm setting myself up for an unconquerable task by trying to live the life of an active male feminist. Sometimes it feels so daunting that I consider giving up. But then I remember what got me here in the first place, and it gives me hope. Feminism is something I embrace because it helps me think more clearly about who I am and how I behave as a man in this society. When I keep this in mind, I understand that I'm not about to defeat the patriarchy overnight, but that I can feel a little better knowing I'm not letting it defeat me little by little, each and every day.

THIS IS WHAT A FEMINIST LOOKS LIKE

Derrais Carter

When I entered college I fell in love with two things: hip hop culture and feminism. Surprisingly enough, hip hop led me to feminism. There are a lot of people who see this as impossible. I have been told that my support of a culture that condones continuous references to women as bitches and chickenheads strips me of my title as a feminist. That is one opinion and I can respect it. However, I am quick to acknowledge that hip hop is about more than labeling women. It's a history of the lived experiences of various ethnic groups and classes. It is art, love, hate, envy, exploitation, and more. It is a battlefield of identity. With that said, there is clearly more to hip hop than some would claim. For me, embracing this culture has opened my eyes to new realities. Feminism happened to be one of them.

The first rap tape I owned was by Snoop Dogg. I found it when I was eight years old. I listened to the lyrics, and I thought to myself, "Who is this and what is he talkin' 'bout?" I quickly rejected rap while my twin brother embraced it. I was always the R&B twin and Snoop wasn't my style. This split continued for years until I got into poetry. I started watchin' *Russell Simmon's Def Poetry* on HBO—most definitely a part of hip hop culture. I fell in love with sistahs like Sarah Jones and Georgia Me. These women ushered me into an arena that projected strong woman in such a way that I just had to know what they were fighting. To hear these two artists combat the labels imposed on them by society brought an air of respectability and desire at the same time. All of a sudden, I'm like "Damn, I need to get it together." I don't want to be that "nigga" who acts so stereotypical that I no longer recognize myself as the somewhat confident, respectable, black man my family raised me to be. I want to be more than that. Better yet, I want the people around me to feel the same. I began re-examining my CD collection.

I casually started going through my computer to see what music I had saved. Next thing I know, I'm loading tracks by Erykah Badu and Lauryn Hill on my mp3. It didn't stop there, though. I wanted to find males who could hit me with the same shit. I started looking at the usual suspects: Talib Kweli, Mos Def, Common, and, surprisingly, Jay-Z. These artists helped me develop a broader perspective on my daily interactions with women. I began to critically assess my relationships with the people in my life to determine whether they were healthy or not. I found that attraction was more than some pornographic objectification. It was a mental and spiritual connection that these artists alluded to. Eventually, the outlook manifested by these musicians fostered a sense of respect for all women. I began to see women as more than a video prop, extra, and eye candy. I saw them as highly misrepresented figures in society who I had been conditioned to mistreat and ignore.

I often tell my friends that women in hip hop captured my mind and fostered a new appreciation for the black experience. Looking back, I see that artists like Lauryn Hill, Sarah Jones, and Erykah Badu helped me solidify my identity as an up-and-coming activist-scholar and as a black male. Their voices took hold of me in indescribable ways. They project an aura of strength and symbolize areas that I try to explore through feminism.

Discussing the position of women in hip hop beyond the camera's "Hottentot gaze" helps me understand a lot about black male identity. Selfishly, I am drawn to feminism because of this very thing. Feminism teaches me about my position in society. In listening to the songs of these women, I look at myself in a whole new light. Don't get me wrong, I understand the realities they are exploring as women; however, I see these songs as dialogues between the artist and listener. These women are teaching me about love, pride, abuse, destruction, and restoration. They are also teaching me about my role as an ally.

As a black male in college, I am often assumed to be on an athletic scholarship. When I wear my "This Is What a Feminist Looks Like" T-shirt, people have accused me of trying to get laid. Others have said the same about my former position as an office assistant at the campus Women's Center. I have battled this sort of thing for quite some time. I used to get angry about it. Now I see these comments as mere ignorance and the failure to accept that there are men who truly care about women's issues.

In spite of all that I get out of feminism, however, nothing is above criticism. To paraphrase Martin Luther King, Jr., there can be no serious critique where there is no great love. Feminism teaches me a lot but, still, it isn't perfect, and I think it's important that we scrutinize the foundations and perspectives of feminism. Doing this, though, can be risky—especially as a man. Let me explain:

I recently attended a campus roundtable discussion that addressed students' academic projects. My friend Chris presented his work on the negative representations of women in hip hop videos. Surprisingly, his reference to feminism angered the black women in the room. They argued that he should use the term womanist—not feminist—to define what he was doing. Their reasoning was that womanism transcends factors such as race and incorporates a more spiritual dimension. Others in the room criticized Chris because they thought he should use the term black feminism. The whole situation quickly went from a setting for providing constructive feedback to a vicious debate over one specific word. The message was loud and clear: The internal debates over feminism took priority over the substantive issues that Chris wanted to explore. As it happened, Chris and I got caught in the verbal crossfire. It didn't help that Chris also wanted to investigate the limitations of feminism as an analytical tool. In the end, it came down to different women getting offended because he was a male critiquing feminism while exploring black womanhood in hip hop.

Both of us left the discussion feeling pretty disappointed. The arguments showed us how we, as men, could easily be written off as feminist advocates simply because a few people didn't agree with the terminology, or with who was doing the research.

Despite the group's criticism, though, I wouldn't change my political position at all. Being a feminist has provided a platform for change in my life as well as the lives of others. This is where I believe it is important to discuss hip hop culture and its place within feminism. When we discuss women in hip hop, the dominant theme is the video girl who is watched and the man who objectifies her. I think feminism can help us go beyond that. We might openly acknowledge, for example, the importance of black women's social position and the structural determinants that produce the video girl. We could discuss the role of black beauty in an environment that constantly narrows the lens of beauty. Hell, we could argue about the complexity of black womanhood and the expectations of American culture. The possibilities are endless.

I stand tall as a self-proclaimed, black, male feminist. This title is important to me. It reminds me of my responsibilities in regard to the treatment of women, and the importance of respect and dignity. Valuing women's roles as mothers, daughters, wives, lovers, doctors, artists, writers, beauticians, counselors, teachers, scholars, activists, leaders, employers, organizers, and humans is central to appreciating their contributions to society. Feminism means that I see values and qualities instilled in women that I wish were instilled in men, like articulating emotions publicly without fearing accusations of inferiority. Just imagine the kind of shift that would create. Who knows what possibilities it could bring. I feel bell hooks when she discusses black love and I dream of the ties it could create in various communities. This, to me, is the very essence of feminism.

I believe that there will be a shift in the ways we view feminism, the way we see women in hip hop, and how we understand the role of black men in feminism. This is a starting point for a lot of brothas out there. Don't forget the message in the music, the power of the voice, or the strength of feminism. This is what a feminist looks like.

FROM OPPRESSOR TO ACTIVIST: REFLECTIONS OF A FEMINIST JOURNEY

Amit Taneja

My gay friends say I'm part of the "family," but sometimes strangers call me "fag."
I was born in India, but I have been called a "sand n****r."
I became a Canadian citizen recently, but I am still called an "Indo-Canadian."
I am working on my doctorate, but I anticipate being in large debt for my education through my late forties.
I am Hindu, but I am often asked if I have found Jesus.
I am fluent in English, but it is my fourth language.
I am big boned, but I am often mistaken as fat and unhealthy.
I work legally in the U.S., but my official status according to the government is "Alien Employee."

INTRODUCTION

As a poor, immigrant, big-boned, non-Christian, gay person of color who happens to be working in a country where Others are feared, some people would say that I have a lot going against me. And they would be right. However, despite all that works against me, I still feel that I have power. Correction: A lot of power. You see, I was born with a penis and I was taught early on that this simple fact meant I was inherently superior to about half of the human population. The mere sighting of my anatomy at birth outlined my destiny in this life as being smarter, taller, faster, stronger, funnier, and in general just "better" than women. That is what I was taught.

Despite all the messages that were bored into my brain about my supposed male superiority, I have come to a place of questioning, resisting, and actively changing the tape that plays as the background music in my head. I have come to fight the sexist messages that I was raised with and, more importantly, to duck and cover from, deflect, and strike back against the thousands of similar messages that come my way on a daily basis.

I write this essay as snapshots of a life-changing journey. It is not a complete story, or even chronological for that matter. But it is a story of important markers on my path of becoming a feminist. This journey brought me from a place of unquestioned male power and privilege to experiencing oppression myself. The journey ends at my resting place as a life-long, hard-core, die-hard, to-my-last-breath, capital "F" Feminist.

SNAPSHOT #1: GET YOUR BROTHER SOME WATER

Summers in India were hot, and while little girls helped their mommies cook and clean at home after school, little boys could run around being rascals, playing cricket, and flying kites. I remember coming home one afternoon after a long day of playing marbles with the other boys. No sooner had I entered the room, my mom asked my younger sister to get me a tall glass of water with ice. My sister resisted and complained, "Why do I have to get him water? He never gets me water when I come home!" My grandmother immediately chastised her, saying that such talk would keep her single all her life, and that she would never land a husband. (My grandmother was more right than she could have known. My sister is a lesbian and now walks around proudly wearing her "Well-Behaved Women Hardly Ever Make History" T-shirt.)

I remember this story about the water so vividly. I might have made a face at my sister while agreeing with my grandmother. Whatever my grandma said made a lot of sense to me at the time. I was brought up to believe that the man is the breadwinner, the decision maker, the provider, and the protector for his family. Women exist to serve the men and children in their lives. These notions made it seem reasonable that it was my sister's job . . . no, change that to duty . . . to bring me water.

I remember this story because of the way my sister looked at me. There was part contempt, part anger, some pain, and perhaps resignation to her fate as a woman. I don't know precisely what she was thinking, but I remember feeling guilty when she came back with a glass of water. I only took a sip (even though I was parched). Somehow I felt that I didn't deserve that glass of water just because I was a boy and she was a girl. But I knew that to question the system would be wrong. I put that event deep in my memory scrapbook, but the seeds of questioning my male privilege were planted for years to come.

SNAPSHOT #2: ISN'T 99 PERCENT GOOD ENOUGH?

Sonali Mehta* and I were good friends in high school in India. We had a fierce, but friendly, competition over who would get the top rank in math each semester. Sometimes I came out ahead, and sometimes she did. Many a teacher commented that Sonali was very gifted in math and sciences, *especially for being* *a girl*. We both tied with 96 percent on our preliminary practice tests before our provincial board exams at the end of twelfth grade. We both studied hard for our exams and the pressure was on for the final showdown. We took the exam and immediately compared notes. It seemed that Sonali and I both had the same answers to most of the questions.

Fast-forward. Two months later. We nervously opened our grade envelopes. I peeked with one eye open and saw my score was 97 percent in math. Another friend saw my grades and yelled over my shoulder, "Sonali, Amit got 97 percent. How did you do?"

All heads turned in our direction, and I saw Sonali sitting quietly with a tear running down her cheek. Oh no! This was supposed to be a friendly competition. She couldn't have done that bad to be crying! I went over to comfort her and saw her grades lying on her desk. Her crying became louder and more noticeable. The paper read, "Math 99 percent." I was really confused at this point. She got the highest marks, but yet she was sad. I asked why she was crying, and Sonali said that she was upset because she did not get a perfect score of 100 percent. I responded by saying, "You still have the highest grade in our class!" She quietly replied, "I am a girl. I am told over and over again that I am exceptionally good at math as far as girls go. I didn't want to be just exceptionally good. I wanted to be perfect; to prove them all wrong! You wouldn't understand." Suddenly it all made sense. And from that day on, I have cringed (and always confront people) when I hear the words "especially gifted for a girl."

SNAPSHOT #3: THE OPPRESSOR BECOMES OPPRESSED

It was the beginning of my freshman year in college, and my family and I had immigrated to Canada nine months earlier. I had a Presidential Full Tuition Scholarship in Engineering and I was determined to do well in school. I wanted to build bridges because they fascinated and scared me at the same time. While I was preparing for the adjustment to living on my own, I also became fascinated and scared by feelings of attraction toward men. I was actively exploring the idea of accepting my same-sex feelings and eventually "coming out" but, at the time, I felt very unsure.

I was sitting in the dorm lounge watching television during the first week of classes when a gay character came on the sitcom. One of my floormates said how much he hated fags, and another agreed by saying that he would "beat the crap out of any fag" he met. Uh oh! Cancel the coming out. I did not need to be hated on, much less beaten for being gay. The obvious path to avoid this was to deny all feelings for men and be as straight-acting and macho as I could.

I started out small by trying to be a heterosexual man (or what I thought it meant to be a heterosexual man). At first that meant making small comments about women, their bodies, their breasts. But that didn't seem enough. I kept thinking that "real men" would be able to see through my façade, so I had to step it up and be more macho than most men to prevent my dirty secret from emerging. I had to turn into Captain Hyper-Hetero, the imaginary superhero who safeguarded masculinity by being the manliest man possible.

I started talking more loudly in the presence of other men (while avoiding all contact with women). I kept telling others that I was looking for sexual adventures with women (okay it was a lot more graphic than that, but I choose not to repeat or remember the details). Soon word got around about my comments, and the women in my building were avoiding me because I was an all-around sexist jerk.

The plan was working. Men thought I was a player and women didn't want to have anything to do with me. Until one day a female neighbor reached out to me, and pointed out that my comments were hurtful, demeaning, and revolting. I was treating women like "meat," and that was not going to get me anywhere. I realized that I was causing harm and fear amongst the women who lived close to me. This was not really me. I was ashamed of what I had done. I just blurted out, "I am gay, and I am trying to hide behind this mask of being super straight." I knew at that moment that I had a critical choice to make and I could not lead a life of lies. More importantly, I could now relate to what it felt like to be oppressed. It was a life-altering moment, and I found love and forgiveness from the women around me when they heard my story. We stayed up late at night, eating ice cream and sharing stories of oppression and fear, while building dreams of a future filled with confidence and hope. And we also created a list of the most eligible bachelors in our dorm, but that is another story for another time.

SNAPSHOT #4: FITTING THE GENDER BOX

After the demise of Captain Hyper-Hetero I decided to come out more publicly. Life was good and I was trying to fit in with the straight world while finding my place within the gay community. The more out I became on campus, the more I was targeted by messages of homophobia from the straight community and racism and classism from the queer community. Straight men questioned my masculinity and often made assumptions that being gay meant that I had to be effeminate. It seemed like I didn't fit in completely in either the straight world or the gay world. I was too femme for the straight boys, and not femme enough for the pretty, out, campy, white, gay crowd. Drag queens in the gay bars were relentless in making fun of my outfit, my accent, and my looks. I dressed too breeder for their liking and I was told that I needed to "gay it up a little." I was told, "Go get some Abercrombie, honey!"

I went looking for Abercrombie clothing, but I could neither fit in it nor afford it. At the same time, the straight men (and sometimes straight women) would belittle the "queeny fags" and the "butch dykes." It seemed to me that if drag queens and butch dykes did not exist, then straight people would only see the "normal gays (and lesbians)" like me, and there would be little reason for them to hate us. I was being taught the message that those who transgress gender boundaries are bad and should be looked down upon. And I bought that message for a while (until I took women's studies courses, and things changed).

I realized through these experiences that the roots of homophobia lie in sexism. People are taught to be afraid of those who defy gender norms because doing so topples the power granted to men over women. Homophobia is an offshoot of sexist ideology, and even gay and lesbian people are not immune from homophobic thinking because sexism is active and alive in our society.

SNAPSHOT #5: BOYS GO TO COLLEGE

In 2001, I moved from Canada to the United States to pursue graduate studies. I recently shared with an American buddy of mine that being born in India (which is a very gender segregated society) I was exposed to numerous messages about male superiority from an early age. He thought that such thinking was "barbaric and idiotic," and he felt good knowing that we lived in a country where young children are not taught such gibberish. "Whoa, hold on a second. Is that really true?" I replied. "Are young children in the United States not taught notions of male superiority? I don't think it is a lot different here," I said. The messages about gender inequality are a lot more covert in U.S. culture, but they have the same effect.

My friend was not quite convinced so I shared with him the story of a recent visit to my partner's family in Ohio. My partner's brother has two children: a five-year-old boy named Colin and a four-year-old girl named Grace, who was asked by her parents to recite the new poem she'd been taught. In a shy tone she recited the following to us:

Boys go to college to get smarter
Girls go to Jupiter to get stupider

Grace's poem was met with a loud round of laughter from an assortment of adults including grandparents, uncles, aunts, and cousins. Everyone laughed except me. The smiling, laughter, and clapping following the performance signified to Grace that her poem was met with approval. In fact, later that night Grace offered to recite the poem again when new company arrived. It was heart-breaking and eye-opening to see that the adults in the room did not understand the significance of the message that was being taught to Grace and reinforced for everyone else.

From the time they are born, little boys and girls are taught gender "appropriate" behaviors, dress, and hobbies. But they are also taught to dream and aspire in gendered ways. It is no coincidence that little boys want to grow up to be firefighters, police, and pilots, while girls want to be princesses who live in Barbie's Dream House. I wonder what would happen to men and women's self-esteem and career aspirations if children were taught that they could be whatever they wanted to be. I think we should all dream of the day when good-minded men, women, and those in-between make a commitment to egalitarian parenting and continually striving to create social change.

SNAPSHOT #6: THE GLASS CUBICLE: COMPLICATING GENDER

During college, I worked at a fast food restaurant for three summers. Make that three l-o-n-g summers. Nicole,* a co-worker who had worked at the chain for five years, said that she was thinking of leaving. I asked her why, and she responded that she did not see herself getting promoted anytime soon. She explained that except for one woman who worked the weekend graveyard shift, all the managers were men. Nicole said that the vast majority of the male supervisors and managers had worked at the establishment for a lot less time than her, and that she was never promoted.

Frustrated from being passed over for a promotion several times, Nicole approached the owner with her concerns. He denied there was any sexism at play, and mentioned that the men who had been promoted were "just better workers." To prove his point he called a staff meeting and asked if anyone was unhappy with promotions or had any concerns. The owner was known to be moody and petty. Although several women had privately shared their frustrations with me, no one spoke up out of fear. The owner said that since no one had anything to say, there must not be a problem. All too often, silence is taken as a form of agreement when in reality the silence is saying a lot more. Nicole was shortly moved to the evening shifts which conflicted with her family commitments, and she quit within a month.

I share this snapshot because it had profound meaning for me. I always envisioned the glass ceiling as something that affected professional women like lawyers and MBAs. The truth is, though, that working-class women are even more prone to its effects. To this day, women still make around seventy-seven cents on the male dollar. This wage difference is exacerbated by race. And when we consider class, (dis)abilities, nationality, immigration status, and race, it becomes clear that some women don't just experience the vertical push of the glass ceiling. They're getting pressed from all sides. The glass ceiling doesn't tell the whole story: Some women's lives are confined within a small glass cubicle. Feminist ideology recognizes the complexities of how oppression affects us and involves a much larger lens than only women's rights.

SNAPSHOT #7: SEXISM WITHIN THE QUEER COMMUNITY

I was hanging out with some gay male friends, when one of them stubbed his toe and let out a cry of pain. One of the other men in the group yelled "Stop being a pussy and take it like a man!" Later that evening, another queer man claimed that he was "allergic to vagina in every way possible." When I pointed out the sexist and misogynistic undertones of their comments, these men became very defensive and claimed that they had little to nothing in common with women, and they couldn't care less about women's issues. Another one responded that he could "barely tolerate the dykes at the pride marches."

Unfortunately, these comments are part of many gay men's repertoires. Some gay men deal with gender and sexuality by either acting macho, or by being a "mean girl" and hating on other "bitches." While my friends claimed their comments were made in jest and with no ill intent, these words actually have a damaging effect on their individual psyches and on the soul of the queer rights and women's rights movements.

I've struggled to explain gay men's sexist behavior. Queer people are oppressed in many ways by heteronormative society. Maybe some gay men deal with this particular powerlessness by hanging onto their male privilege. Perhaps this is also why some white queers are unwilling to acknowledge their skin privilege and the racism within the gay community.

I think it is important for social justice activists to confront sexism within the queer community and challenge misogynistic thinking. There is a grave problem within our community when some gay men claim that they can "barely tolerate" lesbian women. Only certain people with social position have the power to "tolerate" another human being. Of all people, gay men should know what it feels like to be "tolerated." Those of us who don't have social power are often taught to hope for tolerance at best. For many of us, full inclusion and acceptance are not even on the menu of options. The gender split within the queer community needs to be addressed because our internal and external struggles are connected by sexist and misogynistic ideologies. I have hope that activism from the transgender, intersexed, and genderqueer community will help educate others in meaningful ways.

ACKNOWLEDGING AND RESISTING PRIVILEGE

The preceding seven snapshots portray my understanding of oppression and provide the foundation of my feminism. I want to bring this essay to a close by considering the biggest challenge in my journey to being a feminist: acknowledging and resisting privilege.

I experience oppression in a number of ways because of the intersection of my sexual orientation, race, ethnicity, national origin, class, language, and religion. As I said, I am a poor, big-boned, immigrant, gay man of color. Some days I feel the weight of the world on my shoulders. *I can't imagine what a day without oppression feels like.* Yet, still, I know that I have male privilege. The issues for me are multiple: How do I acknowledge and resist my male privilege? And why should I refuse one form of advantage when I am disenfranchised in so many others?

I've toyed with these ideas for a long time and here's what I've come up with: A common thread links all forms of oppression. It is not possible to fight just one form of oppression while neglecting others. And often we ignore how privilege and oppression are heavily mediated by class; that is, by the power and money that provide access to refuge and support, and open doors for people who are subjugated in other ways. This insight helps me reconcile my struggle between being multiply oppressed while also wanting to keep my male privilege.

I have learned that our personal decisions must reflect and support our political ideologies. We are not relieved from responsibility for politically conscientious action by claiming that our personal and political lives do not mix. Those of us who are oppressed don't have a choice. Our personal decisions are seen and treated as political, whether we want them to be or not! I cannot enter a same-sex marriage and expect that decision to be seen as politically neutral. Neither can I hold hands with my partner in public, nor try to be a foster parent without my actions having political meaning assigned to them.

The Advocate, America's largest gay and lesbian publication, recently posed the following question: "Is the gay community welcoming to people of color?" While I understand the intent of the question, I also see the implicit assumption that the gay community is white, and that white people have the power to accept (or tolerate) queer people of color. We need to problematize these assumptions and how we compartmentalize our identities. While some of our struggles may appear different on the surface, we are all connected through our intersecting identities and through the common experience of oppression.

We need to understand that there is no such thing as completely disconnected identities. Race, class, gender, sexual orientation, age—and all other signifiers of identity—intersect in meaningful and powerful ways to shape our individual and collective experiences. We must always talk about women's rights and gay and lesbian rights while also thinki g about xenophobia, classism, racism, transphobia, etc. Doing so allows us to acknowledge the existence of those of us who carry multiple burdens, but also strengthens all our movements under one collective stance. We should not worry about which oppression is worse than the other, but about the fact that all oppression is worth speaking out against. Many of us are in positions of oppressor and oppressed at the same time. This knowledge must fuel our passion for ending oppression by abdicating and resisting norms that give us privilege over others. Women's rights are the same as civil rights, which are the same as gay rights, which are the same as immigrant rights. We are all connected and only together will we be able to create lasting change.

Lastly, I want to encourage readers to make a personal and political commitment to social justice activism. I am suggesting something well beyond the realm of participating in diversity training or signing an online petition. Some people believe that acts like these absolve them of their moral responsibility to participate in social justice activism. The typical corporate diversity training does little to make us examine our assumptions and merely gives us license to continue to exercise our power while maintaining a superficial front of understanding and tolerance. True social justice work starts with grassroots activism and extends in scope from local to national to global. We need to keep moving forward. We need to work for social justice until we reach a place where equal opportunity exists for everyone not just on paper, but also in practice.

*Pseudonyms used.

IT'S JUST COMMON SENSE

Brandon Arber

Male student: What class did you just have?

Me: Women's Studies.

Male student: Oh, shit. Is that a requirement?

Me: Naw.

Male student: Are you stupid? Then why the fuck are you taking it? HaHa. I always knew you were a faggot. Isn't the class full of, like, feminists? Are you the only dude in the class?

Me: Well, I mean, I consider myself a feminist.

Male student: Mmmpff! You gotta be kidding me.

Me: Being a feminist just means I don't think girls should be raped, abused, discriminated against, or denied health services, especially if they get pregnant. What, you disagree with that?

Maybe my definition of feminism is too . . . easy. The way I was raised, however, was that fighting for women's rights was synonymous with fighting injustice in general. So saying that I am a feminist is as easy as saying I'm hoping for the best for all people, and trying to act accordingly. Some might think that this definition robs the word of its gravity, or maybe a sense of total commitment. But I'm not fighting a holy war here. I don't see political or social struggle as a zero-sum game. And my moral beliefs don't come enumerated in some rulebook, whether conservative or liberal. I aspire to more pragmatic, humanist values: caring for all people and using reason to bring about a better world. It's hard to deny that women have been screwed over. So I don't think I'm being revolutionary in saying I'm a feminist. It just makes sense.

Another male student: Whatever, man . . . I was in this Comm class last year that was, like, all girls and we were talking about how there's a male bias in the media, right? And the evidence they used for it was that Meryl Streep was obviously such a better actress that DeNiro, but DeNiro gets all this recognition and makes so much more money and shit. Fucking Meryl Streep? So most of the time I just kept my mouth shut 'cause I knew these girls were just being bitches, right, and the professor would obviously be on their side. But this time, I just said, "Hey, maybe it's not bias. Maybe it's because DeNiro is actually a better actor." The whole class just blew up at me, calling me ignorant and shit. I got the dirtiest fucking looks for the rest of the semester. They couldn't even think that maybe it was their own preference that made them think there was a bias in the first place! No, I understand what you're saying. I'm not sexist, but feminists are fucking crazy.

For many guys, sitting in a room full of feminist women doesn't sound like the most comfortable way to spend an afternoon. This negative reaction to the idea of taking a women's studies class is not just a reflection of ignorance. Liberation can get very personal. Sometimes people feel alienated or personally blamed for being the oppressor. At the same time, too many activists speak their piece, and then pat themselves on the back about how righteous and ground-breaking they are. Or they take radical action just for the shock value. But there is power in being willing to engage in confrontation, and this is important.

The problems we are fighting are systemic. They are aggregate con-sequences of individual decisions. What seems more widespread than overtly bad action is complacency and apathy; a refusal to engage. I think our political emphasis should be on opening eyes, not hardening hearts.

You might ask, who is this white man coming out of nowhere, claiming he's a feminist, and who then proceeds to tell me how to run my movement? Well, I don't care if I'm not welcome at first. I'm patient. I'll wait. As a college athlete, as a beneficiary of white, upper-middle class male privilege and access, I know that feminism is still a dirty word from the locker-room to the board rooms that are still dominated by men. And it's not only because all men are pig-headed. Of course, many men are still insensitive, homophobic, sexist, or abusive. And even the best-intentioned men perpetuate oppression by the language we use and the jokes we make.

But there is also a great potential for men as allies. Many of us see ourselves as victims of prejudice by virtue of being black, Asian, Muslim, or Jewish. And, whether we know about it or not, most of us probably have had a friend, girlfriend, sister, mother, or wife who was abused or sexually assaulted at some point in her life. So it's not the goals and concerns of feminism but, rather, feminism's reputation that keeps a lot of men from dealing with the issues. Ultimately, though, we have to step up. When we need to make decisions either in our own private lives, or regarding public policy, a feminist perspective has to be a viable option. Because when it's time to dig in, we are going to want the true feminist majority behind us. The potential is there. It's just common sense.

Part IV

Points and Perspectives

INTRODUCTION

The authors represented in this section describe both success and challenges. They describe dealing with gender politics in settings that are hostile—or only slowly warming—to new ideas about men and women. Reflecting on their personal experiences, these nine men discuss being sons and fathers, teachers and students. They pose questions, and provide some answers, about living, working, thinking, and learning in a sexist society.

In "Abandoning the Barricades: or How I Became a Feminist," masculinities scholar and anti-sexism activist Michael Kimmel describes the origins of his gender awareness. Written in 1975, Kimmel's essay reflects back to his experience transferring from an all-male college to join the first men attending Vassar. One of the oldest women's colleges in the United States, Vassar College became coeducational in 1969. This experience transformed Kimmel's relationship with women while providing him with new ways to deal with men. Looking back, thirty-two years later, Kimmel metaphorically turns to see who is coming up behind him in the quest for gender justice. He is encouraged to see generations of young men mobilizing in support of gender equality.

Rob Okun's "Confessions of a Premature Pro-Feminist" recalls his involvement with the antiwar movement opposing U.S. involvement in Vietnam. While becoming politically active during the early 1970s, Okun sees how discrimination against women didn't just happen "out there," but also was present within seemingly progressive, activist circles. This spark of awareness drew Okun into a lifelong commitment to pro-feminist activism and social change. Now the Director of the Men's Resource Center for Change, based in Amherst, Massachussets, Okun writes, "despite media reports smugly belittling activism as just a phase in a young person's life," the movement for social justice is alive and well and "worth tapping into over the course of a lifetime."

Bob Lamm also provides historical context for understanding feminism in his essay, "Learning From Women." In 1974, Lamm first taught a course titled "Men, Masculinity, and Sexism" at Queens College in New York. Lamm saw himself as an open-minded professor who would impart wisdom to his students about men's and women's lives. But Lamm discovered something he had not expected when female students confronted him for his misconceptions about rape and male sexual violence, and then held their own classes for women only for the final six weeks of the semester. Lamm realized that he had much to learn by listening to women. "The truth," he writes, "is that I knew virtually nothing about the reality of women's lives . . . I had no idea of how much I didn't know."

In "A Tribute to My Father," Chris Dixon explains how shifting gender expectations in the 1970s impacted his relationship with his dad. Dixon's father was a progressive role model who was involved with men's groups that were exploring new ideas about manhood. But the elder Dixon's personality and parenting were complicated by his homophobia, a volatile temper, and his alcoholism. Dixon expresses love for his father and acknowledges his dad's simultaneous success and failure. The most sincere way of expressing my love, Dixon explains, "is by learning from [my father's] mistakes and accepting the responsibility of not repeating them."

Jeremy Adam Smith also writes about fatherhood, but from the perspective of a stay-at-home dad. Smith weaves personal narrative with national trends and data about men as primary caregivers in his essay titled, "Playground Vertigo." Smith comments that while it might still seem radical today, men as full-time parents could become an accepted routine for the next generation. More men are choosing this option and we are no longer as shocked by the idea. The transformative potential for gender-neutral parenting that Smith anticipates extends beyond the home: Equally shared parenting and housekeeping will mean that the workplace and other institutions will have to respond to families' needs and realities in meaningful ways. Revising the family so that men are full and active participants in parenting may go a long way toward easing gender restrictions in caregiving and in improving the experience of parenting.[1]

"Judging Fathers: The Case for Gender-Neutral Standards" opens with Donald N.S. Unger driving north through Connecticut on the Merritt Parkway. His daughter, Rebecca, eight years old at the time, is sitting with him in the car while Harry Chapin's song, "Cat's in the Cradle," plays on the radio. As Unger talks with his daughter about his decision to be a fully engaged father and take an active role in her life, he also notes that society makes this difficult for men. For instance, it took a lawsuit to get changing tables installed in the men's restrooms along the very stretch of road he is driving on. By the time that finally happened, his daughter was toilet trained and Unger no longer had a personal need for these facilities. However, Unger writes, it is necessary that society hold gender-neutral standards for parenting and accept men as competent, capable caregivers. Things are starting to change, but pop culture's tendency to portray men as bumbling, overgrown teenagers doesn't help, he says.

In "What's Wrong With Fathers' Rights?" Michael Flood exposes the toxic myths of so-called men's and fathers' rights groups. According to Flood, the fathers' rights movement claims that men experience discrimination in cases of separation, divorce, and custody. Flood explains that fathers' rights groups are based on "a profound denial of the systematic gender inequalities which privilege many men and disadvantage many women." Using debatable claims of gender symmetry in domestic violence, these groups actually represent an organized backlash to feminism. In the final analysis, fathers' rights groups give more weight to fathers' privilege for contact with their children over their children's protection from violence. Men who are going through separation or divorce certainly deserve support, Flood notes, but they're not well served by organizations that stifle men's healing process and encourage men to engage in malicious, destructive, and unproductive legal strategies. This effort to win at all costs has high costs for children, for women, and for men.

On a different topic, Kyle Brillante writes about his experience as a male student enrolled in a graduate women's studies program. "Engendering the Classroom" opens with Brillante exasperated at being the token male feminist. Yet he is also puzzled by why he is so often overlooked, ignored, or rejected by professors and other students. Do they fear his queerness, or his passion, or do they assume that gender studies simply should not include men? Today, a growing number of men are enrolling in courses on women's and gender studies. Although there are those who prefer women's studies as a women-only space, it is reasonable that men should join in the academic project of deconstructing and critiquing gender expectations and stereotypes, and counterproductive to exclude men, or gender variant students, through explicit or implied means.[2] Brillante pioneers an important conversation about men in gender studies and gives voice to the challenges he has found there.

Rounding out this section is Bryan Talbot Morris's "Gender in Jakarta," an essay on the power of language and discourse. The essay opens with a conversation between Morris and two friends over Scrabble, coffee, and clove cigarettes in an Indonesian café. Quickly, the discussion reveals to Morris how men's double standards about women and sexuality are alive and unwell. In a country with the world's largest Muslim population, Morris's superficially gender-savvy friend, John, describes his views on the politics of the veil. He liked having casual sex with a woman he met in a club, but wanted to date a woman who wears a *jilbab*, the Islamic headscarf, in effect reinforcing stereotypes of the first woman as a whore and the second as a good girl. As Morris spent more time in Indonesia, he found that John's statement was merely the start of troubling ideas he heard come from other men. "Whether listening to diplomats, expatriates, NGO [non-governmental organization] staff, friends or acquaintances, the daily banter reflected a fundamental and ingrained disconnect between egalitarian discourse and the way men live our lives." This disconnect, Morris surmises, indicates although men may be publicly committed to equality, they have not yet integrated this belief. Men may be trained in gender sensitivity, Morris tells us, but it's time to walk the talk and to pay attention to how speech can reinforce men's agency and women's silence.

1. Oriel Sullivan argues for a conception of change within household gender practices that is "slow and uneven, [and] in which daily practices and interactions are linked to attitudes and discourse, perhaps over generations." See Oriel Sullivan. "Changing Gender Practices Within the Household: A Theoretical Perspective." *Gender & Society*. Vol. 18, no. 2 (April 2004): 207. In response to essentialist arguments that women are naturally better suited to parent children, Alexis J. Walker and Lori A. McGraw point out that while professionals may broadly agree on what children need to thrive emotionally and physically, there is no empirical evidence that these needs must either be met by a man or a woman. Alexis J. Walker and Lori A. McGraw. "Who Is Responsible for Responsible Fathering?" *Journal of Marriage and the Family*. Vol. 62 (May 2000): 563–9.

2. For discussion on some of the potential problems invoked by men in women's studies, see Michael Flood. "Bringing Men Into the Light? Women's Studies and the Problem of Men." Presented at *Casting New Shadows: Australian Women's Studies Association Conference*, Sydney, Australia, 31 January–February 2, 2001. www.xyonline.net/downloads/womensstudiesandmen.pdf.

ABANDONING THE BARRICADES: OR HOW I BECAME A FEMINIST

Michael S. Kimmel

There's a well-known story, probably apocryphal, about an encounter between Henry David Thoreau and Ralph Waldo Emerson. Thoreau had been arrested and was in jail for tax resistance, and Emerson came to visit him. (I always imagined the scene as a sort of Hollywood set in which Emerson would lean against the outside of the brick building and peer through the bars on the window at his incarcerated friend.) "My friend, what are you doing in prison?" Emerson is said to have asked. "My friend, what are you doing out of prison?" replied Thoreau.

I have always thought of this story when, over the years, people have asked about the origins of my political activism for gender equality and my interest in studying men and masculinities. The question—why would I, as a man, support women's equality?—is the wrong question. To my mind, the only right question is why doesn't every man support women's equality? After all, equality is right, just, fair, and supposedly as American as apple pie. More than that, though, gender equality is the only way for men to have the sorts of relationships we say we want to have—with women, with other men, and with our children.

But every story does have a beginning—or, more accurately, several beginnings. The narrator, always unreliable, gets to choose which of these stories is most fitting for the occasion, and it gradually becomes the master narrative, the font from which other subsequent narratives seem to flow inevitably and ineluctably.

So, when I'm asked, I often tell stories that date from graduate school: about helping to found an activist group dedicated to ending rape, about joining a men's consciousness raising group, about the founding of a national organization for pro-feminist men that would eventually become the National Organization for Men Against Sexism (NOMAS). Or I describe how I was challenged, pushed, and confronted by feminist women friends to examine my own behavior. Or the experience of encountering, for what I assumed then was the first time, women who had been battered or raped, and my decision to try to do something—anything I could—to work with men to stop.

There are, of course, other stories, earlier stories, about my gender socialization as a boy, my experiences with boy culture, sports, and the small violences we both do and are done to us to extract an uneasy conformity to norms of masculinity that we neither created nor particularly like.

During graduate school, while I seem to have accumulated all those other stories I would rely on as pieces of an explanation, I reflected on my undergraduate experience, and how participating in an unusual historical moment—the first coeducational class at Vassar College—had affected my political development and my support of feminism. I wrote the following essay in 1975 with no particular outlet in mind, more as a way to try and begin to sort those experiences into a coherent narrative.

Vassar provided what we sociologists often refer to as "taking the role of the other." Being in such a small but visible minority afforded an angle of vision that was rare and in some ways precious: I was able to witness male, predatory, sexual behavior not from the point of view of the perpetrator (although there was surely plenty of that) but from the point of view of those upon whom such behavior was being launched.

This essay is the product of that initial immersion into thinking analytically, sociologically, about the political engagement I was inching toward. It was an essay written to try and map a personal trajectory toward a politics I hadn't yet quite defined.

Typically, when reading an article or essay I wrote many years before, I often wince at the sorts of glaringly dumb things I said. Yet occasionally, there is a moment, a sentence, a phrase, that sings to me still, that resonates for me today, that makes me feel some affection for the boy who wrote it.

Reading this essay now, I wince, wondering about the sophomoric formulation, the self-congratulatory posture, the self-righteousness, and the moral high ground I somehow found easier to occupy at age twenty-five than I do thirty years later. For example, I soon backed away from calling myself a "feminist" and developed a rhetoric of "pro-feminism" to try and position myself relative to the women's movement without appropriating the term.

But I also smile in recognition of the effort, and identify with the young man struggling toward something that he didn't know at the time would come to define his adult life.

Sure, there are a few sentences that are no longer true, a few where I was carried away on the wings of hyperbole. And yet there are a few that are even more true. The Denver Broncos aren't notable for holding hands in their huddles anymore—but so many other teams do!

The impulse to "turn around and see who's behind you" has, today, two meanings for me. It pushed me to look back to the rich, historical legacy of men who supported gender equality. The documentary history, Against the Tide: Pro-Feminist Men in the United States, 1776–1990 offered a collection of original statements, pamphlets, speeches, and articles, so those men's actual words might continue to inspire new generations of men.

Today, it also means that I look behind at new generations of young men who are now taking the lead in efforts to mobilize men in the support of women's equality. True, it is somewhat disconcerting to realize that my work now can be filed under the category of "history"—as the present always straddles past and future, I'm afraid I've now begun to list toward the past. Yet there is something immensely gratifying for having been part of a rich tradition of men publicly supporting women's equality, and *also for working with others to continue that legacy. I offer this essay now to that new generation of men as one small part of that history, that legacy.*

I've left the text as I wrote it in 1975, changing only a few grammatical errors and inserting a line or two here or there for clarification.

I do so not because I stand behind every word I wrote more than thirty years ago; indeed, I would take a few things back, mute or sharpen various points, or change the language. No, I leave it the way I wrote it not because I stand behind every single word, but because I still stand with the young man who first wrote them.

In the spring of 1973, noted anthropologist Margaret Mead, speaking at Vassar College, mentioned the exciting new relationships between women and men she had been observing at Yale. She remarked that most of the male–female relationships had been reoriented around non-sexual friendships rather than sexual involvement. In fact, she noted that many of the dormitories reminded her of enormous extended families, characterized by an inviolable incest taboo, with sexual coupling maintained only outside the dorm.

As I left the lecture, my friends commented how laughably incorrect her perceptions of Vassar were, and that, with the introduction of coeducation, the college had been transformed "from a convent into a roller derby" in which indiscriminate promiscuity was the norm. Although I had been away from Vassar for almost a year at the time, I argued that Mead was more or less accurate in her perceptions and they roughly matched my experiences at Vassar. My years there as a student were far from a sexual free-for-all; in fact, it was in that context that I first began to take sexual involvement seriously. These notes are an attempt to describe the ways in which the character of my interpersonal relationships was begun to be transformed.

AVANT LE DÉLUGE

I would be lying if I was to write that my sexual development into an American man has been even, smooth, or consistent with the value patterns that seem most common. But it would be similarly incorrect to say that I am somehow different than most men. I grew up in the same society, with the same sets of values, as everyone else.

I was raised in a comfortable, upper-middle-class suburb near New York City. Largely white and predominantly Jewish, high school was seen mostly as an uncomfortable but necessary obstacle to hurdle on the way to college. A high level of social order was maintained by the simple, omnipresent threat that any wrongdoing would immediately "go on your college record." The thought of being prevented from going to college was so powerful that most of us docilely stayed in line. In fact, among my peers, the mere fact of going to college was not nearly as important as where one was going. We were judged, and judged each other, by the academic reputations of our chosen schools. And although there was hardly a moment during my high school life when I wasn't morbidly preoccupied with women, often to the point of distraction, I knew that a "quality" education could only be obtained at a men's college.

My preoccupation with women was probably a substantial motivation to desire a single sex college. Women *were* a distraction, the finest distraction ever invented, to be sure, but a distraction nonetheless. A friend, who had gone to Dartmouth, had given me some brotherly advice: "You should have your work during the week, and your women on the weekends. Never let them overlap." Indeed, they couldn't overlap. Women were soft and cuddly weekend playthings, and weekends were a time for a rapid retreat from the intellectual world. The work-week was reserved for study to understand the world, with either the desire to make it or overthrow it (sometimes both). The last thing that was to be on our minds was serious intellectual discussion on a weekend designed for fun. That "fun" I was told early in my freshman year meant "the three Bs: booze, broads, and (foot)ball."

The better part of my first year at that all-male school was spent making many of the symbolic gestures that would demonstrate my opposition to what I saw around me. My definition of myself was a residual category which was composed of the negation of what I observed around me. What they were, I would not be. They drank for relaxation, I advocated temperance; they enjoyed athletics, I wrote poetry; they seemed happy, I vacillated between a desperate depression and maudlin self-pity; students were oriented toward engineering and sciences, I would major in philosophy and art; they lived in fraternities, I would live in a commune (which, it strikes me now, are not so different as we once thought); they wanted to use their education to climb higher on the social ladder, I wanted to use mine to topple the ladder.

By the middle of my second year, it seemed futile to continue in an atmosphere in which I couldn't grow except in opposition. I was too well socialized, though, to abandon education altogether and drop out. I decided to transfer.

UNLEARNING THE LIES

The entire fabric of my interpersonal relationships was dramatically changed during the years I was a student at Vassar. In this section, I will try to sketch some of the ways in which my relationships with women were transformed, while the next section will deal with the new ways I found to relate to men.

The changes in my relationships with women was the result of the confluence of three factors, each in itself necessary, yet none sufficient by itself to foster that change. First, I began to deal with women in the context of a high level of intellectual discussion. Second, I was able to observe from a unique position the complex and subtle ways in which men relate to women, as an observer of the men from nearby men's schools and the men at Vassar, as well as a participant in the working out of my own relationships. Finally, and most importantly, all of my development must be seen in a larger social and political climate that characterized the dramatic changes that were felt throughout American society in general, and the focus of a large part of that change on the institutions of higher education. In particular, there was a sense of attempting to make one's personal relationships consistent with one's political convictions; that is, recognizing the political element in personal relationships.

When I first arrived in the fall, 1970, Vassar was in the midst of an institutional identity crisis. Having made a commitment to coeducation, the school was in the throes of a cataclysmic collective reappraisal of its intellectual and social priorities. Now that they had decided to admit men, what were they going to do with them? The college had taken a major step in defining the terms of the coeducational transition as "coequal" which meant, in essence, that neither sex would receive deferential treatment, and the college's orientation would not be ordered solely on criteria of gender.

There were, however, some substantive changes that were brought about with the coming of the men. As with many single sex colleges in difficult (or inaccessible) locations, Vassar on a weekend often appeared as it does during a summer: a campus abandoned to the lonely or excessively studious. Most women simply packed up and left for a nearby men's college committed to providing adequate cultural diversions for its residents. (Most of the more popular men's schools were also located in or near a major city, which independently generates its own cultural diversions.) In fact, until 1971, the college still chartered at least one bus to transport Vassar women to Yale for the weekend. (As I had a good female friend who had transferred to Yale that first year, I believe I hold the distinction of being the first male to ride the Yale bus.)

With the arrival of men as a permanent fixture on campus, the weekend exodus began to wane. The college began to organize weekend cultural activities, developing, for a college of its size, a remarkable number and wide range of things to do. And if Vassar women were as likely to stay around campus for the weekend, the men from the nearby schools would be sure to come to Vassar. And when they came, I found myself in the uncomfortable position of observing in operation those very values that had initially led me to go to a single sex college. This time, however, I found myself on the other side.

Friday evening dinners in my dormitory were often characterized by the obtrusive entrance of a small, but conspicuous group of men. Upon entrance, they would separate into pairs and trios, single out a table that had a number of attractive women who appeared to be unattached, and begin the long symbolic dances of seduction. Most of the women I knew reacted with a combination of indignant anger and curious fascination, coupled with an uncomfortable anxiety that they might, if approached, be unable to get rid of these men. I was, at first, embarrassed to be a man and watch the spectacle enacted by many other men, and to see the effect it was having on my friends.

I felt angry at the men and protective toward the women. How could these men, I asked, who know nothing about these women, with whom I live, expect to spend the night with them? I believed that if I wasn't going to sleep with them so indiscriminately, neither should they. I felt then as I had earlier felt with my younger sister. Her sexual involvement would develop when it was her choice to develop it, not on the momentary whim of someone trying to convince her that it was her choice. I wanted to protect her from those calculating bastards. I knew their routines too well; I had tried them myself. And neither my sister nor my friends in the dorm had to stand for that nonsense.

For a while, I was committed to subverting the blatant attempts of the "intruders." When I saw a friend being harassed, I would often walk up to her table and, pretending to be her lover, lead her away from her suitor. When masses of West Point cadets would show up, a number of men responded more systematically; once, for example, a telephone call to the dorm receptionist from "Colonel Taggart" ordered all cadets back to the West Point bus for unannounced evening maneuvers. In all, though, my self-concept was still derived negatively, relative to the men from the men's colleges.

It was an uncomfortable position. I am, after all, a man. Yet I was finding, in my own relationships, that the traditional male behavior patterns were not capable of letting me develop relationships that were satisfactory either to me or to the women with whom I was involved. There was always a residual fear that my resistance to these men's behaviors might mean I was gay, yet I was pretty sure I was heterosexual. I began to search for new ways of relating with women based on new criteria for relationships.

The classroom became the first arena of personal struggle. Quite often (since there were so few men in the school at all, and fewer still junior transfers—my graduating class of 478 included only 26 men) I was the only man in a class. But rarely, if ever, did I dominate the discussion. I was somewhat surprised—and not always delighted—to discover so many women who were as bright (if not brighter), verbal, and articulate as I was. But there was something else, far more profound. While my previous classroom experiences had been successful, they had always left me feeling isolated and alone as each man tried to outdo the other for precious grades. My classes at Vassar were not only characterized by a high level of intellectual rigor, but a warm, non-competitive atmosphere that was both stimulating and supportive.

My education had previously been a form of delayed gratification in which certain tasks, however distasteful, had to be learned for externally defined ends. At Vassar, however, I began to see something inherently gratifying and exciting in intellectual pursuits. By learning in a non-competitive atmosphere, I was unafraid to become personally committed.

This commitment was heightened greatly by the content of the courses as well as by the context. In the social sciences, we were dealing with issues of immediate consequence, and classroom discussion was often highly personal and political. Sometimes the two were fused. I believe I learned more during these discussions than at any other time.

But this, too, must be kept in perspective. My college days were at a time of great social and political unrest, which was largely, but not entirely, centered around universities. I do not agree with those critics who argue that the withdrawal from active encounters and confrontations with the symbolic agents of the war-crazed establishment was the result of the failure of the student movement to generate any meaningful changes. Rather, I think that any political movement that will be worth anything must periodically undergo serious self-examination of its own internal dynamics to make them congruent (as much as is possible) with the society one is trying to build. And Vassar women, with their long tradition of fighting in the forefront of the women's movement, were painfully aware of their position in a sexist society. Many women at Vassar were involved in the carving out of new, positive identities for themselves as women, not in relation to the occupational role of a man (like being a "lawyer's wife") but relative to themselves as women.

I felt, for myself, that in feminism was the ability to break free of arbitrarily defined modes of behavior that had been defined for me by someone else and to finally develop ways of relating that were consistent with both my personal experiences and my political philosophies.

LEARNING TO LIVE THE TRUTH

The fact that there is such a widespread women's movement in modern America implies the very obvious fact that women are not equal. And while it is not the function of this piece to develop either the characteristics of the subtle mechanisms that systematically oppress women, nor to suggest the logistics of the demystification of sex roles in a sexist society, it is useful to recall here Sally Kempton's words: In the war against sexism, "the outposts of the enemy are in our own heads."

Women are, to be sure, the victims of centuries of domination. But women, too, daily reproduce those very mental structures which have oppressed them, and in the transmission of those values with each other, victimize other women. The underlying logic of women's consciousness raising is a logic of collective struggle to unlearn the lies of their lives. It is a process of learning to unlearn, an internal battle with an enemy both without and within.

While men have collectively been the front-line army of the victimization of women, they are themselves victims of the perpetuation of those same values. The same mental structures have been internalized, in no less a profound way, deep into the inner reaches of the male unconscious. Men develop myths about both women and men that perpetuate the existing value structures. Although different in kind from the myths that women develop about themselves (but which nonetheless serve the same function of keeping them alienated from one another), male myths are no less deeply rooted and no less profound.

Some of these myths deal specifically with our relationships with women. Women, we are told, are designed biologically to be more naturally disposed toward domestic tasks. They do not experience the same passions or drives that men experience. They need not have an orgasm to enjoy sex, but men must experience orgasm. Their reactions are more likely to be emotional than logical. The list goes on and on. Most myths are designed to soothe our fragile ego from serious vulnerability in sexual encounters.

The myths we maintain about ourselves with other men are equally profound. Young boys, kissing their father goodnight, will someday (at an "appropriate" age) be told that grown men do not kiss, they shake hands. It is unnatural for men to show any physical affection for one another. (Except, of course, the more-than-male athletes, who can get away with it. I am yet to hear anyone accuse the defensive unit of the Denver Broncos, who hold hands during their huddle, of being homosexual.) It is not manly to show any type of emotion at all. Men are always rational. Men do not cry.

In short, women are reduced to whimpering, mindless, house servants and men to calculating, emotionless rocks. And if we are going to change our relationships with women to develop non-exploitative relationships, we must simultaneously alter the ways in which we deal with other men.

My experiences with other Vassar men were fundamental to my becoming able to take the leap from the secure plateau of traditional relationships into the uncharted void of non-exploitative relationships. Although I will return to this shortly, I cannot overemphasize the positive functions of social support. It is a powerfully lonely experience to attempt the transformation of the values that have, for so long, made one whom he or she is. And it is both a relief and an impetus to continue when we discover other men involved in the same struggle.

But one reaction after taking those early steps is to turn around and see who's behind you. My steps were not individual steps, but social steps. I was determined to turn around and help those who were first struggling to take those same risks. I became a freshman counselor in my dormitory, and through that experience, found that many students were still somewhat traumatized at the thought of seeking professional help. Consequently, a number of students, Vassar's resident psychiatrist, and I organized ourselves to develop a peer-counseling program to augment the already overworked professional staff.

In my experiences as a counselor, I dealt with other men who were having difficulty in establishing healthy relationships. A number of men, who had not had any successful dating experiences in high school, had declined offers of admission to superlative men's schools to come to Vassar because they felt they could not only receive an excellent education, but could meet and date a variety of women. When, after three or four months at Vassar they were still unable to develop those relationships, they frequently turned the situation on themselves, believing themselves to be "natural" failures with women. Many men I spoke with voiced fears about their own sexuality, and a sizable number were anxious about possibly being latent homosexuals. Many men, measuring their successes quantitatively, expressed some reservations about the quality of their relationships. Nearly all of them spoke about their inability to develop meaningful friendships with men.

The atmosphere I tried to create with each of the men I met was one of empathy and support. I could not help but relate personally to so many of their fears and anxieties, and consequently was not able to ever achieve the dispassionate distance that often characterizes "professional" relationships. Nor did I seek to achieve it. I wanted instead to understand the dimensions of each man's emotions and to share with him the sense that I was able to feel, and had felt before, what he was expressing.

Rather than feeling alone in my attempts to reconstruct my relationships along more trusting lines, I began to realize how many men were struggling with similar problems and identical causes. We are never taught how to relate to one another; instead we are taught how not to relate. The rules that govern our most important activity as human beings, the formation of interpersonal relationships, do not tell us what we should do, but what we should not do. And seeing so many men in a similar position led me to the feeling that men, too, need a positive collective experience with each other to better come to terms with our individual transformations. Male consciousness raising should not be seen as the activity that men participate in because their women are involved in women's groups. On the contrary, we developed our male group as a positive response to our perception that men must become part of a collective process of redefinition of our identities within a context of mutual trust and support. This is the essential feature of consciousness raising groups. And while the overwhelming majority of the men who participated did so, at first, because of a desire to understand their relationships with women, we soon realized that we were simultaneously and irrevocably altering our relationships with each other, and, by extension, with other men.

WHERE WE ARE GOING

Men in the modern world face perhaps the most serious challenge to their traditional modes of behavior that we have ever faced. Traditional male roles are one of the single largest causes of a great deal of the anxiety, fear, confusion, and unhappiness that we experience. Not only have men become insecure about our identities at work (when so many of us are easily replaced by machines that are so much more efficient) but profoundly insecure about our identities at home. Because of our training, we are afraid to show these anxieties, for the compounding fear of being viewed as weak.

The sexual revolution, like any political revolution, has left many casualties in its wake. We have been brought up in a world of evaluations based on our performances, and our most intimate performances are also our most vulnerable. Men are not the only gender that is capable of evaluating lovers on the basis of their performance, and many men have simply dropped out of the race for fear of losing. As Stirling Moss once wrote: "There are two things no man will admit he can't do well: drive and make love."

We are afraid to relate to other men for fear that we might be secretly gay, or that they might be, or that "things" might just get out of control. It appears far more secure and far less risky to simply avoid the issue, thus cutting us off from any expression of trust between men.

It would be far too facile to throw the entire burden of this very complex problem on individual men (or individual women) and argue that if only we could clean up our personal lives, everything else would fall into place. This line of reasoning ignores a very fundamental issue: The society in which we live is maintained precisely through the perpetuation of our traditional behavior and reinforced by myths about natural predispositions.

On the other hand, it is a convenient shirking of individual responsibility to fail to confront ourselves as the microcosmic reproduction of these very social values on the individual level. We cannot afford to simply wait for the great social transformation to happen of itself, and in its wake sweep aside old modes of relating.

Instead, both levels of action are necessary. At every level, we must collectively confront the maintenance of a system based on competition instead of cooperation, profit as opposed to pleasure; a system that teaches callous manipulation of others for our own ends rather than the development of sensitive and trusting relationships as ends in themselves. But we must also be constantly in the process of transforming ourselves into the people we want to be.

This personal transformation is by no means easy. For me, it has barely begun. And that beginning has been frightening and painful. It means leaving the comfortable security of social behavior that has been well defined over the years and carefully delimited by easily discernible sets of rules, and jumping into a netherworld of non-exploitative relationships for which there are no rules. Without those rules, there is no basis for evaluation and no knowledge of the expectations of others involved. And it is very scary to be making up the rules as you go along.

It means working out the logistics of sexual demystification, in which sex is no longer maintained as a scarce commodity but a beautiful facet of human expression. It means transforming our deeply rooted definitions of behavior. For example, it involves the transformation of our definition of weakness from the inability to conceal one's emotions to the inability to express those emotions. Conversely, we must transform strength from the impermeability to pain to the ability to express whatever we feel. It means giving up standard behavior patterns (no matter how successful they are by someone else's criteria) for the discomfort of not knowing exactly where you are. It means not playing the games in which someone else has made up the rules, but taking active control of our own lives. It means abandoning the enemy's outposts in our heads, and beginning the process of dismantling the barricades sexism has erected in our lives. It often means being very profoundly alone.

There are a number of things that I have found, that, while they don't eliminate the loneliness and the fear, nonetheless provide the grounding so I can continue. Feminist women have constantly supported me in my struggles and shared the problems and the anxieties (as well as the exhilaration) of their struggle to transform their selves and their environment.

The greatest impetus has been from other feminist men, who are similarly trying to deal with the ways in which we relate to women, to ourselves, and to each other. In both structured situations (like consciousness raising groups) and informal discussions with friends, I have felt both sensitive understanding and support for my own development. The process is by no means complete. I wish that I could report to you, at this time, that I have successfully undermined all those traditional values and replaced them with new "liberated" values. But I haven't. In fact, I have barely begun a struggle that will probably last for my lifetime. And yet I am convinced, even at this early stage, that I have begun to develop qualitatively superior relationships, with both men and women, than any I have ever known. The process is still frightening and painful at times. But it isn't so lonely anymore.

If anything is clear from my personal account of my development into a male feminist, it is this: I am not an exception, who by virtue of the presence or absence of one particular component, or the existentially unique composite of a number of components, has been thrust into the void of non-traditional relationships. Rather, I am part of a growing number (and I am amazed at how rapidly it is growing) of normal, "regular guys" who have started to reclaim their lives as their own. Once taken, it is a long and difficult road to keep control of it. But we cannot give it back.

CONFESSIONS OF A PREMATURE PRO-FEMINIST

Rob Okun

I look out at the expanse of lawn before me to a sea of lighted matches held aloft, dotting the dusk sky with sparks of brightness like white caps on a rolling ocean. The Washington Monument looms large—a stoic rear guard ready for another gathering of volunteers reporting for anti-war duty on a balmy evening in the nation's capital. It is May 8, 1970. I am a sophomore at George Washington University.

From my perch in the corner of a temporary stage, I can see both the intense, bearded poet at the microphone inviting the assembled to hold up their "lights of peace" and, before me, the illuminated, outstretched arms of thousands of my brothers and sisters. Now, holding his harmonium up to the microphone, Allen Ginsberg begins playing and chanting, mixing a spiritual longing for peace among all beings with acerbic, poetic jabs at the current occupant of the White House—the architect of a brazen, disastrous Vietnam War policy—Richard Milhous Nixon. Days before, the Commander-in-Chief had announced to an increasingly divided nation that he had ordered a new assault, a bombing campaign in Cambodia. Outraged, students around the country began staging hastily planned demonstrations to protest this audacious, illegal widening of the war outside of Vietnam. On May 4, at a demonstration at Kent State University, Ohio, the National Guard shot four students dead and wounded several others. Days later, Mississippi state troopers killed two students and wounded twelve others at Jackson State University. The war had come home.

Situated just four blocks from the White House, George Washington University was a geographically appropriate campus host for national demonstrations. I played a small part organizing the gathering on the evening of May 8, a cultural prelude to the massive demonstration scheduled for the next day. Along with hearing Ginsberg's poetry, before the night was over we also listened to Judy Collins sing "Where Have All the Flowers Gone?" and to Abbie Hoffman symbolically silencing Nixon, speaking to the nation through a giant, cabinet model television placed at center stage. Before the weekend was over a widening crack in the shaky consensus to wage war in Southeast Asia was exposed.

In the late summer of 1968 I was eighteen years old and beginning college. The 1960s had been like a wildflower growing in a New England meadow that needed minimal sun and rain to thrive. The era was rife with the light of possibility and the storms of injustice, offering me a heady mix of social conditions in which my political awareness quickly grew. It had just been a matter of time. In those days it would have taken real effort not to be aware of the anti-war and civil rights movements: Walter Cronkite brought them to our supper table every evening through the black and white portable television on the kitchen counter. Our family debated both over mom's meatloaf. The women's movement, however, was not part of the conversation. Even though a number of years had passed since Betty Friedan published her catalytic book, *The Feminine Mystique*, the ideas and activities of women's liberation had not yet intruded upon the American family's dinner hour. So when I arrived at George Washington University on a steamy August afternoon—the shocking display of Chicago mayor Richard Daley's police brutally beating student protestors at the Democrats' presidential convention still on the front page— the women's movement was not what I saw. It would be some time before I understood women's second-class citizenship as a central component in the social-change puzzle I was beginning to try to solve.

My parents had barely said goodbye that August day in 1968 when I hopped on a bus for a view of the "Other Washington." As an alternative to the university's sugar-coated bus tour of the city's landmark monuments, radical politicos had organized a tour through areas of the city the university did not want students to see: the parts scorched and burned by angry, grief-stricken African Americans outraged at the assassination of Martin Luther King, Jr. just four months earlier. On that bus were many students who, I would discover, shared my passion for social justice. They were the people I would come to know. Like me, they were hungry to find and shape an alternative culture.

Looking at the boarded-up buildings from the window of the bus, witnessing the rubble in front of vacant storefronts, I felt tears welling up in my eyes. "This is the 'Other Washington'—and the 'Other America,'"—I thought. My college education had begun. The bus ride I took that weekend set a course for my life.

Back on campus—in clean, white, well-appointed Northwest Washington—I was struck by what the bus driver had asked toward the end of the tour: "It's been four months since Dr. King was murdered and the riots happened. No one in this city has yet to begin rebuilding. Why?" To my eighteen-year-old eyes the gap between whites and blacks, haves and have nots, could not have been more apparent.

My alternative orientation to university life continued the next day with a protest of the Soviet Union's recent invasion of Czechoslovakia. I accompanied a group of activists on an otherwise conventional tour of Washington D.C.'s Embassy Row. At the Soviet Union stop, however, while a Moscow hack spouted the party line, at a prearranged signal a handful of us stood and held signs aloft decrying the invasion. Mine, if memory serves, simply read, "For Shame."

As the fall semester unfolded, only my Journalism and American Civiliza-tion classes—which sometimes referenced news of the day as text—nudged me to class. Otherwise, school was a major distraction from my education in the streets. I could feel my connections with my new tribe deepening and, as they grew stronger, I began to enlarge my definitions of friendship, of family, and of community. And it was through that loose collection of hippies, freaks, and activists that the first glimmers of my awareness of gender politics began to glow.

Decades later I recognize how uninformed I was about the politics of women's liberation, not to mention gay rights. Neither was visible to me during my years in Washington. What I did sense was a vaguely articulated question posed by an inner voice: *If I'm promoting peace over war in Vietnam, and integration over segregation for people of color, what about equality over subjugation for women?* At the time, though, I had neither the language nor the community to spark an inquiry into women's second-class citizenship. At George Washington University in 1968 women's studies classes did not yet exist and feminist newspapers like *off our backs* had not yet begun publishing. It would be four years before the first issue of *Ms.* magazine arrived on the newsstands. What I had to go on was a vague feeling something wasn't right; it was a feeling I didn't always pay attention to.

Anti-war political meetings in those years were loud, boisterous, and dominated by white males. We were a flamboyant group—men in olive, army fatigue jackets, red and blue bandanas around our throats or foreheads, tie-dyed T-shirts, faded blue jeans with carefully sewn patches at the knees. Women often wore peasant blouses and long denim skirts. Our footwear was unisex: army boots in winter; moccasins, sandals, or bare feet in summer. The irony of appropriating army culture, on the one hand, and Native American clothing, on the other, was lost on us, obscured, perhaps, by our hair. Which was everywhere—long, straight, and parted down the middle; men's to their shoulders, women's at least to the middle of their backs. The wispy beards that some of us had at eighteen, grew thick and full by twenty-two. Curly-haired white guys let their hair grow out into Afros, another obvious cultural appropriation. Think Jerry Garcia meets Jimi Hendrix.

While I'm sure I didn't consciously take note of the gender makeup of our meetings, in a roomful of twenty there were usually no more than five or six women. As hip and as cool as we were, it was usually guys who spoke out—whether planning the next demonstration or organizing a trip to a Grateful Dead concert (or just the next trip). They spoke with a sense of entitlement that could only be described as white male privilege, a term not yet coined and clearly not widely understood by men. What was it that allowed me to make the connection between whites' privilege and oppression of blacks—which we all saw clearly by then—but not men's privilege and oppression of women?

I suppose I can fall back on my eighteen-year-old naiveté, my lack of experience in how the world worked. But deep down, I knew something wasn't right. In the tiny anti-war movement office on G Street, a storefront sandwiched in between a deli and a dry cleaners, we drank coffee and Coke, smoked cigarettes and pot, separated women from men. Well, not exactly. The separation was more along the lines of women and children in one category; men in the other. As young and innocent as I appeared, I was initially steered to the women's section of our revolutionary ship of state. But since in the late 1960s our movement—unlike the Titanic—hadn't run aground or hit an iceberg, it was women and children last, not first. The women and the younger men made coffee, ran the mimeograph machine, hit the streets to put up posters, tried to convince other students to join the cause. Occasionally, a woman or two took the floor at a meeting and passionately and powerfully talked about an upcoming action, but this was the exception. There was a blindness among the male, anti-war movement leaders, a presumption that as men they were entitled to be in charge.

Long before the photograph of Cuban revolutionary leader Ché Guevara became a famous T-shirt, it seems our movement had claimed as its own the romantic, masculine vision his portrait represented. There was little room for women's ideas, women's ways. It is no surprise that an independent women's movement would evolve alongside—and independent of—the anti-war movement. And it is no wonder that the insights of feminism would contribute so significantly to social change consciousness in subsequent decades.

As long-haired, rebellious young men moving to the pulsing drumbeat of the anti-war protest movement, many of us saw our path to adulthood diverging from the path our peers were taking in the jungles of Vietnam. I remember one spring driving on the Washington beltway in my brother's VW, seven of us packed in en route to Baltimore for a Janis Joplin and Big Brother and the Holding Company concert. We came upon a caravan of seven or eight open-backed army trucks tightly filled with soldiers in camouflage uniforms, topped with matching, flat-rimmed caps over closely shaved heads. We were keeping pace with them, us in the left lane and them in the right, heading, for the moment, in the same direction. We were all the same age yet we were taking such different roads to manhood. In those days when I saw soldiers I'd shake my head dismissively, not understanding what drew them to the military.

My friends and I were part of a movement that rejected militarism as the defining ideal of a masculine identity. We knew that anti-war activism meant we risked being seen as less than "real men" (even though a popular slogan from the period read, "Girls Say Yes to Boys Who Say No"). Sadly, we never tried to find common ground on which to meet with those who were soldiers.

But tonight, as we rode alongside the caravan, I asked myself, "Who were these soldiers?" Were they shipping out soon for Nam? What was it like to be leaving behind everything and everyone you cared about? I was riding in the front passenger seat nearest the caravan. The folks on my side of the car rolled down our windows and started flashing the peace sign at the soldiers. Miraculously, the soldiers flashed it back, a sea of hands raised high, index and middle fingers spread wide. In that moment I felt joined by our youth and our idealism, even if we lived in a parallel universe.

As we passed the lead truck, I locked eyes with a soldier who reminded me of a kid from my hometown in Massachusetts. He looked tough and unemotional. I was beginning to get an inkling about how some guys my age were playing out their passage into manhood and I understood that the smooth stock of a rifle could actually be a comfort to him. I didn't yet know what my brand of masculinity would end up looking like, but I knew it would not include sleeping with my rifle, a soldier's best friend.

Midway through the concert that night, when the darkened Baltimore hall was hazy with marijuana smoke, the image of the caravan of soldiers came back to me. I had never heard Janis Joplin sing live before and her voice that night tore "a little piece of my heart" as it scratched, cried, and caressed. She spoke to us as members of the tribe and I felt hopeful, buoyed. Somewhere in the jumble of memory and emerging adult consciousness was a young man finding his way.

I remember a gathering in the G Street movement office where we were planning a demonstration some weeks before the 1968 presidential election. We were going to hang effigies of the three major candidates—vice-president Hubert Humphrey, former vice-president Richard Nixon, and Alabama's segregationist governor, George Wallace. (Like many of my friends, I supported the candidacy of black activist, social critic, and comic Dick Gregory but I was only eighteen and, in those days, I wasn't old enough to vote.)

At the meeting I was sitting near an "older" woman in her twenties who, like me, was closely following the conversation. What distinguished her, I recall, was that frequently during the meeting she made insightful comments, offering at one point an idea about when to unveil the hanging figures for most dramatic effect. An older, second-tier leader with long, dark hair and a handlebar moustache kept casting furtive glances at her while she spoke. Maybe he was interested in her but I remember feeling his expression more closely resembled the one parents shoot children when they want them to shut up. I felt vaguely upset and confused but wasn't quite sure why. It would be a long time before I'd be able to translate those feelings into words. If I had they would have been something like: *This woman is too smart to be running the mimeograph machine. She should be running the meeting.*

The light is beginning to fade as Judy Collins walks out to perform before the throng assembled that Friday evening. The stage we are on is large enough to hold about twenty people. I am in a good spot in the back corner, able to easily see the performers, speakers, and the crowd. Judy's luminescent, blue eyes assess the scene as she stands for a moment acknowledging the sustained applause. Then she strikes a chord on her guitar and begins to sing. She rallies us, inspires us, enthralls us—her sweet, soaring soprano gliding overhead, its angelic vibrations a blessing. For a few moments she carries me beyond the vulnerability I am no longer able to mask, beyond the widening war I can't slow, beyond the callous government I can't awaken. And then she sings, "Where Have All the Flowers Gone?" ending with the verse that asks, "Where have all the young men have gone? . . . Gone for soldiers, everyone. When will they ever learn? When will they ever learn?"

I can no longer choke back the jangle of raw emotion I've been stuffing down. Tears begin to well up as all the pain and confusion, all the anger and despair I am feeling about the war, my country, my life, come flooding out. The very feelings that invincible young men are never supposed to show are there for all to see. The group on stage had packed in tight while Judy was performing, but now they part as she steps away from the microphone creating an aisle for her to walk through, guitar at her side. I am at the end, a longhaired manchild looking as if he'll burst into tears any second. She keeps walking and, even in my fragile state, I can tell she is headed straight for me, her wide, robin's-egg blue eyes brimming with compassion. I don't know what she did with her guitar but the next thing I remember is she gently held my face in her hands, looked at me with great tenderness, and leaned forward to plant a soft kiss on my lips. Then she was gone, taking with her much of the pain that overwhelmed me.

I have carried that memory with me all these years not just because Judy Collins kissed me, but because that moment was the beginning of a passage. It was years before I knew what the passage meant, years where I would slowly begin to live its meaning—allowing myself to be more vulnerable, allowing myself to show up more for my feelings. For a man coming of age in the last third of the twentieth century to express *any* feelings—besides anger—was rare.

It would take the next two decades to recognize that the tears I shed that night were not the sign of boyish weakness but were a healthy expression of being a man. During these years I began to improve my "Emotionalese," a language I long-sensed that the women in the anti-war movement office on G Street spoke fluently. Activist women seemed to know how to forge a new politics that integrated fluency in the language of emotions with a fiery passion for social justice and liberation. This was the moment defined by the feminist realization that "the personal is political." Like many men, though, I wasn't yet comfortable with the notion of integrating my inner and outer life. If more of us had, perhaps we would have worked alongside the activist organization

"Another Mother for Peace." There would have been a parallel organization founded by fathers. After all, fathers—and men—are as interested in protecting their children from war as mothers and women. It may be hard to believe from today's perspective, but social conditions in the late 1960s were not yet ripe for men to say so.

The struggle women were waging to free themselves from the yoke of patriarchy became one I embraced. Not all at once, and not perfectly. But as part of the student protest movement I began to realize that women were being denied full access to power and privilege in a seemingly progressive political movement. This smoldering truth has never been extinguished. And while championing feminism became integral to my life, the embers of that support began to glow most brightly once I started working in a men's center. This work sparked a vision of gender reconciliation and of creating generations of strong, independent girls and sensitive, caring boys.

As my awareness of inequality grew, I began to see glimmers of the privilege I enjoyed. As a young, white male I felt entitled to do whatever I wanted. Even the specter of anti-Semitism didn't often intrude upon my life. The queasy feelings I had that women were marginalized had no real outlet beyond my slowly emerging consciousness. It seemed as if there was nothing I could do.

I'm certain women I knew at the time would have had reason to characterize me as sexist; perhaps a "kinder and gentler" version, but nonetheless far from a full-fledged ally. Few people outside of the burgeoning women's liberation community recognized the glaring blind spot in the vision of male leaders in the 1960s anti-war movement. Women who exercised leadership in that movement had to do so by emulating their male counterparts, often adopting a confrontational male style. Shifts in gender roles and sharing power more equitably became noticeable during the anti-nuke movement in the mid-1970s where women exercised more leadership and had more of a voice. Nevertheless, sexism remained rampant in most progressive organizations.

My own path kept moving closer to actively engaging in gender politics, first by championing feminism and then working to redefine masculinity. During the 1980s as a proponent of feminist political art and, in the 1990s, as an advocate of male positive, pro-feminist, gay-affirmative, anti-racist men's work, I came to discover the missing piece in my own social change puzzle. The halting voice of a timid eighteen year old recognizing that women in the anti-war movement were being given short shrift had matured into a man who was speaking up and speaking out. Today I direct the Men's Resource Center for Change, a progressive men's center that is seen nationally and internationally as a model for action. I take great satisfaction in the close collaborations we have developed over the years with battered women's shelters, rape crisis centers, women's newspapers, and feminist foundations. My wife and I live in an egalitarian household where my daughters proudly describe themselves as feminists and my son is an outspoken pro-feminist.

I developed my political awareness and became an activist not in isolation, but in community. My commitment was fueled by the camaraderie of kindred spirits walking block after block through late night Washington, often beginning in the shadow of Richard Nixon's borrowed White House. My friends Buzz, Larry and Claire, Rob, Larry K, David—and their yearnings for justice and peace—kept me going. They inspired me and supported me because we shared a burning passion to change the world. The convergence of age, place, and time was nothing short of alchemy. The energy I felt coursing through me at eighteen triggered a lifetime's supply of political adrenaline—a mix of idealism, passion, practicality, and determination slowly seasoned, over the years, with patience.

My life has been shaped by being a part of 1960s history. I could feel it in 1972 when I interned at a Summerhill-inspired, "free" school in Maine, sharing with young people a vision of a world without war or discrimination. The feeling was there five years later when I committed civil disobedience trying to halt the construction of nuclear reactors in Seabrook, New Hampshire. And it was there in 1982 when, while serving as editor of the alternative energy/anti-nuke magazine, *New Roots*, I was arrested in front of the Soviet Consulate in New York City two days after a million people marched demanding a freeze of the nuclear arms race. Even the responsibilities of parenthood couldn't dampen a committed heart. In 1985, when my daughter was six weeks old, she rode in the back seat of the family station wagon in the middle of the night as her mother and I slipped out every block or so, painting human silhouettes on the streets of our town, symbolically representing the vaporized victims of the atomic bombs dropped on Hiroshima and Nagasaki on August 6 and 9, 1945.

Despite media reports smugly belittling activism as just a phase in a young person's life, a period before supposedly one settles down to join the daily commute toward consumerism and apathy, the spirit and heart of a movement for justice—call it the Children of Woodstock Nation, the Spirit of Seattle, the name doesn't matter—is alive and well. It's a renewable energy source worth tapping into and returning to often over the course of a lifetime.

LEARNING FROM WOMEN

Bob Lamm

The following essay is drawn from a speech delivered to the Queens College Women's Student Union on October 28, 1975.[1]

I want to begin by stating how much of a pleasure and an honor it is for me to be speaking here at the invitation of the Women's Student Union. Sometimes, when speakers make these declarations, it's a matter of form and courtesy. But it's a very special honor for me to be here, because I owe a very great debt to the women I've known at Queens College—many of whom worked with the Women's Student Union, with Queens Women Against Rape, and on the annual Women's Festivals.

Officially, in many cases, I was the teacher of these women. But, in reality, they were *my* teachers, and I come here today to try to discuss what I learned from them. Despite all my male and professorial resistance, they taught me quite a bit about their lives and oppression as women, about feminism, and about my own sexism.

When I began teaching courses on "Men, Masculinity, and Sexism" at Queens in the summer of 1974, I was very much impressed with my own qualifications. I thought I knew a whole lot about men's lives and masculinity. And (although I was too clever to say this out loud) I thought I knew a whole lot about women's lives.

The truth is that I knew virtually nothing about the reality of women's lives. The truth is that I came here with no serious background in feminist literature. The truth is that I had no understanding of how absurd and sexist it was for a man to teach a course on men, masculinity, and sexism without a good grasp of feminist literature. The truth is that I had no idea of how much I didn't know.

And the most glaring truth is this one: There's nothing unusual about what I've just said. It's quite common. This afternoon, once 2:00 comes and classes begin again, lots of male professors are going to start telling women students about their lives as women. Some male professors may call this teaching process biology or psychology or history or literature or anthropology. I would call such teaching what many feminists have called it: male supremacy. This so-called educating goes on in every part of this college and in every part of the world—except for the few small bits of turf that feminists have managed to fight for and win.

Thus, there was nothing unique about my coming here to teach at Queens College without much understanding of women's lives or of feminism. But something rather unexpected happened to me. Unlike many male professors, I didn't get away with my act so easily. Lo and behold, there were many strong, eloquent, angry women in my courses who weren't awed by my professorial power or by my radical politics. And these women changed my life.

My course on "Men, Masculinity, and Sexism" in the summer of 1974 was intense and explosive. It lasted six weeks, three nights a week, but it felt like a year. The students in that course—both women and men—were among the most honest people I've ever met in my life. As a result, those classes included moments of risky and revealing self-disclosure. They were also the scenes of bitter and shattering political fights. Women students, speaking out of their anger as victims of a sexist society, wouldn't sit by quietly and be insulted and patronized. Male students, speaking out of their fear and hostility to feminist challenges, wouldn't sit by quietly and listen to attacks on their patriarchal privileges.

One thing I learned was the importance of men listening to women, *listening* to women's feelings and anger, and fighting off our potential for serious backlash. I had repeated conferences with a few male students and found myself telling them again and again to listen to the women in the course. Not to freak out, not to strike back in anger, but instead to work hard at hearing what the women were saying.

The more I found myself in that advisory role, the more I realized how little I myself listened to what women students were saying. The more I observed the backlash and misogyny of male students, the more I had to notice my own backlash and misogyny. And, as I moved increasingly away from a mediating teacher role to active personal involvement, some of my own woman-hating anger began to emerge right in front of me. By the end of the course, it was clear—as one male student wrote—that I was just another fucked-up, insecure man, only with more power than the male students.

During the first week of the course, a woman student asked if she could present a special session on rape—a subject that my syllabus did not cover. I reacted favorably and we set up the class for the next week. Now, at first, my consent may seem like an enlightened act, but it wasn't. It was an act of uninformed, male liberalism. I had no idea of the political and educational importance of having a class on rape in a course on men, masculinity, and sexism. I was simply being amiable or cooptive, depending on your point of view.

My misunderstanding of rape went something like this. I perceived rape to be a serious crime, somewhere between mugging and murder. I was vaguely aware that men were the perpetrators and women the victims of this particular crime. But I never considered the political implications of these obvious facts or the connection between rape and our norms of masculinity.

My mental image of rape was of a sex crime, of what men continue to call a "crime of passion." My image of rape victims contained a subconscious suspicion: What kind of women would *get themselves* into that kind of position? Thus, I had in my head every vicious, woman-hating stereotype that society promotes about rape, right down to blaming the rape victim rather than the rapist for the crime. I had no understanding of the politics of rape—or of how my own power and privilege as a man might have some bearing on the continual rape of women by men in our society.

Women students changed all that. The class on rape and the discussions that followed shattered all of my traditional male prejudices about rape. Women students taught me that rapists are not peculiar, abnormal men. Rapists are very normal, masculine men. There is no exact profile of a "typical rapist" because rapists come in all sizes and shapes, all races and nationalities, all ages and social classes. Many are white, middle-class husbands and fathers.

Women students taught me that rape is neither a sex crime nor a crime of passion. Rape is often premeditated. And rape is a crime of *violence* rather than sex. It is a crime of violence against women. It is an attack by men on women's bodies, on women's feelings, on women's very existence.

Women students taught me that rape is not an isolated, brutal crime against women. It is only one part of a systematic pattern of male violence against women in our society. Some women are raped in their homes or in the streets by men who we call strangers. Some women are raped in their homes or in the streets by men who we call psychiatrists, doctors, college professors, friends, lovers, husbands, and fathers.

Women students taught me that rape can involve psychological as well as physical coercion. Many men, if asked, "Have you ever raped a woman?" would quickly respond in the negative. But what if the question was: "Have you ever, at any time, in any way, through direct physical attack or subtle psychological manipulation, coerced a woman into close physical contact?" How many men could easily answer *no* to that question?

Thus, women students taught me that rape is something in which I myself am deeply implicated—directly in my relationships with women but also indirectly since I benefit from the male privilege that legitimizes rape. For rape is one of the most savage and yet one of the most accurate metaphors for how men relate to women in this society. It is a political crime committed by men as a class against women as a class. Rape is an attempt by men to keep all women in line. It is a clear expression of the hatred of women that pervades our society and our visions of masculinity.

One final thing I learned about rape was about rape jokes and warnings. Every time that a man calls a woman a "bitch," the threat of rape lies behind his hostility. Every time a man calls a woman a "witch," he reminds her of the slaughter of millions of women whose independence and medical knowledge threatened male dominance. And every time a man makes a joke about rape or wife-beating, he issues a warning to women. But, if I learned anything at all from women students, I learned this: Rape is no joke.

My second course on "Men, Masculinity, and Sexism" took place in the spring of 1975. It was as intense as the first but in a very different way. When women spoke out in the first course, men responded out of self-righteous indignation and all hell broke loose. When women spoke out in the second course, men evaded the issue or pretended to be sympathetic. This made honest interaction impossible. The eventual result was that the six women students decided to split. They came in one afternoon and announced that they were holding their own separate classes for women for the last six weeks of the semester.

The women spent those weeks meeting without male students or a male teacher. Their final papers unanimously proclaimed what a valuable experience the all-women's classes had been. As one student wrote: "Our common bonds as women enabled us to discuss topics with our feelings. We can express our thoughts openly because of the oppression we share. We don't have to *prove* what we say is valid. We trust each woman's words and respect her feelings." Every woman wrote about this experience in similarly glowing terms, even those who had been most hesitant at the time of the split.

As a male teacher whose women students all left his course, what did I learn from this experience? Before this course began, I already had some understanding of why women wanted their own space to control as they saw fit. As a result, I accepted and supported the women's split and didn't try to stop it. But talking to the women students at the end of the term, and reading their final papers, taught me some vital lessons about the value and necessity of women's space. And when I say "women's space," I mean this in a very general way. I mean space and time that women exist in and control without male presence or dominance. I mean women's courses, women's studies programs, women's centers, women's self-help clinics, women's consciousness-raising groups, women's coffeehouses, women's bookstores, women's newspapers, women's music, women's communes, women's farms, and, of course, women loving other women. When I speak of the importance of women's space, I'm speaking of all these things and a whole lot more.

I don't need to dwell too long on an obvious point: Men in this society have *no concept* of the importance and beauty and necessity of women controlling their own space, their own bodies, their own lives. Every bit of our socialization as men tells us that we're indispensable, that women simply can't get along without us. We're told that women can only find love from a man. We're told that women have nothing to say or to give to each other.

But here's what I learned as a male teacher. The best college course I've ever been formally responsible for—the very best—was the one where I wasn't there, where I gave no professorial direction, where women controlled their own classroom time.

And that says something very crucial to me, something that men had better begin to learn. The notion that men are indispensable to women is the worst kind of lie. Not only can women function and grow quite well without us being there; in many situations, women can function and grow *much more easily* without us being there. So if men really want to help women, as we always claim, one concrete step is often to get out of the way.

Women students in my course learned more from each other than they ever could have if I had been there. That fact crashes rather heavily into my male ego and my professorial conceit—but it's true and it won't go away. And it helps me to understand a little better that word that frightens and angers men so much: separatism.

Which brings me to a final point about the split. I *did* have ultimate power; I could have stopped the split but chose not to. I could have threatened those women with no credit or with flunking grades or with other academic perils. As long as male teachers have that kind of power over women's lives, it doesn't matter all that much whether they choose to use it or not. Things will be different only when women in the academic world—and in the rest of society—don't have to answer to *any* man, even one that is supposedly sympathetic.

I've tried to touch on some of what I've learned from feminism and from women students I taught at Queens College. Needless to say, I'm still very much at the beginning, and the same is true of every man in our society. Each of us, if we're serious about learning from women and dealing with our sexism, has a lifetime project ahead. If we sincerely want to learn and change, we've got to start reading every available bit of women's writing and feminist literature. This includes women's novels, poetry, history, political literature, autobiographies, biographies, newspapers, journals, and the like.

Also, if we sincerely want to learn and change, we've got to try to shut up and listen to women. This is still the hardest thing for me to do, and yet it is the most essential. In a conversation, men rarely let women get a word in; if a woman speaks, a man often interrupts; and even if a man doesn't interrupt, men don't listen anyway. We're too busy mentally formulating our next bit of oratory. If we want to learn and change, we've got to begin by listening to women and trying to really hear them.

Beyond this, I'm not sure what to say. I know it may seem bizarre or suspicious for a man to speak this way. I know that every time a man says anything halfway reasonable about sexism, it can simply be one more male game, one more way of trying to manipulate women and control women's lives.

But I honestly wish that things were different. I wish I could live in a society where women *truly* were free, where male supremacy seemed so perverse as to be totally unimaginable, where the kind of masculine sickness that still shapes my personality didn't exist. I wish I could live in a society where all of us here really could be friends and respect one another and be apart or together as any of us saw fit. I wish I could live in a society where a Women's Student Union wasn't under pressure from administrators to include a male speaker on its program, where a speaking program *of women only* and *for women only* was considered fully legitimate and appropriate and beautiful.

I know all these things are very far off, but I hope that they're possible some day. Too many men have ruined too many women's lives already. I've seen more than enough, and I've done more than enough, and I want it to stop.

1. "Learning From Women," Copyright © Bob Lamm 2003. From Peter Murphy, ed., *Feminism and Masculinities.* New York: Oxford University Press, 2004. Earlier versions of this essay appeared in *Morning Due: A Journal of Men Against Sexism*, Vol. 2, no. 2, 1976; and in Jon Snodgrass, ed., *For Men Against Sexism: A Book of Readings*, Albion, CA: Times Change Press, 1977.

A TRIBUTE TO MY FATHER

Chris Dixon

My dad was different. Sure, he and I played catch and wrestled, watched sports and enjoyed *Star Wars* together. But he also talked about feelings, cooked dinner regularly, and encouraged me to play with dolls and action figures alike. He didn't even flinch when my mom began painting my toenails pink. Although I wouldn't realize it until later, my father was the first pro-feminist man to touch my life. Growing up, I knew him as a man uncomfortable with manhood. I saw him openly struggle with his own entrenched sexist and homophobic socialization. I watched him try to break down rigid gender roles, with mixed success, in his relationship with my mother. And in the process, I learned a lot about patriarchy and heterosexism, not the least of which is their frustrating resilience.

These kinds of experiences are uncommon. Most of the progressive men that I know don't have much praise for their fathers, particularly when it comes to the issue of sexism. Indeed, more than a few define their anti-sexism in deliberate opposition to their dads. Even so, I think this demonstrates how fathers are so central to our formative experiences as men around gender and sexuality. Many of us have our first run-ins with patriarchy through the older men in our lives, frequently our dads. Consciously and unconsciously, lovingly and punitively, they teach and model being male for children who are expected to identify as boys and unquestioningly accept prevailing notions of masculinity.

In order to understand how patriarchy is perpetuated it makes sense to look first to those who most embody it—men, fathers, and sons. And yet we must also locate the unlikely chinks in its formidable armor: the sites of refusal and struggle in which men, often hesitantly, have challenged patriarchal privilege. That's why I think it's useful, perhaps crucial, to revisit our dads with both sincere compassion and unflinching criticism.

Here I'll start with my late father. I want to pay tribute to him. And I don't mean that in any kind of simple, celebratory way. Rather, this is a tribute worthy of him, one that brings together the good and the bad. In the real world, where domination and oppression intertwine with all aspects of our lives, there are no easy, uncomplicated sources of inspiration. But there are lessons. I look to my dad, then, for lessons about how to struggle against sexism and homophobia, as well as for lessons about the structures of patriarchy and heterosexism that lurked inside him and continue to lurk inside me. In his example, I find both inspiration and warning, inseparably tied.

BEGINNINGS

My dad was born in Fort Worth, Texas, in 1934, in the middle of the Great Depression. My grandmother was young, seventeen years old at the time, and she had just married my grandfather. Six months later they moved to California, where my father spent the rest of his childhood.

My dad grew up white, male, and working-class, an only child in a family constantly struggling to make ends meet. Along the way, he inherited a healthy distrust of wealth and power, largely through his own troubled father, a self-identified socialist as well as an outright racist. Tellingly, his parents gave my dad the middle name "Eugene" for Eugene Debs, the turn-of-the-century radical labor leader. And though my dad came of age during the deeply conservative 1950s, he never lost his gut sense of egalitarian ethics. Decades later as I was becoming politicized, my dad confessed that, at heart, he was forever a socialist. He was convinced that the staggering economic inequalities of our society are fundamentally wrong. I suspect that this core ethic contributed to why he accepted feminism, however imperfectly.

Poverty and hard work framed my father's young adulthood. High school offered very little, so he skimmed through while also working as a gas station attendant. After graduating, he did a stint in the army, narrowly missing the Korean War. Finding nothing redeeming about military life, my dad then entered college, worked his way through, and entered his first marriage, a union that lasted just long enough to bear four children, my half-siblings. By the 1960s my father worked for the State of California.

At first glance, my dad's story looks deceptively like a pulled-himself-up-by-his-bootstraps tale of hard-won success and class mobility. But it isn't; his opportunities and identity were clearly shaped by his access to white, male, straight privilege. Without this, he would have followed a markedly different path. To some extent, my father realized this. He wasn't oblivious to the social movements of the 1960s and 1970s or the openings that they created. My dad would later recount how the civil rights struggles forced him to clarify his values and consider his own position as a white person. Likewise, the women's liberation movement, burgeoning as he met my feminist mother in the early

1970s, challenged him to rethink his manhood and, to a limited degree, his sexuality.

INSPIRATION

My parents married in 1973, on the cusp of a major shift in gender roles and relations that would come to alter kinship, parenting, sex, work, socialization, and so much more. For sure, it was an incomplete shift, but a significant one nonetheless. I sometimes wonder how my dad took it: As the patriarchal landscape around him shook, as some of his privileges as a straight man were called into question, what did it mean to him? How did he learn to change?

One way or another my father embraced some of these shifts in roles and relations. In many ways, I grew up with and learned from a surprisingly nontraditional man. His contributions to household work, for instance, stretched far beyond occasionally barbecuing hamburgers or fixing broken appliances. And contrary to the storylines on TV sitcoms, these weren't duties begrudgingly performed just because my mother asked for help. My dad consistently prepared meals, he washed his share of dishes, and when it was time to clean house, he chipped in just like the rest of us. He changed plenty of dirty diapers, cared for me when I was sick, and carted my brother and me around as my mom worked. Throughout—indeed even after my parents separated in 1994—my father was emphatically dedicated to what he called co-parenting: working together with my mother on equal terms in all parenting decisions. While American pop culture was ambivalently and belatedly coming to terms with Mr. Mom, my parents were figuring out—not always so easily—how to share chores, responsibilities, and decisions. Although seemingly incon-sequential at the time, their innovations shaped how I've come to understand gender, work, and authority.

More than once, I asked my father, "Are you a feminist?" And his reply was always the same: "Yes." For him, that choice transcended our home and his relationship with my mother; it also posed a more general challenge to masculinity and men, himself included. In the late 1980s, his search for answers took my dad to the budding men's movement, a broad (and often contradictory) conglomeration of men's initiatives and organizations. His main participation was with a fairly progressive men's group, including both queers and straights, which met weekly to discuss issues like gender socialization, male role expectations, pornography, and homophobia.

This last topic was especially weighty for my dad, judging from the stories that he shared. When I was nine or ten, for example, he told me about a meeting in which pairs of men in his group had taken turns holding each other's hands while walking around the block outside. Some of them simply couldn't. Their fear of touching other men—their internalized homophobia—

was too deep-rooted. But my father said that he had been able to hold hands the whole way. I saw how scared he had been, and I was proud of him.

Some years later, when I was in my early teens, my dad invited me to attend a local men's conference with him. I still vividly remember the workshops. In the morning, we joined a discussion with lesbian activist and musician, Libby Rodrick, who provided a historical overview of the feminist movement, pulling out lessons for us men to grapple with. "You all," she offered conclusively, "have a lot of work to do among yourselves." In the afternoon, we participated in a lively, multigenerational "dialogue between gay and straight men." For me, still exploring my own sexuality, this was an eye-opening, exciting encounter. And our presence as a father–son duo was especially significant—for the dialogue, because we represented a tangible bridge between generations, and for me, because we momentarily moved outside the assumed heterosexuality that so often pervaded my family and my experience. As I look back, I realize that it took a lot of courage for my dad to participate.

Truth be told, though, many of the most inspirational moments with my father weren't during these major events, but throughout our daily experiences. I treasure memories of the time he explained homophobia to me or, later, our rich, ongoing conversations about gender wherever we went. At the airport with him, for instance, I remember watching and talking about gender roles in greetings and goodbyes: While men were expected to be calm and collected, women were frequently tearful and openly affectionate. Of course, we couldn't, by ourselves, do away with such role limitations, but we found solace in one another as we looked and pushed at them. These were enlightening, memorable times. In them, my dad, along with my mother, taught me a way of critically eyeing the world—a way that he carried courageously into his last days.

WARNING

There was also a flipside to my dad. That is, he was far from untouched by patriarchy or heterosexism. Some of the more poignant lessons I take from him have to do with his failings. My father's shortcomings and his worst demons were inextricably linked to the workings of our social order. At best, my father determinedly pushed at the boundaries of masculinity. Yet for all of his critical self-awareness, he was still a man at times drowning in his own toxic socialization and entrenched in his privilege.

In the late-1990s, my dad finally admitted to his lifelong battle with alcoholism. I have no doubt that this struggle was tied to his larger battles with manhood itself. For most of my life he was largely dry, but he still had his moments of slurred sentimentalities as well as sheer ferocity. For him, alcohol was a coping tool. Depending on the circumstances, it was a means for male bonding, isolated withdrawal, emotional avoidance, or playful oblivion. In short, it was a copout, and a predictably masculine one at that.

Not unconnected was my father's volatile temper. In chilling detail, my mother sometimes tells horrendous stories of his most controlling, explosive states. By her accounts, his care and sensitivity were real, but they also concealed a capacity for intense rage and characteristically masculine entitlement. I definitely experienced pieces of this, but not the full brunt that my mom endured. And as she points out, even as he tried to mend and reconcile in his last years, he never took authentic responsibility.

Certainly my dad should be understood within the larger context of a society founded upon structural inequalities, like patriarchy. Single lives cannot easily bypass institutional realities. However, in some areas of his life, my father worked to challenge this context. So why the incongruity? I suspect that his failure to deal with his behavior stemmed, in part, from his difficulty reaching out and finding support. Despite his encouraging efforts with men's groups, he still relied heavily on the woman in his life—my mom—for emotional caretaking, a dynamic that many men are quick to fall back on. The gendered roles and expectations of the nuclear family—breadwinning father and nurturing mother—don't die so easily.

And while my dad generally frowned on such limited and limiting gender roles, he still sought a fixed masculinity, essential, timeless, and natural. Indeed, he was bothered by my playfulness around gender and worked to police my incursions against gender boundaries. Pink toenails when I was little may have been okay, but at fifteen, I recall his hostility while explaining to my confused younger brother that my beautifully French-braided hair perhaps signaled that I was "gay, or even transsexual." My brother didn't understand that explanation too well, and although the labels didn't bother me, the contempt was biting. From then on, I was careful to keep my more transgressive explorations of gender and sexuality safely away from my father.

Undergirding all of this was the basic fact that my dad's understanding of sexism and homophobia was regrettably shallow. He largely saw feminism as granting women rights in the public arena. He deplored individual, prejudicial, sexist acts. He saw gay rights similarly. Yet he neglected many of the patriarchal and heterosexist structures and patterns inscribed in his own heart. Consequently, his approach to the men's movement, like that of many other men, focused mainly on the obstacles and suffering among us, not the privileges that we enjoy. Sadly, he never quite grasped the whole picture.

LESSONS

My father's story has a natural conclusion. On a wintry day in December of 1999, he collapsed and died, stunning my whole family. But for me, this was less an end than a startling beginning. Since that fateful day, I've come to reflect on my dad in all of his flesh-and-blood complexity, strengthening my connection with him while also creating my own sense of closure and farewell. The process is tricky, for he was full of pointed contradictions: a pro-feminist who angrily vented upon my mother; a gender-role skeptic who nonetheless reinforced gender boundaries; an anti-sexist who failed to confront some of his most sexist patterns; a sensitive, reflective man who fled from his own feelings, long using alcohol to aid his flight. Only in recognizing these can I piece him together.

On the one hand, I acknowledge his successes and the inspirational role he has played in my life. Simply put, I would not be the person that I am today without him. He helped equip me with some essential, reflective tools for challenging systems of oppression. He embodied a (not entirely) different way of "being a man." And he taught me basic things: to confront my own homophobia, to contribute equally in household responsibilities, to never forget how to cry. In this sense, I carry him with me.

On the other hand, I acknowledge my dad's failings. I love him, and the most sincere way I know of expressing my love, particularly in his absence, is by learning from his mistakes and accepting the responsibility of not repeating them. As a (mostly) straight man, the son of my father, I, too, have the capacity to dwell in my rage and entitlement, to sink into avoidance and isolated withdrawal, to rely exclusively on the women in my life for my emotional caretaking. I, too, can choose to ignore my privilege. To forget any of this would be the greatest disrespect to my dad. In this sense as well, I carry him with me.

Somewhat optimistically, bell hooks recently noted in *Talking About a Revolution*, "We have for the first time a generation of men coming to adulthood who were not born into a world automatically submerged with sexist socialization that says that women are not the intellectual or work equals of men." I am of this generation of men. But for all the tremendous social shifts and major feminist successes, I, like others, haven't wholly escaped sexist or heterosexist socialization. This struggle will be a long one. I'm fortunate, though, because my father has left me with some inspiring tools and difficult lessons to help me along the way.

Thanks, Dad.

PLAYGROUND VERTIGO

Jeremy Adam Smith

The day started ordinarily enough. I came home from my office at noon. My wife Shelly went to work. I took our toddler Liko to a cafe for lunch and then we strollered to the playground.

From noon until 7:00 p.m. on weekdays, I'm a Mr. Mom—a term that bothers some stay-at-home dads as a knock on their masculinity. Personally, it doesn't bother me. The reader will not be surprised to hear that I'm usually the only dad I see at Liko's swim and music classes. I don't mind that, either. After a period of adjustment, I came to accept the relative isolation that goes along with my role.

But on the day in question we stepped through the playground gate into a parallel universe where the laws of gender bent and vanished (cue *Twilight Zone* theme): Liko and I found ourselves surrounded by . . . men. Three men playing with three toddlers. No women in sight.

One dad left, but another arrived. At 1:00 p.m., it was still only dads and kids. Naturally, we dads compared notes about the unprecedented situation in which we found ourselves. It emerged that one of us was a full-time, stay-at-home dad but looking for a job; two of us had quit careers to take care of our kids, but still, out of necessity, worked part-time as freelancers; the fourth was finishing a Ph.D. All four of our wives worked more hours than we did.

This was the second time around for the Ph.D., Nick; he has a two-year-old and a seven-year-old. "There are definitely more dads on the playgrounds now than there were five years ago," Nick said.

At about 1:30, the first mom arrived with her baby. Liko and I went home for a nap. This incident raised the question: How many of us—and by "us" I mean men who are primary caregivers—are out there?

The 2004 census says that there are 147,000 stay-at-home dads caring for 245,000 kids younger than fifteen. That's about 1.7 percent of all U.S. parents who are taking care of children, a pretty marginal group, but it's also double the number who stayed home in 1995, which suggests a trend. And the Bureau of Labor Statistics says that about two million dads work part-time for "non-economic reasons" that include childcare, a category into which I fit. Census data also show that homes headed by single dads are the fastest-growing family type.

So what? Those numbers are still small, and it's still mostly women taking care of children, often pulling double shifts as workers and mommies. If there is a trend toward more paternal involvement in child rearing—and there is, no question, and that's a good thing—we should still keep it in perspective.

When Father's Day rolls around, we stay-at-home dads are the freaks. I'm happy to fly my freak flag, while acknowledging that today it's hard for any parent, male or female, to find enough time for their children. In her report, "One Sick Child Away From Being Fired: When 'Opting Out' Is Not an Option," UC Hastings law professor Joan C. Williams found that only 16 percent of working-class families enjoy the luxury of having one stay-at-home parent.

Williams discovered many, many examples of blue-collar workers (mostly women, but some men) who were fired for offenses like being three minutes late because of a child's asthma attack. For many moms and dads, staying home is not an option, and a "balance" between work and family is not possible. What white-collar workers gain in flexibility, they often lose in boundaries: How many of us have spent evenings and weekends massaging PowerPoints and spreadsheets?

Most stay-at-home dads I've met are relatively privileged, creative guys doing what they want to do, and they're happy doing it.

"None of us at-home fathers go into it in order to be some sort of social role model," says Stephen de las Heras, thirty-eight, a digital artist who lives in Manhattan and is the primary caregiver to his four-year-old son. "We don't deserve medals. At least not for that. If anything, the correct response from people would be a completely neutral one. But we do have to put up with some shit from the less enlightened crowd, and face some additional obstacles in a mom-centric world. For that, a pat on the back once in a while can be nice, but is not required."

Exactly. In my view, dads-at-home are significant primarily to the degree they are bellwethers of a wider change in the culture, toward more flexible definitions of masculinity and femininity. Thanks to feminism—which has tried to teach us to ride the shockwave created by massive economic change—women now have more choices. So do men.

When I was born in 1970, my parents debated only whether my mom would work or stay at home. "We opted for her to stay home," says my father,

Dan. "That was the question of the day. The idea that a mother could have a career and be a mom was the radical thought of the time. The option for Dad to stay home was not considered. If it was, nobody told me, and the thought never entered my head." Since then, families have changed a great deal. In 1970, men spent three hours a week on childcare. In 2000, they spent seven hours a week taking care of kids—that's up 62 percent from 1995. During the same thirty-year period, the time women spent on childcare remained roughly constant at around thirteen hours a week. Meanwhile, divorce became normal, more moms went to work, same-sex couples started families, and many heterosexual couples decided not to marry even after having children together. According to Yale University professor Kyle Pruett, nearly two-thirds of the kids born in the last three years of the twentieth century will reach the age of eighteen in "a non-nuclear family configuration." The twenty-first century dad can be single, queer, straight, stay at home . . . she can even be a "lesbian dad" who earns the money that supports her wife and children. (If you doubt me, check out blogs like Lesbiandad.net or icallherjohn.blogspot.com.)

Families are evolving. So are men and ideas of masculinity. Conservatives (and some feminists) argue that men are by nature conquerors, breadwinners, and emotional dolts. But when Canadian sociologist Andrea Doucet studied stay-at-home dads, what constantly surprised her about these fathers "were these clear and loud male voices speaking in what scholars would call a 'language of care' or an 'ethic of care' that embraces qualities of relationality, connections, interdependence, responsiveness, and responsibility." As numerous studies are revealing, it seems that biology is not destiny. "Could it be that when men speak in a language of care," writes Doucet in her book *Do Men Mother?*, "it creates a sense of social and political vertigo?"

In caring for Liko, never have I felt more secure in my masculinity; at the same time, never have I felt less "masculine." I'm learning, slowly, to let go of the link between my self-worth and the contribution I make at work; more and more, I measure myself against women I see as successful mothers. Does that make me effeminate? Is there a reason why I should care? I'm not replacing my wife, who is Liko's mother. For seven or so hours a day, I'm simply adopting a role that in my father's day was automatically assigned to the biological female. In caregiving I have found enormous, vertiginous freedom.

In many respects, a man out in the middle of the afternoon with his toddler, who is known to neighbors and neighborhood shop clerks and waitresses as a "Mr. Mom," is a man in drag, and queer in the most political sense of the term. That's fine with me. Yes, I've gotten criticism from relatives ("A man is supposed to support his family, and a woman is supposed to stay home"). I've also gotten sneering reactions to my blog and articles about stay-at-home daddyhood. "It's hard to believe this dude was capable of procreating," writes one blogger about me. "I'm thinking a turkey baster was involved." I know that I'm facing an uphill battle when I get back into the full-time job market. I'd be lying if I claimed that I have no doubts.

But mostly, I don't care what anybody says. When Liko and I are blasting Yo La Tengo or the Strokes or Blondie (his favorites; he has a thing for punk, new wave and indie pop; anything that bounces, really) and I'm dancing and he's careening down the hall, arms flailing, hopping from one foot to the other, and then he runs up and hugs my leg and yells "Dada!"—life can't get any better. I helped make a new life, and that's staggering: a new human being, and a new life for me. I don't want to give him to a nanny or daycare; as much as possible, I want to take care of him and see him grow.

Many dads, both breadwinners and caregivers, seem to share my desire. A 2006 careerbuilder.com survey found that 40 percent of guys would consider staying at home with their kids. A 2004 Spike TV poll put that number at a fantastical sounding 56 percent.

Though the exact numbers are questionable (why should anybody trust a Spike TV survey?), it reveals a para-numerical truth about changing attitudes. I suspect the number of dads-at-home will continue to grow and I'll keep getting more and more male company on the playground.

Now here's the really interesting question: What impact will our choices have on the next generation? When Kyle Pruett studied kids raised by stay-at-home dads, he found that they didn't seem to care all that much about fixed gender roles. "Gender polarization seemed a marginal, rather than central, issue for these youngsters on the threshold of their adolescence," Pruett writes. "Their equanimity concerning gender issues in their peer relations was striking because of the usual anxiety and conflict at this stage." The kids were drawn to peers who shared their views on gender roles. "None of my girlfriends want to be housewives," says one girl. "None of my guy friends want nothing to do with their kids—they think kids are cool."

And so it goes, from one generation to the next. Liko might not see "mothering" and "fathering" the way I do. If current trends continue, there could be a huge generation gap between us and our children, with many unexpected consequences. Revolutions—maybe I should say evolutions—have a way of leaving the revolutionaries behind.

JUDGING FATHERS: THE CASE FOR GENDER-NEUTRAL STANDARDS

Donald N.S. Unger

It was Sunday night and my daughter Rebecca and I were heading north on the Merritt Parkway, through Connecticut, back home to Massachusetts, after a weekend of visiting friends and family in and around New York City. Harry Chapin's song, "Cat's in the Cradle" was on the radio.

It was 2003. Rebecca was eight at the time, and I was in the middle of two years of teaching as a visiting professor in the English department at The University at Albany, SUNY, some 140 miles from where we lived. It was a five-hour, round-trip commute; a trip that I made about twice a week. Any time I told people where I was teaching and where I lived, they asked if—or sometimes simply assumed that—I was living in Albany half the week. It was a question that always irritated me. Would they make the same assumption about a mother with a young child?

I turned up the volume on the radio and told Rebecca to listen closely to the song. When it was over, I asked her what she thought it was about.

"That the father is sad he didn't see his son grow up?" Rebecca asked, only a little tentatively.

"That's right," I told her, proud, like any parent, that my daughter intelligently answered the question, even if I was the only one there to hear what she had to say.

Rebecca paused.

Then she said, "That's why you don't have an apartment in Albany, right? Because you don't want to be like the man in the song."

"That's right," I said again, working on keeping the emotion out of my voice, concentrating on the road ahead of me.

"I'm glad," Rebecca said.

"Me, too."

"Did you get the idea from the song?" she asked me.

"No," I told her.

That Rebecca was good at analyzing this song's lyrics made sense: I've been talking, writing, and complaining about fatherhood issues since before she was born. But I'll get to that.

It also made sense that we were having this conversation in the car; that's where a good deal of modern-day, parent–child relating seems to take place. When Rebecca was younger and my wife Cynthia was working toward tenure—both during and after the two years or so that I was the stay-at-home parent—my daughter and I regularly drove that route to New York and often discussed these things. Sometimes music was the trigger; sometimes it was something more basic: like rest stop bathroom facilities.

When Rebecca was three-and-a-half—with the *pro bono* assistance of Deborah Ellis, a law professor at New York University and former legal counsel for the National Organization for Women's Legal Defense and Education Fund[1]—I got the Mobil Oil Corporation to comply with state law in Connecticut and New York state and install changing tables in the men's rooms in the rest stops along Route 15, which encompasses the Wilbur Cross, the Merritt, and the Hutchinson River Parkways. Justice grinds slowly, of course; by the time this was done, my daughter was already toilet trained. Nevertheless, I take a measure of satisfaction in this accomplishment to this day, every time we make that trip and I see those changing tables.

It's worth noting that federal law offers no cause of action in such a situation. Achieving gender equity in college athletics is a federal matter—with which I have no quarrel. Whether fathers can change their children's diapers indoors while traveling, however, is a "state's rights" matter with which the federal government chooses not to trifle.

For months after the case, any time I took Rebecca into a men's bathroom, she would look around and then ask me, "Are you going to make them put a changing table in here, too?"

I would if I could and I don't think that's something I'm alone in.

Professor Ellis had a running start in taking on Mobil on my behalf: A few years earlier, her husband, also an attorney, had taken similar action against the Lord & Taylor department store chain for *their* failure to have changing tables in men's rooms.

He won, too.

It may be that the tide is beginning to turn, in terms of how we see fathers and how fathers see themselves, in how we talk about parenting, and how we represent parents in the media, in popular art, in everyday language.

As far as I'm concerned, these changes can't come fast enough; I've been waiting for them almost all my life.

When I was a teenager in the 1970s, the gender messages being broadcast were decidedly mixed. On the one hand, the feminist movement was a force to be reckoned with. Women and men who wanted change—both full civil and economic rights for women and also a more comprehensive fracturing of gender roles over all—were visible, vocal, and, in many ways, ascendant. The Equal Rights Amendment was working its way through state legislatures; many people thought it was on its inevitable way to ratification.

As a teenage boy who did babysitting in addition to mowing lawns and washing cars, these issues were directly relevant to me. There were people who were definitely happy to see a boy taking care of children. Yet, while babysitting, I still received the occasional phone call from a grandparent or friend of the family for whom I was working that clearly indicated that a male voice claiming to be the babysitter was reason for some alarm.

Now and then, I was quizzed on difficult things like the child's name, as if I might have been a slightly dim home invader who had yet to learn that it was poor form to pick up the phone, mid-rampage.

My family circumstances also made these issues more concrete than abstract. My mother was a Zionist socialist who, on graduating high school, left New York City for Israel shortly after the declaration of statehood. In part, she said in later years, she was looking for a living arrangement that dispensed with a good deal of the gendered division of labor. A few years of living on a kibbutz convinced her that Israel was not to be the home of this, then-radical, alternative. She returned to New York and took a job as a public health nurse.

My parents divorced when I was in my early teens, and my younger sister and I stayed with my father. I remember the theory that we were each to make dinner two nights per week; I don't remember clearly how cleaning chores were divided up, although I have some dim memory of charts. This system did not work smoothly or easily, but I don't believe we were undernourished. And if the house was somewhat dingy, and at times in disarray, I don't recall filth at the level of health hazard. So somehow we must have done the cooking and cleaning ourselves, with my father actively participating, as well as playing the crucial, supervisory role.

In the larger society, during the same period, while there was intense cultural and political battling going on, there was also genuine and growing support for women to take on "non-traditional" work roles, which at that time still meant almost anything outside of secretarial work, teaching elementary school, or nursing.

On the domestic front, things were beginning to change, as well—in part as a result of increased workforce participation by middle-class, white women. Intermittent glimpses of men doing housework, cooking, and taking care of children were visible, like a broadcast television station at the edge of the signal, flickering through the interference. But those changes among some men seemed at least as controversial as women moving into the workplace, if not more so.

John Irving's novel *The World According to Garp* came out in 1978, when I was in high school. The title character was a writer, a stay-at-home father, and a great cook. Sounded cool to me. But to a lot of people Garp seemed to be more wacky than admirable, more literary magic than realistic option.

John Lennon was holed up in The Dakota at this time, having essentially given up making music to bake bread and take care of his son Sean. Some people saw this as a positive model, I certainly did. But others interpreted the way that he was living his life as just another example of how he had been emasculated by Yoko Ono. There were ugly strains of misogyny and racism; she was a "Dragon Lady," in this view, who first broke up the Beatles and then broke John's spirit. How else to explain his choice to care for his son rather than continue his career? How else to explain the famous photo of Yoko, lying down, clothed in black, John curled against her, naked and fetal?

On television, there were commercials that depicted men performing domestic labor. But I am hard pressed to remember any which showed this in a positive light. For the most part, in my memory, these commercials boil down to riffs on a stereotypical exchange; the sort that we continue to see today.

Open on:

Wide shot. Suburban household. Day. An inept father is standing in the kitchen, the sink piled high with dirty dishes, something burning on the stove, a two-foot dike of detergent foam leading the way to the clothes washer, around the corner, in the laundry room.

Father (yelling to his wife, off screen): Honey, should I take the kids out of the dryer now?

Cut to:

Close up. Suburban household. Day. Wife's face as she surveys the mess, from the kitchen doorway. A mixture of amusement and disdain at his incompetence clouds her features before she moves in to displace him and restore order.

Popular culture critic Mark Crispin Miller has dubbed these sorts of scenarios examples of pseudo-feminism. A focus on male domestic incompetence gives a surface appearance of recognizing the power and authority of women. But one doesn't have to read too deeply into the subtext to see that the message is neither liberatory nor egalitarian.

What conclusion can one draw from such a scene, other than it would be sheer madness to "allow" men to continue to contribute to cooking, cleaning, and childcare? It implies a willingness on the part of men to do such work, but quickly demonstrates that we are simply not up to the task. The message seems to be, "We bow to your superior skill. Now, back to the kitchen, Honey."

What much of this suggests is that I shouldn't have been so quick to dismiss Rebecca's question about whether my behavior was cued by Harry Chapin's song. It's a song I grew up listening to. And of course—in addition to family, economics, politics, and a whole knot of other influences—books, language, advertising, television, and music *did* do a lot to shape my ideas about what kind of parent a man should or could be. How could they not have?

Today, we're at a funny moment, an interesting juncture. We may be on the cusp of fundamentally—and to my mind, positively—shifting to a much more open definition of family and of caregiving. I *hope* we are broadening what is possible—or, perhaps more accurately, what is *acceptable*—for a man to do with his life.

In the near future we may see the home open up to men in the same way that the workplace began to open up to women in the 1970s. I believe this would be a good thing, for men, for women, for children. But I would never assume that change is always easy nor that it is ever neat. We still have minefields to cross, the nature/nurture debate high on the list.

It was clear as soon as our daughter was old enough to navigate the playground that I was willing to allow her greater physical risks than was my wife. Children periodically fall down and I don't think that's always a bad thing. In many ways, it's an important learning tool, far more effective than any safety lecture that I could give.

I wasn't being callous or indifferent when I gave Rebecca a bit more freedom. I didn't walk away from her when she was attempting something new and difficult, but when she was a toddler on the playground my hand was more likely to be six inches away from her; my wife more often remained in direct contact.

I've never felt that we had any meaningful, philosophical differences there. I don't complain that my wife is smothering Rebecca; my wife doesn't accuse me of neglect. But our approach to parenting is clearly different. Go to any playground in America and you'll probably see a similar parenting split, often along gender lines.

Observations of this kind lead some people to argue that male–female differences have innate, biological sources. Others ascribe differing parenting styles to nurture rather than nature. We might be more confident about being able to change our gender roles if we believe these parenting tendencies are learned through our culture rather than being hard-wired, inborn differences.

I don't have the answer. And I have no interest in picking a side.

Instead of trying to resolve the nature–nurture debate, what I want to advocate instead is respect for personal choice and individual difference. If geneticists find a variety of genes that they have been hunting for some time now—the genius gene, the criminal gene, the gay gene, the mothering gene, the super-athlete gene, the warrior gene—will this really put a smooth end to a variety of ideological and sociological debates about women, men, and parenting that have been roiling societies for generations?

It seems unlikely.

We do better to look at actions in context and judge them apart from labels, to look at what is being done, rather than who is doing it. In observing a parent on a playground then, the question becomes not "Is that child being maternally smothered or paternally neglected?" but, rather, "Does the level of attention being given to the child fall within reasonable parenting practice?"

In other words, *Is that person taking care of the child?*

Not a perfect solution. This approach loses some of the warmth and specificity of either "maternal" or "paternal" and has a slight utilitarian tinge to it.

But what I'm asking for as a fully engaged father is essentially the same thing that women have been fighting for in the professional sphere for forty years or more: a gender-neutral standard of assessment.

Judge me on whether or not I am an effective parent, not on whether or not I'm a pretty good parent *for a man*.

1. Now known as Legal Momentum.

WHAT'S WRONG WITH FATHERS' RIGHTS?

Michael Flood

Twenty years ago I joined my first anti-sexist men's group. I've had a passionate commitment to profeminism ever since, nurtured through men's anti-violence activism, women's and gender studies, editing a profeminist magazine, and now pursuing a career in feminist scholarship. Men's violence against women is an obvious area for anti-sexist men's activism, as it's one of the bluntest and most brutal forms of gender inequality. I've organized campaigns in groups like Men Against Sexual Assault, run workshops in schools, helped run a national White Ribbon Campaign, designed violence prevention programs for athletes and others, and done research and writing on violence against women. But I've also been forced to critique and confront anti-feminist men in so-called men's rights and fathers' rights groups. Their efforts are having a growing influence on community understandings of, and policy responses to, gender issues.

MEN'S RIGHTS AND FATHERS' RIGHTS

Any man who publicly supports feminism will find himself up against negative stereotypes of, myths about, and hostile responses to feminism, feminists, and the men who support them. "Men's rights" and "fathers' rights" groups represent this in concentrated and toxic form.

The fathers' rights movement argues that fathers are subjected to systematic discrimination as men and fathers, in a system that is biased toward women and dominated by feminists. Fathers' rights groups overlap with men's rights groups and both represent an organized backlash to feminism. Fathers' rights and men's rights groups are the anti-feminist wing of the men's movement, a network of men's groups and organizations mobilized around gender issues.

Two experiences bring most men (and women) to the fathers' rights movement. The first is deeply painful marriage breakups and custody battles; the second is when non-custodial fathers are dissatisfied with loss of contact with their children or with regimes of child support. Fathers' rights groups are characterized by anger and blame toward ex-partners and the legal system, believing that both have deprived men of their rights to contact with their children and to be free from financial child support obligations.

LIES AND DENIAL

All this matters to profeminist men because men's rights and fathers' rights advocates and organizations are doing harm to the causes in which we believe. They are our political opponents. These anti-feminist networks are hindering progress toward gender equality, and in some cases, they're even making things go backward. Fathers' rights groups are well-organized advocates for changes in family law, and vocal opponents of feminist perspectives and achievements on interpersonal violence. And they're having some successes. I'll return to this in a moment.

I try to push feminist and profeminist perspectives in the public domain, by giving media interviews, writing op-eds, making speeches, and producing accessible information like fact sheets and articles for the lay reader. As part of this, I've critiqued the claims made by anti-feminist men's groups. I also monitor their activities and agendas, by checking on their websites and reading their literature. And sometimes, I've engaged in direct debate. I used to go to the mainstream men's movement events around Australia, large men's festivals and men's gatherings of 100 to 200 men. Committed anti-feminist men are regular participants in these. Profeminist men are a much smaller minority and anti-feminist or, at best, non-feminist notions are part and parcel of the men's liberation perspectives shared by most participants in the men's movement. More recently, I've posted comments on fathers' rights websites, and responded to others' postings on the blog of the Australian White Ribbon Campaign.

I don't think that every profeminist man has to engage in direct debate with men's rights and fathers' rights activists. But we all have to deal with anti-feminist reactions and beliefs in society in general, as well as the pernicious influence of these more organized agendas. We should know what they're saying, what's wrong with it, and have other ways of responding to the issues they claim to address.

So, what's wrong with men's rights? Above all, anti-feminist men's per-spectives are based on a profound denial of the systematic gender inequalities which privilege many men and disadvantage many women. Yes, some men are disadvantaged and some women are privileged, but these have more to do with other social divisions—class, race, age, and so on—than they do with gender. Yes, there are times when individual men are harmed or cheated by individual women—we are all human, after all, but such instances do not support anti-feminist men's claim that men are the "new Jews," suffering under, what they call, a global, "feminazi" regime. Men's and fathers' rights groups offer a bizarre and fundamentally inaccurate portrayal of feminism as anti-male and fail to see the enormous hope for and goodwill toward men which it embodies. Fathers' rights groups tell lies about the extent of women's false allegations of abuse or domestic violence. And both men's rights and fathers' rights advocates make dodgy claims of gender symmetry in domestic violence based on studies using problematic and much-criticized tools of measurement and highly selective readings of the literature.

Violence is a key area of fathers' rights activism because it's a common issue in family law proceedings. We know that the time around separation and divorce is one of the riskiest in terms of women's subjection to violence by an intimate partner or ex-partner. More widely, violence against women is a confronting example of gender inequality and thus central to struggles over the meaning and shape of contemporary gender relations. Violence is one of the most worrying areas in which men's and fathers' rights groups are having an impact.

FATHERS, VIOLENCE, AND FAMILY LAW

There are three ways in which the fathers' rights movement has had a damaging impact on the field of violence against women. These are readily apparent in Australia, and probably evident in the United States and elsewhere, as well. First, fathers' rights groups have negatively influenced laws and policies that affect the victims and perpetrators of men's violence against women, particularly when it comes to cases of separation, divorce, and child custody.

Above all, fathers' *contact* with children has been privileged, over children's *safety* from violence. In large part due to publicity efforts by fathers' rights groups, an uncritical assumption that children's contact with both parents is necessary now pervades the courts and the media. In Australia, the Family Court's new principle of the "right to contact" is overriding its principle of the right to "safety from violence." In short, family law increasingly is being guided by two mistaken beliefs: that contact with both parents is in children's best interests in every case, and that a violent father is better than no father at all. Greater numbers of parents who are the victims of violence are being subject to further violence and harassment by abusive ex-partners, while children are being pressured into contact with abusive or violent parents. The Court now is more likely to make interim orders for children's unsupervised contact in cases involving domestic violence or child abuse, to use hand-over arrangements rather than suspend contact until trial, and to make orders for joint residence where there is a high level of conflict between the separated parents and one parent strongly objects to shared residence.

Second, fathers' rights groups have had a negative impact on community understandings of violence against women and children. They have discredited female and child victims of violence by spreading the lie that women routinely make false accusations of child abuse to gain advantage in family law proceedings and to arbitrarily deny their ex-partners' access to the children. The Australian evidence is that allegations of child abuse are rare, false allegations are rare, and false allegations are made by fathers and mothers at equal rates. In any case, allegations of child abuse rarely result in the denial of parental contact.

Fathers' rights groups also claim that women routinely make up allegations of domestic violence to gain advantage in family law cases and use protection orders for vindictive reasons rather than any real experience or fear of violence. Again, Australian research finds instead that women living with domestic violence often do not take out protection orders at all, and when they do it is only as a last resort in the face of severe violence.

Another dimension of the fathers' rights movement's damaging impact on community perceptions is to do with men's versus women's violence. Advocates encourage the mistaken belief that domestic violence is gender-equal. I've debunked this claim in detail elsewhere, but here is a lightning-quick critique: It's simply not true that men and women assault each other at equal rates and with equal effects. To support the claim that domestic violence is gender-symmetrical, advocates draw almost exclusively on studies using a measurement tool called the Conflict Tactics Scale. But anti-feminist groups use CTS results only selectively. More importantly, the CTS is a very poor method of measuring domestic violence: it asks only about violent acts, ignoring their initiation, intensity, context, history, consequences, or meaning.

Let's say that I've been systematically abusing my wife over the last year. I've hit her, I've constantly put her down, I've controlled her movements, and I've forced her into sex. And once, in the midst of another of my violent attacks on her, she hit me back. My various strategies of power and control have left her physically bruised and emotionally battered. And her one act of self-defense just made me laugh. But according to the CTS, we've both committed at least one violent act. So the CTS counts us as equivalent. (Note here that, if our positions were reversed and it was my *wife* who'd been systematically abusing *me*, the CTS would still be a poor measure of the violence. It's crappy either way.)

There's a whole mountain of evidence—crime victimization surveys, police statistics, and hospital data—that domestic violence is not gender-neutral. Men do under-report, but no more than, and probably less than, women. Yes, some men are victims of domestic violence, including by female partners. And there are important contrasts in women's and men's experiences of domestic violence. When it comes to violence by partners or ex-partners, women are far more likely than men to be subjected to frequent, prolonged, and extreme violence, to sustain injuries, to be subjected to a range of controlling strategies, to fear for their lives, to be sexually assaulted, to experience post-separation violence, and to use violence only in self-defense.

There are obvious signs that the fathers' rights movement's attention to domestic violence against men is not motivated by a genuine concern for male victimization. The movement focuses on domestic violence when the great majority of the violence inflicted on men is not by female partners but by *other men*. For example, a four-year study of admissions to the Emergency Department of a Missouri hospital found that among the over eight thousand men who had been assaulted and injured, only forty-five men were injured by their intimate female partners or ex-partners, representing 0.55 percent of male assault visits and 0.05 percent of all male visits. Boys and men are most at risk of physical harm from other boys and men.

In addition, the efforts of the fathers' rights movement to modify public responses to the victims and perpetrators of violence harm female and male victims of domestic violence alike. This is the third kind of impact the movement has had on interpersonal violence. The fathers' rights movement tries to erode the protections available to victims of domestic violence and to boost the rights and freedoms of alleged perpetrators. The Lone Fathers' Association and other groups argue that claims of violence or abuse should be made under oath, they should require police or hospital records as proof, and people who make allegations that are not then substantiated should be subject to criminal prosecution. They call for similar limitations to do with protection orders. Fathers' rights groups also attempt to undermine the ways in which domestic violence is treated as criminal behavior. They emphasize the need to keep the family together, call for the greater use of mediation and counseling, and reject pro-arrest policies.

These changes would represent a profound erosion of the protections and legal redress available to the victims of violence, whether female or male. This agenda betrays the fact that the concern for male victims of domestic violence often professed by fathers' rights groups is hollow. Fathers' rights groups often respond to issues of domestic and sexual violence from the point of view of the perpetrator. And they respond in the same way as actual male perpetrators: They minimize and deny the extent of this violence, blame the victim, and explain the violence as mutual or reciprocal. Fathers' rights advocates have expressed understanding or justification for men who use violence against women and children in the context of family law proceedings. And, ironically, they use men's violence to demonstrate how victimized men are by the family law system. Fathers' rights groups also attack media and community campaigns focused on men's violence against women and harass community sector and women's organizations that respond to the victims of violence.

Yes, male victims of domestic violence deserve the same support as female victims. And we don't need to pretend that they total 50 percent of victims to establish this. And we're certainly not doing them any favors by attacking the systems and services set up to support and protect them or the women who put the issue on the public agenda in the first place.

SUPPORTING FATHERS

Men who are going through a separation or divorce certainly deserve services and support. But they're not well served by fathers' rights groups. Fathers' rights groups stifle men's healing processes, constrain and harm their relations with their children, and directly compromise the wellbeing of children themselves. First, many groups offer their members identities based only in victimhood, centered on hostility toward and blame of the legal system and their ex-partners, and colored by misogynist norms. Such approaches fix men in positions of anger and hostility, rather than helping them to heal. Some groups encourage their members to engage in malicious, destructive, and unproductive legal strategies.

There is no doubt that many of the individual men in fathers' rights groups want a greater involvement in their children's lives, but these groups have done little to foster fathers' positive involvement in children's lives, whether before or after separation and divorce. The fathers' rights movement focuses on fathers' "rights" rather than the actual care of children. It prioritizes formal principles of equality over positive parenting and the wellbeing of women and children. It conflates children's welfare with parental equality, ignores actual caregiving divisions of labor, and neglects the real obstacles to shared parenting both in couple families and after separation or divorce. Many fathers' rights groups seem more concerned with re-establishing fathers' authority and control over their children's and ex-partners' lives than with actual involvement with children. They neglect the real challenges of maintaining or setting up shared parenting after divorce, arguing for one-size-fits-all approaches based on joint custody, which won't work for most families.

Fathers' rights groups also have been willing to compromise children's wellbeing. They've tried to force parental contact on children regardless of children's wishes and wellbeing, to reduce non-resident parents' obligations to financially support their children (although some aspects of current child support regimes *are* unjust), and to undermine the protections and support available to child victims of abuse and domestic violence. Through their hostile and misogynist depictions of resident mothers and their attempts to control mothers' management of finances, parenting, and contact, fathers' rights groups also have fueled interparental conflict, leading to more problems with contact and further stress for children.

BEATING THE BACKLASH

The achievements of the fathers' rights movement are already putting women, children, and even men at greater risk of violence and abuse. The fathers' rights movement has exacerbated our culture's systematic silencing and blaming of victims of violence and hampered efforts to respond effectively to the victims and perpetrators of violence. Fathers' groups have done little to encourage fathers' positive involvement in parenting, whether before or after divorce, and in some ways they've even made things worse. More generally, men's rights and fathers' rights groups are hampering progress toward gender equality or pushing it backward.

However, the new politics of fatherhood has not been entirely captured by the fathers' rights movement. There is potential to foster men's positive and non-violent involvement in parenting and families. Key resources for realizing the progressive potential of contemporary fatherhood politics include the widespread imagery of the nurturing father, community intolerance for violence against women, growing policy interest in addressing divisions of labor in childcare and domestic work, and men's own investment in positive parenting.

Responses to separated fathers should be father-friendly, accountable, and oriented toward encouraging positive and ongoing involvement in their children's lives. We should be working to respond to separated fathers, not only because of the emotional and practical needs they have, and not only to encourage their ongoing and positive involvement with children, but also because doing so will lessen the recruitment of separated fathers into the fathers' rights movement. In other words, providing compassionate and constructive services for separated fathers is important in part because it diverts them from participation in fathers' rights networks. And doing this is desirable because such networks are harmful for law and public policy, for women and children, and for separated men themselves.

At the same time, we must confront the dangerous ambitions and dishonest claims of the men's and fathers' rights backlash. We need to directly subvert these groups' agendas, spread critiques of their false accusations, and respond in constructive and accountable ways to the fathers (and mothers) undergoing separation and divorce. We must step up efforts to engage men in positive ways, building partnerships with supportive men and men's groups and with the women's movements. All this is part of a broader profeminist effort to build a world of gender justice.

ENGENDERING THE CLASSROOM: EXPERIENCES OF A MAN IN WOMEN'S AND GENDER STUDIES

Kyle Brillante

I am exasperated.

It's my roommate. He tells me about a group on campus conducting a speaker's series. The series topic is about feminism today, and the group wants several students to talk about their relation to feminism, and to describe their lived experiences as feminists in the twenty-first century. They are seeking a diverse panel, and the woman in charge—a friend of his—asked if he knew of a man who might be willing to speak on the panel. They'd love to have a man speak about his support of feminism, she says. Perhaps they could even find a real-live male feminist. The woman tells my roommate that they can't find a genuine male feminist and asks if he knows one. She's heard he has a roommate—a man—who is interested in feminism. The woman begs my roommate to help her find a man willing to talk about his identification as a feminist. They *really* want a diverse panel. Does he *puleeze* know of any man who might be able to speak?

My roommate casually relays this information to me over dinner. In the midst of my second helping of green beans, he implores me to participate. As the only male in a women's and gender studies graduate program at one of the largest universities in the country, I'm exactly the person they want. After all, being the self-identified feminist that I am, he tells me, I am perfect for the panel and I'll have a lot to say. I have a lot of experience; ergo, it'll be easy. Not to mention, he adds, my participation will also help make the panel diverse. My chewing slows. As my roommate speaks, I feel the first helping of green beans begin to reverse its course.

I imagine it in my mind: Woman-in-charge verifying the panel's diversity. African-American feminist (check), Anglo-American feminist (check),

Chicana feminist (check), radical lesbian feminist (check), and of course, somewhere down the line, in between ecological, post-third-wave, vegan feminist (check), and the anti-feminist feminist (check), me: one non-fratboy, not posing-as-a-feminist-to-get-chicks, probably gay, real-life, we might-have-to-touch-him-to-make-sure male feminist. (Check?)

My stomach heaves and I emit a disgruntled sigh. I'm being asked to speak about my feminism to a bunch of feminists. I'm the token, a novelty on display. I make a quick dart to the bathroom expecting the next wave of intestinal tremors.

Later, on a conference panel in New York about men in women's studies, I experience some of the same pangs. In between speakers, I look around, gauging the attention span of the audience, numbering thirty-five or so. The audience, as far as I can tell, is predominantly female. Aside from me and the one guy next to me, I count two other men in the room. Four men in attendance on a panel about, of all things, men! I wonder where the rest of the men are; I await their arrival.

The woman to my left is speaking about being a women's studies professor and her experience of having a male student in class. I bite my lip. She details her discomfort with him in the classroom. He's the only man in a course full of women about women in literature. The woman is uncomfortable with his presence because she feels he might have an ulterior motive to enrolling, and quite frankly, acknowledges that she doesn't understand why a man would— of his own volition, too—enroll in a class dedicated to women. I look around the room; I see a few heads nodding in agreement with her sentiment. I can't help but wonder if she, and perhaps many of the others in the room, is also uncomfortable with me sitting here. My gut clenches. Despite a swoon of thoughts about her student's—and by extension, my—ability to disrupt and unsettle, I lean closer to the woman.

Now she has to revise her syllabus. Bradley, the male student who audaciously enrolled in her women and literature course, will not be able to journal, along with the other women, his experiences as a woman in relation to the texts. With a quick control+c, attendance and participation are now worth double. The woman moves on, discussing Bradley's performance in class. She and the female students are initially critical of Bradley because he doesn't understand. From her account, Bradley is probably a good student, but for the life of him, does not know much about what makes women's literature, and for that matter, a woman. Indeed, he challenges the professor, entreats her to explain the why, how, and so-what of the texts, and to make explicit the connections between the texts and women. In the end, everyone learns to appreciate Bradley, including himself and the professor. Turns out he's not a jerk after all, he has no ulterior motives, and despite his maleness, and perhaps an odd desire to read about women in literature, does have insightful comments to contribute (though as of yet, he remains unable to journal his experiences as a woman in relation to the texts). The professor's story, it seems, is yet another classic example of mistaken identity.

Poor Bradley. I feel for him. I wonder if he ever took another class about women again. I speculate as to whether he took the class intentionally. I wonder if the women of the class with their expectations and their discomfort drove him away from enrolling in future classes about women. Counting Bradley, there are five of us men in women's studies at the conference—enough for a basketball team. We're the men-who-like-to-take-classes-for-women basketball team. For exhibition only.

When I return from the conference, I hear about what I missed from some colleagues. Evidently, while I was gone, one of my classmates made a remark about how it's so great to be in a class with only women. It's so safe. And comfortable. The teacher drew attention to an empty seat, "But what about Kyle?" she asked, pointing to where I usually sit. "He's part of the class, too." Silence filled the room. Someone else added, "And what about Nicky? Nicky is trans and doesn't identify as a woman." Silence again. Their questions remained unanswered. Upon hearing this anecdote my mind races. *Am I one of those—dare I say it—men who make people uncomfortable and unsafe in class because I challenge implicit expectations about gender and women's studies?* And what about Nicky? Is Nicky like one of those men, too, because ze refuses to identify as biologically female? Or maybe Nicky will always be an outsider, never able to take the men's classes or the women's classes. I wonder if men ever sit in class and think, "Thank God there are no women in here. I feel so safe, so comfortable." Thinking back to my conference in New York, I can't help but consider that maybe I'm the Bradley of this class. The women resent my presence because it prevents them from writing in journals about how their woman-ness relates to the texts.

Yet I also wonder whether we *should* feel safe and comfortable in class. Isn't class the space where we rub up against and explore issues that are uncomfortable and make us feel unsafe? Feeling unsafe and uncomfortable is necessary because it promotes the critical and reflexive thinking that education is all about. This discomfort in experiencing new ideas drives the learning process. Therefore feeling unsafe is good; feeling uncomfortable can be worthwhile. Indeed, are not those feelings the impetus to create change? And yet, my stomach still aches at the thought of causing people discomfort. I don't want to be the one who creates unease. I don't want to be the one who makes people feel unsafe in the classroom.

I wonder, too, though, if I don't count in the classroom because I'm queer. Perhaps I'm inoculated against man's dis-ease and therefore it's perfectly acceptable for me to be in a women's studies class. Maybe it's perfectly acceptable for other effeminate, girly, womanly, femme, and queeny men to be here because on all accounts we're more like women than men. We can relate to women, so they say. By that token, maybe it's okay for Nicky to be here, too, because ze still has some semblance of female anatomy. Nicky can still empathize about what it's like to have a period, even though ze probably never felt completely like a woman. These thoughts bristle in my mind.

I'm presenting a paper in a graduate seminar on feminist theory. My stomach is churning. I hate presenting to people I know. I get afraid because they know me. Since they will see me afterward it feels like there is no room for error. I mentally practice my sentences, making sure to come off sounding articulate and composed. The female panelist to my right has just finished, and I get the signal from the moderator. I breathe, smile, trying to appear brave. The class faces the panel members. Directly across from me, right in my line of sight, the first person I see when I look up, is the other man in the class, Matt. I can tell he doesn't want to be here. He looks annoyed, fidgeting in his chair, looking to his right toward the window. I focus and begin reading my beautifully crafted introduction, hoping that I'll be able to draw Matt's attention through my words. In between sentences I survey the room. All eyes are on me, except for one pair. It's Matt, my brother, my fellow male compatriot in class. I feel the beginnings of intestinal pain, starting near my diaphragm. I shift my legs, hoping to quash the rumblings. I'm hurt.

Together I thought we'd guide each other, venturing forth as the sole males brave enough to take this course. We'd debate, argue, and gradually show everyone else in the class that, yes! it's possible, indeed necessary, for men to be a part of feminism. We are invaluable contributors to the movement. We are the next wave. But now, I continue reading, somewhat dismayed. I think to myself, *Matt—Brother—why do you forsake me in my time of need? When I most need your support, your encouragement, your attention to my project, you're not here. You're elsewhere. In fact, you are actively disengaged.* I pause, turn the page, keep reading, fighting to win over his attention. *My words have spurned you*, I think. *They've alienated you*, I know. They must have, because you're mad now. You refuse to make eye contact. I keep trying, all the while reading, beseeching you with my words to make contact, looking up to meet your approval. I'm practically screaming my message to you across the room. Why won't you listen? Why won't you hear what I have to say? Don't you understand that it's for you that I read this; for you, and for us.

It's too much for you. You cannot stand it any longer. Just as I near the midway point of the paper, the point at which I am at my strongest, both rhetorically and orally, you make your calculated move. You reach for your long, yellow notepad. I see it flicker from the corner of my eye. I look up, see it all in slow motion. Your hands move first, then your elbows, your arms—all together in unison, reacting sharply to a timed impulse. With calculated perfection, you mechanically center your frayed yellow pad in front of your face.

PFFFFFFFFFFFT. Your swift movement sounds and feels like an airplane landing, narrow, quick, vacuum-like. I can no longer speak to you. My words, my looks, my body, my feminism is obstructed by your impenetrable paper shield. The pad you once used to write and collect our class thoughts now stifles our dialogue. There's no hope now for our male-feminist revolution. My body quivers. My eyes, my belly, my voice internally combust. Momentarily, I am incapacitated.

Is it my queerness that you fear, I wonder? Maybe that's what turned you away. Or perhaps it is the conviction with which I speak that scares you, frightens you from action. Maybe it is my personality, I consider, or my quirky habit of sitting with my leg both over and under the other. Did I say the wrong words? Did I come on too strong, expect too much too soon? That's it, I know it: I tried too hard. Tell me, I demand to know, what it is that caused you to so willfully enact such passive violence. What did I do to deserve such disrespect? During, of all times, the moment I was most anxious about my reception, the time at which I was brave enough to let everyone be privy to my most profound and personal desires for change. Why?

Though shaken, I refuse to speak to your notepad, Brother. Everywhere around me eyes are watching, hearing, blinking with the cadence of my words. I see, for now at least, my words are for them, and not you.

Back in New York, at the conference, it's my turn. I argue for the need to legitimate and recruit males as students of women's studies. It is a paper in which I imagine my audience as mostly women, a paper driven by passion and a motive to incite change. In it, I write:

> To achieve our goal of valuing men in women's studies, as I see it, women's and gender studies must embrace the experience of gender in the classroom and promote, teach, and offer their classes from gendered perspectives. Teachers must approach perspectives which are not gender neutral, but rather, gender-positive, gender-open, and gender-fluid. Fluidity and openness about the necessary reality of gender in our lives, as well as its various inflections, must preface any attempt to foster a gender-egalitarian class, which successfully attracts all people. The presence of men and other genderqueer and gender-variant identifying folks as teachers will facilitate the openness and fluidity of gender in the women's studies classroom. They should also be welcomed and recruited by women's studies scholars as capable purveyors and proprietors of feminism and women's studies scholarship. Together, past, present, and future embodied representatives of feminism in women's studies classrooms, coupled with courses which emphasize gender and feminism as applicable to everyone, will be the first foundation by which we can bridge the gender gap in women's studies. It is the first and foremost action that is necessary for the future and viability of men in women's studies.
>
> Feminism's goals, as I understand them, are to identify and end all oppression; not only women's oppression, but class oppression, racism, heterosexism, homophobia, and, yes, men's oppression, among many others. Women's studies, then, exists as one, if not the main, academic

arena for promulgating the critical tools and methodologies to recognize, understand, and combat those oppressions. By prohibiting men's involvement as women's studies students through disavowal and neglect, women in women's studies programs make themselves the only ones knowledgable and capable of fulfilling feminism's goals. A women's studies class comprised of most, if not all women, precludes the opportunity for all of us to achieve feminism's goals in our daily lives. Women's studies must recognize the value and utility of education for anyone and everyone, and solicit men *as men* in women's studies.

As I finish reading my paper, I feel my voice give way. I reach for water, and its soothing relief tingles my salty upper lip. I sit back, the cold sweat I produced during my reading now pressing close against my chest. I look around the room, ready, open to feedback. I wait anxiously during the Q&A for someone to acknowledge my paper and its strengths and weaknesses. There are no questions.

After the panel concludes, I gather my things methodically, inching my way across the room. The only comment I receive occurs upon my departure. As I hold open the door for a woman, also exiting, she smiles at me. I return her smile. I remember her from the audience, third row back, second chair from the end. The door shuts, and I begin to make my way down the corridor. Before we both walk the remainder of the hall in silence—she always one-and-a-half steps in front of me—she turns around briefly, pausing to say how nice my paper was.

At times I feel more like a man than I ever have. Usually, it's in class, as the sole male—the token—when all of a sudden my biology becomes acute and divisive. I am no longer a student anymore: I become a disinterested, unable-to-understand man, my classmates all presumably understanding because they are women. "You don't understand," I'm told by one female colleague. Even though the professor tries to intervene, mentioning, once again, something about empathy, it's too late. The woman is right, I think: I'll never truly understand. I know it. "I'm sorry," I tell them. "I didn't mean to offend." But though I still try, I can't help but feel that as long as women like her—my peers, my classmates—continue to remind me that I don't get it, that I can't get it, that I won't get it, I'll always remain distant in their eyes, my maleness forever an impediment. What I really want from my classmates, peers, and other women, is for them to realize me for who I am, who I can be, and who I want to become; that I am someone who is willing and wants to understand.

Other times in class, I feel hollow and alone, more un-manlike than any of the men I read about. Maybe this is good; I don't want to be that kind of man we decry, deride, and single out. If that's what being a man is, then I'll have none of that, I say. But secretly, I'm afraid. When my classmates look at me perhaps they see that misogynistic, chauvinistic, wife-beating, child-molesting, rapist. After all, we have the same Adam's apple, facial hair, broad chest, hairy arms, hairy legs. My female classmates read me as man, like those same men I strive not to be, but who, despite my efforts, will always look and sound like me. I am most definitely not one of those misogynist men we study. Yet again, I have a silent fear: that the women in my classroom will be unable, or will refuse, to look again, past my physicality, and really see me. They'll see me as "one of them," but that's all they'll do.

These thoughts pummel me at night. I lay awake questioning, wondering, thinking—and wishing I could just rest. How do I, as a man, fight for feminism? How do I convince my brothers and my sisters that men are not a lost cause? How can I prove that we're not all like "those men," that we, too, can be a part of feminism? How do I take something that is on many levels married to women and make it resonate with men? How do I function in a world dominated by homophobia, racism, sexism, and capitalist exploitation? How do I do justice to the depth and breadth of my maleness in an exercise about describing my gender identity? How do I cope with the legacy of whiteness on my own white body? How do I survive as a man in women's and gender studies?

The questions are inexhaustible. Sleep eventually overcomes my mind's rambling, and I'm able to rest for now. But this is in no way means these questions have subsided. They continue to haunt my life with an intensity that is channeled to my body. My complete digestive track bears the brunt of my anxieties and ambivalence, absorbing my sadness, the disappointment, the loss, and all my lived experience as a male, token, queer, feminist student in a women's and gender studies program. My body takes them, sequesters them, and funnels them away so that I can temporarily function.

An urgent call interrupts my late-night reading. It's a colleague. There's news about one of our grad school peers. It's Dave, the new male in the program. He's withdrawn from school, she tells me. It's his mental health. No, he's not coming back. No he's not answering his calls. No, no, no . . . I put my book down. I can't read anymore. I think back several weeks ago to when Dave and I, grabbing a beer, commiserated about our experiences. "It's nothing like what I thought it'd be," he says in between sips. "Never thought it'd be this difficult." We comforted each other that night, laughing, drinking away our frustrations. Now, just a few weeks later, he is gone, five class days away from completing his first semester in graduate school. My eyes are closed, I am thinking about him. Where he is, what he's doing, if his mental health has improved now that he's gone. My stomach rumbles softly. I press my hand close and try and force it to stop. I can't help but wonder if my same colleague, the one that called me about Dave, won't make a similar phone call one day about me. I can hear her voice now: "Stomach ulcers. Yep, that's what I heard. Something about how his whole stomach, intestines, everything just ate each other up. Yeah . . . I had no idea either."

As my experience in a women's and gender studies graduate program indicates, gender affects learning. This is especially true when professors make assumptions about their students based on gender. Women's and gender studies classrooms are not exempt from these incidents, even when they purport to interrogate and deconstruct gender. As teachers and students we must be mindful of gender in the classroom, attending to our own gender biases, and constantly working to create space for everyone to equally and accessibly encounter knowledge. Left unchecked, gender-based judgments not only inhibit the learning process, but also undermine the goals of feminism. If feminism is a movement that teaches us to identify and end oppression—in all its manifold forms—then feminism is not solely a single-gender interest. It is a process, a way of learning and thinking that continually invites us to reconsider its purpose and meaning. I believe there is a feminism that includes men. And I know that the feminist classroom can exist without, or in spite of, gender.

GENDER IN JAKARTA: LESSONS ON DISCOURSE AND DISPARITY

Bryan Talbot Morris

In 2004, just days away from Christmas and sweating in the thickness of a rainless evening in central Jakarta, I sat down over coffee with two friends for what I had thought would be a casual chat. The three of us were new researchers in Indonesia, fresh from graduate school, young and excited. We met in an Indonesian language class a year earlier, and had agreed to meet up, swap stories, and compare informal notes on our experiences in a new country.

The conversation that ensued created for me a heightened awareness of the political significance of what men say when we talk about women, sexuality, and ourselves. It would not be the only experience I would have in the following year that honed my understanding about what we say, the language we use to say it, and how this reflects existing gender imbalances.

As we sat in that café, talking over Scrabble, coffee, and clove cigarettes, our conversation wove in and out of topics, from the challenges of doing research in another language, to the recently drafted Indonesian anti-pornography legislation and, ultimately, to anecdotes from our personal lives. We, three white Americans, felt perhaps a fleeting camaraderie of a shared experience that allowed us to talk freely.

John, as I'll call him, began recounting various escapades with women who he'd encountered at bars or clubs, malls, and karaoke bars while living in Yogyakarta, a smaller city also located on the island of Java. His face conveyed obvious surprise as he commented to us, "I just didn't expect it to be like this; it has been crazy." This was John's first time in Indonesia, and while we, his audience, had spent only slightly more time in the country previously, we exchanged curious glances with each other and urged him to continue.

"There was this one woman and we, you know, hooked up. I guess I just didn't expect casual sex to be so easy here," the implication of "here" perhaps meaning "a country with the world's largest Muslim population." John went on to explain that he met an Indonesian woman in a club a couple months earlier and that they spent a couple of nights together. She became angry when he said that he did not want to be in a relationship with her. When we pressed John for details, particularly about her line of work, he immediately responded, "She wasn't a prostitute." We pressed on, but John was unwilling to seriously consider the situation further. He ended our query by saying, "She didn't ask me for money."

The three of us began joking back and forth about the woman and how exploitative sexual relationships don't necessarily require women wearing fishnet stockings, spiked heels, and working a corner sidewalk. Then, John shocked us into silence when he said, "I like the *jilbab* (Islamic head scarf). I think women who wear the *jilbab* are attractive. I want to date a woman who wears a *jilbab*. I want to date a good girl." He was dead serious.

My initial impulse was to call John an idiot. But this would have gotten us nowhere. My reaction was stifled by my shock at John's statement. Here was a man with a college diploma who was pursuing a master's degree in Southeast Asian studies; a man surrounded by development professionals and academics sensitive to global gender injustice, and particularly injustices in Indonesia. Here was a man who said, in effect, "I will sleep with whores; I want to date a good girl. Whores are useful; virgins are the marrying type." Even worse, here was a man who wasn't just reinforcing—but truly believed—that a woman who wore a headscarf did so because she was good and pious, and that the headscarf advertised this piety to the world. John thought that women who did not wear the headscarf were making a statement announcing their sexual availability. Ultimately, John thought that statement was bad. Women without headscarves could be slept with, but not married. Marriage was to be saved for the virgins, the headscarf-wearing good girls, the girls that didn't frequent the bars, clubs, and karaoke halls where he himself went looking for the bad girls.

John's remarks revealed several disconcerting issues. First, despite the fact that John agrees theoretically with the concept of gender equality, his comments point to the gap between what some men know they're supposed to say and what they actually believe about women. Second, John's statements indicate that the virgin–whore complex is alive and unwell. Many men have no problem sleeping with women casually and using the discourse of liberation as justification. When it comes to dating and marriage, however, many of these same men still want the virgin. Third, and slightly more complicated, is the introduction of the headscarf to the scenario: What we say about ourselves, our sexuality, and our gender does not come only from verbal cues. The headscarf speaks symbolic volumes about sexuality, yet we're not always sure what these messages are.

Ask almost any Indonesian woman if one can tell if a girl is sexually chaste or not based on the presence of a *jilbab* and most of them will laugh out loud, as if the question is ridiculous. Just because a woman wears a headscarf doesn't necessarily mean she's sexually inactive. That, at least, is the conventional wisdom in Jakarta. If he was thinking clearly, this knowledge should have complicated the picture for my friend John. But he wasn't and it didn't. According to John's confused logic, wearing the headscarf is simply a choice women make. Nothing more.

I do not share John's view of the headscarf. I don't think wearing the *jilbab* is a matter of simple choice for a woman. The *jilbab* reflects a value system that intends for women, and not men, to be covered, limited, and hidden. When young, female children are dressed in a headscarf—well before puberty—it can be a challenging, iconoclastic decision to take it off later in life. There is enormous social pressure for women—from community members, from peers, from family members—to wear the headscarf. John would perhaps be surprised to know that an Indonesian friend of ours in graduate school, who does not don a *jilbab* in the United States, wears a headscarf whenever she is in Jakarta. It's not a matter of simple choice for her: She wears the headscarf because her parents insist on it. In fact, they say, when she visits she may hang out with whomever she wants and stay over at female friends' apartments, as long as she wears long sleeves, long pants, and a headscarf. She is in her thirties.

My point, though, is not solely about the *jilbab*. While I am questioning men's entrenched power over women as symbolically expressed through the headscarf, issues of gender and power don't just happen in far-away countries and in cultures that seem so different from our own. My intention here is to highlight how gaps between men's good intentions and what we really say are power issues, too. As Westerners we're not off the hook when it comes to critically looking at how we exert power over others. As men, we're certainly not off the hook. We can't point our finger at those "Others" (in this case, Indonesian Muslim culture that encourages and pressures women to wear headscarves). We need to examine how our own culture, with fundamentalist religious influences, continues to reinforce gender injustice and how we participate in that injustice when we open our mouths without thinking about what we're saying.

My point is that what we say about gender relations reflects an imbalance in agency, choice, and voice between men and women that is so ingrained that some of us do not recognize it when it shows up over coffee and Scrabble among friends—even when it comes out of our own mouths. I'm using my friend John as an example, but he's certainly not alone. We have been trained, after all, in gender-sensitive speak and we are unlikely to say anything that would obviously contradict our support for gender equalities.

As my year in Indonesia continued, I would find John's statement only the beginning of the troubling things I heard come from men's mouths. From diplomats, expatriates, NGO staff, friends, and acquaintances, the daily banter reflected a fundamental and ingrained disconnect between egalitarian discourse and the way men live our lives.

Approximately halfway through my research project, I was invited by the Public Affairs Officer at the U.S. Embassy to informally present findings from my research and lead a discussion over lunch about my experience in Indonesia. At the time, I was working with Jakarta's oldest women-focused non-governmental organization, an advocacy, information, and communications center. During our discussion that day, I explained how the NGO I worked with used program evaluation as a mechanism of accountability. Within the context of this specific NGO, I was discussing the difficulty organizations have in measuring their programs' impacts—for example, measuring an economic empowerment program's effect on widowed tsunami survivors —and how there are challenges in relating specific impacts from programs with the original mission and purpose of the NGO.

Because we were using women's economic empowerment to discuss impact assessment and accountability, it was no surprise that the conversation veered a bit to include development programming targeting women. During the course of this discussion, an Embassy officer made a statement both slightly off-topic and highly problematic. He said, "Well, what you've got are NGOs working from a feminist perspective. This is basically a Western ideological import. Is it suitable for the Indonesian culture?" His point was that an NGO that worked toward equality for women, and that was based loosely on feminist principles, was obviously going to have difficulty evaluating their programs' impacts because their mission was based on an ideology that was not indigenous, that was instead allegedly imported from the "West," and was therefore not easily integrated within an Indonesian sociocultural context. "How could they measure something so foreign to them to begin with?" the Embassy officer seemed to imply.

I was so angry I wanted to firebomb the room. This U.S. State Department representative had expressed an incredibly flawed, inaccurate, ethnocentric, and condescending perspective. First, he presumed that gender equality is an exclusively Western idea. Second, he assumed that if feminism were a Western import, then women in Southeast Asia would be incapable of, or resistant to, thinking they deserved equality. Third, this man's comments suggested that the Indonesian women I had been working with were not interested in changing a culture with such ingrained gender inequality.

Why would an American State Department representative dismiss progressive possibilities for Indonesian women by claiming that feminism is a Western import and therefore irrelevant? Apparently he felt comfortable ignoring the fact that the Indonesian government signed on to the United Nations' Convention on the Elimination of All Forms of Discrimination Against Women (CEDAW) in 1980. As of 2006, the United States had yet to ratify CEDAW.

Feminism in Indonesia is uniquely Indonesian. Although it may be connected with Western-based feminism, it is specific to the cultural and social needs of Indonesia. Dismissing Indonesian efforts toward human rights and equality for women under the guise of paternal cultural sensitivity is particularly troubling. Indonesian women who want gender equity do not operate on the basis of Western values. Gender equity is a status that they work toward based on their assessment that they deserve it, as does any other woman in any other country, culture, or society. To think that Indonesian feminists simply imported a Western notion further limits the voices of these women. American women do not agree on all the goals and theories of feminism; the same is true in Indonesia. Yet there is a shared fundamental belief in both countries regarding the equal rights and treatment of women *vis à vis* men. Equality is not a Western import. It doesn't even exist thoroughly in the West.

So what is the link between my friend John and the representative from the U.S. Embassy? The relevance of these two stories is this: Feminism, and its profeminist actors, is a movement aimed at increasing the agency of women in a world in which there are many groups searching for movement, for agency, for increased freedom. The things we say and the language we use reflect the reality we participate in—the contradictions, the imbalances of power, the literally and symbolically structured silence of some, and the booming voices of others.

Men speak out constantly. Most disconcerting about our speech is how oblivious many of us can be about how our language reflects existing power relations. The agency men have is a fundamental benefit we reap from a social structure that allows us freedom of voice. This structure silences others in ways that are literal and symbolic. Men can speak out without realizing that what we say oftentimes reinforces the restricted agency of women to do the same. We speak out loudly without thinking about how easily our voices carry. We speak out loud in ways that reflect the breadth of our agency and unexamined power over the women around us. It happens over coffee, during luncheons and presentations, in the ways we look at and communicate with others. This essay is a reflection on the things we say.

Part V

Taking Action, Making Change

INTRODUCTION

M en are frequently not engaged with feminist politics because they do not feel welcome, because they do not think the issues pertain to them, or because it simply does not occur to them to get involved. At the same time, feminist groups may intentionally or inadvertently exclude men. Without men's active participation in feminist political organizing, however, three problems emerge: First, feminism without men inadvertently essentializes a political perspective while paradoxically arguing against essentialist foundations; second, a purportedly inclusive social movement risks framing itself in exclusionary terms; third, a political movement that has among its goals the equal access to the goods of society—and an equitable division of domestic work—renders itself responsible for doing the "dirty work" of fixing sociopolitical and interpersonal gender problems.

Feminism is comprised of both activism and knowledge construction. While these spheres inform each other, they are also qualitatively and politically distinct. Because some aspects of men's participation are more controversial than others, it is crucial to first unpack feminism: Feminism is a practice, a perspective, and a process; it includes constructing new frameworks for understanding politics and power while simultaneously setting concrete goals for change. The fact is, feminism can be both loudly political and deeply personal. The essays in this section reflect both sorts of change.

The question is what are—or, what ought to be—men's roles in feminist activism and knowledge production? And do the challenges of men's participation and inclusion vary accordingly?

There are reasonable arguments for being cautious about men's participation in both knowledge production and in more applied forms of feminist political organizing. It may bother some women if men show up for a feminist rally, or run a campus women's center, but the issue of men's feminist activism is perhaps easier to deal with. By comparison, men's role in knowledge production is a far trickier proposition because this raises issues of identity, experience, and the privileging of perspectives. But the bottom line is that when men get involved, there is the potential for achieving great success in reaching feminist goals—both personal and political.

In the first essay of this section, "Sport, Strong Women, and Feminist Epiphanies," New Zealander Richard Pringle describes the deeply personal and individual experiences of young male athletes who emulate the traits of dominant masculinity. Pringle documents the moments of epiphany by which these young men find reasons to change and to become critically aware of the sorts of choices they are making in regard to sexism, masculinist behavior, and their relations with others. Pringle highlights the significant role of strong, positive women as catalysts for change in these young men's lives.[1]

In the essay "Violation," Eli Hastings tells the story about a group of guys avenging a sexual assault on their female friend during high school in Seattle, Washington. Hastings raises important issues about what it means to respond to male violence with more violence. This essay invites us to think carefully about how our perceived options impact the form of action we choose to take. Hastings points to the fact that we need the right tools of social awareness in order to avoid recreating that which we seek to end; in this instance, sexual violence.

"Steel-Toed Boots" is the story of Cliff Hixson, a working-class guy who grew up in the housing projects of Pittsburgh, Pennsylvania. Author Tal Peretz chronicles his friend Cliff's radical transformation from a racist skinhead to a progressive-minded student. Cliff, who wants to be a rehabilitation counselor in the inner city in order to make a positive difference in young people's lives, first crossed paths with Peretz in their college women's studies class. How does someone learn that hate and aggression are seemingly viable choices for "doing" masculinity? And what does it take to change their view?

Ben Atherton-Zeman, a spokesperson for NOMAS (National Organization for Men Against Sexism), looks at recent instances of highly publicized youth violence, demanding that we must call it what it really is: *male* violence. "Men's Manifesto" argues that we must redefine masculinity and manhood to include both toughness and vulnerability. Doing so, Atherton-Zeman states, is what will provide better role models for other men and boys and will encourage respect, equality, and shared power in relationships with others.

In "Breaking the Silence One Mile at a Time" Grantlin Schafer describes his experience following college graduation when he took part in a national tour to educate men about ending male sexual violence against women and helping assault survivors recover. The program Schafer joined was conducted by the group One in Four, an all-male group of peer educators.[2] Ending violence against women is a specific topic area around which men are organizing actively and visibly. Men have a role in caring about and taking action against sexual violence for five reasons: Because men rape, men *are* raped, rape confines men, men know survivors, and because men can stop rape.[3]

In "Being a Social Justice Ally," Jonathan Ravarino provides a ten-point plan for men who are social justice allies, particularly those working to end male violence against women. Ravarino provides tools for identifying and dispelling myths about masculinity and sexual violence. He points out why it is politically important that men develop "the capacity to shut up and listen to the actual experiences of women" and why men's role in stopping violence against women is so crucial. Ravarino ends by highlighting mindfulness meditation as an important aspect of doing meaningful and consciously political work.

"Good Ol' Boy: A Tale of Transformation in the Rural South" is a story of profound personal change. Author Jay Poole grew up in the southern, rural countryside. His parents were fundamentalist Christians and members of the Ku Klux Klan. In complete contrast to everything he had been taught was right, Poole realized he was gay. "Good Ol' Boy" describes his dramatic change in perspectives as he leaves behind the racist, hegemonic surroundings of his childhood to become a progressive-minded adult.

The final essay in this collection, written by Chris Crass, is titled "How Can I Be Sexist? I'm an Anarchist!" A long-time anarchist and community activist, Crass confronts his surprise upon realizing his own sexist tendencies. These are subtle—almost invisible—patterns, but no less powerful than overtly sexist practices. Crass explains that history and contemporary life are full of examples of women's ideas gaining legitimacy only after men appropriate these views. This leads the public to believe that men are the primary culture producers. Crass provides clear-cut suggestions for men who are working for gender justice so that they can do so in ways that confront sexism, while avoiding the arrogance of privilege.

1. Pringle's observations echo R.W. Connell's comment that most men he knows support feminism because of important personal relationships with women. See R.W. Connell. "Long and Winding Road: An Outsider's View of U.S. Masculinity and Feminism." In Judith Kegan Gardiner, ed. *Masculinity Studies & Feminist Theory: New Directions.* New York: Columbia University Press, 2002.

2. For further information see www.oneinfourusa.org/index.php.

3. www.feminist.com/resources/artspeech/mensvoices1.html; www.mencanstoprape. org. Accessed February 3, 2007.

SPORT, STRONG WOMEN, AND FEMINIST EPIPHANIES

Richard Pringle

The oval shaped football had been kicked with height, it had the meta-phoric "snow" on it, and it was now falling back to earth with me standing under it. It was not a location I relished yet I knew as an eleven-year-old that I had to catch it; there was no room for error. My teammates depended on it and I had to *prove* that I could do it. So with adrenaline and heart pumping, I judged the ball's trajectory and secured it in my arms. With a sense of satis-faction and relief, I now heard the calls from my teammates: "go man go," "come on," "run." Perhaps I looked frozen and this is why they were yelling at me, but I snapped back to attention and sprinted off toward the touchdown line. Looking back from the opposition goal line and sucking in the sweet air of success, I could see three bodies on the ground. These were the bodies of the boys who had missed their tackles: bodies that weren't injured but, nevertheless, were somehow defeated and slow to get back on their feet. This vision from the try-line, of the boys on the ground, is one that is strangely etched into my memory. Even though it is now over thirty years ago I can still remember with great clarity the warmth of the sun on that spring day, the color and texture of the grass, and the names of the players on the ground—my old school friends Proctor, Greenie, and Burton. So, unlike many other childhood memories, why hasn't this one faded?

With the benefit of adult hindsight, I now have an understanding of the significance of that youthful sporting moment. Although only a moment of several seconds, it contributed to my burgeoning understanding that I was good at sport; that I was a sporting boy. And this gendered identity—this story of self—made me feel good, valued, and somehow worthy. These feelings were seductive and I began to actively craft my identity by immersing myself further into the world of sport. This comforting story-of-self influenced my choice of after school activities, friends, and even shaped my education and career pathways. (I now teach in a sports department at a university in New Zealand.) In this manner, I believe there is truth in the cliché that "sport builds character." Yet through my many years of experience in various sporting codes, I am not confident to suggest that sport always builds *good* character.

In fact, I am acutely aware of how the homosocial culture of male sporting teams can, at times, encourage males to believe that it is *manly* to be stoic, play when injured, not express emotions, drink lots of beer, and be aggressive. And how *some* sporting males can also develop beliefs that they are superior to females and better than *softer*, less-athletic males. I am, accordingly, concerned that sport can help build sexist, homophobic, and violent characters. Yet my aim in this essay is not to expose the inner workings of sporting cultures and the production of hypermasculine males. Instead, I want to provide three vignettes to illustrate how some men learn, within male sporting contexts, to think critically about sexism, to empathize with feminist ideals, and, in some cases, to become pro-feminist men. I collected these stories while I was interviewing men about how sports influenced their understanding about what it means to be manly. Each of these stories recounts epiphanies, turning points in which the men (named with pseudonyms) began critically reflecting on issues of gender discrimination. Each of these experiences involved the influence of a strong, politically aware woman.

THE TWENTY-FIRST BIRTHDAY PARTY: BRUCE'S STORY

Well, it is embarrassing for me to tell you this story and I guess we have all done things we regret and this was one of those moments in my life. It's something I wish I could forget but, at the same time, I guess it helped me grow up. Anyhow, I'll start from the beginning: I was only seventeen and that year I had been invited to play in the senior men's football team (rugby union in New Zealand). This was a real honor for me; it was my big break in my sporting career and I was determined to make the best of it. My dream was to be a professional player, but I was having trouble fitting in. These guys were all at least four years older than me. Of course they respected what I could do on the footy field and that helped. But I felt like "the kid" and so I would try different things to fit in and be accepted. My prime way of attempting to fit in was by drinking a lot and doing stupid things. This was my special skill. I was known as "Crazy Bruiser." And, looking back, I know now that I did do some really stupid things: drink and drive, do all sorts of drugs, and get into fights. I guess I was just lucky that I didn't get injured in a car crash or arrested or something.

Anyhow, it was at the end of my first season and our team had just been beaten in the finals—it was bloody good that we even made it to the finals so we weren't disappointed—and everyone was high-spirited. We all had a few drinks in the clubrooms and then headed off to Mitch's house. It was his twenty-first birthday and we were all looking forward to a big night. At Mitch's house there was a nice buffet dinner and a bar where we could all help ourselves to drinks. So I started drinking. By about midnight, most of Mitch's family and elderly guests had left the party and it was just the football boys outside. And that is when I thought it was appropriate to demonstrate my special skill. So I downed two big jugs of beer in quick succession and then I urinated into the jug and drank that, and then promptly vomited into the jug and I had a go at drinking that also. The boys were all clapping and laughing so I thought that my "stunt" had worked a treat.

But I didn't realize that Mitch's mum had been watching. And she was a woman that I totally respected; she had done a tremendous job of raising her three boys by herself. On top of that, she had taught me at high school. She was a top woman. So I was completely humiliated when I realized that she had been watching. She came over and literally grabbed me by the ear and pulled me into the kitchen. She told me to sit down and she let me have it: told me straight about how if I wanted to be accepted as a man then I had to stop acting like a fool. Told me that what I had done was disrespectful to her. That she had saved a lot of money to help make this a special occasion for Mitch and how this was an emotional day for her, how this was about family, and life, and love. She had me in tears.

Then I realized she wasn't telling me off; she was trying to help me. So we started talking and she talked about her life. She told me about her husband and how he had had a drinking problem and wasn't man enough to raise his boys, how he had turned his back and walked out. And soon she was in tears also, which made me feel even worse. But it hit home a message to me; it was about responsibility and care—about care for yourself and care for others. And I had just been acting like a bloody idiot. She was telling me about how to be a good man and to recognize that what men do has a big influence on the women who surround them. This was something that I had never thought about before.

It has now been ten years since that incident and people still remind me of it and, of course, it is embarrassing. But after that night I gave up being Crazy Bruiser. That night had a real big impact on me. Yet one of the things I now think about is, why didn't some of the older guys on the team—like the coach—why didn't he talk to me about my drinking and doing stupid things? Why didn't he give me some advice? Why wasn't it a man that told me about how to be a respectful man?

GENDER AND POWER IN THE CLUBROOMS: MIKE'S STORY

Ever since I was old enough to walk I have been hanging around the football club. My old man was president of the club when I was young, and by the time

I was five I was out there on the field. I was big for my age and with all the coaching from my dad I was soon making representative sides. By the time that I was a teenager I would train on Tuesday and Thursday nights at the club, on Monday and Wednesday for the rep team, then I'd play on Saturday and sometimes Sunday. The only day away from footy would be Friday and even then I would probably go and kick a ball around with some mates. I enjoyed everything about footy: I liked the smell of the massage oil in the change rooms, the feel of the ball, the hard training sessions, and, of course, running with the ball. There was nothing better than getting the ball out in the open and carving through the opposition.

Every Saturday, in the winter, it was footy day and that was how it was until I was twenty-one. I played sixteen straight seasons and only missed three games due to injury. But by the time I was twenty-one I realized I wasn't enjoying the whole football scene anymore. It was sort of hard to put my finger on why I wasn't enjoying it but I guess it was related to Anne. We got married young—we were both only twenty. Anne and I were both at university at the time. She was reading a lot about feminism and gender issues, and I was training to be an architect.

After we got married I continued to play football and I invited Anne down to the clubrooms. She came along a few times but then stopped. I tried to encourage her to keep going but she told me that she felt very uneasy about the whole atmosphere. She explained that she didn't like all the talk about knocking people over during the game, or putting in a punch, or taking somebody out. She thought the talk somehow celebrated violence and she didn't really like all the drinking either. I mean, she likes to have a glass of wine or two, so she's not a teetotaller or anything. But she said the prime reason that she felt uneasy was because she didn't like how she was looked at and she didn't like how the guys talked about women or made dirty jokes. Initially I defended the guys, I said that they were all good people and they were just having a bit of a joke and she shouldn't take it all so seriously. I then told her that all that feminist reading she was doing at university was just making her anti-male. And after I said that I could tell that she was really disappointed with me. And then we agreed not to talk about it anymore.

I kept playing footy for the rest of the season and Anne didn't come down to the clubrooms anymore. But I guess our argument, if you want to call it that, had some influence on me. I started to think about what the boys actually talked about in the clubrooms, and how we talked about women. And I was surprised because I had never really thought about it before, but it was just terrible. They were always talking about scoring with women. If someone had started dating a girl, all the team wanted to know if they had had sex yet. That was the ultimate question: "Have you done her yet?" As if sex was somehow the answer to life. And it was a great source of humor if someone was still a virgin.

It became a team mission to get one of the young guys laid. His nickname was actually "Virgin." We could all be on the field talking about our tactics in a game and people would say, "Okay, you flick the ball to Virgin and then I'll double round and blah, blah, blah." I could talk about these sorts of examples all night and there is much worse. One of the guys I remember actually called his girlfriend the "rootbag." You know, she would walk into the clubrooms to drive him home because he would get drunk every Saturday night and he would say something like "here comes my little rootbag" or "how are you going my rootbag?" I know it sounds terrible. And what is worse is that she would actually hear these sorts of comments and didn't seem to mind! Another guy, Colin, he called his wife the "handbrake" because she was always stopping him from doing things. And another was nicknamed the "Ayatollah." You get the picture?

It was all totally disrespectful. But, you know, I wasn't initially surprised because I guess I had grown up with that sort of talk all my life. I never really stepped back and thought about how it frames women and what sort of impact it must have on the men's relationships. And when I thought about the culture, it felt very much like an immature boy's club. So I started to agree with Anne, and I began to feel uneasy about the whole club scene. Anne was happy that I now felt that way and we talked more about feminism. One day she asked me what I was going to do about all the problem talk in the clubrooms. This surprised me, because I still loved the game and I didn't want to give it up, and I wasn't going to be some martyr and try and change all the boys. But I decided, at the least, to not participate in that sort of sexist talk. Yet this was sort of hard to do, because some of the jokes I actually found funny. But over time it became easier to do and the more that I separated myself from that sort of talk, the more I felt dissatisfied with the whole footy culture. So, to make a long story short, I played one more season and then retired from footy.

I became really interested in talking to Anne about feminism and various political issues and I started reading all of her books and lecture notes. I noticed that she had quite deep friendships with her girlfriends and that they could talk about all sorts of emotional things. I was quite envious about this. I realized that I didn't have a lot of male friends; that I actually preferred Anne's friends. I also realized that with the one or two male friends I had, we never talked about how we felt, or our relationships, or what we wanted from life. It sort of felt shallow. It was like we didn't know how to talk about important things. At around this time I changed my career plans and started studying to be a teacher. While I was at university I helped set up this men's support group. We wanted to help men become more aware of gender issues and problems with violence and to help men to feel good about being a man. I guess I helped set up this group because I needed a bit of help myself. I was struggling with some of those tensions of how to be manly but also be a feminist.

So that's my story of how I became a feminist. It all really started with Anne and the problems she saw in the footy club. She was a big help in helping me see things differently.

RUNNING AWAY FROM PREDATORS: HARRY'S STORY

By the time I was twelve my schoolteacher said that every boy had to play a sport and we could select between soccer and footy. Yet that wasn't really a choice; we all knew that we were meant to play footy because soccer was not a respected sport for boys. But I wasn't ready to play footy, I wasn't really confident about all the tackling and heavy-contact stuff. So I lined up in the soccer line and my teacher said, "Harry, aren't you Darryl's brother?" He was my older brother—a gifted sportsman—and I said, "Yes." And he said, "Well you are in the wrong line," and he physically directed me into the footy line. Which was okay, I guess, but I never really liked the game. I played it because I thought I had to, and I played it to fit in, to be one of the boys. I played for another two seasons, until I was fourteen or fifteen years old.

I was always afraid of getting hurt in the game but I never talked about this. I played on the wing because there was less chance of getting the ball out there. If I had to tackle somebody, I would just try and hang on to them long enough until someone else got there. If someone wanted to run around me they could. It was embarrassing at times. I hated getting the ball, I wasn't very fast, and I felt like a small animal running away from a predator. Because I was slow, I knew that it was just a matter of time before they would catch me and knock me to the ground. So I always played in this state of fear. But I felt that I had to play.

During one of the games, I let this big guy run straight past me and he scored a touchdown. I didn't even try to stop him. In fact I let him do it three times over the game. I knew that my teammates were upset, but I was scared and by the end of the game I started to cry a bit. After the game, this one guy in my team started calling me a wimp and a girl for not taking the tackle. Soon the whole team was hassling me and the coach didn't stop them. People were saying things like, "Hey, Harry! There's the girl's hockey team over there. Why don't you go and see if you can make the tackles with the girls?"

These hassles continued for several weeks and then I decided I'd had enough, so I quit the team. I told the coach and all he said was to make sure that I returned the uniforms by the end of the week. When I got home, I told my mum that I had quit and I asked her if she would tell Dad. I was quite worried that he would be disappointed. She said that she would but she wanted to know why I had quit. It was hard to tell her what had happened but she was real understanding and supportive. Mum said that she had always worried about me playing the game. She worried that I would get hurt and she thought the game was dangerous. She also thought it was terrible that the coach had heard all these comments about me and didn't step in or stop them. And then she explained to me why she thought it was wrong for boys to be bullied by being called "girls." It was quite a long explanation but the clear part of the message, that I understood, was that it was not only abusive to the boy but it was also putting down girls. The person being called a girl was being called this because they believed that girls were no good, not skilled, not strong, or whatever. So, in essence, girls or females get positioned as pathetic or useless.

Later that afternoon I came in from playing outside and I heard my mum on the phone to the school. She was talking to the principal of the school and complaining about the coach. About how he had witnessed all this abusive and sexist talk and just let it happen. My mum was saying stuff like the coach was complicit with sexist values and was not fit to be a leader of young men. I was immediately embarrassed but listened quietly from the hallway. I didn't want any further trouble and wished that this wasn't happening.

After my mum had hung up I heard her call out to me, "Harry is that you? Were you listening?" I said that I had and she explained that she didn't want to hurt me but she felt that she had to let the school know what was going on. She said that if she just ignored what had happened then she would be a bit like the coach: weak and part of the problem, not the solution. A few weeks later the coach phoned and talked to me. He apologized for not stepping in. He said he was truly sorry and that he'd learned from it all. I was still a bit embarrassed by all this, but I told him not to worry about it and said that I was fine.

It wasn't until years later that I had the language to understand this whole bullying incident and what my mum had done. The language that I had learned was feminism. My mum had given me a lesson in how to be a feminist; she had exercised her sense of ethics, not only in supporting me, but also in speaking out about an issue of gender that she was concerned about. Although I'd been a bit embarrassed at the time, I also felt proud that my mum had stuck up for me, spoke out about what she believed, and was strong enough to do so. I learned that ethical and emotional strength was much more important than physical power.

SOME FINAL WORDS

Bruce, Mike, and Harry's recollections are stories of optimism. They show the importance of ethical, strong, and critically aware individuals. They let us know that individuals can play a significant role in helping shape others' beliefs and actions. Sometimes it can feel like individual efforts to change gender relations are futile. But these stories remind us that we can all play a part in helping promote social change and justice.

In each of these stories, the impetus for change in men's lives stemmed from the actions of women. I have heard many stories about men being influential in shaping ethical understandings of gender: I wanted to emphasize the role of women in shaping men's understandings of feminist issues. My reason stems from a recent spate of pop psychology books on how to raise boys that have gained considerable media attention in Australia and New Zealand. I am concerned that these books promote the message that men are more important in raising boys and that women need to step back from a parenting role, particularly when boys are teenagers. The underpinning and flawed message in books like this is that men have inherent knowledge about masculinity and that women are deficient; thus it takes a man to raise a boy. In contrast, the stories of Bruce, Mike, and Harry illustrate the value of caring and strong women in shaping young men's understanding of gender issues and power relations. Yet I stress that this process is not linked to the sex of an individual, but to how influential individuals choose to think, act, and interact with others.

Lastly, I want to mention that sports are not good or bad. Sports are not the problem; sexism is. What is important is paying attention to the language we use in sporting contexts, and encouraging coaches and team cultures to produce ethical gender relations. In this way, the sporting world can offer great opportunities for producing critically aware narratives about masculinities and gender relations.

VIOLATION

Eli Hastings

For a while I watched the boughs creak and moan and how the raindrops slid and magnified the dance. I dusted off my desk. I looked at the clock six times in five minutes. I tried turning on KUBE 93 FM—ads. I tried C-89—Richard Marx. I tried silence. It wasn't coming out. I wasn't used to having to actually produce anything and I was rusty. The history paper had blindsided me; it was the old bat's way of getting back at us for skipping her class or coming in stoned and tipsy every other day. Apparently she no longer shared our high school's *de facto* policy of turning a blind eye.

The old oak stairs creaked and trundled. A light tap on my door followed and I turned, glad to be distracted. Kristy entered the room. She looked beautiful: her big amber eyes were in full effect and swollen raindrops winked on her lashes. She had her arms wrapped around her from the chill. We'd broken up a year ago. A snap and crackle of lust was born and died in me as I reminded myself she was my surrogate sister now.

She settled in and in the way her gaze darted around the room we'd haunted so many times with our amateur fumbling, I could tell she had something on her mind. She'd been shy about leaning on me since we'd parted; I desperately didn't want her to feel that way. I coaxed her into speaking, but even when she did she wouldn't meet my eyes. She watched the boughs dance through the rain, too.

"Something happened with Craig . . . I . . . I don't know if you know but I was kind of seeing him for a little while."

I didn't know. I winced inwardly, nodded.

"It was in March. He and Eric came over when my mom went to Vegas." She stopped and walked over to the window, giving me her alarmingly thin back. She crossed her arms again and her shoulder blades rose like wings. "We were fooling around and we . . . got to a point where . . ." she hesitated, looking for language. "You know, I wasn't really serious about him." She blew out a breath that was deep but staggered by anxiety anyway. "He tried to rape me."

What crept from my center outward would best be described as nothing— but a very cold nothing. This was more troubling than rage, because with the stillness and the void of emotion, came the promise of its end.

The next morning at eight o'clock I met Fog, Hugh, and Jamie behind the church. We smoked a lot of grass; someone produced a forty-ounce of Mickey's to share. We'd meant to confer—that had been my intention in calling them all the night before. It wasn't supposed to be so quiet between us. The autumn winds beat the church's brick savagely and ripped leaves down over us. Every few minutes one of us would say something like *Man, I can't believe that little fucker* or *I tried so hard to believe he was a homie.*

Thing was, Craig was allegedly a friend. He'd come late to our high school and our crew and determinedly made his way in. He was a scrawny, tenacious kid with beady eyes and shaggy, dirty-blond hair. His doggedness on the soccer field and ability to intimidate in the process of drug deals was unlikely given his build. And the velocity with which he set aside the healthy, childhood pastimes like soccer, and the zeal with which he dove into the dark lake of drugs was disconcerting even for us. We were all experimenting, of course, and most of us were overdoing it. But Craig was the type of kid that liked to take LSD and sit in a darkened room.

It would be easy to call him a spoiled kid with a Napoleon complex from a dysfunctional (possibly abusive) home—and all that was certainly true. Whenever he tired of a night out, even at age seventeen, he'd call his mother who would drive the half-hour or more from their North End home to whisk him away, no matter what state he was in. And, the way that his mother averted her gaze and spoke deferentially, the bags under her eyes, suggested that things weren't ninety degrees straight behind that family's closed doors. But there was something additional, some black thread woven through Craig's spirit that went beyond all this. Something wicked and mocking in his humor, his laugh, his gaze, and something disturbing in his fanatic adoration of Jim Morrison, the sicker songs of Tool, and, of course, Kurt Cobain.

Then again, one on one, there was an intimacy that was almost irresistible. He was generous with food, drugs, what have you, solicitous of advice, humble, and sometimes hilarious. If he could tap into your anger at a mutual friend (or avowed enemy), he'd unload biting mockery on your behalf, emphatically agree with your assertions. We were all adrift in those days, wandering between the school, city parks, parent-free homes, downtown, ducking into whatever crevices we could find to take a swig or a toke. In the pitch and roll of those waters he was expert at lashing his raft to others—but his motives always felt somehow sinister though none of us could point to much in particular. The shared laughs and parties and kindnesses were simply underwritten by an invisible toll.

My skepticism of his true nature remained, even after splitting to California with him for a two-week road trip. Everyone had tried to shed their doubts, but, as it later came out, doubts had continued to roil in everyone's guts. As the forty-ounce emptied and the silence swelled that October morning, I realized I'd conjured a posse. And I realized that's exactly what I'd meant to do; it was no conference.

When he walked out of the decrepit, old building at second period break, Craig had his earphones on. When he saw the way we were standing around, he took them off. Gusts of wind lifted plastic bags and leaves, sent them spiraling past. The word had leaked and nearly seventy kids hung around to see what the Frink Park Kings would do with one of their own—to see, without a doubt, whether FPK had the heart it claimed. On this typically wet and cold Seattle morning came our opportunity to show we were something more than typical, more than a frivolous, little, white, party crew. He approached Hugh. I know that Hugh still didn't know what he would do. But when Craig spoke, there was simply nothing to say.

"What's up?" The literal question lurked behind the casual greeting. His small brow wrinkled up. He still didn't know; it'd been nearly six months. How could he know?

It's funny, but what I saw in Hugh's face when he swung was not rage, but restraint, pain, doubt. His boxer's fist collided with Craig's insubstantial chest, but not all that hard. Hugh's left hand took him by the neck. I looked in Craig's eyes when my left hand hit his stomach, and I felt the same things I'd witnessed in Hugh. I looked over his shoulder at the frozen football field and distant barbecue joint and housing projects when my right hand connected with his face. I backed off then, feeling equal parts sick and excited. Jamie put all of his 250 pounds behind every kick that he landed. Craig's earphones were tangling his neck and arms. His backpack was heavy and threw him off even more each time he tried to stand. It wouldn't have mattered; Jamie was aiming for his legs now, keeping him flat on the pavement. When the chain-smoking French teacher Mr. B put himself between the two and politely asked Jamie to back off, he did. Mr. B lit a cigarette and strolled away. He was no fan of Craig either. There was no expression on Craig's face as he hauled himself into a crumpled but vertical shape. He was not breathing hard. He met none of the dozens of gazes that burned on him. He trudged away down Alder Street in silence. My friend Ryan half hugged and half restrained me, but it wasn't necessary.

"Don't ever come back, punk," I screamed after him.

And he never did.

The first vague haunting of regret stirred in me as soon as I hit that kid. Of course, the overwhelming emotion was anger, followed closely by sadness, and then guilt (at not having listened to my gut and distanced myself from him sooner). Regret was a distant fourth or fifth and didn't roll close to the surface for many years, really. But, as early as that afternoon, I was told by a female friend that what we'd done was wrong. She was always evolved, sensible—a strange creature to be roaming the scrappy, boozy hallways of high school.

"Rape is an act of violence, you know. Choosing violence to punish it won't work. It will only make things worse in the long run," she said, or something to that effect. I'm sure that I averted my eyes and nodded vaguely at the linoleum floor as I did whenever savvy and mature girls lectured me in those years. The truth of what she was saying didn't press itself upon me for a long time to come.

As months and then years flashed past, it seemed that more people who'd at least tacitly condoned our actions that day changed their minds. It wasn't that the incident was even discussed very often. In fact, Craig's name became a kind of taboo, as if some Godfather of Garfield High School had commanded that he *never be mentioned again in this house*. But the few times the subject did arise—mainly after high school had concluded and we'd gather for reminiscing—and I tested gazes around the room, I could sense condemnation as a few of them turned away. Had anyone overtly questioned or judged our action (aside from well-meaning girls), I would have unloaded invective on them. My attitude, though never stated as such, was: We did *something*, we took action. It fell to us and we had the balls.

Of course I realized as time went on that my female friend had been right—the futility of answering violence with violence, of punishing a would-be rapist with humiliation, was undeniable. And, indeed, when word of Craig filtered back to us, it sounded like he was a mess: squatting somewhere selling drugs, out of school, wandering around with his headphones looking dangerous, and, eventually, living in California where word was he'd been fired from a restaurant for assaulting a female coworker. It's likely that the beating— or more precisely, the humiliation and banishment, because he wasn't truly injured—only compounded the vile need in him to exert power. To say it plainly: We probably made it worse.

But what was the alternative anyway? Try and coax Kristy into the agonizing, shameful, laborious, and probably unsuccessful process of prosecution? Drag her through more noxious emotional fallout than she'd already endured? Allow that little bastard to keep firing his evil eyes at her every day in the hallways, half-taunting, half-warning (as he'd been doing for months)? Allow him the time to frantically assemble allies, to convince (and he was a conniving creature) a small, key group that Kristy was a liar? No, these options conjured nothing but unbridled disgust in me—and, I assume, in Hugh, in Jamie, in others who stood by in solidarity. In that context, at that age, in that school, there was nothing to do but stand up and be men—in the flawed and undercooked way that we knew. And I forgive my friends and myself for our age, our culture, and our warped sense of justice. And I'm still proud that we stood awkwardly up.

Recently, a friend of mind told me she had been sexually assaulted—not rape, but not negligible either—by a mutual friend. As I listened to her cautiously unfold the incident, I realized I was scarcely angry. My placidity was partly due to the odd compassion she felt for her assailant, how she mixed that into her account. This came in stark contrast to Kristy's story; Kristy's revelation was partly a plea for retribution.

But it wasn't only that. It was also how my attention flew to our common friend, how I revised him in my mind—not so much as a sexual predator but as someone who is fucked up, suffering, disturbed. I thought about how easy it'd been before for me to ignore the fact of his pain and his struggles and I knew, without a doubt, that his suffering was at the root of his action. That's not to excuse it, of course—if my female friend had pursued prosecution, I would have supported her.

I'm left to wonder if this truly represents evolution in me. I can't help but feel the lack of rage attends a lack of emotional health: After all, such acts *are* reprehensible any way you slice it and *should* cause outrage. Have I come *too* far from the ignorant, delinquent kid that I was then? Have I studied too many Buddhist texts, do I ascribe too much to the power of suffering? Is my loving-kindness overdeveloped? Or have I simply become too cynical by the battering of years, by watching people I love wrong themselves and others with carelessness, selfishness, and even with the best of intentions? I'm not sure.

But I do know a couple of things.

One: While compassion may have twined with anger in my first, surging reaction, a profound sadness at the caprice of betrayal, at the violation of trust and intimacy—things so golden and fragile in this life—remains a very close second.

Two: Neither compassion nor overwrought cynicism are adequate excuses for not breaking out of our fear when it comes time to really *be* men, to stand up against the timeless and shameful tradition of abusing women.

STEEL-TOED BOOTS

Tal Peretz

I am finally starting to understand Cliff Hixson. Seeing him in a women's studies class is striking, even confusing: Standing nearly six feet tall, with his red beard and earlobes stretched over an inch wide, dressed in black jeans with a band T-shirt reaching over his thick, tattooed arms, Cliff looks like a cross between a boxer, a biker, and a bulldozer. It isn't his physical size that gives this impression, but something about his persona, his personality projecting into the world around him like backlighting, like a personal soundtrack.

Seeing Cliff outside of class, working on a project with his steel-toed boots on a classroom table, he fits right in. He seems perfectly at home cutting out circles of paper for buttons bearing feminist slogans like "*There is an ASS in sexual harassment for a reason!*" As he talks, a big friendly grin offsets the smooth scar slashing across his left cheek. During a childhood fight, someone picked up a board with a nail and threw it at him, hitting Cliff in the face and ripping his cheek open. The scar dances as he speaks in a relaxed, sandpaper baritone.

"That was my thing—I was angry, and I expressed it through fighting. I always enjoyed fighting. I really liked it."

"I've only got into one fight at Penn State," Cliff begins, holding up his index finger for emphasis.

"A friend of mine likes to play basketball. I suck at the game, but I'm the guy who makes the teams even. I just run around the court, get the ball and miss, and everyone gets mad at me and won't give me the ball again.

"One day I go to the gym. I have on a black hoodie with an Iron Cross over my heart. The back of that jacket has a big Iron Cross on it, too. It says 'Hated and Proud.' Across the shoulders it says 'American.' On the bottom it used to say 'Skinhead.' I still have that jacket at home.

"I'm in the locker room, unlacing my boots, getting ready to play basketball, and I see this guy go by. He gives me a stutter-look, a double take. I've been in enough fights to instantly know that something is going to happen. I start tying my boots back up.

"He comes up and I'm ready. My boots are tied and I'm like, 'What's up?' He's like, 'You got a lot of interesting patches on that jacket.' And I go, 'Yeah, what's the problem?'

"Well, what do they all mean?"

"'All of them, or just one specifically?' I asked, because already I know what he's talking about. 'That Iron Cross,' I tell him, 'is a symbol of pride. It's also a symbol for Independent skateboards. It's also a symbol for . . .'

"I start being a jackass about it. He's like, 'It's not a symbol of white pride, is it?' I say, 'To who? It depends on who you're talking to. But since you're talking to me, it's none of your fucking business what it means. Do you have a problem?' And he goes, 'No, no, it's cool . . .' and he walks away.

"I take off my boots and go to play basketball. Like I said, I'm not a good player so when the guys pick teams I don't get chosen. My buddy does, though, and when I tell him I'm leaving he asks me to take his ball back to the dorms. So I'm holding his basketball, and my gym clothes, and I come out of the bottom of Rec Hall, going up the steps. I get to the top, and I have my hood pulled over my head, and I hear, 'What's up now, you racist motherfucker?'

"Just as I look up, I'm grabbed right where the Iron Cross is and hit with a hard right. I mean, this guy hit me across the face with everything he had, and I was stunned. I look up, the blurriness is going away, and he's holding out his arms going 'Whassup now? Whassup?'

"I just hit him one time, but—y'know when you're a little kid and you fantasize about hitting someone as hard as you can? It was that hit. His head snapped back. There was instant blood. He flew back maybe six steps, turned around, and took off running."

Cliff is a born storyteller. If we still valued that talent, he'd be made for life. As it is, he just got fired from his job as a janitor at the Pennsylvania State University after organizing the union workers against a supervisor known for sexual discrimination, harassment, and threatening employees. Cliff is also taking classes, studying to be a rehabilitation counselor. He wants to help kids like himself escape the effects of negative masculinity.

"The idea," he explains, "is to work with inner city gang kids, specifically boys, and find out why they feel the need to act out their masculinity in violent ways. Because what happened with me is that after I started learning about masculinity, things started to click."

Presently, Cliff and I are working on a group project for a men and masculinities course, the first of its kind at Penn State. Cliff is sharing concerns about his final presentation for the class; his plan is to describe his transformation from racist skinhead to socially conscious feminist.

"I worry a little about how people will perceive me, because I still have some of that racist skinhead image. I still have all the tattoos . . . but, you know, most of them aren't really me anymore. Like this one here." Cliff rolls up his sleeve as he speaks, pointing to a tattoo that reads, "I feel the blinding rage." It's inked in red. Cliff holds out his arm so we can see the jagged lettering above the thick, black barcode and just below the black, shadowy face of a screaming man.

"I'm a little concerned," Cliff continues, "because I don't want my presentation to sound like, 'This was my life; end of story,' because my life-story is still changing."

And so Cliff's description comes out disjointedly, in convoluted bits and pieces, because it is a real, true story. Life isn't linear; it doesn't follow a neat story arc. Life doesn't often make nice, neat sense and, for Cliff, the unfolding of his life is far from over. He weaves metaphors and side-stories, takes tangents, fields questions, and gestures emphatically in the air.

Cliff's story starts in the projects of Uniontown, a poor neighborhood south of the steel city, Pittsburgh, PA. Cliff grew up in a loving family, although there were some problems with alcoholism and violence.

"My father was always a big fighter. He told us stories about how he beat up a teacher, or beat up two guys. Those were his glory stories. I remember watching my dad beat a guy until he was a puddle of piss and blood. When the guy started begging and crying for an ambulance, my dad dragged him out into the street. The guy probably would've died out there but my mother called the paramedics. As a kid, you watch something like that and you learn that the way to deal with anger is to get satisfaction from someone else's sorrow.

"By second grade I was already such a troubled kid that they put me in a class for learning disabilities. There was only one LD class for the whole school and I was the youngest kid in the room. Not only was I still fighting, but now I was fighting fifth and sixth graders."

Hearing this, I start to see how Cliff developed that look of determination, that nonchalant aggression. Facing down boys twice your size when you're only eight years old could easily ossify through years of social pressure. I begin to wonder how Cliff managed to break down such habits.

"I don't think I would be the person I am today had it not been for Lindsey," Cliff explains, referring to his wife. They've recently married, though they've been together for eight years.

"I've taken some women's studies classes, but I never would have taken them without her. She's the one who motivated me to be something, who told me, 'You're not stupid.' Honestly, if it wasn't for that I would not be a student and I never would have gone to college. College wasn't for me. I was proud to be working class. Lindsey encouraged me to apply, to make something of myself."

Although Cliff has learned so much in college and he has swapped words for fists, he still has something of a penchant for confrontation. Cliff seems to recognize that this is left over from old habits, but he also sees this aggression as an inherent part of his personality. Since it's something he can't get rid of, he turns it to good use.

"Like, today, I'm walking from class downtown, and I see these guys standing on the corner of the street, holding a big sign that says 'Abortion Kills Children' and something about Hitler.

"I walk up to one of the guys, and I ask, 'First of all, where are you from?' The guy tells me they're from Ohio, so I ask him why they came this whole way to stand here and bother us in State College, PA. He says, 'We're here to educate people, young women at Penn State.' So I ask him 'You think you know all about abortion, huh? You've studied it? Have you ever talked to a woman about it? Maybe a woman who has had one? Are there any women here with you?'"

I listen to Cliff, nodding my head; I've noticed that there are never any women with these groups. I wonder how it is that Cliff's immediate instinct is to confront people so directly.

Cliff continues his story noting sarcastically, "I'm glad a group of guys are here telling women about their reproductive rights.

"It's just funny to me," he continues, "the way these people come around, holding these signs up. They want to show where they stand, they want everyone to know their position, but they don't want to be challenged.

"I have a very hard time passing people and letting something go. Back when I was an angry person, if something made me mad, I was in your face about it. I'd get in your face for looking at me wrong, for looking at Lindsey wrong—for anything I didn't like. I still react strongly to things, only now I'm confronting different issues, like when I hear someone call someone else a fag, or when I see some guy staring at a girl's breasts."

I ask Cliff what changed, and he doesn't seem to have a clear answer. "It was a long process," he explains. He continually points to Lindsey's influence, but neither of us thinks it was just her. At some point Cliff started questioning his own identity choices, and eventually he began making or taking other paths. Lindsey helped, as did starting school, taking women's studies classes, meeting new people, and hearing new viewpoints. Ultimately, when the opportunity arose, Cliff made the decision to change himself. He tells me a few other stories that mark his way, but we both know change this radical can't be spelled out in a few stories.

Cliff backtracks to high school, when he started shaving his head and cultivating his angry image. "In high school, no one messes with a skinhead. You look at a skinhead and you know they're bad news," Cliff tells me, as if I need this reminder. By the time he moved to Chicago, standard dress included bomber jackets or black, hooded sweatshirts with patches, punk aphorisms and band names, skinhead slogans emblazoned across the shoulders in red-stitched fabric, and sometimes that Iron Cross over the heart.

"I was at this club in Chicago checking out some band, and this girl comes up to me and gets all up in my face. She starts grabbing my jacket, talking about my patches, telling me she can't stand me and stuff. I don't even know the girl!

"Now she's right in my face. She's talking and yelling, her spit hitting my face. I can feel the warmth of her breath just boiling my blood. She's grabbing at my patches, my Iron Cross, and I tell her not to touch me. She tells me her friends are waiting for me outside. When I go to leave, I see eight or nine multiracial skinheads—there's an Asian guy, a couple black guys, some white guys. They're in full skinhead gear; bombers, braces and boots, and they're just waiting for me.

"I start looking around the back of the club, off to the sides of the stage, you know, to see if there's a back way out. Then I just said, 'Fuck it' and went out the front door. I looked around, and I just start talking. I'm saying things like, 'Yeah, you guys might beat my ass, but you'll know it took all of you to do it,' and I just keep talking to them.

"Turns out, these guys were SHARPs . . . " Cliff has to pause and spell it out: Skinheads Against Racial Prejudice. They dress like skinheads so most people think they're Nazi, white, power guys, but they're almost like an anti-racist gang or something.

"If I would've run from the SHARPs waiting outside the club they would've come after me because they would've known I was alone and scared. But because I walked right up to them just started talking in their face, they thought I might have been part of a set-up.

"When they finally realized I was alone, they were too impressed with my mouth to start kicking my ass. One guy actually came up and said 'Let's go have a drink,' but I didn't drink. He said, 'No, it's on me,' but I still refused. He said, 'You've got some fuckin' balls.'

At about that time I was just getting out of being an angry racist guy, but I still wanted to keep that skinhead image of aggression. I liked the intimidation factor. So I started calling myself a SHARP for a while.

"I realized that I wasn't as racist as I projected. Basically, I realized that I hate all kinds of people, so it must not be a special race thing."

Once Cliff told this story, I started piecing together why he wanted to hang onto his skinhead look and badass attitude: People have something to gain from adhering to a certain mindset, persona, or set of norms. Understanding why some people hang onto negative perspectives can help redirect their energy to more productive purposes. Perhaps what Cliff got from identifying as a racist skinhead was the protective image of aggression and a sense of community. Seeing the chance to maintain a similarly protective image and community, but without the dehumanizing racism and negativity, may have helped create the opportunity for Cliff to change. I asked Cliff just what he got from the skinhead identity, and he surprised me with his reply.

"I still like the image, the idea and the unity behind it all, the non-conformist attitude of it. I like the edge of it, and that's where I feel comfortable. For me it's about working-class attitude, not about race. Being a skinhead was to me about being a strong person and being true to myself.

"I remember in seventh grade, this one teacher called me to her desk on the first day of school, and I hadn't even done anything yet," Cliff tells me. She says 'I know how you are, I know what kind of student you are, and I'm not going to deal with it.' She takes me to the hall and stands there pointing at a spot on the floor saying, 'If you sit here, don't make any noise, don't cause any trouble all year, you'll pass.' So that's what I did, and I passed.

"Now I look back and wonder why I don't have an education . . . I can't read, I can't write, and I feel the effects of it now that I'm trying to get a college degree. For a while, Lindsey would actually sit down and help me, just to get a little better understanding of how I read. I'd read out loud to her, and she'd be like, 'Oh, okay, you really can't read!'"

Cliff laughs, self-effacing, and then modifies his statement: "*Well*. Can't read *well*. I've actually walked out of classes. The first day of my first women's studies class, the professor was handing out the syllabus, and different people were taking turns reading it out loud. When it got near to me, I got up and went out into the hall. I waited in the hall until it was way past me, and then went back in and sat down like nothing ever happened. I didn't want to look stupid."

Sitting across from him, watching him relate easily to the other members of our study group and hearing him discuss feminist philosophy, I find this hard to believe. First, Cliff doesn't strike me as the type to be afraid or ashamed of anything. He exudes self-confidence like an octopus leaking ink. Harder still for me to believe, though, is that Cliff would have trouble with something I consider so basic and so fundamental, like reading. It certainly isn't apparent when talking to him.

"Once I was in college and took an intro to women's studies class I really started to open my eyes to a lot of things. That's when I started to critically look at myself, what opinions I had, and why I had those opinions. I started really thinking about it and realized that I definitely had a kind of masculinity, an aggression, in me, but yet at the same time—it took looking at myself critically to realize that I wasn't really being me."

Cliff still wears his steel-toed boots, but not because he's constantly ready for a fight. And he doesn't go out of his way to look aggressive. But most significant is his simple presence in class as one of the most outspoken voices for gender equity, human rights, and progressive change.

"I don't dress like a skin anymore, although I do still have my old hoodies and jackets. Actually, the other day I put on some old, cuffed-up pants and my Doc Martens because I didn't want to dirty any of my newer clothes, and

Lindsey said, 'You're not going to start dressing like a skinhead again, are you?' But I'm not the old Cliff anymore. The only fight I've been in since moving here was the one at Rec Hall, carrying my friend's basketball. I'll admit it, though, I was really thinking about pounding those guys on the corner with the signs today."

Reading this piece as I'm drafting it, Cliff starts getting emotional.

"It's good, because it's true. This is stuff I talk about all the time. I'm always telling people my story. Maybe there's someone like me, early me, who might read something like this and go, 'Y'know . . .'" He trails off, imitating some earlier self, reconsidering his life choices.

Cliff has a new job working part time at a florist's shop. I think that says a lot about the changes in his views about masculinity. I find myself wondering if he seems as out of place at work as he does in our women's studies class, but then I look around and realize that he isn't out of place at all. This semester Cliff is taking classes in feminist philosophy and rehabilitation education. And of course, his story is still going, and he's still telling it.

MEN'S MANIFESTO

Ben Atherton-Zeman

Reports of men's violence against women dominate our headlines. In Colorado high schools, in Pennsylvania Amish country, in homes in the United States and around the world, my gender is perpetrating violence against women in record numbers.

In 2001, eleven-year-old Nestor Nieves was stabbed to death outside a Springfield, Massachusetts, movie theatre by another boy his age. Subsequent news reports indicated that Nieves was going to the movie with a girl that the other boy wanted to date. "That other boy was jealous and got mad," said Nestor's stepfather, Angel Herrera.

In recent years, this kind of event has been described as "youth violence" rather than what it really is: male violence. Many of the highly publicized shootings of recent years have involved some kind of dating violence—usually a girl wouldn't go out with one of the boys. In each of these shootings, though, the attackers have all been men. Media analysis of these tragedies usually misses this important point.

When I read about Nestor Nieves' murder, it made me think about my own experiences going to middle school in Springfield. I learned many things there about what it means to be a man. There were some good lessons: Be strong about your opinions, stand up against injustice, take initiative rather than standing back, and so forth. But there were some lessons I could have done without: Always have a girlfriend, always have the biggest car or make the most money, don't show vulnerable feelings. If a girl doesn't want to kiss you, kiss her really well and she'll "melt." If your girlfriend doesn't do what she "should," it's all right to bring her into line. And if she's going out with someone else, you have the right to a jealous, even homicidal rage against that other person—or against her.

All the popular guys in the Springfield Middle School, as in the other schools I attended, embodied these qualities. They were the guys I wanted to be like, and I tried my hardest to embody what Jackson Katz calls the "Tough Guise." These same role models were on TV, the movies, and in our popular culture. Any guy who deviated from this got labeled a sissy, gay, or somehow girl-like (the worst thing to be called as a young boy, which is a problem in itself).

I, for one, am sick of it. One of the reasons our sons are killing is because we have encouraged it. One of the reasons our brothers and fathers have abused their wives, girlfriends, and partners is because we haven't said, with a unified voice, that this is not a "manly" thing to do. We need to do more work to change what it means to be a man, what it means to be one of the "cool" and popular guys. Toward this end, I propose a Men's Manifesto.

We will be our own role models, and the role models for other men and boys. Rejecting some of traditional masculinity, we will embrace what is useful to us and sometimes create new definitions of what it means to be a man.

We boys and men claim the right to define what's cool. It doesn't have to mean aloofness, toughness, unreasonable jealousy, and possessiveness. We declare that it's cool to be tough sometimes, and vulnerable some others. We declare it cool to support the women (or men) we date in their independence: Love isn't about control and sex isn't about coercion.

We will stand up against injustice. We will speak out against it, and we will listen without defensiveness when it is pointed out in us. Rather than hiding behind "I didn't mean to," we will listen to the effects of our actions, not just point out our good intentions. Strength as men will be measured not just by how many barbells we can lift, but by how well we can listen.

We will not use homophobic, sexist, racist, or other oppressive slurs to gain the upper hand with someone else. And when we're called sissy, fag, or girly, we will take it as a compliment. Strength as men will not be measured in opposition to women and things female, but in unity with those things.

We will be men in this way with determination—sometimes quietly, sometimes proudly, and always unapologetically. We will write country western, rap, and rock songs with these voices. We will raise our sons this way, and raise our daughters to be strong and articulate. We will refuse to accept it if others say this isn't the way to be a man. This is our way to be men, and we will not be denied our self-defined manhood.

We are sick of violence from intimate partners. Gay men, bisexuals, heterosexuals, lesbians, and transgender folks all have the rights to joyful relationships free of violence and control. Since most of this violence is males controlling females, we pledge to never commit, condone, or remain silent about this violence. We choose to respect, listen to, seek equality with, and share power with the women in our lives, and to encourage other men and boys to do the same.

Nestor Nieves didn't have to die. The other boy could have gone and talked to his friends about how jealous he felt, how frustrated he was that the girl went to the movies with someone else. Every murder is preventable, especially if we can change our culture of violent masculinity. We must stand with our boys before these things happen, and stand with each other as we boldly define a new form of manhood.

BREAKING THE SILENCE ONE MILE AT A TIME

Grantlin Schafer

Plenty of stares, some thumbs up, a middle finger, countless inappropriate jokes, and the miracle question: Why are you doing this?

Our thirty-seven-foot RV complete with our non-profit name, the National Organization of Men's Outreach for Rape Education (NO MORE), was the vessel soliciting those reactions during our national tour of fifty-nine colleges, one U.S. Navy base, a national conference, forty-two states, and 35,000 miles. I spent an entire year with three other recent college graduates as part of the One in Four RV tour to educate men about ending rape and helping survivors of sexual assault. The name "One in Four" comes from the national statistic that one in four college women have survived rape or an attempted rape.

We were taking action. We were speaking out. We were breaking the silence: Men were finally talking about men's violence against women. We spoke in a way that gave us credibility. We were not academics lecturing. We did not stand on soapboxes looking down at our audience. The four of us had experienced that approach and knew it did not work.

As we looked out at our audience, we saw reflections of ourselves from a few years earlier. We crafted our message to speak to our peers as guys who did not want to hurt women. Instead, we wanted to empower them to learn how to help survivors and take action to end sexual violence against women.

Change starts with language. We know that most men do not think they are rapists or that they hurt women in any way, so it is not effective to approach men with the assumption that they do. Most men want to be a better friend, boyfriend, family member; presenting ways to be good allies keeps ears open and defense mechanisms down. When we talk about preventing rape and sexual assault, we provide small, simple things that guys can do and say immediately after they see our presentation. We talk about not joking or kidding around about rape and sexual assault. Jokes like "that team just got raped" take away from what rape really means, so the solution is simple: Don't use the word rape out of context.

We can help prevent violence toward women by paying attention to how we talk to our friends, teammates, and peers in locker rooms, on sports fields, and athletic courts. When we hear teammates or friends yell, "Get up, don't be such a pussy" or "You threw that pass like a girl," they are probably not intending to hurt women. However, this language equates women with being less valuable than men. Some men will use this language to justify treating women as though they are weak and inferior. Another simple solution: Don't bring gender into joking.

Finally we urge guys to step up and say something when they hear bragging about getting a girl wasted at a party the night before, taking advantage of her, or other tales of conquest. It is likely that other guys hearing this kind of talk at the breakfast table or around the lockers are feeling uncomfortable, so by standing up and saying something, the others will respect you. Even if some guys act like they don't respect you, remember that you were the one who had the courage to do the right thing.

Our presentation is part of *The Men's Program* entitled "How to Help a Sexual Assault Survivor: What Men Can Do." It works. Men who see this presentation have reported a dual benefit from the program: Learning how to help women recover from rape while decreasing men's acceptance of rape myths. Studies show that men who have attended this program report a lower likelihood of raping. When it comes down to lighting a spark of change, our presentation effectively asks guys to make a simple change of language. We do not order them to join activist marches or become different people. We believe that language influences and guides action, so if we can change our language a change in action will follow.

Even though I knew about the research on the success of programs like ours, I was not personally convinced that One in Four's peer education program would work until I went to a national sexual assault prevention conference. I listened to academics give presentations on how to get through to young men. Sitting there in the audience, I felt talked down to. It sounded too much like a classroom lecture. Lectures struggle to be effective because the message is not real, tangible, or applicable to young men. This is precisely why the RV tour does things differently. Giving suggestions to men about how they can help prevent violence is the first step in creating change, but it is not the last.

This movement is working its way toward creating what writer Malcolm Gladwell calls the tipping point. The One in Four program is a realistic and effective catalyst for change. We give the men who are thinking about gender equality and ending male violence against women a chance to put these ideas into action. To date, twenty-five colleges and one U.S. Naval base house chapters of One in Four. This is just a start. As the number of chapters and members of One in Four continues to grow, our communities will become infused with the message that it is not okay for men to rape.

A goal of the One in Four movement is to bring this message to younger men in the military, college, high schools, middle schools, and throughout our communities. Young adults are experiencing times of growth and learning; these are formative periods. We want prevention and mentoring to thrive. Establishing One in Four chapters in high schools means that members can serve as mentors for middle-school boys. This will work to change social norms from a scene where younger teens often learn sexist attitudes from older boys to environments that model true respect.

The broad goal of the men's movement is to change the definition of what it means to be a man. We are committed to including men as part of the solution to end discrimination, classism, sexism, and violence against women. This new definition and this new generation of men will produce fathers who are outspoken against sexism and who set an example of positive behavior.

One day while we were on the road, a woman approached our RV. She told us about her father's violence. His abuse included repeatedly raping her well into adult life and led her brother to commit suicide. That moment in a grocery store parking lot outside San Francisco refocused me on the big picture. If our message can empower one guy to become an informed, active agent of change, we have fulfilled the movement's goal for that day. We have to take it one man and one mile at a time.

BEING A SOCIAL JUSTICE ALLY: A FEMINIST'S PERSPECTIVE ON PREVENTING MALE VIOLENCE

Jonathan Ravarino

Becoming a feminist has been one of the most important steps I have taken in my adult life. It requires continual critical thinking, unending self-reflection, and risk taking in multiple spheres of my life. The benefits are well worth the effort. I've gained a better understanding of my position as a man in interpersonal relationships and how to make choices that consider my community. Feminism has offered me a sense of freedom from the shackles of male socialization and the bondage of male privilege. Feminism teaches men something that patriarchy ultimately ignores; that when others are oppressed, no one is free.

My decision to become a feminist—or social justice ally—is a form of activism because it involves risk. I have learned that I must go beyond simply adopting feminist principles or engaging in critical dialogue among the safety of my friends. I and other men must serve as social justice allies by actively supporting women. This role involves making a commitment to work directly with men in the interests of women. This can be difficult, to say the least.

Helping to prevent violence against women is an important way of serving as a social justice ally to women. I hope the ten suggestions I offer here demystify the process of feminist activism and provide men with specific strategies to incorporate into their social justice advocacy.

1. CHALLENGE THE MYTHS ABOUT MASCULINITY, PATRIARCHY, AND SEXUAL VIOLENCE

One starting point in becoming a social justice ally is to begin deconstructing masculinity. A useful strategy is to critically examine one's own socialization.

For example, you might start by asking yourself, "What qualities have I been taught makes a man, a man?" Traits like *tough, strong, intelligent, unemotional, provider, protector, and pimp* will probably come to mind. When I've asked men this question, the response has alarmingly and frequently been something to the effect of "not a sissy . . . not a wimp . . . not a fag." Recognizing the misogynistic and homophobic underpinnings of such comments is important because men's collective commitment to rejecting anything female or gay contributes to violence against women and sexual minorities.

Being a social justice ally involves deconstructing patriarchal ideas. If patriarchy is a political system designed to privilege and ascribe power to men, while oppressing and marginalizing women, then we must look at this impact. Patriarchy operates according to myths about gender and this interferes with genuine human development. When I was young, I was encouraged—*required*, actually—to engage in rough and aggressive competition with other boys. And while I often heard the saying "boys will be boys," it took decades before I fully understood the impact that boys' and, later, men's violent behavior has on others. I have come to see the connection between condoning school-aged aggressive behavior and rationalizing the actions of politicians who start wars against less powerful nations.

Men are also taught myths regarding sexual violence against women. One example of how this works is through the rape and sexual assault trials that are highly publicized in American media. Newscasters minimize the behavior of the men by offering statements such as, "So these men got a little crazy . . . What do you expect when men get drunk and there is an exotic dancer in the room? . . . Do you really think men like that could rape a woman? . . . Those men don't have to rape women. They could have anyone they want." Equally frightening are the sheer numbers of people who question the behavior and allegations of a sexual assault survivor. Sometimes people doubt a survivor's integrity by saying things like, "She asked for it by turning him on . . . She didn't have to stay, she could have left . . . She is falsely reporting to get the money."

My point here is simple: Myths about sexual violence silence sexual assault survivors and, at the same time, condone men's violent behavior. Men who challenge myths about male socialization, patriarchy, and sexual violence are well on their way to becoming social justice allies to women.

2. SHIFT YOUR LENS OF UNDERSTANDING

Becoming a social justice ally requires developing the capacity to shut up and listen to what women have to say. Doing this means men must shift their lens of understanding. This is not easy since a facet of patriarchy and male privilege is to ensure that men have minimal awareness of the issues affecting women and other targeted groups. One component of male privilege is that men do not have to think about how their presence and behavior impacts women.

Listening to women means understanding their experience and the political issues affecting women's communities. Reproductive rights, independent financial security, equal division of labor at home and at work, and a criminal justice system that is accountable to the people are central issues for women in today's world. I am reminded of a comment made by a feminist friend who recommended, "Listen before speaking and understand before acting."

One area in which I choose to listen more deeply to women involves the issue of violence. I have learned that women engage in multiple strategies to ensure their safety from men's violence. Examples include locking the car door upon entry, walking to one's vehicle while holding keys in the form of a weapon, exercising with mace readily accessible, going to the washroom in groups, and not walking alone at night. I am embarrassed to admit, but I once believed that locking the car door was irrational and that women went to the washroom in pairs only because they wanted to gossip. By doing so, I minimized the legitimate safety concerns of women in my life and likely missed an opportunity to be supportive.

3. ACCEPT THAT MEN HAVE A PRIMARY ROLE IN STOPPING VIOLENCE AGAINST WOMEN

Violence against women is as much a men's issue as it is a women's issue. Helping men accept that they have a primary role in stopping violence against women is not easy. This often requires patience and understanding.

Because men's violence against women does not happen inside a vacuum, dismantling myths about male violence is crucial. One example would be to critically examine the multibillion-dollar pornography industry that equates violence against women with eroticism. Second, is exposing the dangerous idea that if women can't prevent violence then they didn't try hard enough, or they must have done something to provoke it. Some men operate according to this lie. This myth is dangerous because it blames the victim. Whatever a woman does before, during, or after an episode of violence is done in order to survive.

Men are responsible for men's behavior and thus only men can stop men's violence against women. Nothing women do—and I mean absolutely nothing—warrants sexual violence or domestic assault.

4. AVOID WORKING ALONE

Political activism requires the emotional and physical support of others, and becoming a social justice ally to women is no exception. It is crucial that men join established organizations that work for gender justice and that hold men accountable. This encourages long-term engagement in the struggle. As a mentor once stated, "Women don't need fly-by-the-seat allies; women need men who are committed."

There are many organizations focusing on social justice and the issue of violence against women, including The White Ribbon Campaign and Men Can Stop Rape. Becoming a member of established organizations enables allies to become informed about issues affecting women and to learn ways of becoming politically active. The White Ribbon Campaign, for example, is an international organization committed to supporting the lives and safety of women and has become an invaluable resource for networking and receiving important mentoring services. Barring all else, one way to get involved is to give money. Financial contributions are central to helping social justice groups stay afloat and enable them to conduct outreach and educational programming. Financial support also helps rebuild organizations when they are attacked by vandalism or organized efforts to distort their message.

5. DON'T REMAIN ON THE SIDELINES

Becoming a social justice ally requires more than simply joining an organization and putting a logo sticker on one's car. Allies get involved on a political and personal level. Being an ally requires taking serious risk in the face of possible ridicule and alienation—or even hate and discrimination—from others.

The good news is that there are an infinite number of ways to become involved and they do not all call for intense large-scale personal risk or political action. The first step in determining how best to become involved is to make an inventory of your specific strengths and skill sets. You may be good at organizing events, writing newsletters, or speaking to children. You may be better at teaching, research, or facilitating small-group dialogue.

The subject of violence against women is a sensitive one and people tend to feel awkward about discussing sensitive issues. Often we don't want to offend someone or become too emotionally connected to the issue. Failing to engage in a difficult conversation with other men out of fear of making a mistake is a hurdle for both the growth of individual allies and the feminist movement. I encourage men who wish to become social justice allies to keep speaking up and moving forward. Silence feeds violence and we must refuse to be silent. We will all make mistakes along the journey. We must keep working to improve on this.

6. RECOGNIZE MALE PRIVILEGE

Men who are social justice allies are in a unique situation. While we choose to challenge systems of patriarchy, many of us cannot—or do not want to—give up male privilege. Coming to grips with how we continue to experience privilege that we have not earned is a challenge for men to work through.

One thing I do is to take responsibility for my privilege by using it to work for good purposes. Emerging research indicates, for example, that college men are more receptive to learning about rape myths and sexual violence if men provide the workshops or education sessions. In other words, as men, we have unique access to other men. This same-sex dynamic means that men can be effective social justice allies in addressing sensitive topics. I try to stay focused on recognizing the responsibility I have to educate men who, because of persistent sexism, may not otherwise entertain statistics or comments about male violence if presented by a woman.

In my experience facilitating programs on sexual violence, I have noticed that men seem caught off guard when a man gets in front of them and discusses violence against women from a feminist perspective. It could be that men feel less shame and guilt when a man tells them about the impact of violence. I make use of personal disclosures about my own process of learning about violence against women. This seems to help men see me as human, and more like them.

Social justice allies should not run away from their privilege as men but, rather, find ways to use it in the interests of women and social justice. At the same time, it's important to remember that for centuries, female feminists have been confronting men's violence against women. It's not as if male allies invented this concern. We must publicly recognize the contributions and mentoring we have received from women who make up the feminist move- ment. Men must remain accountable to women's leadership and be open to feedback at every level of the process.

7. CONTINUALLY EVALUATE YOUR GOALS AND INTENTIONS

My professional role as a therapist has given me an understanding that men are socialized to derive self-esteem and self-worth from action-oriented tasks. Men are taught to engage in activities with a specific goal in mind and to do whatever is needed to accomplish their objective. While this may be viewed as determination and discipline, it can also be understood as self-centered behavior that is overly concerned with outcome rather than with process. Social justice allies must therefore maintain an awareness of men's tendencies toward dominating, monopolizing, or competing with others—even while we are working toward justice and equality. This does little in the way of helping women or challenging institutional structures. Allies must lose the notion that "size matters" and focus less on outcome and more on process. This will enable men to notice the incremental change emerging as part of all social justice activism.

Becoming a social justice ally is a worthy cause but it is nothing special. I have seen some men carry unproductive and exploitative behaviors into the realm of social justice work. Men who assume this work must do so out of authentic commitment and compassion. Allies must continually evaluate their intentions and focus on the collective goals of the social justice and feminist movement. I have seen first-hand how some men have become glorified and glamorized as activists, or even by sharing housework and childcare duties at home. Women do not need men to take over a movement and use it for self-serving purposes!

8. ALWAYS BELIEVE IN MEN'S CAPACITY TO CHANGE

It is important to remember that individual men are not the problem; rather, the problem is within our larger institutions. Knowing this allows us to maintain compassion and empathy for individual men caught in the system. Feminism allows men an opportunity to gain a sense of freedom: Fighting to end violence against women will result in liberation for men, too.

Sometimes men can seem resistant to change. But holding our experience of male socialization close at heart ensures that allies maintain the skills to work with some of the most guarded men. When I come across men who manifest counterproductive traits, I understand them as being somewhere on the journey and capable of change at any minute. After all, my goal as a social justice ally is to help each man move in the direction of compassion and empathy, hoping that they will continue to encounter people and experiences that will move them even further. Maintaining this sense of compassion means believing in the potential of individual men to make changes; it means believing in the capacity of larger institutions to become more equitable and accountable to our community. At times when I am challenged by the most stereotypically defensive men, I like to say to my peers, "Remember where you started. Anything is possible."

9. RECOGNIZE THE LINKS BETWEEN VIOLENCE AGAINST WOMEN AND OTHER FORMS OF INJUSTICE

Becoming a social justice ally to women means developing the skills to under-stand multiple forms of social injustice. The intersectionality of gender, race, sexual orientation, disability, and class is evident at every level of social justice. bell hooks reminds us in *Ain't I a Woman*, that at no point is a woman only a woman; she is a constellation of traits as a gendered, racial, sexual, and classed being. While gender has been the most salient trait in my life, I must not forget that my position as a white, heterosexual male plays a significant role in the work I do and in how others perceive me. Learning our history and locating ourselves on the privilege/oppression continuum helps ensure that we engage in social action without contributing to social oppression. I say this because I have made mistakes in this area.

When I was speaking to a group of activists, a woman asked how my work took into consideration black men's experience and relationship to women. I understood her question perfectly, but I was incapable of responding in a meaningful way. This served as a catalyst for the work I needed to do to become a multiculturally competent social justice activist.

10. PRACTICE SELF-CARE

The final step I encourage is to incorporate self-care into one's life. This is valuable with respect to ensuring that social justice allies remain committed and balanced as men. Unfortunately, I have noticed that we often only offer lip service to the notion of self-care. This is unhealthy and can interfere with the activist process. As a therapist and educator, I believe self-care is central to finding both meaning and joy in life.

One specific method I practice is called mindfulness meditation. This incorporates the skills of acceptance, nonjudgment, and present-moment orientation into my daily life. Mindfulness has been defined as a non-judgmental awareness of the present moment. This may sound simple, but many of us struggle with slowing down and finding peace inside our self. I have found that the effort required in social justice and anti-oppression work benefits from the balancing energy of mindfulness meditation. Similar to other strategies of self-care, it has been critical for me to engage in mindfulness meditation daily and devote time to my practice.

Other social justice activists have commented on the benefits of practicing mindfulness meditation when engaging in social action. Thich Nhat Hanh, one of the pioneers of bringing Buddhism to the Western world, speaks of observing strong emotions toward others instead of acting them out. Observing one's anger or fear while witnessing or reading about acts of violence allows social justice allies to not be overwhelmed or paralyzed by anger or negative emotions. Thich Nhat Hanh further suggests that individuals can learn to understand forms of violence inside our own minds as a way of understanding how to combat violence outside the mind. He offers the simple but powerful truth, "The only antidote to hate and violence is love." As a social justice ally, I use this notion to help me generate compassion and love for men who engage in violence against women. Hate is not helpful in this process, and social justice allies who are able to move beyond this are better served as members of this movement. Although mindfulness meditation represents a method I personally choose to use to maintain compassion and energy as an ally, it is not the only method. I think it's important, though, for social justice allies to identify self-care strategies to combat cynicism and hate and cultivate love and compassion for others.

Men can help change the institutional conditions that impact the safety and lives of women and the freedom of men to be authentic and compassionate beings. In sum, here's what we need to do: Increase awareness by listening and learning from women and other allies; develop the capacity to take personal risks as well as to support other allies and organizations; and believe in the capacity of all humans to end personal and collective forms of violence. Being a social justice ally is a way of gaining freedom and of expressing responsibility to our communities. Like Alice Walker said, "Activism is the rent I pay for living on this planet." Being a social justice ally to women has become the rent I pay for my privilege as a man.

GOOD OL' BOY: A TALE OF TRANSFORMATION IN THE RURAL SOUTH

Jay Poole

My mother and father were in the Ku Klux Klan. Yes, you read that correctly. Both of them became members in the late-1950s as rumbles of integration grew into loud booms across the southern United States. Mom and Dad were both raised in the rural South. They were born during the Great Depression and spent their adolescence in a post–World War II environment that witnessed a resurgence of opportunities to seek the great American dream. Dad dropped out of high school during his senior year to work in a veneer plant and Mom, despite her hatred of being singled out for ridicule over what she wore, managed to graduate from high school. (Mom only had one brazier, two skirts, two blouses, and one pair of penny loafers.)

My mother always said that she married so that she could have a bathroom—the house she lived in as a teenager had no indoor toilet, only an outhouse. Mom was bright and managed to land a job at Sears in customer service (a very appropriate job at the time for a female—it was, after all, a service position). Mom was very successful at Sears and she and my father saved up enough money to buy the house that would become my home. So, with working-class parents who held traditional southern values and who believed in the superiority of white, Christian, heterosexuals, I was bound for a journey that would take me into the throes of trying to become a "good ol' boy." I arrived, though, at a place of despair about knowing who I was and who I wanted to become.

I was born in 1962. Great social changes were beginning to occur and people like Mom and Dad were frightened at the prospect of living and raising a child in a world that was going to be so different from the one they knew. I suppose it was this fear that fueled their decision to join an organization like the KKK that promised to keep the social order of the South intact.

My early years were spent in a world dominated by a masculine power structure that emphasized the superiority of white men over all other people (and creatures, for that matter). A woman's role was defined as inferior and subordinate to men. I was born with the "privilege" of being a white southern male, and with the expectation that I would follow in the footsteps of my father and his father before him to become a hard-working, productive, and respected man in the community.

What I came to recognize was that men in the rural South were, if anything, supposed to be rocks. They were supposedly invincible. It was understood that you should develop a love of sports, particularly those involving physical contact. Basically, any opportunity to beat the hell out of another guy should be your greatest desire. You must not cry when being beaten or battered on the playing field—or off it. A southern boy (particularly a rural southern boy) must love hunting. You should have your first BB gun by the time you are ten and your first rifle by the time you are thirteen.

I went on my first hunt when I was eleven years old. We spent the entire night in the woods following the hounds on the trail of several raccoons. I remember the smell of cigarettes and chewing tobacco mixed with the faintest odor of whiskey as my father, myself, and three other men tore through the underbrush on that cold November night. Hunting taught me that "real" men can conquer just about anything, and that hunting and killing is testament to the power that men possess. I noticed that most women did not hunt. My mom's role was to see that my father and I had a good meal and warm clothes before we ventured into the woods. She was supposed to be concerned about us until we came safely back home. I learned about competition as I listened to my dad and his friends talk about whose dog was best at tracking the prey and which football or basketball teams were going to win during the season. They never talked about being sad or about love. Those were sissy things and I quickly understood that these topics were off limits for men. About the only thing that resembled tender emotion were discussions about turning to Jesus in times of trouble or concern. It was in the southern Baptist Church that I learned about the power of God the father, God the son, and God the Holy Ghost—all presumably male.

Dad never went to church. It was Mom who dressed me in my Sunday best and took me to hear weekly sermons about the awesome power of the heavenly father. The preacher spoke with great passion about the fires of hell and how we were dangling over them. That's why being saved was of utmost importance. Living a good life meant that you had accepted Jesus as your Lord and Savior into your heart. The stories we studied in Sunday school emphasized the role of the man as the decision-maker and the leader of the family. Women were to support their husbands and serve as the men provided for the family. Certainly being a man was much better than being a woman; at least that seemed to be the position of my local church and community. By the time I was in my teens, I was a fundamentalist Christian and I desperately wanted to be successful in my role as a man. It was here that I encountered problems.

Some early photos in the family album caught my eye as a teenager. There I was, a two-year-old in my mom's heels with her patent leather purse draped over my arm. I was beaming! In another picture, I am standing with Mom at the kitchen counter mixing a bowl of cookie dough, again smiling from ear to ear. There were more! One of me ironing; another folding clothes; and yet another sitting with my legs crossed to one side delicately holding a kitten. What did this mean and why were these pictures in the family photo album? I certainly did not appear to be doing things that I had learned boys were supposed to do. Far from it; I was doing "girl" things.

I knew that successful boys were athletes. And I learned in school that popular boys had several girls swooning after them, proving their sexual prowess. By these terms, I was not a successful boy. My attempts to be an athlete failed miserably. I could not hit or catch a ball of any kind. I loved talking to girls, but none seemed interested in dating me and the feeling was mutual. I began to realize that I was sexually attracted to other boys, a feeling that rocked the very foundations of my identity. Boys were not supposed to like other boys, so why did I? I did not see myself as sissy . . . but, then, there were those pictures. I was supposed to be a man and, now, my definition of what that meant was completely knocked out from under me.

My upbringing taught me to despise and fear those who were sexually "perverted." I found myself in an existential crisis as I had my first sexual experience with another male. On the one hand, it felt wonderful, natural, and so right. On the other hand, it was gut-wrenching—a sin punishable by death as the preacher said many times quoting verses from the King James version of the Bible. "Queers" were sick and God forbid you were one.

My identity as a man was spiraling down a dark hole leaving me with a void in knowing who or what I was. I avoided appearing feminine at all costs for fear of being discovered. I made every attempt to cross my legs at the ankle, not the knee. I was careful about gestures I made with my hands and practically sat on them if they did "womanly" things. I tried to walk like the jocks at school. Most of all, I dreaded gym class because my lack of athletic ability was exposed to the world, diminishing my ability to pass for a "normal" guy. Later, I would come to recognize that society had made up these rules about gender by which I was so desperately trying to live. At the time, though, the ideals of masculinity and femininity seemed completely real and I thought I had to conform.

By the time I was a young adult, everything that I had been taught by my church, at school, and at home was under suspicion. I began to question those narrow-minded values that Mom and Dad worked hard to instill in me. I distanced myself from the standards by which I grew up and it was in this displacement that I began to discover who I was and who I wanted to be. I recognized the importance of social activism in the gay liberation and feminist movements in bringing attention to the inequity, prejudice, and discrimination toward women and men who express their gender and sexuality in a manner that some people find unacceptable.

As I began to associate with people outside my very insulated hometown and church, I recognized that there are many differences among people and that difference is not negative. My initial reaction was to feel anger, rejection, confusion, and disgust toward my family, church, and hometown. At some point, though, I needed to make sense of where I'd come from and where I'd arrived.

I'm not excusing bigots and homophobes for marginalizing or discriminating against others, but I recognize now that people reflect what they know. And what they know is what has been taught to them. As we are exposed to new ideas, or if we expose ourselves to new information, we may initially react with trepidation. But, if we spend some time with this new information—whether we find it in books, movies, people, or situations—we can be transformed. I have learned that informing one's self is a key to change and growth.

Our society is filled with so many beliefs and stereotypes about all sorts of people. It seems important that we each assume responsibility for taking the frightening step toward encounters with unfamiliar people, places, and experiences. Doing this can help dispel the sort of thinking that has caused so much harm and grief.

My personal journey has enabled me to recognize the importance of questioning what we believe, grappling with why we believe it, and ultimately, facing the challenging task of de-centering ourselves so that we have the opportunity to grow. Many of us sit comfortably in belief systems that are handed to us. It is from that comfortable place that prejudice, discrimination, and oppression are often born.

The questions I now ask myself focus on challenging those beliefs that are most comfortable for me. I have come to understand gender and sexuality—and race and religion—in much different ways from the way I understood them as a teenager and certainly, much differently from the way my parents understood them. Perhaps, as I stretch my thinking even more, the concepts I have around gender will be redefined once again. As a fifteen-year-old, I never would have believed that I would come to challenge what I learned about being masculine and feminine, straight and gay, black, white, Latino, and any number of categories that defined my position in this incredibly diverse world.

We are all students and we are all teachers and it is within the appetite of human curiosity that we begin to discover all that is around us, leading us to think, re-think, and imagine new possibilities. If my mother and father had been able to recognize the benefits of asking questions about the world of hate and fear that they came to know, perhaps they would have opened the space to embrace those who were not like them and my battle with my own identity would have not been as arduous a journey.

HOW CAN I BE SEXIST? I'M AN ANARCHIST!

Chris Crass

"**W**hat do you mean I'm sexist?" I was shocked. I wasn't a tough guy jock. I didn't hate or assault women. I wasn't a bad guy. "But I'm an anarchist! How can I be sexist?" I was anxious, nervous, and my defenses were up. I believed in liberation, in fighting against capitalism and the state. There were those who defended and benefited from injustice—and then there was us, right? I was nineteen years old. It was four years after I'd gotten involved in radical politics, and my sense of the world was slipping.

My girlfriend, Nilou, held my hand and patiently explained. "I'm not saying you're an evil person, I'm saying that you're sexist and sexism happens in a lot of subtle and blatant ways. You cut me off when I'm talking. You pay more attention to what men say. The other day when I was sitting at the coffee shop with you and Mike, it was like the two of you were having a conversation and I was just there to watch. I tried to jump in and say something, but you both just looked at me and then went back to your conversation. Men in the group make eye contact with each other and act like women aren't even there."

This can't be true, I thought. Maybe it's just her deal. Maybe she's just having a hard time and we can get past this.

She continued, "For a long time I thought maybe it was just me, maybe what I had to say wasn't as useful or exciting. Maybe I needed to change my approach, maybe I was just overreacting, or that it was just in my head and I needed to get over it," she explained. "But then I saw how the same thing was happening to other women in the group, over and over again. I'm not blaming you for all of this, but you're a big part of this group and you're part of this dynamic." While I struggled to understand what she was telling me, this conversation changed my life. Fundamentally, Nilou Mostoufi pushed me to realize that in order to work for liberation I needed to make a lifelong commitment to feminist politics and practice against male supremacy.

So how could I better work for change? And what could I suggest to gender, class, or race-privileged guys who were also committed to positive social transformation?

More and more gender-privileged men in the anarchist movement are working to challenge male supremacy. We recognize that patriarchy exists, that we have material and psychological privileges as a result, and that sexism undermines political movements. Women, transgender, and genderqueer people have explained it repeatedly and said, "You all need to talk with each other, challenge each other, and figure out what you're going to do." We need to listen to them. However, there are also men in the movement who agree that sexism exists, but deny their personal participation in it.

Lisa Sousa, who is part of the San Francisco Independent Media Center and AK Press, told me that in recent discussions she's had in groups about sexism and gender, she's heard the following responses from men: "We are all oppressed"; "We should be talking about class"; "You are just using gender as a way to attack such and such."

These comments sound so familiar. While it is tempting to distance myself from men who say things like this, it's important that I remember that I've made those comments, too. As someone who believes in movement building and collective liberation, it's crucial for me to be honest about my experiences, mistakes, and learning process.

When I think back to that conversation with Nilou and her explanation of how sexism operates, I remember trying not to shut down, trying to listen. The word "but" repeated over and over again in my mind, followed by: "it was a misunderstanding"; "I didn't mean it that way"; "if I knew you felt that way I wouldn't have done it"; "I wasn't trying to do that"; "I would love to see you participate more"; "no one said they didn't want to hear what you had to say"; "we all believe in equality"; "I love you and would never do anything to hurt you."

Looking back ten years later, it's amazing how often that same list of "buts" comes running to mind. I'm more like those "other" men than I'd like to admit. Many of us who have been challenged on sexism get stuck in the defensiveness and frustration of not knowing what to do. Or, in the rush to solve the problem, we overlook the depth of the problem to begin with.

Nilou, who comes from a middle-class, Iranian family, spent hours talking with me about sexism. It was tremendously difficult for both of us and only in retrospect can I comprehend how courageous it was for her to do this. A clearly defined dualistic framework of good and bad shaped my politics. If it was true that I was sexist, then my previous sense of self was in question: I must have been bad. Nilou pushed me to develop a more complex framework. She helped me begin to locate myself in a complex power analysis of society in which I had material and psychological privilege as a man. I knew this was a profoundly important moment in my growth and it still felt like shit.

Two weeks later as our anarchist study group meeting came to a close, Nilou raised the concern that "sexism is happening in this group." "Oh my god," I thought, "What am I going to do?"

She listed the examples she had told me. The five other men in the room now amplified the defensive reaction that I'd had. Other women started speaking up. They had experienced these dynamics as well and they were tired of it. The men were shocked. They began listing all the reasons why claims of sexism were simply misunderstandings, miscommunications, and misperceptions. With genuine sincerity they said, "But we all want revolution."

To understand the situation we were in, I should give some background history. We were members of the United Anarchist Front. It was an activist youth group formed by political punks in Whittier, a suburb in Southern California, in the late-1980s. Focusing on animal rights, we regularly held anti-corporate protests at McDonald's and passed out literature on vegetarianism in our high school classes. (For information check out www.mcspotlight.org.) The driving force in the group was Mike Rejniak, a sixteen-year-old, working-class punk who dressed like a Catholic school student, regularly used something called the Internet, read philosophy, and was enormously popular at school in almost every clique and scene. We were heavily influenced by English anarcho-punk bands and, for the first few years, the UAF was essentially a group of teenage guys who grew up together doing politics. In 1991 the Gulf War radicalized us. We participated in mass peace marches in Los Angeles, repeatedly covered our school in anti-war chalk graffiti, passed out anti-capitalist, anti-militarist literature, argued U.S. foreign policy with teachers during classes, and faced off with the young Republicans in the debate club—and won. Through all of this we developed a visible left–anarchist pole at our high school that gave legitimacy to radical politics.

While the UAF itself was comprised of a handful of people, our social scene grew to a core of over forty people. Our frequent parties brought together young people from multiple high schools and colleges in the area who were mostly feminists, anarchists, progressives, and queers. By 1992, more people began working with the UAF, including April Sullivan who was the first woman in the group. We worked with other anarchist groups around Southern California and joined the Love and Rage Network that put forward a revolutionary anti-imperialist, feminist, anti-racist, anarchist politics in their monthly newspaper, a publication that we distributed at punk shows and at school. The Rodney King verdict in 1992 further galvanized us: We went to black-led, anti-police brutality marches and argued with students and teachers about the meaning of the L.A. riots. As many shook their heads saying, "They're animals" or "It's senseless violence," we argued—in classroom debates, in the school newspaper, and in flyers we handed out—that people were responding with justified rage against unemployment, poverty, police violence, and white supremacy.

Out of this momentum a few of us decided it was time to bring more organization to the UAF. We started having regular meetings and invited people from our social circle to join us. Soon we had a dozen members. We divided our activities into work committees and launched a study group to help us develop our political analysis. This was a major transition because prior to this we had done our work informally over coffee or beer. The down side now was that generally two or three of us made the decisions and took all the organizational responsibility. We wanted to bring more people into the work and expand our activities. Without mentors or role models, we experimented. We were about six months into the process of building a collective when Nilou raised the issue of sexism in the group.

While people debated whether sexism existed in the group, April, who came from a white, working-class, Irish family and had been in the group for well over a year, sat me down. She, too, gave me example after example of sexist behavior. Men in the group didn't trust her to handle responsibilities, even when they were newer to the group; she wasn't looked to for information about the group, nor were her opinions asked for on political questions. People turned to my friend Mike and me for political direction, but she was usually ignored. Others joined our conversation, but when April gave examples that she had just clearly explained to me, the men denied any claims of sexism as a misunderstanding. A few minutes later, I restated the exact same examples given by April and this time the men agreed that perhaps these incidents were, in fact, sexist.

April called it out immediately and explained what was happening. Her ideas, coming from my mouth, were being taken seriously, when they were dismissed coming from her just minutes before. There it was. I still didn't want to believe that sexism was happening, but now I saw it. It felt horrible, like a kick to the stomach. Nilou and April were desperately trying to get us to agree that there was a problem. How could this be happening when I hadn't intended it to and all of us were so committed to being revolutionary? I was scared to say anything.

Two months later, I was sitting silently in a men's caucus. We didn't know what to talk about. More specifically, we were nervous, unskilled, and without experience. We had not developed an agenda or a plan to help us have a useful discussion about sexism. Nilou and April proposed that the UAF spend a day talking about sexism. It was decided that we'd start with separate, gender-based caucuses and then come back together to discuss what we'd learned.

Once we broke off into our small group of men, we awkwardly tried to talk about sexism. For the most part, though, we anxiously waited for the women to return.

The women came back into the room walking arm-in-arm, while the men stood around feeling uncomfortable. The women had come to a shared understanding of their experiences with sexism and, furthermore, explored ways that sexism within the UAF was pitting them against one another.

While the women's caucus had reached depth and honesty, it was quickly apparent that the men's caucus had barely scratched the surface. Rather than report back anything meaningful, men began questioning what the women had said, and the women were now defending the points they had made. "We need to just listen," was the most that I could contribute to the conversation.

Several people left early in tears, disillusioned, and overwhelmed.

Over the next few months an important development took place. We regularly read anarchist newspapers and zines from around the country as a lifeline to a broader movement. We began looking to other groups for examples to bring to our work. The journal *Free Society*, based in Minneapolis, devoted an entire issue to anarchist groups' experiences dealing with gender and power dynamics. We devoured the articles and this transformed how men began relating to our discussions about sexism. "It's not that we're just fucked up, these issues are coming up in groups all over the country" and "they sound exactly like what women in the UAF are saying," we said. Women used the articles to highlight what they had been telling us: "Sexism is systemic like capitalism, and it's not just about you."

It was becoming clear to me and to other men that challenging sexism was about far more than learning how to make eye contact with women and asking them what they thought during UAF meetings. Indeed, it was a political commitment to challenging a system of power that operates on the political, economic, social, cultural, and psychological levels. My lack of direct eye contact was one of a thousand subtle ways that male supremacy enforces the worldview that women's work is insignificant, marginal, or non-existent. While I wanted to just stop being sexist, I was learning that this would involve a long-term collective struggle to transform the world in which we live.

THIS STRUGGLE IS MY STRUGGLE

> I haven't the faintest notion what possible revolutionary role white heterosexual men could fulfill, since they are the very embodiment of reactionary-vested-interest-power.
>
> —Robin Morgan, from the introduction to *Sisterhood Is Powerful*

I have periods of hating myself, feeling guilty, and afraid. I know in my heart that I have a role in liberation struggle and that there is useful work that I can do, but still the question haunts me: "Am I just fooling myself into believing that I am more useful than problematic?"

I find Robin Morgan's quote useful to struggle with (but not to get stuck on) because I grew up believing that I was entitled to everything. I could go anywhere and do anything and wherever I went, I would be wanted and needed.

Patriarchy and heterosexism taught me, in subtle and blatant ways, that I was entitled to women's bodies, that I was entitled to take up space and express my ideas and thoughts whenever I wanted to, without consideration for others.

This privilege came from growing up in a society that is indeed designed by and built for people like me.

This is a very different reality from that of most people in this society; people who are told to shut up, keep it to themselves, hide who they really are, get out of the way, and to never forget how lucky they are to be allowed here to begin with.

I think it is healthy to not assume I am always needed, to learn to share space and power, to work with others, and to realize the roles that I can and should play. What is unhealthy is how rarely gender-privileged men talk with each other about these issues and how little we support each other through the process of challenging sexism and developing a healthy male identity.

I still struggle every day to really listen to women's voices. My mind wanders quicker when a woman is speaking and my instant reaction is take men's opinions more seriously. When I walk into a room full of activists I instantly scan the group and divide people into hierarchies of status according to how long they've been active, what groups they've been part of, what they've written, and where it's been published. I position myself against them and feel the most competitive with men.

I'm not proud to say this, but I'm just being honest here: When it comes to women, I add their sexual desirability to my status hierarchy tally. I have almost never zoned out on what a man was saying because I was fantasizing about him. But I have repeatedly found myself sexually distracted while listening to women speak, women who are organizers, leaders, and visionaries. I'm all about crushes, healthy sexual desire, and a pro-sex orientation. That is not what I am talking about. This is about owning up to power, entitlement, and my own role in marginalizing women's leadership in a society that is violently misogynistic.

I wish I didn't get defensive on a regular basis, but I do. I get frustrated and shut down by conversations about how power operates between my partner and me. I get defensive about how the world interacts with us and how that influences our dynamics. I know that there are times when I say, "Alright, I'll think more about it" when really I am thinking, "Leave me alone."

Male supremacy negatively impacts how I communicate with my partners, friends, and comrades. It negatively impacts how I want, express, conceptualize, and make love. It negatively impacts how I live my life and how I organize. Male supremacy hurts men's relationship with themselves, with women and people of all genders, and with the earth. It has shaped our emotional lives so as to effectively advance a violent, militaristic, misogynistic, anti-queer, brutally competitive economic system. I am enraged by the resulting damage I see in men's lives all around me.

Patriarchy tears me up. Every person I meet bears the scars of patriarchy.

bell hooks writes that love is impossible where the will to dominate exists. I want to believe that I can genuinely love and that it is possible to forge a non-patriarchal political practice for men—a political practice that moves men to meaningfully join with all people in a collective struggle to re-organize our society toward systemic liberation.

And in this fight we, as men, will realize that even in the face of these systems of oppression, our love, beauty, creativity, passion, dignity, and power grows. We can do this and we need to love, support, and take care of one another as we challenge, push, and encourage each other.

WE MUST WALK TO MAKE THE STRUGGLE REAL

While it's necessary to get into the hard and murky emotional issues of radical political change, there are also concrete steps men must take to challenge male supremacy. This essay is primarily focused on lessons from my own struggles in living a feminst life. However, there is a danger of emphasizing the individual over the group. I believe that organizations can also provide us with opportunities to practice our politics in a collective way that maximizes both the effectiveness of the work and the depth of learning from the process of putting theory into practice.

In the mid-1990s, the United Anarchist Front made some organizational changes. The primary move was to start a Food Not Bombs (FNB) chapter in Whittier. FNB is a network of volunteer-based economic justice; people-before-profit groups that share free food in public spaces to provide a direct service and protest homelessness and poverty. There were numerous reasons why we started a FNB group, but one was to confront sexism. We were trying to address the critique that men held all the power in the group. FNB represented an opportunity for everyone to participate in a meaningful way. There were dozens of easily identifiable roles and responsibilities for people to take on, rotate, and share. Women played leading roles in FNB, positively shifting the dynamics in the group, and yet sexism did not end as some of us had hoped. There are three key lessons that I drew from this experience.

First, some of us (across genders) were equating challenging patriarchy with making women feel comfortable in the group. While this is important, it was becoming the end goal as opposed to transforming the relationships of power. This often led us to abandon things that created discomfort rather than struggle to figure out how to actually change them. For example, sexist dynamics persisted in our study group. But instead of finding creative ways for everyone to feel empowered in developing their political analysis, we de-emphasized the importance of having analysis and ended the study group. People continued to study politics individually, but we moved away from developing our collective analysis. We opted to maintain an unexamined peace rather than deal with the tensions.

Second, a dynamic developed amongst some of the men that detracted from our egalitarian goal. Our view was that if we believed in equality then it should exist right now. This led men to feel guilty for having skills and experience because this reflected the patriarchal privileges that enabled us to have this know-how to begin with. Instead of sharing this knowledge with the women in the group, our reasoning was that if we were all equal then nobody should take the hierarchical role of teaching someone else how to run the show. But we were deluding ourselves with this flawed logic. What really happened was that the historic and institutional system of male supremacy was blurred into a practice that left few possibilities for actual positive change. What's more, women's actual skills, experiences, and analyses were still overlooked and minimized and we felt a sense of despair.

Third, we didn't have an organizational frame of reference for understanding the complexities of internalized sexism and its impact on women and men. Instead, collective political challenges of the UAF were perceived as personal issues between individuals. Lacking an adequate framework led men to feel personally blamed instead of being able to hear women's critique. What we needed was a process by which all of us could begin to see ourselves as part of classes or categories of people rather than just individuals. Only then could we imagine social change, organizational change, and individual change to challenge male supremacy and develop liberatory practices.

We continued to do our work and the UAF gained momentum. We beat city hall when they tried to stop our Food Not Bombs servings. We worked against student fee hikes and for an ethnic studies program at the community college many of us attended. We brought in more new people and we continued to have fun together. However, we saw our inability to end sexism as an organizational failure rather than interpreting our ongoing commitment to challenge male supremacy as a strength to build on over the long haul. This led to conflict and divisions rather than the pursuit of collective political goals.

This experience with the UAF pushed me to recognize that we needed to go through transformations of our own while simultaneously working for revolutionary change in the world. And while this may seem ambitious, there are some things I've learned along the way that I hope can benefit others who are actively working for positive social change. To that end, below are my suggestions.

TOOLS FOR GUYS (AND OTHERS WITH PRIVILEGE) WHO ARE WORKING FOR SOCIAL CHANGE

1.   Practice noticing who's in the room at social, professional, and political gatherings. How many are gender privileged (biological) men? How many are women, transgendered people, white people, and people of color? Is the majority in the room heterosexual? Are there out queers? What are people's class backgrounds? Don't assume to know people, but also work at becoming more aware by listening to what people say and talking with people one on one.

2. Count how many times you speak and keep track of how long you speak. Likewise, count how many times other people speak and keep track of how long they speak.

3. Be conscious of how often you are actively listening to what other people are saying as opposed to just waiting your turn thinking about what you'll say next. As a white guy who talks a lot, I've found it helpful to write down my thoughts and then focus on what other people are saying. Frequently others will be thinking something similar and then you can support their initiative.

4. Value other people's knowledge and experiences. White guys tend to talk among themselves and develop strong bonds that manifest in organizing. These informal support structures often help reinforce informal leadership structures as well. Asking people what they think and really listening to their answers is a core ingredient to healthy group dynamics. So practice asking more people what they think about events, ideas, actions, strategy, and vision.

5. Pay attention to how many times you put ideas out to the group you work with. Support other people by asking them to expand on their ideas and get more in-depth.

6. Think about whose work and what contributions to the group get recognized. Practice recognizing more people for the work they do and try to do it more often. Offer support to other men and actively challenge competitive dynamics that men are socialized to act out with each other.

7. Be aware of how often you ask people to do something as opposed to asking other people what needs to be done. Logistics, child care, making phone calls, cooking, providing emotional support, and following up with people are often undervalued responsibilities performed by those we hold in low esteem.

8. Struggle and work with the model of group leadership that says the responsibility of leaders is to help develop more leaders, and think about what this means to you. How do you support others and what support do you need from them?

This includes men providing emotional and political support to other men. How can men work to be allies to each other in the struggle to develop radical models of anti-racist, class-conscious, pro-queer, feminist manhood that challenges strict binary gender roles and categories? This is also about struggling to recognize leadership roles while also re-defining leadership as actively working to build power with others rather than power over others.

9. Remember that social change is a process, and that our individual transformation and individual liberation is intimately interconnected with social transformation and social liberation.

10. This list is not limited to white guys, nor is it intended to reduce all white guys into one category. This list is intended to disrupt patterns of domination that hurt our movement and hurt each other.

Finally, remember that no one is free until we are all free.

BIBLIOGRAPHY

Adams, Rachel and David Savran, eds. *The Masculinity Studies Reader*. Malden, MA: Blackwell Publishing, 2002.

Alcoff, Linda and Elizabeth Potter, eds. *Feminist Epistemologies*. New York: Routledge, 1993.

Anzaldúa, Gloria E. and Analouise Keating, eds. *This Bridge We Call Home: Radical Visions for Transformation*. New York: Routledge, 2002.

Bailey, J. Michael. *The Man Who Would Be Queen: The Science of Gender-Bending and Transsexualism*. Washington, DC: Joseph Henry Press, 2003.

Baumgardner, Jennifer. *Look Both Ways: Bisexual Politics*. New York: Farrar, Strauss and Giroux, 2007.

Bird, Sharon R. "Welcome to the Men's Club: Homosociality and the Maintenance of Hegemonic Masculinity." *Gender & Society*. Vol. 10, no. 2 (April 1996): 120–132.

Boykin, Keith. "No Blacks Allowed." http://www.temenos.net/articles/12-23-04.shtml.

Breines, Winifred. *The Trouble between Us: An Uneasy History of White and Black Women in the Feminist Movement*. New York: Oxford University Press, 2006.

Brod, Harry. "They're Bi Shepherds, Not Gay Cowboys: The Misframing of *Brokeback Mountain*." *Journal of Men's Studies*. Vol. 14, no. 2 (Spring 2006): 252–253.

Butler, Judith. *Gender Trouble: Feminism and the Subversion of Identity*. New York: Routledge, 1990.

Califia, Patrick. *Speaking Sex to Power: The Politics of Queer Sex*. San Francisco: Cleis Press, 2002.

Cannick, Jasmyne. "Gays First, Then Illegals." http://www.advocate.com/exclusive_detail_ektid28908.asp.

Carey, Benedict. "Straight, Gay, or Lying? Bisexuality Revisited." *New York Times*. July 5, 2005.

Chaudhry, Lakshmi. "Growing Up to Be Boys." http://www.alternet.org/story/33801.

Collins, Patricia Hill. *Black Feminist Thought: Knowledge, Consciousness, and the Politics of Empowerment*. New York: Routledge, 2000.

Collins, Patricia Hill. "Book Review: *Separate Roads to Feminism: Black, Chicana, and White Feminist Movements in America's Second Wave*." *Acta Sociologica*. Vol. 49 (2006): 231–233.

Combahee River Collective. "A Black Feminist Statement." In Carole R. McCann and Seung-Kung Kim, eds. *Feminist Theory Reader: Local and Global Perspectives*. New York: Routledge, 2003.

Connell, R.W. *Gender and Power: Society, the Person and Sexual Politics*. Stanford, CT: Stanford University Press, 1987.

Connell, R.W. *Masculinities*. Los Angeles: University of California Press, 1995.

Connell, R.W. "Reply." *Gender & Society*. Vol. 12, no. 4 (August 1998): 474–477.

Crenshaw, Kimberlé. "Demarginalizing the Intersection of Race and Sex: A Black Feminist Critique of Antidiscrimination Doctrine, Feminist Theory, and Antiracist Politics." In Katharine T. Bartlett and Rosanne Kennedy, eds. *Feminist Legal Theory: Readings in Law and Gender*. Boulder, CO: Westview Press, 1991.

Currah, Paisley, Richard M. Juang, and Shannon Price Minter, eds. *Transgender Rights*. Minneapolis, MN: University of Minnesota Press, 2006.

David, Deborah S. and Robert Brannon, eds. *The Forty-Nine Percent Majority: The Male Sex Role*. Reading, MA: Addison-Wesley, 1976.

Demetriou, Demetrakis Z. "Connell's Concept of Hegemonic Masculinity: A Critique." *Theory and Society*. Vol. 30, no. 3 (June 2001): 337–361.

Dicker, Rory and Alison Piepmeier, eds. *Catching a Wave: Reclaiming Feminism for the 21st Century*. Boston: Northeastern University Press, 2003.

Digby, Tom, ed. *Men Doing Feminism*. New York: Routledge, 1998.

Doucet, Andrea. *Do Men Mother? Fatherhood, Care, and Domestic Responsibility*. Toronto, Canada, 2006

Drummond, Murray J.N. "Asian Gay Men's Bodies." *Journal of Men's Studies*. Vol. 13, no. 3 (Spring 2005): 291–300.

Enloe, Cynthia. *Bananas, Beaches and Bases: Making Feminist Sense of International Politics*. Berkeley, CA: University of California Press, 2001.

Faludi, Susan. *Stiffed: The Betrayal of the American Man*. New York: Harper Perennial, 2000.

Flood, Michael. "Bringing Men Into the Light? Women's Studies and the Problem of Men." http://www.xyonline.net/downloads/womensstudies andmen.pdf.

Gardiner, Judith Kegan. *Masculinity Studies and Feminist Theory.* New York: Columbia University Press, 2002.

Gellene, Denise. "Men Found to be Anorexic, Bulimic Also." *Los Angeles Times.* February 1, 2007.

Giddings, Paula. *When and Where I Enter.* New York: Bantam, 1984.

Grant, Judith. *Fundamental Feminism: Contesting the Core Concepts of Feminist Theory.* New York: Routledge, 1993.

Griffin, S.A. *Unborn Again.* Los Angeles: Phony Lid Books, 2001.

Harding, Sandra, ed. *Feminism and Methodology.* Bloomington, IN: Indiana University Press, 1987.

Harding, Sandra. *Whose Science? Whose Knowledge?: Thinking From Women's Lives.* Ithaca, NY: Cornell University Press, 1991.

Hernández, Daisy and Bushra Rehman, eds. *Colonize This! Young Women of Color on Today's Feminism.* Emeryville, CA: Seal Press, 2002.

hooks, bell. *Ain't I a Woman: Black Women and Feminism.* Boston, MA: South End Press, 1981.

hooks, bell. *Killing Rage: Ending Racism.* New York: Owl Books, 1996.

hooks, bell. *Feminist Theory: From Margin to Center.* Cambridge, MA: South End Press, 2000.

hooks, bell. *Where We Stand: Class Matters.* New York: Routledge, 2000.

hooks, bell. *All About Love: New Visions.* New York: Harper Paperbacks, 2001.

hooks, bell. *Sisters of the Yam: Black Women and Self-Recovery.* Cambridge, MA: South End Press, 2005.

Hunter, Andrea G. and Sherrill L. Sellers. "Feminist Attitudes Among African American Women and Men." *Gender & Society.* Vol. 12, no. 1 (February 1998): 81–99.

Jensen, Robert. "A Call for an Open Discussion of Mass-Marketed Pornography." http://alternet.org/mediaculture/47677.

Jhally, Sut, dir. *bell hooks: Cultural Criticism and Transformation.* Northampton, MA: Media Education Foundation, 1997.

Johnson, Merri Lisa, ed. *Jane Sexes It Up: True Confessions of Feminist Desire.* New York: Four Walls Eight Windows, 2002.

Jones, Adam, ed. *Men of the Global South.* London: Zed Books, 2006.

Jones, Daniel, ed. *The Bastard on the Couch: 27 Men Try Really Hard to Explain Their Feelings About Love, Loss, Fatherhood, and Freedom.* New York: Harper Paperbacks, 2005.

Kimmel, Michael S. *The History of Men: Essays on the History of American and British Masculinities.* Albany, NY: State University of New York, 2005.

Kimmel, Michael S. *Manhood in America: A Cultural History.* New York: Oxford University Press, 2005.

Kimmel, Michael S. and Thomas E. Mosmiller, eds. *Against the Tide: Pro-Feminist Men in the United States, 1776–1990.* Boston: Beacon Press, 1992.

Kimmel, Michael S. and Michael A. Messner, eds. *Men's Lives,* seventh edition. San Francisco: Pearson, 2007.

Kitlinski, Tomek and Pawel Leszkowicz. *Love and Democracy: Reflections on the Homosexual Question in Poland*. Krakow: Aureus, 2005.

Kraemer, Kelly Rae. "Solidarity in Action: Exploring the Work of Allies in Social Movements." *Peace & Change*. Vol. 32, no. 1 (January 2007): 20–38.

Labaton, Vivien and Dawn Lundy Martin. *The Fire This Time: Young Activists and the New Feminism*. New York: Random House, 2004.

MacKinnon, Catharine A. "Not a Moral Issue," *Yale Law & Policy Review* 2 (1984): 321–345.

Mann, Bonnie. "How America Justifies Its War: A Modern/Postmodern Aesthetics of Masculinity and Sovereignty." *Hypatia*. Vol. 21, no. 4 (Fall 2006): 147–163.

McCann, Carole R. and Seung-Kyung Kim, eds. *Feminist Theory Reader: Local and Global Perspectives*. New York: Routledge, 2003.

McCaughey, Martha. *The Caveman Mystique: Pop-Darwinism and the Debates Over Sex, Violence, and Science*. New York: Routledge, 2007.

Miller-Young, Mireille. "Hardcore Desire," *ColorLines*. (Winter 2005–2006): 31–35.

Milne, Carly, ed. *Naked Ambition: Women Who Are Changing Pornography*. New York: Caroll and Graf, 2005.

Mirandé, Alfredo. *Hombres y Machos: Masculinity and Latino Culture*. Boulder, CO: Westview Press, 1997.

Moraga, Cherríe L. and Gloria E. Anzaldúa, eds. *This Bridge Called My Back: Writings by Radical Women of Color*. Berkeley, CA: Third Woman Press, 2002.

Morgan, Robin, ed. *Sisterhood Is Powerful: An Anthology of Writing from the Women's Liberation Movement*. New York: Vintage, 1970.

Morgan, Robin, ed. *Sisterhood Is Forever: The Women's Anthology for a New Millennium*. New York: Washington Square Press, 2003.

Murphy, Peter, ed. *Feminism and Masculinities*. New York: Oxford University Press, 2004.

Nagle, Jill, ed. *Whores and Other Feminists*. New York: Routledge, 1997.

Ouzgane, Lahoucine, ed. *Islamic Masculinities*. London: Zed Books, 2006.

Pruett, Kyle. *Fatherhood: Why Father Care is as Essential as Mother Care for Your Child*. New York: Broadway, 2001.

Quinn, Beth A. "Sexual Harassment and Masculinity: The Power and Meaning of 'Girl Watching'." *Gender & Society*. Vol. 16, no. 3 (June 2002): 386–402.

Rieger, Gerulf, Meredith L. Chivers, and J. Michael Bailey. "Sexual Arousal Patterns of Bisexual Men." *Psychological Science*. Vol. 16, no. 8 (2005): 579–584.

Sadler, Anne G., Brenda M. Booth, Brian L. Cook, and Bradley N. Doebbeling. "Factors Associated With Women's Risk of Rape in the Military Environment." *American Journal of Industrial Medicine*. Volume 43, Issue 3 (March 2003): 262–273.

Seidler, Victor J., ed. *Young Men & Masculinities: Global Cultures and Intimate Lives*. London: Zed Books, 2006.

Shor, Francis. "Hypermasculine Warfare: From 9/11 to the War on Iraq." http://bad.eserver.org/reviews/2005/shor.html.

Snitow, Ann, Christine Stansell, and Sharon Thompson, eds. *Powers of Desire: The Politics of Sexuality*. New York: Monthly Review Press, 1983.

Snodgrass, Jon. *For Men Against Sexism: A Book of Readings*. Albion, CA: Times Change Press, 1977.

South End Press Collective. *Talking About a Revolution: Interviews With Michael Albert, Noam Chomsky, Barbara Ehrenreich, bell hooks, Peter Kwong, Winona LaDuke, Manning Marable, Urvashi Vaid, and Howard Zinn*. Cambridge, MA: South End Press, 1998.

Spieler, Jennifer Zahn. "Soldier's Harassment Claim Leads to Court Martial." http://www.womensenews.org/article.cfm/dyn/aid/2980/context/cover.

Staples, Robert. *Black Masculinity: The Black Male's Role in American Society*. San Francisco: Black Scholar Press, 1982.

Strossen, Nadine. *Defending Pornography: Free Speech, Sex, and the Fight for Women's Rights*. New York: New York University Press, 2000.

Sullivan, Oriel. "Changing Gender Practices Within the Household: A Theoretical Perspective." *Gender & Society*. Vol. 18, no. 2 (April 2004): 207–222.

Tarrant, Shira. "Who's Accountable for the Abuse at Abu Ghraib?" *off our backs*. Vol. 34, Issue 9/10 (Sept–Oct 2004): 15–16.

Tarrant, Shira. *When Sex Became Gender*. New York: Routledge, 2006.

Tarrant, Shira. "Stepping Out of Bounds: Feminist Men and Political Organizing." Presented at the Western Political Science Association Annual Conference, Las Vegas, Nevada, March 9, 2007.

Taylor, Verta. "Review. *The Trouble between Us*." *Gender & Society*. Vol. 21, no. 1 (February 2007): 136–138.

Tea, Michelle, ed. *Without a Net: The Female Experience of Growing Up Working Class*. Emeryville, CA: Seal Press, 2003.

Tong, Rosemarie Putnam. *Feminist Thought: A More Comprehensive Introduction*, second edition. Boulder, CO: Westview Press, 1998.

Valerio, Max Wolf. *The Testosterone Files: My Hormonal and Social Transformation from Female to Male*. Emeryville, CA: Seal Press, 2006.

Vance, Carole S. *Pleasure and Danger: Exploring Female Sexuality*. London: Pandora Press, 1989.

Verloo, Mieke. "Multiple Inequalities, Intersectionality and the European Union." *European Journal of Women's Studies*. Vol. 13, no. 3 (2006): 211–228.

Walker, Alexis J. and Lori A. McGraw. "Who Is Responsible for Responsible Fathering?" *Journal of Marriage and the Family*. Vol. 62 (May 2000): 563–569.

Walker, Rebecca, ed. *What Makes a Man: 22 Writers Imagine the Future*. New York: Riverhead Books, 2005.

Williams, Joan C. "One Sick Child Away From Being Fired: When 'Opting Out' Is Not an Option." http://www.uchastings.edu/site_files/WLL/One SickChildovervu.pdf.

Young, Iris Marion. *Justice and the Politics of Difference.* Princeton, NJ: Princeton University Press, 1990.

Young, Josephine Peyton. "Review. *Masculinities, Gender Relations, and Sport.*" *Gender and Society.* Vol. 15, no. 5 (Oct 2001): 778–779.

INDEX

heteronormative pornography 65–6
high school 136, 155–6, 255–6; sexual violence 246–50; youth violence 258–60
hip hop culture 17–23, 151–3
homophobia: in gay community 61–2, 94–7; internalized 198–9; and misogyny 95, 96, 97; and sexism 157–8
homosociality 60, 70–3, 239
hooks, b. 11, 37, 99, 102, 201, 269, 281

India 155–6
Indonesia 169–70, 227–31
Iraq, sexual harassment/assault of women officers in 108, 124–30
It's Time for Guys to Put An End To This (booklet) 113, 121, 122

Jewish community 96, 109, 136
johns 65–6, 67
jokes 37, 81, 84, 100, 148, 164, 193; rape 193, 262; and sexual harassment 125–6, 127; sports culture 241–2, 262; *see also Life Without Shame* (TV show)
Jones, D. 9–10
Joplin, Janis 186

Katz, Jackson xxi–xxiv, 121, 259
Kempton, S. 177
Kimmel, M. 106; and Messner, M. 10
knowledge production 235–7

Labaton, V. and Lundy, D. 107
League of Polish Families 95, 96
lesbian identity 30–1, 32, 33
"Let Us Be Seen" campaign, Poland 94–7
Life Without Shame (TV show) 114–23

macho stereotype 47–55; gay men 156–7, 160
macho women 50–1
MacKinnon, C. 59–60
male bonding *see* homosociality
male insecurities and transformation 179–81

male privilege: acknowledging and resisting 160–2; recognition of 267–8; *see also* patriarchal system
male sexual assault/rape 62, 100–2
marriage 36–7, 134–5
masculinity 1–3, 9–14; challenging myths about 264–5; gay men of color 92–3; multiple masculinities 3, 10; traditional/hegemonic 2, 10–12; *see also* black masculinity
masturbation (johns) 65–6
media advertising 115, 118, 209
media images 39, 74, 83, 84; gay men 87
media perspectives 80–1, 82–3, 85; anarchist 280; anti-war activism 189; gay rights 96–7; *Life Without Shame* (TV show) 114–23; military journalism 124–30
membership of activist organizations 266–7
"Men, Masculinity and Sexism" course 190–5
men–women relationships 24–9, 246; Affirmative Action for 134–5; marriage 36–7, 134–5; political–personal relationship 175, 177, 187–8
men's groups 99, 100–1, 179; anti-sexist 99, 100–1, 116; fathers 169, 212–13
Mexico 47–55
military: and anti-war activists 185–6; sexual assault/assault of women officers 108, 124–30; violence 47–8, 49–50
mindfulness mediation 270–1
Mirandé Sex Role Inventory (MSRI) 54
misogyny 20, 25, 191; and homophobia 95, 96, 97; and racism 121–2; transgender identity 33, 35
Modleski, T. 107
Morgan, R. 280
mothers 36, 98, 247, 272; and football culture 240, 243, 244; *see also* family
multiple identities 4
multiple masculinities 3, 10
music: anti-sexist 140; Harry Chapin 206–7, 209–10; Judy Collins 186–7; dancing 40–2; Duldung, feminist

United Anarchist Front (UAF) 278–9, 280, 282–3

Valerio, Max Wolf 30
violence: and alcohol 48; fathers as perpetrators 253; "Let Us Be Seen" photo exhibition 95–6; male–male 215–17, 251, 252, 254, 266, 267, 268; military 47–8, 49–50; murder 36, 38–9; women as perpetrators 50–1; youth 258–60; *see also* rape/sexual violence
violence against women: avoidance strategies 266; domestic 48–9, 53, 214–17; *It's Time for Guys to Put An End To This* (booklet) 113, 121, 122; *see also* pornography

Walker, A. 271
Walker, R. 9–10
white domination: of feminist movement 107, 134; of gay community 87–90
White Ribbon campaign 121, 212, 213, 267

whore–virgin concept of women 228
women: bisexual 83, 84; and football culture 240, 241–2, 243–4; in hip hop culture 18, 19–20, 151, 152–3; learning from 190–5, 249, 253, 254, 265–6, 276, 277–8; lesbian identity 30–1, 32, 33; macho 50–1; male myths about 177–9; in sex industry 60, 65, 66, 67; violence against 48; *see also* black women; family; girls; mothers; *specific issues*
Women Against a Violent Environment (WAVE) 113–20
women-focused NGO, Indonesia 230
women's bodies *see* objectification of women; pornography
Women's Student Union 190–5
women's studies 163–4, 169, 219–26, 251, 253, 256, 257
Womyn's Issues Now (WIN) 138–41, 144–6
working class culture 53–4, 236, 272

Young, I.M. 10–11
youth violence 258–60